A Cultural Hist
of the Arabic Lan

ALSO BY SHARRON GU

Language and Culture in the Growth of Imperialism
(McFarland, 2012)

A Cultural History of the Chinese Language
(McFarland, 2012)

A Cultural History
of the Arabic Language

SHARRON GU

McFarland & Company, Inc., Publishers
Jefferson, North Carolina, and London

LIBRARY OF CONGRESS CATALOGUING-IN-PUBLICATION DATA

Gu, Sharron.
   A cultural history of the Arabic language / Sharron Gu.
      p.   cm.
   Includes bibliographical references and index.

   ISBN 978-0-7864-7059-4
   softcover : acid free paper ∞

   1. Arabic language—History.   2. Arabic language—Poetry.
3. Arabic language—Social aspects.   4. Language and
culture—Arab countries.   I. Title.

PJ6075.G8 2014
492.709—dc23   2013035496

BRITISH LIBRARY CATALOGUING DATA ARE AVAILABLE

On the cover: Moroccan doorway (iStockphoto/Thinkstock)

Manufactured in the United States of America

*McFarland & Company, Inc., Publishers
   Box 611, Jefferson, North Carolina 28640
      www.mcfarlandpub.com*

Table of Contents

Acknowledgments

I would like to express my appreciation to my editor Norman A. Christie. He not only edited most parts of this book but also provided a valuable perspective, the perspective of my potential readers who were born and educated in the English literary tradition, have interests in Arabic poetry and literature, yet do not read Arabic originals. Without his help it would not have been possible to write a book that adequately describes the evolution of a thousand-year-old literary tradition in a single volume. I thank Mr. Christie for his constructive criticism and suggestions. All the shortcomings that you may find in this book are mine.

Preface

This is a brief yet wide-ranging study of the history of the Arabic language. It is written for scholars and educated readers of Arabic and Islamic culture whose first language is not Arabic. It also may be useful for native Arabic speakers who are interested in knowing how their heritage is seen from a global perspective. This work focuses on what is unique about Arabic compared to other major languages of the world—Greek, Latin, Hebrew, English, Spanish, and Chinese—and how the distinct characteristics of Arabic took shape at various points of its history. It is intended to provide a linguistic and cultural background for understanding social and political institutions, religious belief and religious practice in the Middle East.

Humans are cultural beings rather than linguistic, ethnical, or psychological stereotypes because they are shaped by their immediate cultural environment. Cultural history is a complex process during which various forms of expression accumulate, interact, and transform. Each generation born into a specific culture (or more precisely, a certain stage of development of a given culture) inherits a distinctive repertoire of expressions in its music, oral, literary, and artistic languages that shape its attitude, imagination, and wisdom. To understand a people one must comprehend the cultural inheritance that has allowed ideas and worldviews to evolve. Hopefully, this book inspires readers to regard Middle Eastern history and the contemporary Muslim world in a different light.

The Arabian civilization is one of the most misrepresented and misunderstood in the West. Besides the political propaganda fueled by international conflict, the language of social and political science, in whose terms the world has been described and debated for the past two centuries, has perceived other cultures and their people in foreign (English, German or French) terms, disregarding the unique cultural and linguistic setting of Arabic. As a result, the history of Arabic and Islam as written in English

1

has presented various distortions according to the fluctuation of self-image of the cultures of Western Europe and North America. In this book, readers will recognize many familiar characteristics in Arabic history shared with their own cultural history and others that are beyond their horizons. That has occurred not only because literary Arabic has a longer history compared to modern European languages but also because it has produced a mature literary canon, including writings of law, science, philosophy, and historical narrative, centuries before the West.

One of the most illustrative examples of historical differences derived from this gap in time between the Arabic and English cultures is the highly developed and refined poetic expression in Arabic that has set it apart from other languages in the world. This mature and refined poetry has exceptional capacity to cultivate and activate fluid emotions. Unlike in the West, where poetry is the vocation and pastime of elite intellectuals, Arabic poetry lives on the street (and in the coffee houses), in the mosques and in private homes. Poetic imagery and rhythm derived from it remain in the ears and minds, and on the lips, of Arabic speakers. There are not any people in the world more readily attuned to and motivated by words than Arabs. This is the reason why Islam, the youngest world religion, commands wide and lasting influence throughout the world. The power of Islam lies in Qur'anic poetry and the poetry of Arabic language.

My acquaintance with the Arabic language initially was an accident. I was born in China during the Mao period, when every citizen's life was dictated by the state of politics, especially education and career. The beginning of the Cultural Revolution marked the end of my academic dream (of getting into the best universities to pursue whatever I pleased) because of my family background. I was born into a "black" family, a Chinese term referring to families of wealth and education under the communist regime. My ancestors had many properties throughout the country and held high positions in the old regimes because they were scholars and lawyers trained in Western Europe, Japan, and North America. As a member of the now undesirable part of society, I had to go to the countryside to wash off my family (intellectual) heritage and wait for my turn to be reborn as an acceptable revolutionary. After three years of gruesome hard labor, I thought that I was reformed enough to go to university and pursue my delayed dream. But it was not quite enough in the eyes of the regime, who believed that poverty and ignorance were the best human virtues. As I enrolled in university, I was not allowed to learn English, my first choice, because my parents were English professors and translators. At first, it broke my heart that I had to settle for Arabic.

What happened was that learning the Arabic language and its literature became a positive influence in my life. Arabic equipped me with a vision and sensibility that was beyond any of those provided by modern Western languages and my native (Chinese) culture. In China, the sound of music and poetry as an expression of true emotion had died long before I was born. As poetic words lay frozen in books on dusty shelves, Chinese culture and scholarship crystallized and became increasingly analytical. As feelings were overly processed and eventually numbed by verbal reasoning, the sparkle in the eye and body gesture disappeared in expression. Travel to the Middle East provided much more than a breath of fresh air. The capacity to perceive and comprehend a high degree of poetic sensibility that no other language of the world can yet express was a blessing for my intellectual growth and my later career as a researcher and writer in world cultures.

After spending several years in the Middle East I had poetry in my ears and was surrounded by people whose emotions often danced with rhythm in front of my eyes. I became convinced that there was a connection between poetry and the cultivation of human emotion and spirit. I saw a similar display of fluid emotion in North America and Europe activated by modern music; however, music could not carry meanings as specific, well defined and eloquent as poetry. The lyrics in contemporary music, although often representing some of the best modern poetry written in English and Spanish, remain centuries behind contemporary Arabic poetry in terms of formal maturity and refinement.

If one believes (as I do) that world literatures in various languages share a common growth, maturity and aging process, reading and meditating on Arabic literature, especially its poetry, can certainly open one's eyes to the direction that English poetry will follow as it evolves. If the mighty river of literature will eventually grow cold and frozen as Chinese has done, let's jump into Arabic poetry to enjoy the warmth and vitality that words create.

Introduction

This is an introductory history of the Arabic language. It differs from those written by linguists and literary theorists in three main ways. First, its perspective is global in nature. It does not portray the language and culture as completely opposite to those of the West nor suggest that it is a divinely inspired and yet misunderstood civilization that seeks to challenge and convert the world to its religious doctrine. Rather, it emphasizes that which is unique about Arabic when it is compared to other languages; in other words, the ways in which Arabic is similar to and differs from Hebrew, Greek, Latin, English, and Spanish and the types of historical experience that cultivated its distinctive characteristics. This work illustrates how Arabic emerged from a hub of interaction and mutation of ancient oral traditions of the Middle East that finally distilled it into an exceptionally well developed poetic medium. It demonstrates how Arabic prose expanded and regulated its poetic vision and created clear, penetrating, and comprehensive worldviews. It illustrates that Arabic literature contained as well as elevated ancient poetry by embracing various non–Arabic expressions (Greek, Persian, Hebrew, and Spanish), and that this constantly enriched and reinvented literature further nurtured a variety of regional traditions around world.

Second, this history deliberately transcends the boundaries of academic disciplines, such as language (as in speech), literature, music, theatrical performance, and visual arts. It sees various forms of non-literary expression as inspiration that contributes to the evolution of literary language. The degrees of refinement of the literary language shape the main characteristics and historic development of the non-literary expressions. In other words, this history considers the interaction and reciprocal transformation between various verbal and non-verbal forms, other than abstract ones, to be the main dynamic of the linguistic evolution of Arabic. Third, it proposes an original theory of language through rewriting (or revision of) the history of a language that is much more refined and poetic than those of European origin.

The history of the Arabic language is an experience beyond the horizon of any linguistic and literary theories that have been produced by European languages. The most important and distinctive characteristic of Arabic is its profound poetic form, which was cultivated and refined before Arabic became a written language. Poetry, the oldest and most developed genre of Arabic literature, laid the foundation for the sound, rhythm and structure of Arabic prose, and it remains a dominant form in modern literature. This poetry was deep-rooted in ancient Semitic traditions that evolved over thousands of years and later formed the basis for several written traditions. Although none of the ancient scripts have survived as a universal language (of the Middle East), Semitic culture (very much like various Celtic traditions) kept evolving in many other forms: music, oral poetry, ritual performance, and liturgical composition. Semitic written language was discontinued and reoriented several times while its words continued to be spoken; and its stories were told, recited, and performed for thousands of years before the emergence of Arabic. This under-codified and under-sanctioned oral poetry (in the absence of a continuing script to guide it) became exceptionally fluid and expressive. Like highly fertilized soil waiting for new seeds to grow, the pre–Islamic Middle East was ready for a new universal language, a language that could regulate and embrace its diverse poetic traditions.

As the latest reincarnation of its ancient ancestral poetry, Arabic inherited and reinvented these traditions and elevated them into a brilliant literature during an amazingly short period of time. Arabs needed only about two hundred years to produce a highly sophisticated literary canon. In comparison, seven to nine centuries (depending on how one defines formative and mature literature) were required in English, French, and German, and the Chinese process covered more than a millennium. Classical Arabic rapidly codified and assimilated the ancient and diverse cultural expressions of the Middle East and southern Europe as the Islamic cultural center traveled from the Arabian Peninsula to Syria, Iraq, Egypt, Persia, southern Spain, and Turkey. During this Islamic expansion, and as in the expansions of Greek and Latin before it and English, Spanish, and American after it, Arabic encountered many local cultural and linguistic traditions whose influence left a remarkable impact on Arabic, further enhancing its literary language.

Translating Greek literature into Arabic created a brand new universe of general and abstract concepts that fostered the development of science, law, arts, and philosophy. Like Latin ten centuries earlier, Arabic radically expanded and reinvented itself from a tribal poetic medium into a language of high learning, linguistics, law, religion and political administration. However, with its deep Semitic roots in the Middle East, Arabic did not die with the decline of the Islamic Empire. Like undying embers that fuel new fire, it survived and kept burning because it managed to spark in the sound and rhythm of its spoken and written poetry. Living on the lips and in the ears of its speakers, Arabic maintained its backbone and inexhaustible resources to create a highly diverse and vibrant culture.

The form of the Qur'an, the first rhymed prose in Arabic literature, inherited the audibility and theatricality (in delivery) of its ancient poetry. Unlike the commonly perceived concept of literature, especially literature as opposed to speech, early Arabic literature was written to be read aloud and heard (in public) rather than in solitude and silence. The word *Qur'an* is derived from the Arabic verb *qara'a* (to read or to recite). An important meaning of the word is that it is heard through the act of reciting. A great portion of Hadith, the second canonical piece of literature in early Arabic, was a collection of recorded sayings attributed to Muhammad and narrated scenarios in which Muhammad's words were uttered. The evolution of Arabic that sounds similar to the formative history of Biblical Hebrew and pre–Imperial Latin stops here. Arabic was unique in the sense that it did not lose its oral roots as it evolved into a language of learning during and after the Islamic period. There were always learned and popular branches of Arabic that functioned at different levels of a given society, but they never lost touch with each other. This unbreakable link was entrenched in the language of the Qur'an, a literary language carried by the sound and rhythm of a spoken tongue; a highly refined literary oral poetry.

This closeness between spoken and written language and between poetic creation and public recitation can still be witnessed in mosques and heard on the streets of the Arab world. Unlike the ritual of synagogues and Christian churches, Arabic religious ritual does not include music because its language is already musical in the ears of its speakers. The emotional and rhetorical power of Arabic had emerged before the scriptural invention of Islam, and this made Allah's words extremely engaging and persuasive. The parallel power of poetic metaphor in Arabic has only recently begun to be seen in the poems of the best English and Spanish poets during the twentieth century. But it has been common in the poems of Arabic poets for centuries. This is because the Arabic literary language has been steeped in poetic creation and recitation for thousands of years and has crystallized in the poems of many generations of Arab poets. Most importantly, this poetry belongs to every Arabic speaker.

The idea of recording spoken words with script promoted a revolution and rebirth for Arabic. As literature, the Qur'an was the first work in Arabic of significant length (114 *surat* [chapters], which contain 6,236 *ayat* [verses]); it had a far more complicated structure than earlier literary works. It contains narratives, injunctions, dramatic dialogue, homilies, parables, direct speeches, wordplays, and instructions, and even provides direction on how it should be received and understood. The Qur'an is admired for its layers of metaphor as well as its clarity. Like the religious literature of Judaism and Christianity, the newly invented Arabic produced an impressive body of literature devoted to complement the commentaries (*tafsīr*) and interpretation of the words of the Qur'an. One of the most important of this literature was Hadith, which recorded the words and deeds of Muhammad. Research into the life and times of Muhammad, and determination of the genuine parts of the *Sunna*, were important early projects of scholarship of Arabic language. This was also the motivation for the collection of pre–Islamic poetry, as some of these poets were close to Muhammad, and their writings illuminated the times when these events occurred.

The Qur'an exegesis also led to preoccupation with Qur'anic language, its grammar as external structure, and its interpretation as internal understanding. Some of the earliest studies of the Arabic language were conducted in the name of Islam and were patronized by the Islamic states. Prose replaced poetry as the dominant literary form during the sixth and seventh centuries. Arabic grammarians played an important role in codifying the language in both oral and written forms. By the tenth century, most of the language had been systematically codified and theories of prosody, music and grammar were in place.

As Ionic prose had accomplished for Greek literature, Arabic prose gave its language the discipline, organization, and sanction that were missing from its original loose and fluid poetic form. Now Arabic was not only able to express feelings such as love, hate, praise, and condemnation. It could introduce wisdom in the highly limited scale of life in the desert. It could also expand its stories (narrative) to include a life, a village, a nation, and even a world. It acquired the ability to form a worldview. The rapid accumulation of biographical and travel literature and the emergence of historical writing are only a few examples of this linguistic and literary development. Arabic gradually grew into a complex literary, legal and philosophical language with increasingly varied genres and with tighter formal boundaries.

Tracing the emergence of Arabic in terms of its concrete interaction with various sub-verbal idioms, music, theatre, and visual imageries is only a part of the story of this language. The other part is how Classical Arabic, the universal language of the Middle East, nurtured a variety of local literatures. The specific characteristics of the formation of each local literature, Arabic or otherwise, are portrayed as a historic interaction between Arabic and the local oral and literary tradition that carried a history of its own. Local oral or literary traditions, each with its unique degree of maturity and refinement, reacted differently to the Arabic influence, and they competed with it on their own terms. In most cases, a variety of cultural fusion was established as Arabic brought innovative expression to reshape the old local traditions. In the cases of Iraq, Egypt and Arabian Peninsula, Arabic provided a script or an alternative script for the mature and distinct local traditions that had been articulated for centuries. These ancient traditions flowed into the mainstream of Arabic as they were rewritten, enriching Arabic literature while substantially entrenching the continuity of the local tradition.

A major contributor for the formative Arabic literature was the ancient civilization of Persia, whose poetic tradition was as old as Ancient Semitic. Unlike Hebrew and Arabic, Old Persian was a fully alphabetic script that contained 37 consonants and 16 vowels that presented the sound of its spoken language more accurately than any of its contemporary Semitic scripts. Pre-Islamic Persian poetic tradition had a more direct ancestor, Old and Middle Persian (Pahlavi) that had been cultivated in oral tradition, religious (Zoroastrian) chanting and recitation. Arabic revitalized the Persian poetry that had become polarized into an elite literature (Avestan) and a vernacular (Pahlavi) and unified these two seemingly mutually incomprehensible languages, channeling them into a single literature. The codification of Persian poetry initiated an interaction between the emerging Arabic and the reviving Persian and contributed enormously to the formation of classical Arabic poetry. The scope of this interaction as well as the distilled literary reforms that emerged from Arabic are unique when compared to the evolution of the major world language groups.

* * *

An understanding of the history of the Arabic language can be helpful for students of Western culture because it presents an experience beyond the horizon of contemporary speakers of Western languages, whose literatures have just started to mature during modern times. The study of an ancient language provides glimpses into the future of one's own language. A mature literary language is often overly inflated with codes of law and diverse legal philosophy, and supports a political system maintained by increasingly sophisticated media rhetoric. Western scholars of social science and humanities may also benefit from this study. Within Arabic cultural history, they can find explanations for many major issues that have been haunting historians and cultural theorists for decades. How does language relate to worldview and political institution? What happens to law after its language loses absolute boundary and binding power? How do music, visual, and theatrical images influence literature, especially a mature literature? How does an established language and ideology penetrate and cultivate the collective consciousness and unconsciousness by creating endless repetition of seemingly varied images and tones?

Part One, "The Sound and Rhythm of Poetry," describes how the Arabic language emerged from ancient Semitic traditions that were steeped in music and poetry over thousands of years. It focuses on the historic cultivation and continuation of the sound and rhythm of ancient oral traditions on the periphery of major literary traditions such as Akkadian, Babylonian, Assyrian, or Hebrew. This voice of the old tongue is portrayed here as the real source and dynamic of linguistic evolution that finally was distilled into Arabic. Comparison with the careers of other ancient Semitic languages explains why Arabic is the first language and the only language of the Middle East that could grow into a literary language without losing the oral roots of its speakers.

Chapter 1, "Music and Poetry Before Arabic," is a brief history of the poetry of ancient Semitic languages. Like Ancient Greek and Ancient Chinese, Semitic languages emerged intact with their music. The voice of the poetry of ancient Mesopotamia was heard in religious rituals that took place at the great temples, the center of cultural activities at the time. The first poetry was sung, accompanied by drums and harp, and performed to gods and goddesses. As musical ceremonies lengthened they incorporated various instruments of percussion and wind as well as processional movements of choirs. This type of religious performance rivals those Roman or Anglican devotions that occurred much later.

Testifying to the influence of this elaborated musical culture are several highly advanced poetic traditions that have evolved since the fourth millennium B.C. Among the hymns of the great temples dated to the middle of the third millennium is a tablet collection that contains 42 hymns of 545 lines. After the Ur III period (21st to 20th centuries B.C.), hymns were longer and narratives more complex. As poetic narration developed, it separated from music and was uprooted from ritual performance. By this time, poetry could sing, recount, and motivate with its words alone. Hymns evolved into prologues inserted into mythology. Short prayers became long laments that contained personal confession and even political commentary.

Chapter 2, "Recording the Sound of Poetry," is a brief history of how the Semitic script was invented and how alphabetic script became the chosen writing form in the Middle East. Contrary to the established theory that asserts that Akkadian, the first Semitic language, adopted a non–Semitic script, this history considers Sumerian as the initial form of writing of the ancient Semitic, which was graphic rather than phonetic. Like the ancient Egyptian and Chinese pictographic scripts, early Sumerian cuneiform emerged from a prehistoric tradition of visual and symbolic presentation. Sumerian was unique only in the timing of its process of abstraction, a process which took place earlier and in a more extreme fashion than it did in Egypt and China. By the fourth millennium B.C., Sumerian cuneiform had shed all of its pictorial elements, and it became completely phonetic by the middle of the third millennium B.C. (at which stage it is called Akkadian by linguists). However, it took many more centuries and many linguistic changes for the Semitic script to complete its transition from syllabic to alphabetic. Babylonian, Assyrian, Ugaritic, Phoenician, Hebrew, and Aramaic were the more important stages of this long evolution. Qur'anic Arabic was the first Semitic language that codified its phonetic presentation (a complete recording of its sound and rhythm), and this finally brought linguistic stability to Semitic.

Chapter 3, "Rhythm from Poetry, to Prose, to Speech," is a history of the codification of the sound of the Arabic language. It demonstrates how the Qur'an inherited and elevated pre–Islamic poetry into a rhymed prose and engraved its rhythm into the memories of Arabic speakers, and how Arabic grammarians accumulated a mountain of literature as an extension to the Qur'an and Hadith to reinforce the correct reading and understanding of the Holy Book. Unlike the Holy Books of other religions, the Qur'an knew no institutional sanction (such as church, temple, or holy men); the only sanction that it established was the sound and rhythm of its language, which was and is accessible by all individual Muslims without a filter. (The reformation movement of the Christian churches during the early modern period made the same attempt.) This filter in each letter of the language and in the mind of each speaker was the greatest success of Arabic as a literary language because it became instantly oral, spoken, understood and motivating.

Part Two, "The Formation of Arabic Imagery," describes the evolution and accumulation of imagery in Arabic literature. Islam gave the ancient poetry a new voice to sing, new subjects to envisage, and a new devotional life. As the Arabic vision expanded with its rapidly growing vocabularies, its imagery became more precise, enlarged and more abstract during the classical period. The boundaries between God and world, between God and his believers and between believers and non-believers had to be established. As this obsession for boundaries transformed into abstract art forms, it became a pattern of shapes and colors, a pure form of beauty without any concrete figuration. It took several centuries for this broad vision to refocus and fill with detailed and refined imageries that were fluid enough to alter with changing mood. After imagery became more and more polished with individual variations, the world and God himself became personal and intimate again to the artists.

Chapter 4, "Imagery of the World: Poetry and Prose," shows how the imagery of early Arabic poetry painted a world narrow in scope yet refined in depiction. Like later Chinese poetry (from the Song Dynasty), the number of subjects that were described in the poetry shrank while their portrayal became more varied and the emotional engagement deepened and become more subtle. Arab poets gave more attention to eloquence and wording than to structure. They produced poetry of strong vocabulary and short ideas in their loosely connected verses. The seemingly simple imagery (such as a ruin that reminds the poet of his beloved) was pregnant with layers of meaning that activated a real sense of vision, touch and smell in the minds of readers.

Chapter 5, "Imagery of the Universe: Arts and Literature," focuses on the widening of literary vision and abstraction of its imagery. This process is seen and analyzed in the emergence of Arabic prose that laid a foundation for religious, philosophical and legal writing and the creation of artistic and architectural patterning without figurative images. The best example for this attempt to universalize language and thoughts is demonstrated in Islamic arts and architecture that projected grand vision with decorative motif. They presented a majestic unity, seemingly anti-image, yet were open to increasingly detailed and refined individual expression and creativity.

A similar attempt to create a majestic unity to juxtapose various literary genres was found in the *maqāmā* (assembly), a rhetorical style of rhymed prose. It was used to tell basically simple and entertaining stories in an extremely complicated and fictitious style. With no attempt to present a realistic tale, *maqāmā* displayed the author's eloquence, wit, and erudition in a dramatic or narrative context to provide both social commentary and moral enlightenment. The first collection of such writings was the *maqāmā* of Al-Hamadhani (968–1008). It consisted of picaresque stories presented in alternating prose and verse woven around two imaginary characters. The genre was revived and finally established in the 11th century by Al-Harīrī of Basra (Iraq), whose *maqāmā* is regarded as a masterpiece of literary style. Like artistic and architectural expression, the *maqāmā* became increasingly refined, ornamental and even rigid in the hands of writers of later generations.

Chapter 6, "Imagery of Man and His Feelings," describes the emergence of Arabic poetry since the Islamic period. Arabic prose built a verbal universe during the first two centuries of Islam, and its poetry began to create a brand new world of emotion and desire during the second half of the eighth century. By this time, the Bedouin poetry that eulogized the harsh and simple desert life and was recited around a campfire ended, although its theme could still find modern adaptation from time to time. The more settled, comfortable and luxurious life in Arabian courts led to a greater emphasis on poems of love (*ghazal*).

Like the European literature of courtly love, early Arabic love poetry described distant and unobtainable love and a lover's inner struggle between his desire for immediate fulfillment and his awareness of the virtue of striving for the unattainable; between the self-imposed state of submission and the overwhelming need to express pain and resentment. However, while it took English, Italian, and French several centuries to overcome the agony of these antitheses, Arabic poetry completed this transition from idealistic or heavenly love to human emotion (regardless of social and religious morality), physical attraction, and even intoxication in one generation, within even the life a single poet (Abu Nuwās, 754–814).

Unlike modern European poetry that completely abandoned medieval religious ideals and replaced them with modern notions of romantic love, devotion, and desire, Arabic poets simply utilized the inherited repertoire of imagery to enlarge the containment of the old images. They successfully refocused and intensified the meanings of the worn-out images by enhancing and re-juxtaposing them. For example, the age-old recurring image of wine was embracing the motif of *ghazal* (love) and *nasib* (elegiac prelude) to gain the audience's involvement. The *nasib*, an ancient device used by pre–Islamic poets, depicted the poet stopping at an old tribal encampment to remember the happiness he had shared there with his beloved and his sorrow when they parted. The new wine poetry embraced elements of the old poetry to serve two separate goals: the contrast of emotions, and the narrative focal point of seduction. This combination tightened the structure of narrative and cast a shadow on poetic language.

Chapter 7, "The World in Arabic Fiction," shows how the ancient poetic origins of Arabic literature determined that its narrative form did not evolve separately from poetic and rhetorical expression as happened in many younger languages that developed a phase of linear (realistic) narrative. Arabic narration was always tangled with non-narrative themes that displayed the author's ideas, learning, and eloquence. For Arab writers the form of the narration was as important as its content. *Maqāmā* was only one of these examples. In a highly artificial manner the storytelling appeared to be fragmentary, held together in purposeful juxtaposition that included lengthy prose and verse quotations, as well as many independent essays and anecdotes instead of a story line.

There are three main reflections of the complex narrative traditions in modern novels: the use of multi-leveled meaning in imagery (abstract, symbolic, or concrete meanings), multi-dimensional plot movement and characterization, and close connection between the author's grand theme and his detailed (sometimes realistic and powerful) depiction of everyday events.

The Conclusion summarizes this work with the idea that the most distinct characteristics of the Arabic language are its exceptional fluidity and the diversity of its origins and forms. The boundaries between words, literary genres, literature and philosophy, reality and fiction, have leveled out and intermingled during its literary evolution. A literary mind that is trained in its entire repertoire acquires a much larger and more multi-dimensional perspective than one that emerges from a younger culture.

PART ONE

The Sound and Rhythm of Poetry

This part is a history of the evolution of the sound and rhythm of Arabic. It first describes the cultural and linguistic context from which Arabic emerged: the ancient Semitic traditions steeped in music and poetry over thousands of years. It then focuses on how these ancient and active oral traditions shaped the sound and rhythm of Arabic and how Arabic distinguished itself from other Semitic languages to become the most influential and universal Semitic language in the Middle East since ancient times.

Arabic inherited from ancient Semitic languages not only vocabularies and grammatical forms shared by many other Semitic languages, but also its forms of expression, story-telling, and poetic performance. It was this public performance that engaged the majority of speakers and kept the sound and rhythm of the older language alive, thus providing a historic vehicle to constantly reframe the meaning of the language and redefine its social, political, religious, and spiritual functions. It was this dynamic articulation of poetic voice as manifested in composition, recitation, and public reception that kept oral tradition alive even as the goals of the composer and political and social significance of the message changed. This was also the reason that poetry and its varied narrative frameworks could transcend the dialectic and linguistic borders that emerged throughout the centuries by oral transmission and public performance. As the poems of the poets repeated and reworded the ancient stories, the lips of the audience were reciting the words and recreating the old sounds while they became installed in the hearts of all.

These continuing oral traditions (vernaculars) did not remain undeveloped or under-developed, as many scholars assume. Oral language does not always naturally evolve into written, and written form does not always guarantee linguistic survival. Compared to other ancient tongues, such as

Greek, Celtic, Chinese, Italic, and Hebrew, the transformation from Ancient Semitic to Arabic is a unique case in linguistic history. Arabic poetry evolved into increasingly sophisticated and polished expressions before they finally crystallized into written form. The characteristics of ancient Semitic traditions were carried into later literature through constant and active reinvention. The repeated attempt to canonize well-articulated oral languages and dialects (such as Akkadian, Babylonian, Assyrian, Aramaic, and Hebrew) left distinct marks in the historic distillation of ancient Semitic and its eventual transformation into modern languages. Arabic has preserved the largest number of features of the postulated proto–Semitic.[1]

This part focuses on the historic cultivation of the sound and rhythm of the ancient oral traditions on the periphery of major literary traditions, such as Akkadian, Babylonian, Assyrian, and Hebrew. The voice of the old tongue is portrayed here as the real source and dynamic of linguistic evolution that finally crystallized into Arabic. By comparison with the progression of other ancient Semitic languages, it explains why Arabic is the first language of the Near East that could grow into a literary tradition without losing its oral roots, thus remaining on the lips and in the ears and minds of its speakers.

This assessment of the development of Semitic languages may sound speculative at a time when new data is discovered every day that requires years of analysis to be thoroughly investigated. However, without an innovative theoretical framework, these new discoveries could be easily swept under the heavy rugs of established linguistic theories. This book aims to demonstrate that the experience of Semitic, as a language group, is currently beyond the scope of any established linguistic and cultural theories based on the bias of modern Western languages, the majority of which are the youngest literary languages in the world. To squeeze the Semitic linguistic experience that had accumulated over five thousand years into a modern Western paradigm is impossible without the shoehorn of Greco-Roman influence. This book is an attempt to convince scholars and educated readers that Arabic, the latest incarnation of Semitic language, has walked far enough and experienced a long enough history to deserve its own comfortable shoes.

To create a new paradigm for linguistic history, many general assumptions of language development based on western European languages have to be put aside to give Semitic language enough space to evolve in flux and reconstruct itself on its own terms. Language does not always require a unified or codified phonetic system. Many Semitic languages survived and flourished for a long time without such a system. In fact, phonetic diversity (the lack of a unified standard of pronunciation) has been one of the main reasons for the survival and maturity of the Semitic languages. Modern English and Spanish also had this diversity, which is one of the reasons for their popularity compared to French and German. The accumulation of linguistic repertoire does not have to have anything to do with migration. A language does not have to come from a single geographical origin; in fact, many major languages (including many western European languages) emerged from the periphery of a neighboring literary establishment after the latter peaked and passed its golden age. The linguistic and cultural prominence in Europe that traveled from ancient Greece, to Roman, to Southern Spain, to France, German, and to England is an example of this historical cycle. Linguistic reorientation and reconstruction of an older language almost always spawned a new and vibrant literary tradition, the best example of which can be found in the history of European vernaculars during the late Medieval to early modern times.[2]

Based on these new assumptions, the focus for historical study of the Semitic and Arabic languages has to shift its perspective. It has to begin with expressions beyond the rigid definition of language and at the borderline between words and music when poetry was sung. It also has to listen to the sound and rhythm of language before it became written and to experience the meaning that lives beyond the paper margins. Literary language has never lived on paper alone, because once it is no longer spoken, it dies. (For additional details of an alternative paradigm applied to the history of another ancient language, please refer to my *A Cultural History of the Chinese Language*.) Like other ancient languages, the Semitic language emerged and evolved within the context of ancient and active musical cultures. The long history of ancient musical culture is difficult to substantiate because none of the earliest music or its notations have survived. However, the Semitic tradition of music can be verified through four types of historic and archaeological findings. First, the Middle East was the region where the oldest musical instruments were invented and used in chanting and performance. Second, there was abundant evidence of religious ritual that was carried and accompanied by music.[3] Third, without a continued literary tradition, poetry in various languages and dialects could not have survived without music as a vehicle to retain poetic narrative and recitation. Finally, the rhythmic quality of Arabic has illustrated that it had absorbed the musical rhythm of its ancestor languages, as is the case with Latin and Italian, pre-modern Greek, and ancient Chinese.[4]

CHAPTER 1

Music and Poetry
Before Arabic

The Arabic language emerged within the context of ancient Mesopotamia starting in the third millennium B.C., when a well-established and advanced musical culture evolved and nurtured several highly advanced poetic traditions in Akkadian (Babylonian, Assyrian), Hebrew, and Aramaic.

There was abundant evidence of musical cultures in the ancient Mesopotamia, where the first detailed attestation of instrumental music was found.[1] The simplest sound-making instrument was percussion made to produce beat. At Kish (an ancient city of the early dynasties of Sumer, located 80 km south of Baghdad) and Ur (an important coastal city-state in ancient Sumer, located at the site of modern Tell el-Muqayyar) certain curiously curved blades of thin copper (in pairs) have been discovered. With a fixed wooden handle, they were not weapons as some might assume, but dancing sticks. A golden cylindrical seal unearthed at a royal tomb of Ur illustrates how these sticks were clapped by dancers to measured cadence of movement.[2]

The Sumerian word for drum was *UB*, which transfigured to *uppur* in Akkadian. *UB* originally meant something "hollowed out" or "enclosed," which corresponded to Greek word *lephes* or *lepis* (a cup or limpet-shell). It was used in solemn processions together with the double reed pipe, timbrel and other drums. The *BALAG* was a more interesting percussion instrument. Initially it was presented with a pictorial sign in the third millennium B.C. as an hour-glass-shaped instrument with two heads and a strap. Its Akkadian and Assyrian name was *balaggu, balangu, palagga* or *pelaggu*.[3]

As in many other ancient cultures, the sound of drum initially was juxtaposed with the sound of language and other kinds of expressions, such as lamenting, wailing and singing. The drum speech of ancient

18

Mesopotamia (the harmonious sound of drum and spoken words) is revealed in the original meaning of *BALAG* and *DUB* (without determinative). They symbolized not only the instruments but also more abstract ideas such as lamentation and wailing. A similar association occurred between the names of the cross-strung harp (*ZAG-SAL*) (without a determinative), which expressed the idea of "praise" where it accompanied the human voice during worship. The universal implication of the drum was often derived from its sound. The divine associated sound of the drum was said to have filled the forecourt of Eninnu, the Lagash Temple, with joy. When the king performed lustration and divine petition, the sacred drum and horn made the musical offering perfect.[4]

The beating of the drums that created the simple rhythm was further elaborated by the introduction of cymbals. This is illustrated on several cylinder seals from Ur. Various combinations of percussion and other types of instruments appeared. A harpist and two singers were seen clapping their hands; also a lyre player, two cymbalists and a singer; elsewhere a small orchestra complete with a conductor, with his baton on his shoulder and six female performers: a lyrist, two cymbalists and three singers. In all three cases, these musicians seem to entertain guests at a banquet.[5]

Last of the percussion group was a sort of rattle, a hard-baked clay sphere, with clay pellets that clattered when was shaken. Drums of different kinds were often used. They varied greatly in size, ranging from the large bass drum to a small tabor or timbrel held by a woman with both hands. Countless numbers of small figure-plaques of the time of Gudea or the Third Dynasty of Ur popularized a latter arrangement that featured a female musician (perhaps a temple slave or *hierodule*) who did not make any attempt to veil her physical charms. The bass drums pictured on a vase on a stele from Telloh and on the stele of Ur-Nammu from Ur must have measured over three feet in diameter. The parchment stretched over the circular frame was fastened to the rim with huge nails, which also served to strengthen the frame, for the drum could only be moved by rolling it. Two drummers were required for the instrument to produce its full effect. On the Telloh vase is an enigmatic detail: the big drum is surmounted by a human form with the head of an animal. This depiction of a hybrid being has never been satisfactorily explained.[6]

Among the earliest musical instruments that have been mentioned was a kind of flute (*gu-di*) on a cuneiform tablet that is currently in the collection of the Vorderasiatisches Museum in Berlin. The tablet was unearthed in Sumer, the Southern Mesopotamian valley (present-day Iraq) and dated to around 2600–2500 B.C. A pair of badly damaged silver pipes that were excavated from a grave at Ur, dated to 2500 B.C., support the written record. The pipes were crafted with what appear to be finger holes, and it is believed that they formed a pair of tubes or "double-pipes," which were made of reeds. When reconstructed, it consisted of a pair of thin tubes that had three finger holes on one tube and four holes on the other. It could deliver a diatonic scale, possibly C-D-E-F-G-A.[7]

The most typical flute of these early ages was the vertically held simple reed-tub, sounded by blowing across one of the open ends. With three finger holes it was called *TI-GI* in Sumerian and *tigu* or *tegu* in Akkadian, and it was highly utilized during religious rituals. The *TI-GI* was also called *IMIN-E* ("the seven notes"), and was attested in temple records. Praise poetry of the Temple of Enki at Eridu (2200 B.C.) said that the musician on the seven notes brought forth a plaintive sound. Again, the account of a festival at the Temple of Ninab (2000 B.C.) depicted that the sound of the great drum, the "seven note" and the sacred drum was heard from far away, even in the city.[8] The most memorable instance for musical documentation came from the *Epic of Gilgamesh*, in which Gilgamesh interred a flute with Enkidu for his journey in the afterlife. It was made of carnelian, a semi-precious reddish-brown stone that was mined and processed in the East. It was used as early as 4000 B.C. in Mehrgarh, located in present-day Pakistan and the site of one of the earliest centers of agriculture and herding in South Asia (7000–5500 B.C.).[9]

Sections of the *Gilgamesh* tablet (three clay fragments) can be seen in the British Museum. Another brown calcite (limestone) cylinder seal in the same museum depicts a flute player. The long vertical flute, played by a seated figure on a stone cylinder seal of the Akkadian period, is one of the rare depictions of this kind of instrument from ancient Western Asia. Rim-blown vertical flutes are shown in Egyptian wall paintings of the Old and Middle kingdoms (2686–1690 B.C.E.), and this type of flute survives in North Africa, the Middle East and the Balkans. It may well have been common in ancient western Asia, though perhaps of too humble association to be depicted often.[10]

Wind instruments were invented by the early third millennium B.C. A cylinder seal found in the royal cemetery of Ur illustrates a monkey, surrounded by other animals, playing a long flute in the shade of a tree. The tradition of a flute-playing monkey, whether with a single- or a double-piped instrument, persisted for a long time. Actual flutes that were found at Ur could substantiate the story. These flutes had four equidistant finger holes in the silver tubing. It was certainly not until much later, doubtless in the Seleucid period (312–63 B.C.), that the panpipe made its appearance in Larsa (25 km north of Ur and near modern as-Senkereh). This instrument is like a mouth organ whose pipes, though externally of the same length, are actually stopped inside at different lengths so as to change the pitch of the notes. A small plaque discovered in Larsa portrays a woman playing this instrument, thus giving the earliest known demonstration of a method of music-making destined to have remarkable developments in succeeding ages. Although the trumpet was mentioned in Sumerian texts, the earliest known image of the instrument is from the eighteenth century B.C., in a wall painting found in the palace of Mari (an ancient Sumerian and Amorit city at modern Tell Hariri, Syria). In the image, a horn is held in a curious position between the thumb and fingers of the right hand by a bearded man with long hair. In the Temple of Ishtar, another more positive image of a trumpet was found. A statuette in a sanctuary represents a pair of musicians playing horns with a group of temple staff.[11]

Harps were one of the oldest and most characteristic of ancient musical instruments from Mesopotamia. The general name given to the harp was *GIŠ ZAG-SAL* ("wooden cross-strung instrument") because the strings had to pass across from the upright arm to the horizontal sound box. *ZAG-SAL* also had abstract connotations such as "glory" or "honor." This type of harp was also called AL ("sound" or "music") and was ascribed to the great god Enlil. The head of the instrument was made of lapis lazuli, and its voice, with the deep tones of its strings, sounded like that of a horned bull. It was used in the recitation of hymns of fate. It was considered holy, as it glittered as the stars. It uttered speech by day and poured out songs by night. It was said that the heroic god Ninurasha made it for Enlil, and the goddess Nisaba tendered her advice, while Enki, god of music, sang its praises. There was an old legend that a god, who was slain for the welfare of his land and people, actually resided within the instrument and spoke in its sounds. This was the reason that images of gods were represented on the body of the bronze kettledrum, which suggested that god, music (sound), and its instrument became the holy one: music became a part of god and the harp was his instrument.[12]

This verbal connection can be verified by the way in which the ancient harp was made and decorated. In the royal graves at Ur (dated to the earlier part of the third millennium B.C.) a large harp was found. Praise hymns called it a great harp. It has a rectangular sound box embellished with an edging of mosaic (lapis lazuli, shell and red stone). The front of the sound box, deep and wide unlike the shallow resonance-chamber of the lyre, was decorated with four superimposed panels representing mythological scenes, and above these was a bull head of gold leaf over a wooden core, its hair and beard made of lapis lazuli. There were eleven strings fastened to the upright by gold-headed nails. The strings were of gut like the traces of those found on the lyres; they were not tuned by revolving pegs, but passed over metal guides (a typical Sumerian invention) that were twisted around the arm and tightened or loosened by hand.[13]

In addition to this fine example of golden harp, simpler and smaller specimens are also shown in the seal impressions of the early dynasties. For example, images of performances illustrate a pear-shaped lute, with a tiny body and a very long neck. The larger harp was either rested on the ground or placed on a stand by the player; smaller instruments could be carried and played in processions. A lyre figure was found on a Gudea stele. In it a musician was seated behind with his right hand plucking a seven-string harp. A similar or even identical type of instrument (with a bull-head sound box) appeared in other tombs discovered several centuries after the period of the "royal" cemetery of Ur. It became apparent that the bull has more than a decorative meaning for the musicians; the figure-head—bull, cow, calf or stag—symbolized the divine nature of music and even designated the tone of the instrument.[14]

The association between music and animals went back to the very beginning of Mesopotamian history. Early Mesopotamian beliefs and music practices retained this prehistoric association between music and the voices of spirit-animals. This association was reflected in Mesopotamian visual art, wherein animals were portrayed playing musical instruments and gods, kings, and priests were illustrated wearing animal body parts to symbolize that the great men's powers (effected through their vocal pronouncements) were analogous to the powers of the sonically conceived spirit-animals. Eventually, the voices of spirit-animals became the voices of gods. The gods, in fact, were differentiated in terms of their voices. Ea (or Enki), the god of the deep sea, was associated with the drum, the sound of which personified his essence. Ramman, who commanded the thunder and the winds, was the "spirit of sonorous voice." The goddess Ishtar was known as "the soft reed-pipe."[15]

This close and significant connection between gods and music in Mesopotamia made musical performance an important part of everyday life. Mesopotamians worshiped many gods, and they believed that their gods were actually living in the great temples on earth. Keeping gods happy became essential part of their lives and the world that they inhabited. The worshippers played music several times a day as they served the gods a sumptuous meal. The meal, which was often consisted many courses, was set out before the statue of the god or goddess. It could include over a hundred vessels of beer, two hundred loaves of bread, twenty rams, and two bulls. Music was played, and incense was sprinkled. The musical performance in this ritual was as grand and lavish as the feast, and it was played by large ensembles of singers and instrumentalists playing harps, flutes, reed pipes, and other instruments. In a pre-biblical culture (before the words of gods were invented and had evolved into holy script), music was the only language that was believed to be able to reach the ears of gods. Thus, one who had intimate knowledge of musical language would have the most political power because he would know secret formulas and incantations for reach the gods. Each chant had a special quality for communion with a chosen deity or had a definite magical effect on specific god. In other words, the musical language of ancient Mesopotamia became so sophisticated that it was believed to have the ability to fine-tune the mood of gods and alter their behavior.

By the middle of the third millennium B.C., religious musical rituals developed into elaborate ceremonies wherein each god had acquired his or her particular sound, tones, melody and preferred instrument. One of the most ancient of the gods, Ea, the ruler of the deep, had his name written with the sign *balag* (drum); the dreaded sound of the drum became the personification of his essence. For Ramman, there was the spirit and sound of sonorous voice because he commanded the thunder and the winds. Perhaps because the breath of Ramman was imagined to resemble the sound of wind, the reed-pipe tones often represented him. The soft reed pipe presented the goddess Ishtar, the virgin mother, while a gentle poetic vocal was associated with her partner, Tammuz, the god of tender voice.[16]

The musical establishment in the temples consisted of liturgists and psalmists who were charged with the proper conduct of the daily services. In the great temple of Ningirsu at Lagash (one of the oldest Mesopotamian cities, northeast of Ur), a special officer was responsible for training the liturgists and psalmists while another officer was in charge of the choir. The chanters and musicians, both male and female, were organized under several titles. The NAR (Akkadian *naru*) was a musician, who played flute, double-pipe, harp, lyre or drum or sang. The *UŠ-KU, LAGAR* or *GALA* was a liturgical psalmist. In Akkadian the former appears to have been also called *zammeru* and the latter *kalu*, but the names were not well defined, and they often overlapped or were used interchangeably. In the early period, the *GALA* was a liturgist who sang to win the favor of the gods rather than a consecrated priest. Later on, the *GALA* or *kalu* often carried a sacred drum (*BALAB*) associated with religious ritual. The Gudea statue inscription recorded that in the city of cemetery and rituals, no corpse was buried without the accompaniment of the beating of drums and the wailing of the psalmists. There were different ranks of psalmists. The chief psalmist (*UŠ-KU Maḥ*) was a permanent official of the temple with a high salary. He had a thorough education because an Assyrian scriber once called him the wisdom of Ear (god of letters).

Temple ritual was a lavish event. In the frontcourt a large drum (*A-LA*) was set up and in some temples even a large bell (*NIG-KAL-GA*) was placed. Ceremonies of libation and supplication were performed. In the great temple at Lagash and probably also at Eridu (the ancient Sumerian city in modern Tell Abu Shahrain, Iraq) drums and bells were accompanied by the blowing of horns. Within the temple stringed instruments were played to accompany the psalmists and chanters. Harps were also played, especially during the oracular utterances of the high priest. This was the reason why it was called the instrument of fate. Its sound was heard by day and night, sometimes combined with the ritual flute. In a late record, it led an orchestra composed of the seven-stringed lyre (*sebitu*), the "covered" pipe (*kanzabu*), the single-pipe of oboe type (*malilu*), the two-stringed lute (*sinnitu*) and other instruments.[17]

Liturgical chanting was taught at the temple college. The presenters were immersed in the mysteries of their sacred office, including a precise knowledge of the cantillation (*kalutu*) which, like the *prae-cantus* of the Christian church, was an art form of extensive training. The Sumerian language, like the Latin in the Roman Church, was the language of the liturgies although, later, an interlinear Akkadian version existed. As in Christian lands, Mesopotamian presenters were well versed in science. Yet their most important work was to copy and edit the temple liturgies, many of which have survived.

Little can be verified about the actual music of the Mesopotamian temples, although a vast treasure of liturgies, breviaries, psalms, and songs are available to inspect. These records verify and express the mood and sentiment of ancient temple music. Historians believe that a full index of this musical material would rival that of the Roman or Anglican books of devotion. Unlike the Roman and Anglican church music that inherited the Jewish and Greek music repertoire, the public musical rite in Mesopotamia evolved from a single psalm or hymn from Sumerian days. It began as a lamentation (*ersemma*), which strictly meant a psalm or hymn set to a reed pipe. Yet other instruments were also used to accompany the psalm: flute (*tig*), drum (*balag*), kettledrum (*lilis*), and tambourine (*adapa*). Over time, the music came to be known by the name of the complementary instrument. This single psalm service was replaced by the *kisub* before the time of the first Babylonian dynasty (1830 B.C.). The *kisub,* an *ersemma* accompanied by a complete liturgical service, was compiled by the schools of liturgists who had combined several of the *ersemma* type of psalms or hymns that had a common appeal. By this time, they were extremely long services composed of a succession of melodies with changing refrains and musical motifs. Each liturgy was now called a "series" (*iskāru*), and each had as few as five psalms or hymns and as many as twenty-seven. At a later period the term *ersemma* was revived as an intercessional hymn at the end of a *kišub*.[18]

The surviving literary record shows that the ancient liturgical performance not only got longer but also became more varied in its vocal and instrumental forms. It became a long assembly of various songs (named by their first lines) and melodies with individual titles and alternating voice and instruments. This is quite similar to early Latin and English liturgy, in which a rubric might say: a song to the tune of "Thou wilt not cast me down." Another might signify a processional movement on the part of choir. A choral march or a real recessional might follow at the end of the litany (of the *kisub*). Interludes were also found in lengthy litanies, and one may perhaps see in these an explanation of the much-discussed selah of the Old Testament. Even antiphony (*gisgigal*) became fairly common.[19]

In ancient Mesopotamia, musical performance was not only a religious affair. It was also regular public celebration to commemorate a victorious military campaign. In this ceremony, a man holding a lyre with both hands is accompanied by a woman singing behind him with her hands crossed on her breast. Images of singing and dancing women existed as early as the first half of the third millennium and are illustrated by the small statue of Ur-Nina (The Great Singer) discovered at Mari. Besides the complete statue, another damaged sculpture of the same singer was found. Only the torso and parts of a hand holding a musical instrument remained. Ur-Nina, then, played, sang and danced, no doubt with equal proficiency and to the entire satisfaction of her sovereign.

By the time of the Akkadian Empire (2334–2154 B.C.), the word for music that had been inherited from Old Sumerian religious ritual extended to include other forms of entertainment. The Akkadian *Nigūtu* or *ningūtu* (music) carried the connotation of joy and merrymaking. *Alālu* (singing) was included in not only religious music but also popular activities. A seal in the Louvre displays a peaceful scene in which a peasant plays a flute to one of his herd. Music and singing apparently became a popular expression of emotion by people of all walks of life. The toil songs (also known as well songs) were mentioned in Exodus 21:17, and the story of singing Arabs was told by an Assyrian annalist. It is recorded that some Arab prisoners of war who were captured and enslaved by the Assyrians sang to relieve their pain and sorrow. It was also recorded that royal musicians gave public concert to gladden the hearts of the people.[20]

Babylonian and Assyrian cultures apparently inherited various forms of musical performance that originated in Sumer and carried them into following millennia. The best example of this continuity was attested by the archaeological discovery of the city of Nineveh, capital of the Neo-Assyrian Empire on the eastern bank of the Tigris River. Assyrian culture emerged originally as geographical and dialectical divisions of Akkadian, and is believed to have contributed the first universal Semitic language of the ancient Near East.[21] Assyrian archaeological findings share many forms with those of ancient Sumer. Unpainted pottery and metal vases have been found throughout the Tigris-Euphrates Valley and are dated to the late 4th millennium B.C. During the 2nd and 3rd millennia B.C., Nineveh was known primarily as a religious center. The healing powers of its statue of the goddess Ishtar were renowned as far away as Egypt. The unpainted Ninevite pottery dated around 3000 B.C. was similar to that discovered at other Sumerian sites of approximately the same period. It contains a series of attractively painted and incised ware known as Ninevite V, which is a home product distinct from that of the south. Beads found in these strata may be dated to c. 2900 B.C.[22]

The Assyrian bells were embossed with symbols of Ea, the divine patron of music, while the skin head of the Babylonian drum (*balag*) was made from the hide of a bull. For more than ten centuries, the Temple of Ea (*Luma*) was the stage for musical ritual performance. The image of a bull was also a prominent feature on the sound-chest of the grand *kithara*. This depicts an association between animals that play musical instruments and gods, kings, priests, and mummers, dressed in animal or fish-like garb. Well-known art remains also show animals that listen to or attend musical performances.[23]

Ample lithographic material of music and musical instruments survived from the time of Ashur-nasir-pall III (883–859 B.C.). Among these were sculptured slabs illustrating two musicians playing the lower chested harp (*sagsal*). By now, musicians had lost their divine connection and had become skilled employees (or slaves) of the court. For example, when Sennacherib (Assyrian king, r. 705–681 B.C.) invaded Syria, he sent one of his generals to lay siege to Jerusalem. To soften the wrath of the conqueror, Hezekiah (716–697 B.C.), the king of Judah sent his wives and his daughter, and male and female musicians as a gift to Sennacherib hoping that he himself might be spared. A bas-relief carved circa 645 B.C. in Sennacherib's Southwest Palace at Nineveh shows a procession led by musicians playing vertical harps of various sizes and a double-flute player. There is also bas-relief from Karatepe (850 B.C.) showing lyre and double-flute players.[24]

Ashurbanipal (668–630 B.C.) was one of the few Assyrian kings who had a scribal education and could read the cuneiform script in Sumerian and Akkadian. He took it upon himself to learn the wisdom of Nebo, as presented on clay tablets. During his reign he collected cuneiform texts from all over Mesopotamia, and especially Babylon, in the library in Nineveh.[25] The Library of Ashurbanipal is perhaps the most compelling discovery in the ancient Near East. There are over 30,000 clay tablets of historical inscriptions, letters, and administrative and legal texts. There were thousands of divinatory, magical, medical, literary and lexical texts providing archaeologists with an amazing wealth of Mesopotamian literary, religious, and administrative history. Among the findings was the Enuma Elish, also known as the Epic of Creation, which depicts a traditional Babylonian view of creation in which the god Marduk slays Tiamat, the personification of salt water, and creates the world from her body. In this particular version, man is created from the blood of a revolutionary god, Qingu, who led the battle against Marduk on behalf of the legion of minor gods. The *Epic of Gilgamesh*, also found at Nineveh, is a compelling account of the hero and his friend Enkidu seeking to destroy the demon Humbaba. The gods punish the pair for their arrogance, however, by having Enkidu die from illness. After Enkidu's death Gilgamesh seeks Utnapishtim in order to find out the secret of immortality. The library also included hymns and prayers, medical, mathematical, ritual, divinatory and astrological texts. Aside from the many other myths found in Nineveh, a large selection of "omen texts" has been excavated and deciphered.[26]

During the Assyrian period, as the literature of ancient Mesopotamia was read, edited, and preserved, the tradition of musical performance continued. Between a register of foot soldiers evidently singing (since they are clapping their hands in time) as they file past and a scene of horsemen and archers engaged in battle, the intermediate register shows a groom leading four restive, unharnessed horses and behind him four musicians, facing each other two by two. Their postures illustrate that they were on the move, pacing back and forth alternately. Two men on one side are playing a tabor and a lyre (or perhaps a psaltery); those on the other have cymbals and an eight-stringed lyre.

The best illustration of an Assyrian musical scene is the fine relief carving called the Garden Party, from the North Palace of Ashurbanipal (the last great king of the Neo-Assyrian Empire, 668–627 B.C.). The king is giving the queen an account of his Elamite campaign as they sit facing each other and enjoying a banquet. A harpist is playing music in the shade of a tree from which hangs the head of Teuman, the defeated king of Elam. Elsewhere, returning from a successful hunting expedition, the Assyrian monarch pours a libation over the dead animals to a musical accompaniment.

Several ivory pyxes discovered at Nimrud throw further light on the music of ancient Mesopotamia. One of them is decorated with a banquet scene. Seated on a throne is a woman, perhaps a goddess or a princess. With a cup in her hand, she is about to do honor to the dishes set before her on a high pedestal table. Behind her are five young musicians, two playing the double pipes, two the psaltery and one the tabor. Here, then, once again we have a small orchestra composed of all three families of instruments (winds, percussion and strings) described above.[27] From the same period a large sculptured slab commemorates Ashurbanipal's victory over the Elamite king Teuman. Musicians followed by women and children clapping their hands are celebrating the accession to the throne of Ummani-gash, a refugee Elamite prince. Well in view are seven harpists, two double-pipe players and a man with a tabor.

The musical tradition in forms of songs, musical tunes, and liturgical performance continued through various languages in the Near East. Although the sound of the music has not been preserved, literature provides clues as how they were performed over time. For example, the later Akkadian word *enū* meant "answer," "repeat." It may have been derived from the Sumerian *en* (*siptu* in Akkadian). A Babylonian antiphonal lamentation in later Akkadian duplicated a Sumerian original of the time of Narām-Sin (2280 B.C.), when it was sung by two groups of women from different towns. Each half-chorus sang the lines alternately.[28] *The Liturgy and Prayer to the Moon God* was a more moving example of an antiphon; it dates from the time of Dungi (twenty-first century B.C.). With its twin recurring refrains, it appealed to the god Sin to care for flocks and harvests.[29]

The best example of public delivery of ancient poetry with musical setting was the New Year's Festival at Babylon. This celebration, the most important holiday in the Mesopotamian calendar, lasted ten or eleven days, and the entire population participated. According to the Sumero-Akkadian belief, the struggle between order and chaos and the subsequent creation of the world were not permanent acts carrying with them conclusion. This struggle had to be re-enacted at the beginning of each year in order to ensure the stability of the cosmos for the coming year. For this reason the Creation Epic (*enuma elish*) was recited with due solemnity on the fourth day of the New Year's Festival. Kingship, which was considered a gift from the gods, had to be renewed each successive year. On a certain day of the New Year's Festival the Babylonian king had to go through a cleansing and humiliating ceremony. He was divested of all insignia of royal power, was struck on the cheek, and was forced to make a negative confession before Marduk that during the past year he had not been unmindful of the gods, of the city of Babylon, and of his subjects. After the recitation the door was open. All the *ēribbīti* priests entered and performed the traditional rites. Then the *kalū*-priests and the singers did the same.[30]

The ritual has to follow a specific procedure. Two hours from sunrise as the trays of the god Bel and the goddess Beltiya have been set, the *amas-masu*-priest began to purify the temple by sprinkling water on it. The water was from a cistern of the Tigris and a cistern of the Euphrates. He then beat the kettledrum inside the temple. He would always have a censer and a torch with him while entering the temple. While the priest remained in the courtyard he could not enter the sanctuary of the deities Bel and Beltiya. When the purification of the temple was completed, he could now enter the temple Ezida, into the sanctuary of the god Nabu, with censer, torch, and vessel to purify the temple, and then he would sprinkle water on the sanctuary. He was supposed to smear all the doors of the sanctuary with cedar resin. In the court of the sanctuary, he placed a silver censer, upon which he would mix aromatic ingredients and cypress. He called a slaughterer to decapitate a ram, the meat of which the *masmasu*-priest would use in performing the *kuppuru*-ritual for the temple. He was to recite the incantations for exorcising the temple as he was purifying the entire sanctuary including its environs, and he was to remove the censer after that. The *masmasu*-priest and the slaughterer went out into the open country. As long as the god Nabu was in Babylon, they were not to enter Babylon, but to stay in the open country from the fifth to the twelfth day (of the month Nisannu). The *urigallu*-priest of the temple Ekua was not supposed to view the purification of the temple. If he did, he would no longer be pure. After the purification of the temple, when it was three and one-third hours after sunrise, the *urigallu*-priest of the temple Ekua was to go out and call all the artisans. They brought forth the Golden Heaven from the treasury of the god Marduk and to cover the temple of Ezida, the sanctuary of the god Nabu and the foundation of the temple. As the *urigallu*-priest and the artisans began to sing, ritual recitation went on.[31]

Like other Semites, the musical genes of Hebrew speakers came from the centuries-long tradition of ancient Semitic culture from which Hebrew evolved from a dialect to a language. The record of musical culture in the biblical period is mostly from literary references in the Bible and post-biblical sources. The Old Testament reveals how God's ancient people were devoted to the study and practice of music, which holds a unique place in historical and prophetic books, as well as the Psalter.

The music of religious ritual was first used by King David, who is credited with confirming the men of the Tribe of Levi as the custodians of the music of the divine service. The twenty-four books of the Old Testament, and the 150 psalms in the Book of Psalms ascribed to King David, have become the basic repertoires of Judeo-Christian hymnology. Figurines and iconographic depictions reveal that people played chordophones and frame drums, and that the human voice was essential, as women and men sang love songs along with laments for the deceased. Data also describe outdoor scenes of music and dancing in sometimes-prophetic frenzies, often with carefully orchestrated and choreographed musicians and singers within specially built structures.[32]

The Hebrews did not invent ritual music, but they inherited and enriched the musical traditions of ancient Mesopotamia. By biblical times, music had become able to express a great variety of moods and feelings or the broadly marked antitheses of joy and sorrow, hope and fear, faith and doubt. In fact, every shade and quality of sentiment is found in the wealth of songs and psalms and in the diverse melodies of the people. The highly sophisticated musical ritual in King Solomon's Temple included 24 choral groups of 288 musicians and ran for 21 services a week.[33]

Antiphony (also referred to as responsorial singing), which was originally seen in ancient religious rites, became established as a common form of liturgical performance and substantially influenced the form of poetry, whose words were initially accompanied by music. The musical origins of Semitic poetry determined the initial form of literary expression. For example, the majority of Sumerian literature (with little or minimal Akkadian rewriting) came from works of praise (to praise a deity, a temple or a hero king). A speech was directed to someone or something that was cherished, worshiped, but was now gone or had died. Eventually, invisible gods were praised. The verbal praise derived ultimately from the form of incantations. Praise hymns appeared to have roots in the language of spells that were intended to make things happen, to glorify a thing or person, or to prolong the effect of good and desirable qualities. Similarly, works of lament developed from spells to bring back what was gone through the power of spoken words.[34]

The words of spells were spoken in different tunes, tone or rhythm. Music brought extra effect and emphasis to spoken words through tone, rhythm and duration. The lament for Dumuzi was performed in the mourning procession at the annual celebration of weeping for the dead god. The lament of the temple was performed to induce gods to rebuild the destroyed temple. In a way these words created a different kind of language or communication that was higher than the ordinary spoken words. The words were not simply spoken but were performed by singing, weeping, or screaming them to the gods who held man's fate.

Most scholars believe that the recorded words of Sumerian were translated and rewritten into Akkadian, and they began to attain the structure and maturity of a written literature. For example, third-person narrative began to develop, and storytelling became more coherent in the Babylonian versions of epics. However, as Sumerian stopped being spoken (around Ur III period, 2100–2000 B.C.), cuneiform script began to transform from a written language to a writing technology, which could be transformed to write any language.[35] This is somewhat similar to Latin, a verbal and written language that functioned at various cultural and social levels (liturgical, political, legal, philosophical, and religious) as it spread into vocabularies of various European vernaculars, and eventually to alphabets that were used to record different languages. Various Semitic and non–Semitic languages in the Near East, like the European vernaculars, had existed for many centuries before Sumerian script fell out of favor. They were distinct ancient languages. Like the European vernaculars, they evolved as local dialects registered (written) in a borrowed alphabet, but the majority of their speakers had never spoken Sumerian. The literature that they produced did not share the same conceptual foundation as Akkadian.

In the pre–Biblical world, languages of religion had neither distinct levels nor boundaries between them. The words that spoke to gods (hymns and palms), words that described gods (myth) and the words that were spoken by gods were from the same language, the language of storytelling, private or public speech. Since the words that depicted the stories of gods and their divine lives were the same as the words for men, Semitic epics created deities who had much more human characteristics (as did the ancient Greek myths). Like the Olympic gods, Semitic gods had human images and lived among men. They had good and bad days, happiness and sorrow, and they could die like men or suffer enormous hardship in their pursuit of immortality. They had the full range of human emotions—jealousy, rage, and desire—and could feel pain. Semitic gods were close to their worshippers and easy to see and to talk to because they shared a common language with humankind.

As written, Semitic languages did not completely register the sound of the speaking voice (in other words, Semitic languages were not alphabetic writing in the sense of English or the Romance languages) until Arabic; the prosody of neither Sumerian nor Akkadian were perceived as based on rhyme in English sense. The written Semitic languages, unlike the typical European alphabetic script that registers every single sound, were consonantal "skeletons" into which vowels had to be inserted and to which prefixes and suffixes had to be attached.[36] In this specific linguistic and scriptural context, the study of poetic form had to focus instead on the patterning of composition within individual lines of verse or between pairs of lines, or groups of three or four on the basis of meaning and structure; assonance, alliteration and rhyme are based on limited knowledge of their original phonetic characteristics.[37] As the sound of Semitic poetry is somewhat lost in the sands of time, the most prominent continuity of literature will be revealed and adopted in poetic imagery and its organization that moves from one language or dialect to another and from one literary canon to another.

The poetic imagery (or metaphorical language) of ancient Semitic was rich and complex because it had been developing within bilingual or multi-lingual contexts and was revived and re-imagined many times through many different languages and dialects, each of which brought in something new and fresh.[38] Unlike ancient Chinese or Greek, which were enriched within a single language by imagery accumulating from a singular textual tradition, Semitic imageries often were juxtaposed through translation, imitation, or both. Literal and figurative meanings intermingled as different levels of expression flowed forward and away from each other. The best example of the constantly accumulated and syncretized repertoire of images is the names and images of the moon god. Nanna, the son of Enlil and Ninlil, was the god of the moon in classical Sumerian myth. The Semitic moon god Sue'n/Sin was in its origin a separate deity from the Sumerian Nanna, but from the Akkadian Empire period the two underwent syncretization and became one. The name of the Assyrian moon god Su'en/Sin was usually spelled as DEN.ZU, which means "lord of wisdom." He was not regarded as the head of the pantheon even in the period (2600–2400 B.C.) during which Ur exercised a large measure of supremacy over the Euphrates valley. (The head of Sumerian pantheon was his father Enlil.) However, it was at this time that mythology began to elevate Su'en/Sin towards the godhead by describing him as the "father of the gods," "chief of the gods," "creator of all things," and the like. Nanna/Sin also accumulated images associated with light. His chief sanctuary at Ur was named *E-gish-shir-gal* (house of the great light). He became the national deity as Enheduanna, the daughter of King Sargon of Akkad, played the powerful role of En Priestess in the cult of Nanna/Sin.[39]

The first fourteen lines of *Balbale* depict a scene of rural life as well as an impression of a religious rite. The moon god Su'en, the cowhead, was bringing the milk to the table (altar) while many cows were calving almost simultaneously. In this dark night, all the cows, bright, little, and large were grazing at the brilliant risen moon. They could simultaneously be the subjects of offering or the offerings themselves in the hands of the moon god.[40] Semitic poetics inherited these overlapping, vague and specific images and reworked them into new poetry. The best example of the accumulation and reconfiguration of images is the evolution of animal images.[41]

A good example of how literary narrative continued while language itself changed is the rewriting of the Sumerian epic in Babylonian and the

Babylonian epic into Hebrew (biblical stories). Although scholars have been debating the origins and specific transmission of the Semitic narratives, they have never questioned the obvious continuity of the storyline, narrative forms, and patterns of expression of these literatures.

The Sumerian epic was the forerunner of Babylonian epics. The *Descent of Istar*, to take the obvious example, is nothing but a free rewriting of the Sumerian *Descent of Inanna*. Even though the actual story is not proven to be of Sumerian origin, the motifs and phraseology present strong Sumerian influences.[42]

Figurative images were often clustered densely in Sumerian literature. The word *axes* attracted many comparative and super-relative descriptions, some exaggerated for emotional effect: "Stone which has no equal," or "The arm of the man who strikes it will never get tired." A large number of figurative speeches can be found, such as: "Nergal, great battle-net for malefactors covering all enemies! Warrior, you are a great and furious storm upon the land which disobeys your father! You terrify the walled cities and the settlements as you stand in your path like a wild bull, smiting them with your great horns!"[43]

Densely constructed string of images and fragmented stories became more fluid and leveled out after centuries of rewriting. The best example of this long process of re-framing and polishing is the textual history of Gilgramesh, the most famous and influential narrative of Mesopotamia. The story of the king of Uruk (biblical Erech, Gen. 10:10) began with five independent Sumerian poems about Gilgamesh. Four of these poems were used as source material for a combined epic in Akkadian. The first, "Old Babylonian," version of the epic dates to the 18th century B.C. and is titled *Shūtur eli sharrī* (Surpassing All Other Kings). Only a few fragments of it survive. The later, Standard Babylonian, version dates from the thirteenth to the tenth centuries B.C. and bears the title *Sha naqba īmuru* (He Who Saw the Deep). Some of the best copies were discovered in the library ruins of the seventh-century B.C. Assyrian king Ashurbanipal.[44]

The early literary language of ancient Mesopotamia was, like many ancient languages such as Chinese and Greek, a written form of spoken language (recorded dialogue) rather than a language of literature (in the English sense). This is the reason why it did not include the same literary genres as modern literary language. Sumerian literature was often categorized according to performance rather than literary modes. For example, the terms *Sir-gida* (long song) and *ti-gi* (drum) became written according to the way in which they were originally performed. Like modern poetry, Sumerian poetry was untitled, and is referred to by its initial lines.[45]

The term *ŠU-ILLA* ("the lifting of the hand") means a prayer spoken to god privately. Private prayer could also be accompanied by music. This musical setting can be verified by a prayer said and recorded in a hymn titled "Hymn to Ishtar" of the Isin Period (2100 B.C.). The suppliant says, "With the strains of the lyre [*AL-GAR*], whose sound is sweet, I will speak to thee." The lament of a penitent, his crying is likened to the plaintive sound of the reed pipe (*NǍ*), which was probably linked with his petition. Since the time of ancient Sumer, musical accompaniment was required for liturgy. The lute (*TI-GI*) and the square timbrel (*A-DǍ P*) were the favorites, while Akkadian recitations and love-ditties rejoiced in the ten-stringed harp (*eširtu*), the Syrian reed pipe (*imbubu* or *malilu*), the curved pipe (*pītu*) and the covered pip (*kitmu*).[46]

The words-to-music relationship in Mesopotamia liturgy was similar to that of early modern Europe rather than to that of the Middle Ages because similar linguistic reorientation took place in the ancient Near East. The Christian liturgy of medieval Europe was initially sung in Greek and Latin; the hymns were set to music by metrical terms (in alternating short and long syllables). As European vernaculars gradually replaced Latin liturgical singing, composers had to make an effort to suit the rhythm of the emerging vernaculars, whose words and phrasing were different from those of Latin. In the sixteenth century, verbal accentuation began to provide the main rhythm for music and song-writing. More and more prayers were sung in non–Latin language. Musicians had to seize the rhythm of the vernaculars to make song and music more expressive.[47] The religious liturgy of ancient Mesopotamia was in a similar situation because it had already experienced linguistic reorientation. Music had been adapted to accommodate the rhythm of poetry and poetry had begun to cultivate its own rhythm independent of musical measure. Therefore, although many literary languages and spoken dialogues came and went in the Near East, their relationship with music remained constant. As their musical composition often was obsessed with words, verbal accentuation (rather than quantitative measure) was the center of musical evolution, singing, and performance.

In the rarely available example of musical accompaniment recorded in the Sumerian "Hymn on Creation," it is evident that most words were sung in free recitative, the verbal accentuation giving the rhythm, which was reinforced by the harp or the drum accompaniment. To render this correctly and artistically required not only knowledge of a long-standing oral tradition, but also incorporation of contemporary speaking rhythm. In fact the continuation of this tradition, relayed from generation to generation and from language to language, was dependent on more than just professional training in the modern sense; rather, it required the participation of the majority of speakers. In other words, ritual singing and recitation kept Semitic language alive and firmly on the minds, ears and lips of its speakers.

Popular involvement in ritual singing is attested in many historical records. A "Liturgy and Prayer to the Moon God," written during the UR III period, began with six lines, an introduction in which a single chanter appeals to the god Sin, as watchman of the Temple of Enlil and patron of the flocks and the harvest. Then it is followed by ten strophes of four lines each in the manner of a litany. Lines one and three of each section have a recurring refrain beginning, "O Nanna, God of Wisdom art thou" or "God of Light are thou," while the intermediate lines tell of some aspect of the god in respect to the fields. This section would have been rendered by chanter and chorus or by two semi-choruses antiphonally (sung alternately by separate groups). Then there is a short recitative by the chanter describing Enlil's orders to Sin with an appeal for his return to Ur. The liturgy ends with a chorus rejoicing in the anticipated fulfillment of Enlil's commends. Another antiphonal use was presented in a lament written at Babylon in 297 B.C. The lament, which is traced back to the last quarter of the third millennium B.C., was said to be sung by women of various Sumerian and Akkadian towns who were called upon to mourn their fate under the Gutain oppressors. The singers came in two semi-choruses, each singing alternate lines appropriate to their respective groups. It appeared that the compositions in recitative form were preferably allotted to a solo singer because she could perform more freely in tempo and accent than would be possible in a choral rendering. In the transcription of the "Creation Hymn," however, the whole was set in fixed time by the use of crotchets. This crude method has been adopted to indicate roughly the probable accentual stresses placed on the original words.[48]

As time went on, the original music (measured in musical rather than verbal terms) disappeared from the written records of liturgy. They were replaced by syllabic signs, which had no connection with music. It took many centuries for poetry to completely cultivate its own music and for many poetic traditions in various languages to transform musical (strophic or antiphonic) devices into verbal forms of repetition. Several literary languages appeared and disappeared in the Near East. Both the music and sound of the poetry were forgotten, but the rhythm of the poetry and its verbal structure remained.[49]

The most obvious verbal structures inherited from musical accompaniment are repetition of words and phrases (from notes or tones). The following section will depict the process in which the literary repetition (called parallelism) was gradually cultivated and refined through various Semitic languages.[50] It often took many centuries to cultivate verbal repetition to replace musical structure, and the repeated linguistic re-orientations (from Sumerian, Akkadian, Ugaritic, to Hebrew) made it even more difficult. Verbal repetition as an abstract concept had never been a formal idea for the Semitic poets, just as an English poet would never meditate about his own language (in general terms) during his composition. He simply opens his mouth and ears. To say things several times without using the same wording was an inherited linguistic habit for a Semitic poet. To create elegant variations on a single idea was natural to a speaker of biblical Hebrew in the same way that simple, direct speaking was natural for most European languages in early modern times.[51]

This linguistic habit was cultivated by the linguistic history of the Near East, and can be easily seen when reading Akkadian and Hebrew poetry. The liturgical tradition continued even though the language of recitation changed, and poetry began to create its own music prosody based on verbal organization rather than musical measures. Similar prosodic history can be found in English poetry during the early modern and modern periods after it departed from Latin or when it borrowed verse forms from Romance languages, such as French and Italian. It can also be found in Tang Chinese poetry. The first form of verbal prosody often was based on stress, as demonstrated in Akkadian poetry.

After a century of research, scholars are still debating the metrics of Akkadian poetry, but they have agreed that Akkadian meter was not based on counting and measuring syllables as were Latin and Greek verses. Most scholars recognize a "standard" verse that existed during various periods of Akkadian poetry that was based on counting accentual peaks.[52] It has four accentual peaks that appear to balance each other (2/2) as in *Enuma eliš* I:47–48:

> Īpulma Mummu / Apsû Imallik
> sukkalum lā magiru / milik mumīšu
>
> Mummu spoke up with counsel for Apsû—
>
> "Hullligamma abī / alkata ešīta;
> urriš lū šupšuhāt / mūšiš lū ṣallāt."
>
> "Father, destroy that lawless way of life,
> so you may rest in the day-time and sleep by night!"[53]

Similar stress-based rhythm can be also be heard in Babylonian epic:

1 iltam zumrā rašubti ilātim
2 litta''id bēlet iššī rabīt igigī
3 ištar zumrā rašubti ilātim
4 litta''id bēlet ilī nišī rabīt igigī

1 Sing ye of the goddess, the most fearsome of the gods,
2 Praise be upon the lady ruler of men, the greatest of the Igigi!

3 Sing ye of Ishtar, the most fearsome of the gods,
4 Praise be upon the lady ruler of the people, the greatest of the Igigi!
5 šāt mēleṣim ruāmam labšat
6 za'nat inbī mīkiam u kuzbam
7 šāt mēleṣim ruāmam labšat
8 za'nat inbī mīkiam u kuzbam

5 She who gets excited, clothed in sex appeal,
6 adorned with fruits, charm and allure.
7 She who gets excited, clothed in sex appeal,
8 adorned with fruits, charm and allure.[54]

The following Babylonian poetry illustrates how simple repetition or paralleled clauses worked in a long monologue before a formal and mature parallelism began to be a dominant form of Semitic poetry.[55]

"The Righteous Sufferer (*Ludlul bēl nēmeqi*)" is a long monologue in which a noble person told the story about how he met with every conceivable calamity and was eventually restored to health and prosperity by God. It was a written speech using compelling paralleling or contrasting images to dramatize events and achieve emotional effect. For example, "My god has forsaken me and disappeared," "My goddess has failed me and keeps at a distance." "The benevolent angel who (walked) beside [me] has departed." "My sonorous shout is [reduced] to silence." "My lofty head is bowed down to the ground." "Dread has enfeebled my robust heart." "A novice has turned back my broad chest." "My arms, (though once) strong, are both paralyzed." It constructed verbal (rather than musical) repetition, which was a repetition with varied and contrast images. It also used paralleled statements to reinforce the same sentiment: "If I walk the street, ears are pricked"; "If I enter the palace, eyes blink." "My city frowns on me as an enemy"; "My land is savage and hostile." "My friend has become foe"; "My companion has become a wretch and a devil."[56]

"The Dialogue of Pessimism" is a dialogue between a master and slave. The master announces to his slave that he is about to do something, and the discreet slave promptly agrees and points out the benefit of the proposed course of action. But the master has already tired of the idea and declares that he will certainly not do the thing, whereupon the slave equally promptly mentions some of the unpleasant consequences that might have followed the realization of the plan. When the master has thus disposed of all the ideas that he can summon, he finally asks the slave what is worth doing. Now the slave takes the initiative and declares that death is the only desirable end.[57] Here the repetition is followed by a contrary clause and than back to repetition, revealing a verbal structure to be further polished into more formal parallelism. A similar tendency can be observed in pre–Islamic Arabic poetry, where lines were rhymed but not yet dominantly parallelistic, because Arabic poetry at this stage was not an established written poetry yet.[58]

As words and music departed from each other and became independent expressions, poetry began to cultivate its own music (prosody). In the Near East this process began with the emergence of Akkadian, a much more speech-friendly language than Sumerian. The written Akkadian was more suitable to record speech. Therefore written language could more closely reflect the original speech, which provided a vehicle for linguistic continuity. However, it took Semitic languages many centuries and several linguistic re-orientations (Akkadian, Babylonian, Assyrian, Ugarit, Hebrew, and Aramaic) to overcome the inherited discrepancy between written and spoken language. Arabic was the crystallization of this age-long effort.

The path to verbal parallelism varied from language to language among the ancient Semitics. The earliest parallelism in poetry that might be considered similar to that of Hebrew appeared in Ugaritic texts (14th century B.C.). Ugaritic became the first non–Akkadian Semitic script, as the scribes of Ugarit wrote down their own vernacular using the traditional Akkadian script. They exploited the alphabetic principle that had already inspired the invention of the Canaanite alphabet farther south, but devised signs using cuneiform impressions on clay, as in Akkadian. The Ugaritic alphabet consisted of thirty simple cuneiform signs, each one representing a consonant (except for three, which represent the same consonant—a glottal stop—with three different vowels). Ugarit script survived in numerous internal administrative records of the city government, many letters and religious texts, and a few literary texts.

Ugaritic narrative poems were representative of a poetic tradition from which the Hebrew Bible evolved. The Ugaritic versions of traditional tales or motifs were later recast in Hebrew literature. Like Akkadian, Ugaritic poetry was not metrical, and it consistently used parallelism and/or poetic formulas. It juxtaposed phrases or clauses in usually two, sometimes three, and occasionally more, poetic cola of similar syntactic structure and/or semantic import. Poetic formulas included standard epithets for common characters, including gods; standard expressions for the introduction of direct speech, for a character's arrival at or departure from a place, for the passage of time, and so on; and standard pairs of words or phrases used in parallel cola.[59]

Music left deep footprints in the composition of early Ugaritic poetry. Gradually, a verbal measure emerged to organize the rhythm of poetry without music. For example, the words in Ugaritic poetry were initially defined as separate units by the word-divider, a small wedge, stroke or point as inherited from cuneiform script. There were single syllable words such as Ugaritic *p* for mouth (*ph* in Hebrew), *l* for not (*l'* in Hebrew), and *k* for surely (*ky* in Hebrew). However, when Semitic poetry was sung, the singer could expand or contract as he pleased (within certain limits). This free rhythm and phrasing gave poetry an enormous freedom and flexibility when set to music. Free rhythm transformed when poetry departed from singing, making it possible to combine stressed syllables with a considerable number of unstressed syllables and elongate one word into an entire phrase. Thus, the foot of Ugaritic poetry, which had never had a fixed syllable count, could be from two to five syllables.[60]

Ugaritic poetic texts showed a tendency to keep the number of stressed syllables per colon approximately the same through a long poem. The number of stressed syllables had to reduce if it did not fit into the norm. The basic component of Ugaritic verse was the verse-line, which could be divided into two (parallel) half lines. A line could be relatively isolated or clustered in sets that varied from two to seven couplets. The standard strophic form was the couplet, although single lines or monocola occurred very frequently. A stanza was a fixed or variable group of lines that were organized into thematic, metrical, rhetorical, or narrative sections.[61]

Frequently used Ugaritic poetic features included three-clause sentences, the very common appearance of repeated words or phrases in consecutive clauses, and the employment of a stock vocabulary of pairs of words such as proper names and their epithets, standard synonyms or antonyms, and commonly paired ideas, found again and again in consecutive clauses.[62]

Although Hebrew is believed to be highly indebted to Ugaritic, it evolved into a unique literary tradition.[63] The biblical poetry in Hebrew marked the beginning of an important transformation of Semitic literature, in which the form of poetry expanded from merely phonetic (based on prosody) to literary parallelism. The most important of this transformation was delivered by changing three-clause sentences in Ugaritic into basic binary parallelism in Hebrew.[64] This change condensed poetry and made it more terse. Hebrew poetry demonstrated more variations than Ugaritic poetry, which was limited by its relatively strict phonological length parameterization of its three beats and 2:2 units, somewhat reminiscent of martial meter in Hebrew. The dynamics of parallelism at the semantic and syntactic levels in Ugaritic seems less supple and open to variation than in Hebrew. On the other hand, the sound orchestration is much tighter in Ugaritic than in Hebrew on account of the preservation of case endings in the former. One can imagine the text's prosody and a vocalization of the text. Word stress in Ugaritic probably fell on the penultimate syllable, and the poetry needs to be read accordingly in order to get a sense of its rhythm. Both Ugaritic and Hebrew inherited the beginning of fixed pairs (stock pairing words of semantic parallelism); Hebrew's formulaic stock was much richer and more flexible and could be substituted.[65]

Like ancient Akkadian and Arabic poetry, Hebrew poetry did not include a rhythm based on the quantity of meters according to classical prosodic theory. Hebrew poetry contained almost no regular rhyme in an English sense. However, this did not mean that this poetry did not evolve from song (with musical measures). It only meant that it had been separated from song form for a long period of time during which musical forms had gradually been verbalized and standardized into a literary canon.

First, the ancient texts preserved in the Hebrew Bible were written over a period of at least a millennium, during which time the pronunciation of the language had changed. Words that rhymed at the beginning of that period might no longer rhyme at the end. Second, even in one and the same period, different tribal groups or other Hebrew speakers pronounced words differently. Similar phonetic changes took place in every single language, both modern and ancient. For example, the open verses of Chaucer's *Canterbury Tales* are hardly appealing to the ears if read to speakers of Modern English. After considering the phonological alterations that obscure the rhymes of Chaucer after only a few centuries, it is not difficult to imagine what had happened to the sound of biblical Hebrew texts, which had a much larger time span to mutate.[66]

An example of this history of departure from music can be found in the first book of Psalms (1:41), which gives convincing evidence of its origin from song and musical forms. The word for psalm is *mizmor* in Hebrew, meaning "something that is sung," and it cognates with the verb *zamer* ("to sing" or "to hymn"). The overall structure and formal devices of these poems demonstrate that the psalms were composed of a consistent pattern of cantos (stanzas) and strophes, which originated from singing. The formal devices include quantitative balance on the level of cantos in terms of the number of verse lines, verbal repetitions and transition markers.[67]

There were many examples of rhyme and meter in the book of Proverbs, 6:9 and 6:10. It is common in biblical Hebrew texts to observe two verses, split into four lines of poetry, demonstrating both internal rhyme (more common) and end-of-line rhyme (less common in Hebrew but the norm in English rhyming poetry), as well as noticeable meter. The last word of the first line ('AD maTAI 'aTZEL tishKAV) rhymes with the last word of the last line (me'AT khibBUQ yaDAYM lishKAV). In the third line, the second and fourth words create an internal rhyme with each other (me'AT sheNOT, me'AT tenuMOT). Finally, the first word of the second line (maTAI taQUM mishshenaTEksgha) is identical to the first word of the first line, linking those two lines even without obvious rhyme. It is also observed that ancient Hebrew texts demonstrate assonance more often than rhyme. In fact, assonance is prominent in ancient Hebrew texts, as are other forms of sound-matching. An example of assonance is found in the first song of Exodus, 15:1–19, where assonance occurs at the ends of the lines, as in "*anwehu*" and "*aromemenhu*" (15:2). Like in Arabic, the consonance of "*hu*" (= "him") can occur frequently in the Hebrew, because the language allows speakers to affix the object-case as a suffix to verbs.[68]

Not all of the biblical texts had the same degree of musicality as phonetic repetition. The earliest poetry, *The Song of Deborah* (Judges 5), shows a fondness for patterns of incremental repetition. So did the Psalms. Psalms have relatively unified forms. They have two to four beats or stresses per colon, two to three cola per verse, two to three verses per strophe, and two to three strophes per stanza. Although this is far from a rigid structure, the vast majority of poems are bicola while only twelve and a half percent are tricola.[69] As the original sound of poetry in biblical Hebrew had been lost (it was composed about a thousand years prior) by the time that vowels (which gave the poetry its complete rhythm) were re-injected into its texts, this inherited inclination to repeat sound patterns required new inspiration. This inspiration was the rhythm of contemporary spoken language, Rabbinic Hebrew. Like Modern English poetry, especially the poetry of the late twentieth century that emerged with music and song writing, biblical Hebrew inherited an accentual rhythm, based on regulating accented and non-accented syllables. The free and reflex rhythms produced lines with two, three, four, and five accented syllables, between which one to three, or even four, unaccented syllables could be inserted. The poet was unbound from a set pattern. For example, in the lines of Psalm 2: "Serve the LORD with fear" ("*'Ibdu et-Yhwh be-yir'ah*," 2:11), "rejoice with trembling" ("*wegilu bi-re'adah*"), equal length was not the basic formal rule. The majority of biblical verses were naturally iambic or anapestic (two unstressed syllables followed by one stressed syllable), as the words are accented on one of the final syllables.

Parallelism can be found most commonly in the books of Psalms and Proverbs, but also throughout the entire Hebrew Bible. Initially, parallelism was used to express a single idea in two or more different ways (in order to confirm or reinforce it). For instance, in Psalms 119:105, "Your word is a lamp to my feet and a light for my path." One sees two pairs that illustrate one idea ("lamp"/"light" and "feet"/"path"). Another example is "My son, my teachings you shall not forget and my commands your heart shall guard" (Proverbs 3:1), in which "my teachings" is paralleled with "my commands" and "you shall not forget" is paralleled with "your heart shall guard." However, Hebrew parallelism did not stop at verbal repetition, but evolved into a creative dynamic. Psalm 88:12–13: "Will your kindness be told in the grave / your faithfulness in perdition? // Will your wonder be known in the darkness / your bounty in the land of oblivion?" The first set of matched terms confirms and stabilizes the idea by linking a series of the complementary concepts of kindness, faithfulness, wonder and bounty. The second set, however, carries progressive imaginative realizations of death; from the familiar grave to *avendon* ("perdition"), a poetic synonym that is a mythic word that is grimly explicit about the fate of extinction that the grave indicates, then to the word "darkness," a sensory depiction of the realization of death, then a poetic synonym of the underground world, "the land of oblivion," which summarizes the idea of death.[70]

As in music, where different tunes were designed to express specific emotions, certain kinds of biblical poetry that expressed specific emotions employed specific kinds of rhythm. A dirge (*kinot*) (somber song) was an address to God seeking relief. It described suffering or anguish as a petition for help and divine deliverance. The specific rhythm of these poems often began with a longer line followed by a shorter one. Like in the Greek hexameter and pentameter, this change of rhythm was intended to symbolize the idea that a strenuous advance in life was followed by fatigue or reaction. This sad rhythm, often called the "elegiac measure," is found in Amos 5:2 and Jeremiah 9:20, 13:18. It refers here expressly to "the mourning women who in the East still chant the death-song to the trembling tone of the pipe" (48:36). They are found also in Ezekiel 19:1, 26:17, 27:2, 32:2, 32:16, and 32:19–20.[71]

Many pilgrimage songs that were sung and recited at the festivals of Jerusalem were elevated into a special kind of rhythm called *anadilosis*. It became a mode of speaking in poetry, wherein the phrase at the end of one sentence was repeated at the beginning of the next, such as in the passages "They came not to the help of the Lord [i.e., to protect God's people], to the help of the Lord against the mighty" (Judges 5:23), and "From whence shall my help come? My help cometh from the Lord" (Psalm 121). Many similar passages can also be found in Psalms 15:120–134 and Psalms 120:5–7.[72]

Reading biblical texts is a journey through a language history in which an increasingly sophisticated literary form gradually evolved as it outgrew and integrated music and phonetic repetition, and cultivated literary repetition. It assimilated many other types of rhetorical dynamics to elevate its expressiveness. There were different rhetorical forms in the parallelism of biblical poetry. With synonymous parallelism, the second hemistich (half line of verse, or verset as some called it to distinguish it from the half line in other languages) says much the same thing as the first one, with variations. For example, Amos 5:24: "But let judgment run down as waters, and righteousness as a mighty stream," or Isaiah 2:4 or Micah 4:3: "They will beat their swords into plowshares and their spears into pruning hooks." Antithesis is also found where the second hemistich directly contradicts or contrasts with the first. As Proverbs 10:1 put it, "A wise son maketh a glad father, but a foolish son is the heaviness of his mother."[73]

Formal parallelism is used to balance hemistiches, clause for clause, but it does not have to contain synonymy or direct antithesis. Psalms 14:2 says, "The LORD looked down from heaven upon the children of men, to see if there were any that did understand and seek God." Climactic parallelism balances the two hemistiches by adding a thought or completing the first hemistich with a second one. Psalms 29:1 states, "Give unto the LORD, O ye mighty, give unto the LORD glory and strength." An external parallelism achieves balance by creating syntactic units across multiple verses. Here, parallelisms can also arrive not within a line but also between lines. Isaiah 1:27–28 reads, "Zion shall be redeemed with judgment, and her converts with righteousness. // And the destruction of the transgressors and the sinners shall be together, and they that forsake the LORD shall be consumed."

There is a tendency among those scholars whose first language does not inherit parallelism to confuse verbal parallelism and semantic synonyms, because for them parallelism simply means "doubling up." In this case, they do not have the sensibility to see the difference between doubled form and doubled meanings. Paralleling two words does not need to be semantic repetition for a poetic tradition that has outgrown (or is ready to outgrow) phonetic repetition. This was the case in biblical Hebrew. It was in Hebrew that Semitic poetic parallelism began to transform by expanding (rather than replacing) phonetic-based repetition into semantic repetition in which new and dynamic meanings emerged.[74]

It was in Hebrew that Semitic phonetic parallelism extended to semantic parallelism. This worked as a dynamic for creating and expanding the literary repertoire of the language.[75] One of the creative uses of parallelism was to present opposite and contrary aspects of an idea, which could be called negative parallelism as illustrated in Proverbs 11:19–20.

> A1. Righteousness brings one to life
> > B1. Pursuit of evil brings one to his death
> > B2. a twisted heart is an abomination of YHWH
> A2. a mature path is his pleasure

The basic principle of Hebrew poetry is the repetition, elaboration, or variation on the sense of a line. This parallelism may be semantic and/or grammatical. Hebrew poetry uses all the figures of speech of English poetry: metaphors, similes, personification, etc.[76]

Synonymous parallelism repeats the thought in synonymous terms:

> Hear O heavens, and I will speak;
> Hear O Earth, the words of my mouth.
> Let my teaching fall like rain
> and my words descend like dew,
> like showers on new grass,
> like abundant rain on tender plants [Deut. 32:1–2].
>
> A generous man will prosper
> he who refreshes others will himself be refreshed [Prov. 11:25].

Antithetical parallelism contrasts the thought with another, usually introducing the second line with "but":

> A wise son delights a father,
> but a foolish son is a mother's grief.
> Ill gotten treasures will not avail;
> but virtue saves from death [Prov. 10:1–2].
>
> For the Lord watches over the way of the righteous
> but the way of the wicked will perish [Psalms 1:6].

Synthetic parallelism is a "catch-all" variety of forms. In completion or internal parallelism, the second line completes the first:

> Yet have I set my king Upon Zion my holy hill [Psalms 2:6].

comparison parallelism:

> Better a meal of vegetables where there is love,
> than a fattened calf with hatred [Prov. 15:17].

Climatic parallelism, in which a stairstep of lines adds thoughts to the first:

> Ascribe to the Lord, O mighty ones,
> Ascribe to the Lord glory and strength.
> Ascribe to the Lord the glory due His name;
> Worship the Lord in the splendor of His holiness [Psalms 29:1–2].

Chaiastic parallelism is similar to synonymous parallelism, only the second line reverses the first:

> Have mercy upon me O Lord, according to your unfailing love;
> according to your great compassion blot out my transgressions [Psalms 51:1].

In emblematic parallelism the second line serves as an emblem to illustrate the first without any words of contrast:

> A gold ring in a swine's snout
> a fair woman without understanding [Prov. 11:29].

Cold water to a thirsty soul,
and good news from a far country [Prov. 25:25].

Frequently the first of two paralleled lines is a more "general" term, and the following part uses more specific, extravagant, or explanatory terms or figures of speech to intensify and strengthen emotions, sharpen images, or make actions more powerful, real and concrete. The combination of this dynamic parallelism with its vivid figurative language allows for the rich development of themes, meaning, and ideas within the poetry.

The basic unit of poetry is the strophe or stanza. A wide variety of larger parallel structures, refrains, alliterations, repetitions, acrostics or other literary devices may be used to unite the parts into a larger unit. There are distinct forms for some types of poems such as laments, thanksgivings, and praise songs. There is a striking absence of any narrative storytelling in Hebrew poetry, but these poetic forms are often used in the narrative and prophetic writings to make the images or descriptions of events or judgments vivid. Hebrew poetry is also noted for its terseness, as it frequently drops nouns or verbs, or omits conjunctions, temporal indicators or logical connectors.

It should be clear that Hebrew poetry is readily translated, as it is the thoughts and images that "rhyme," not the words:

Praise the Lord, all nations!
Extol him, all peoples!
For great is his steadfast love toward us,
and the faithfulness of the Lord endures forever.
Praise the Lord! [Psalms 117:1–2].

The rigidly symmetrical sound of verse of the early period was lost as Hebrew poetry was composed in silence (writing) during the later period.[77] As phonetic parallelism expanded into literary parallelism the very structure of the poem transformed from having linear connections in sound or meaning to using multi-dimensional references in terms of sound, meaning, imagery, and emotion. Psalms 137 is a good example of how extra dimensions were being built to tighten literary vision. The song in which "by the rivers of Babylon, where we sat down and wept" and hung harps upon the willow also contains these lines: "If I forget you, O Jerusalem, let my right hand wither; // Let my tongue cleave to the roof of my mouth, if I do not remember you" (5–6). While the words "forget" and "do not remember" have identical meanings, they are paralleled by physical discomfort in three body parts, and reinforce the central connection between action and consequence even more tightly.[78]

While Hebrew poetry cultivated a more advanced literary parallelism than did Ugaritic poetry, pre–Islamic Arabic poetry presented a more

mature, varied, and refined poetic tradition. This difference derived from
the specific history of contributing languages, the continuity and discon-
tinuity of their oral traditions, and the timing in which the oral traditions
became literature. When Hebrew was replaced by other vernaculars, it lost
not only its original sound but also the articulation of the language itself
(the very foundation of its linguistic evolution). Arabic, on the other hand,
was a continually active language since the fourth century.[79] The most
important difference was that when Arabic became a written language, it
had already cultivated a mature poetic tradition with varied and sophisticated forms. The continued, rich, and active oral tradition of poetry was
what set Arabic apart not only from biblical Hebrew, but also from other
Semitic languages. As a continually active language, Arabic had never
stopped being spoken as it evolved into its literary form.

Arabic poetry emerged from spoken language rather than literary languages, as did the majority of world literatures. It emerged not from the
minds of intellectuals and literary poets but rather from the lips of soothsayers. It was recited, recreated and memorized by the minds and ears of
its speakers. It was the first Semitic poetry that completed its journey from
phonetic to verbal form, something that biblical Hebrew had attempted
more than a thousand years before. It was also the first Semitic language
that cultivated a literature without losing its vernacular roots. As a mature
poetic tradition, pre–Islamic poetry gave more attention to eloquence and
wording of verse than to the theme and structure of the poem as whole.
This was different from Ugaritic and Hebrew. As a result, its poems were
characterized by a strong vocabulary and short ideas in loosely connected
verses. In place of overall pattern, cultivated forms such as the romantic
or nostalgic prelude commonly opened pre–Islamic poems. In these prel-
udes, a thematic unit called a *nasib*, the poet would remember his beloved
and her deserted home and its ruins. This concept in Arabic poetry is
referred to as "standing at the ruins" because the poet would often start
his poem by saying that he stood at the ruins of his beloved. With this
seemingly uniform beginning, the poet would be focused on his creative
application of the form to express his personal sentiment.

This chapter has described the cultural context from which Arabic
emerged. The historical evolution of Semitic languages, especially their
repeated linguistic and literary re-orientations, seen as the formal foundation of Arabic, defined some of the most basic features of the Arabic language. The forms of poetry being constantly steeped in music, musical
recitation and performance made it possible to produce a highly sophisticated oral poetry. The efforts of adopting and verbalizing musical repetition
into literary expression that had been pursued by generations of poets and

writers in many Near Eastern languages finally crystallized. As the youngest offspring of a very old linguistic and literary family, Arabic inherited characteristics of the Semitic languages: the sense of balance in the sound and images of poetry, and the ability to repeat with original variations through flexible compositions.

This chapter has illustrated all that Arabic shared with ancient Semitic traditions. The next chapter describes what set Arabic apart from other Semitic languages and how these unique characteristics were shaped within the historical evolution of Arabic. It focuses on the evolution of Arabic prosody: the creation of the music of poetry, from oral to written poetry.

CHAPTER 2

Recording the Sound
of Poetry

Arabic is the only continued literary tradition that remains active today from the ancient Semitic literatures. All of the offspring of ancient Semitic have disappeared (for centuries or forever), been reoriented (attempted to be written in various scripts), or been assimilated as a part of a hybrid language (Hebrew), losing many of their Semitic features.[1] This chapter is the history of the continuation and enrichment of Arabic poetry before, during and after the classic period; it focuses on how Arabic, one of many Semitic poetic traditions, evolved, matured, and eventually grew into a refined literature. The main theme of this history is the process of writing (recording, mediating, and transforming) an oral poetic tradition by establishing a poetic rhythm that can be written, read, recited, heard, memorized, and performed by its speakers at large.

Alphabetic writing, the most efficient method to record a spoken language, initially originated in the Middle East; Ancient Phoenician and many other Semitic languages invented the world's oldest phonetic (rather than pictorial or mixed) scripts. However, none of the original languages survived except Arabic. Meanwhile, the use of alphabetic scripts swept the world, especially Europe. The linguistic transformation in the Middle East from oral traditions to written language did not succeed without repeated linguistic reorientation. It took Semitic languages (starting with Akkadian) more than ten centuries to eliminate the visual (pictorial) and syllabic elements inherited from Sumerian cuneiform, a system of pictographs. This transformed the foundation of writing from visual symbols to sound recording, first to syllables and then to single phones. Language change made it possible for the syllabic script to be uprooted from its speech, lose its semantic and visual meanings, and become abstract symbols of single sounds.

The linguistic change from Sumerian to Akkadian narrowed the inherited gap between the representation of the sound of language and that of its meaning. However, Akkadian faced two related problems in its search to become a lasting literary medium. These were to record the sound of language as precisely as possible and to canonize the established sound (pronunciation) of the language. As Akkadian script registered only the consonants of speech, the close relationship with spoken language and dialect allowed a continuing and relentless linguistic regeneration because it made written language too sensitive and volatile to remain constant as it interacted with highly innovative vernaculars. As new languages and dialects kept being recorded and codified, new languages that initially emerged as regional dialects of the given language quickly evolved into distinct languages. As the older and written language became uprooted from speech, it had to adopt different vernaculars, which completed a never-ending circle that widened the gap between script and speech.

It took Semitic languages another millennium to invent a different script to deal with the phonetic instability and ambiguity rooted in their syllabic structure. During this time, many scripts appeared and disappeared until a consonantal alphabet was created in the eleventh century B.C. by a peripheral culture, Phoenician, a branch of Canaanite.[2] The most important innovation of consonantal alphabet was to separate the vowels from consonants by written presentation. Thus, for the first time in its history, Semitic languages successfully identified, isolated, and separated phonemes, the smallest unit of speech, from syllabic script and established a way for the transformation to alphabetic writing to proceed. The Phoenician alphabetic script became capable of registering every single consonant free from the entanglement of vowels in syllables. Compared to Akkadian cuneiform, a consonantal alphabet was a more accurate and efficient way to record Semitic speech.

Scribal reorientation in the Semitic languages proved to be much more complex and difficult in the Middle East than it was in Europe. It took European modern languages, which did not have a rich graphic and syllabic inheritance, only a few centuries (between Italian, the closest to Latin, to Germanic, the most distant from Latin), to produce and accumulate their unique literary traditions. Carrying a much heavier burden of the past, Semitic languages needed more than fifteen centuries to establish another mature literary tradition (Arabic) after the death of Babylonian literature. The long and drawn-out process, which spawned the emergence of Aramaic, Hebrew, Syriac, and eventually Arabic, now is reflected in the maturity and sophistication of the well-developed narrative and polished imageries that finally manifested in modern Middle Eastern languages.

The embryo of alphabetic writing emerged initially from a Semitic language that recorded its speech in cuneiform. The Ugaritic alphabet, which was the second alphabet after the Egyptian and the first within the Semitic languages, was a consonantal alphabet in cuneiform style. The Ugaritic language emerged from Ugarit, Syria, which was the center of literacy in the Middle Eastern world from 1500 to 1300 B.C. It combined the most advanced features of the previously known hieroglyphic and cuneiform scripts, each of which had been experimenting with more syllabic and less logographic writing systems, into an *abjad* (a consonantal alphabet).[3]

The Ugaritic alphabet combined the principles of the Canaanite alphabet with the technique of Akkadian cuneiform. It created Semitic alphabets utilizing various types of simplified Sumerian wedges: the vertical wedge, ↑, the horizontal wedge, ←, the wedge in oblique position, □, and the angle wedge [*winkelhaken*], Δ.[4] A similar process also produced other original alphabetic scripts that evolved from Egyptian hieroglyphics. The best examples of this older attempt were the Wadi el-Hol script (2000 B.C.) and the Proto-Canaanite alphabet (1500 B.C.). The Wadi el-Hol (*wadi al-ḥawl*) inscriptions were carved in stone along an ancient, high-desert military and trade road linking Thebes and Abydos in a wadi in the Qena bend of the Nile. The script was graphically very similar to the Proto-Sinaitic inscriptions, but was older and further south, in the heart of literate Egypt. The shapes and angles of the glyphs best matched hieratic graffiti from 2000 B.C. Most scholars believe that this presented a stage of evolution of the alphabet, which was continuing to further eliminate pictorial features.[5]

Proto-Sinaitic script is best known from carved graffiti in Canaan (Israel and Palestine) and the Sinai Peninsula. Like the Wadi el-Hol script, the Proto-Sinaitic script has graphic similarities to the Egyptian hieratic script, although it suggests a more or less abstract form. It is generally accepted that the language of the inscriptions was Semitic, and that the script had a hieratic prototype that was ancestral to the Semitic alphabets. Proto-Sinaitic soon spread to Canaan; therefore, it carried the name of Proto-Canaanite, or Old Canaanite script. It evolved locally into the Phoenician script, and became a complete alphabetic writing system. For instance, the glyph ꜁, ancestral to the Latin *N*, derived from one of the Egyptian glyphs meaning "snake." The name of the letter was therefore the Canaanite word for snake, *naḥas*. It could be used acrophonically for the phoneme *n*, but also logographically as the word *naḥas* (snake). It could also be used as a poly-consonantal rebus: for example placed with the letter ת *T* (taw), as נת, to represent *nḥšt* (copper).

The Proto-Canaanite alphabet was a consonantal alphabet of twenty-two glyphs. It evolved from the above-mentioned Middle Bronze Age alphabets. It retained some of the original pictographic images. But unlike Sumerian and Egyptian, the pictographs came to symbolize the sound alone without the meanings of the word from which the letter derived. For example, the first letter, *alp* (the ancestor of A in Greek, A in Latin, א in Hebrew and ا in Arabic), was originally a symbol of an ox head referring to the Aramaic word "*alp*" (ox). The fourth letter, *digg* (the ancestor of Δ in Greek, d in Latin, ד in Hebrew, and د in Arabic), was a picture of a fish and referred to the Aramaic word *digg* (fish). The two most obvious letters that had pictographic origins were the letter *mem* and *r'as*. The former was the ancestor of M in Greek and Latin, מ in Hebrew, and م in Arabic and was a symbol for a wave of water, meaning "water" in Aramaic. The latter was the ancestor of p in Greek, r in Latin, ר in Hebrew, and ر in Arabic. This primitive Canaanite alphabet was first attested in Levantine texts of the Late Bronze Age (from the 15th century B.C.). This endured until 1050 B.C., after which it is known as Phoenician according to established chronology. About a dozen inscriptions written in Proto-Canaanite have been discovered in modern-day Israel and Lebanon.[6]

The Canaanite alphabet was a much more powerful tool than the Ugaritic alphabet because of its deep and wide roots in oral and local languages. The relationship between Canaanite and Ugaritic remains a controversial topic today. Almost all of the alphabetic scripts west of Syria seemed to have derived, directly or indirectly, from the Canaanite alphabet, whereas the hundreds of alphabetic writings of the East apparently have derived from the offshoots of the Aramaic alphabet. In general terms, the direct and indirect descendants of the Aramaic alphabet can be divided into two main groups: the scripts employed for Semitic languages and those adapted to non–Semitic tongues. With regard to the Semitic offshoots, six separate alphabets may be discerned: Hebrew, Nabataean-Sinaitic-Arabic, Palmyrene, Syriac-Nestorian, Mandaean, and Manichaean.[7]

The Phoenician alphabet developed from the Proto-Canaanite alphabet during the 15th century B.C., before which time the Phoenicians wrote with a cuneiform script. The earliest known inscriptions in the Phoenician alphabet came from Byblos and date back to 1000 B.C. The relationship between Phoenician and Canaanite could be verified by the native name for the language: *Pōnnīm/Kana'nīm* (Punic/Canaanite speech). With the active trade of its merchants, Phoenician spread around the Mediterranean, particularly to Tunisia, southern parts of the Iberian Peninsula (modern Spain and Portugal), Malta, and southern France and Sicily, and was spoken until the 1st century A.D. A variant of Phoenician, known as Punic, was spoken in Carthage, a Phoenician colony in what is now Tunisia, until the 6th century A.D.

The Phoenician alphabet completely discarded pictographic content and employed the same number of letters as the Canaanite alphabet, many of which had several different forms. Like other Semitic languages, it did not indicate vowel sounds. The current form of Phoenician letters is attested to in the regions now encompassing Lebanon, Syria and Israel, an area then known as Put in Ancient Egyptian, Canaan in Phoenician, Hebrew and Aramaic, and Phoenicia in Greek and Latin, and is believed to have emerged about the 11th century B.C.[8]

Another old Semitic alphabet that emerged from the Arabian Peninsula was Southern Arabic, which remained confined to its region for most of its early history.[9] The Minaean (Madhabic) language was an Old South Arabian (Sayhadic) language spoken in Yemen between 1200 B.C. and A.D. 100. The Sabaean (Sabaic) language was spoken from c. 1000 B.C. to the 6th century A.D. It was the language of the famous kingdom of Saba'a. It was also used as a written language by some other peoples of ancient Yemen including the Hashidites, Sirwahites, Humlanites, Ghaymanites, Himyarites, and Radmanites. Historians are still debating its origin and its relationship with the Proto-Sinaitic alphabet.[10]

Eventually, the increasingly complex and redundant cuneiform, like the Egyptian hieroglyphs, could not possibly compete with the startling simplicity and precision of alphabetic writing. These forms simply vanished after centuries of co-existence, remaining only as religious or administrative language, isolated from speech.[11]

However, in the homeland of alphabet script, literary languages were not easily sustained. Aramaic became dominant as the official languages of two powerful empires, the Achaemenid (500–330 B.C.) and the Arsacid (247 B.C.–A.D. 224) on the land of non–Semitic speaking people. But its dominance did not endure without living vernaculars. Aramaic, although highly structured, had difficulty in keeping up with the active Semitic vernaculars that emerged in different regions of the Middle East, where locals not only spoke the language differently but also were inventing their own distinct scripts. Aramaic's unity as an international medium was short lived.

Hebrew, unlike the highly versatile Aramaic, had an extraordinarily stable early period when compared to various other Semitic languages. After departing from Aramaic due to a vowel change in the Western Semitic group, Hebrew remained essentially the same for many years to come, undergoing changes that appreciably affected its vocabulary but not its basic phonological or grammatical structure. It has been suggested that Hebrew, like many ancient languages, was not a homogeneous linguistic system but a multi-layered mixture in which it was possible to distinguish an early Canaanite layer, very close to Akkadian, and another more recent layer, closer to Aramaic and Southern Semitic.[12]

The reason that Hebrew survived while other Canaanite scripts such as Phoenician and Aramaic did not was Hebrew's constant reinforcement through literary intervention, codification, interpretation, and re-interpretation by religious writers. The pronunciation of Hebrew changed substantially between the early 6th century B.C. Babylonian Exile and the 8th–11th centuries A.D., when Masoretes (Tiberian) vocalized the text of the Hebrew Bible, an attempt similar in principle to the codification of the Qur'an in Arabic but on a much smaller scale. At its formative stage, Hebrew constantly assimilated linguistic changes into script to keep pace with the development of its various spoken forms, yet maintained its solid separation from speech. In other words, it thrived as a religious and liturgical language rather than a political, administrative or diplomatic language. Hebrew was less reliant on government to sustain its influence.[13]

The second reason for the continuity and resilience of Hebrew was the limited development and diversity of its spoken form. Compared to its sister language, Aramaic, ancient Hebrew was a formative speech. As an oral language it never spread outside of Israel. Without international exposure (Israel was a tribal kingdom rather than a multi-ethnic and multi-lingual empire comparable to other Mesopotamian empires), Hebrew never had the opportunity to diversify into regional dialects until many centuries later, when Jewish immigrants dispersed around the world. This oral limitation was a blessing for Hebrew because it did not lose its unity during ancient times, as did Akkadian and Aramaic.

Hebrew prose was utilized as the official language of the courts and educated circles of Jerusalem during the reigns of David and Solomon.[14] Like many ancient languages, Hebrew prose writing further defined its grammatical and phonetic features. For instance, Hebrew was the first Semitic language to create a precise and complex system of verbs that indicated time and aspects of action. Prose writing also attempted to redefine the changing vowel length and place of stress after the oral language gradually discarded its final short vowels.[15] However, Hebrew lost its position as the dominant language of the religion in the 6th century B.C., when Amaraic replaced it.

At this time, Hebrew entered a long-term competition with Aramaic that ended when it lost its battle as a spoken language in the 2nd century A.D. Aramaic was a language spoken in Jerusalem starting in the late 6th century B.C. and may have been the city's majority tongue. Many Hebrew-speaking Jews in Judea would have had various levels of competence in Aramaic as a second language. Since at least the mid–second century A.D., the transmitters of the reading and pronunciation traditions for both biblical and Mishnaic Hebrew were speakers of Aramaic. By the time of the Masoretes, Hebrew had not been spoken for 700 years and the tradition of Hebrew had been overwhelmed by Aramaic linguistic pressure. This pressure from Aramaic not only increased the impetus for change but also determined many features of the Hebrew language.[16]

Hebrew miraculously survived all of these rivalries because of its strength as a written tradition and the age-long persistent writing of its religious scholars. The most important innovation for the development of Hebrew writing was the introduction of a system of vowels into its script, exactly the same issue that had been facing Semitic writing for twenty-five hundred years. Hebrew scribes began to experiment with vocal presentation in the tenth century B.C. The Mesha Stone inscription (850 B.C.) illustrates clear presentation of vowels.[17]

Hebrew did not die, as did many of its Canaanite neighbors. It was constantly rejuvenated by Rabbinical Hebrew to support the articulation of biblical Hebrew, which remained an exclusive spoken language for the Jews.[18] However, Hebrew's influence as a language never ventured beyond the boundary of a minority group in the Middle East. The influence of its ancient literature could only be extended through translation (to Greek, Latin, and European languages). Repeated recycling through translation eventually altered the language so much that Modern Hebrew has lost many of its Semitic characteristics. Arabic, the next surviving Semitic language, lived a completely different life and eventually became the first and only universal language of the region.

The success of Arabic lies in its powerful living poetry, which maintained the musical and ritual heritage of the ancient Semitic. It was the performance of oral poetry that made it possible for Arabic to mature before it became a literary language during the seventh century. As the latecomer to the Middle Eastern literary scene, Arabic had had enough time to develop and achieve a far more advanced and sophisticated poetic form (compared to those of ancient Aramaic and Hebrew) at the time when it became written. The formal distance of degrees of maturity and sophistication resembles the distance between ancient Latin and Greek as they initially adopted alphabet writings, and can be easily observed by reading pre–Islamic Arabic poetry and comparing it with the poetry of ancient Aramaic and Hebrew. The maturity of Arabic poetry and its eloquence and artistic value became a major source for classical Arabic language in grammar, vocabulary and imagery.[19]

By the first few centuries A.D., the most prominent Semitic languages, Akkadian (with its regional divisions of Babylonian and Assyrian), Ugaritic, and Hebrew, had become extinct as spoken languages. Their voices had been replaced by other Semitic languages and regional dialects. In the north, the Aramaic cluster of dialects represented the dominant cultures of the Mesopotamia. It had two main branches: Syriac, spoken by the early Christians, and Nabataean, spoken by the pagan population centered in Petra. In the south, Sabaic had been spoken since antiquity and had developed features similar to those of the southern Arabian dialect that eventually gave birth to Arabic.[20]

Before the sixth century A.D., the poetry of the Semitics was probably only orally articulated and transmitted. There is little evidence of a written literature. Even those attempting to keep written records managed to produce only scattered records of functional (not literary) writings. Unlike the Syriac and Jewish branches of Amaraic that developed written literature, the oral language of the Arabian Peninsula left only graffiti, casual scribbling of names, instructions, and simple messages. During the centuries before Islam, several scripts began to emerge from the north, central, and southern Arabian Peninsula.[21]

The Semitic group from which Arabic evolved was represented by some forty thousand inscriptions mostly located in and around the oasis-towns of northwest Arabia, the sandy desert of the Hisma (north of Tabuk, Saudi Arabia), the basalt desert of the Harra, and the highlands of central Arabia. These so-called north Arabian languages were all fairly close to one another and were mutually comprehensible. The ancestor of classical Arabic, referred to as Old Arabic by scholars, was found among these languages. Old Arabic was distinguished by its use of the definite article *al* (other languages use *h/han*). The Greek historian Herodotus noticed that the Arabs call Aphrodite *Al-ilat* ("the goddess"). Old Arabic was believed to exist as early as the fifth century B.C., but was seldom recorded until a century or so before the advent of Islam. In the very few examples found it was committed to writing by borrowing local scripts. For example, at Dedan near the Sabaean kingdom, a record of Old Arabic written in Sabaean was found before the end of the first century B.C. During the middle of fourth century A.D., two texts of Umru al-Qays, the most celebrated pre–Islamic Arabic poet, were found at the desert southeast of Damascus and at Nemara. There were composed in Old Arabic and yet recorded in the script of Nabataeans, which was a script with inadequate capacity to present Arabic vowels and consonants.

Old Arabic (written Sabaean) was widely spoken throughout the Middle East, as its linguistic features often surface in texts written in other north Arabian dialects or in Nabataean from various parts of Arabia. Nevertheless it remained primarily a vernacular, employed by non-literate people and by those who, for whatever reason, preferred to write in other languages. Texts written entirely in Old Arabic are so rare that the commissioning of them must have been a conscious and deliberate choice. Presumably the intention was to make a statement about their ethnic and/or cultural affiliation, and their Arab identity.[22]

Another branch of ancient scripts, the ancient Yemeni alphabet (*musnad*) evolved from the Proto-Sinaitic alphabet around the 13th century B.C. Its distinct form appeared in Babylon and near Elate of the Gulf of Aqaba around the 8th or 7th centuries B.C. The South Arabian proper appeared around 500 B.C. and continued to be used until around A.D. 600. It was used for writing the Old South Arabic languages of the Sabaean, Qatabanian, Hadramautic, Minaean, Himyarite, and *proto–Ge'ez* (proto–Ethiosemitic) in Dmt (a kingdom located in Eritrea and northern Ethiopia that existed during the 10th to 5th centuries B.C.). There were no vowels in the alphabet. Instead it used the *mater lectionis* to mark them. This script matured around 500 B.C. and expanded the range of its alphabet into 29 symbols with distinctive shapes in order to cope with the phonemic consonantal repertory of the Southern Arabian languages.[23]

It seems that until the advance of Islam, the sustaining power of Arabic lay less in its ability to keep written records than in its vibrant vernacular, performed, heard, recited and therefore alive in the ears and on the lips of its speakers. The survival of pre–Islamic poetry depended on its form of poetic performance. One of the earliest accounts of this performance concerns the illustrious poet Al-Nābighah (d. c. 604). He composed a poem for the poetic competition held in the annual fair of the town of 'Ukāz. The tradition of the poetic competition, a metrical and verbal duel, continues today in several parts of the Middle East. It is performed in a variety of local dialects and metric forms that reflect the journey of Arabic from Arabia to North Africa, south Spain and the Levant. In the *zajal* tradition of Lebanon, two poets, with their separate groups of musicians and choruses, pass the evening hours exchanging verses on the qualities of an opposing pair of topics (such as black and white).[24]

Poetic performance also fulfilled a more ceremonial function in the lives of Arabic speakers, such as in the venue of a tribal gathering, court ceremony, or day of national remembrance. Such occasions would include celebrations of victory in battle, prominent events in the lives of the ruling dynasty (births, weddings, and funerals), and religious festivals. For the most formal gatherings (*majlis*), the subject matter of these poems would follow court protocol. Later in the evening when the ruler gathered with his boon companions and slave-girls, the *majlis* would have a more intimate atmosphere. The topics of poetic performance became considerably less constrained, which was revealed by some of the accounts of the poets Abu Nuwās and Abu al-faraj al-Isfahānī's (d. 967). For example, *Kitāb al-Aghānī* (*The Book of Songs*) contained both formal and informal accounts of musical and poetic performances by illustrious singers on various occasions.

In earliest times the occasion for a poetic performance could be a tribal gathering, whether it involved the members of a single grouping around an evening campfire or a larger annual gathering of tribal confederacies. Current practice in countries such as Yemen may provide some clues about what was going on during these occasions. As first-hand historical recording is absent, the following is the closest depiction of the events. Coffee is served to the noisy group. When the poet is ready, he clears his throat to request silence and then begins his recitation. Each half of the first verse of the poem ends with rhyming syllables, and the poet may repeat the first line so that the audience has a clear sense of both rhyme and meter. The audience is thoroughly familiar with the occasions, motifs, and facets that make up the poetic craft and quickly express approval for excellent lines (often requesting their repetition) and provide criticism of less satisfactory efforts through silence or bodily gestures of disapproval.[25]

Most historians agree that there were distinct forms of music in the pre–Islamic Arabian Peninsula that played an important part in the formation of Arabic poetry. Arabic poetry, unlike the literary poetry of many European languages that is written by literary writers, the Arabic poetry was invented originally by Arab soothsayers (*kahins*). They used incantations of a rhythmic form of rhymed prose known as *saj'* and a poetic meter called *rajaz*. Arab soothsayers were also enchanters and prophets. It was believed that the *jinn* (supernatural creatures) prompted the verses of the poet and the melodies of the musician and connected music, poetry, and magic.[26]

Music's role in ancient Arabia was very similar to that of Akkadian (both Babylonian and Assyrian), Aramaic or Hebrew during the formative periods of their linguistic histories. The temples of Ishtar and Yahveh had their specific chants, and Arabian shrines had theirs. Like the Assyrians, Arab poets worked hard in composing their songs to express their feelings. A performance of music similar to one at a Hebrew banquet would most likely have taken place among the pagan Arabs. The main difference between the Western chromatic scale and the Arabic scales is the existence of many in-between notes, which are sometimes referred to as quarter tones, to indicate finer distinction of sound. In some treatments of theory, the quarter tone scale or all twenty-four tones should exist. According to

Yūsuf Shawqī (1969), in practice, there are many fewer tones. Many Islamic formulaic pronouncements and ritual recitation were originally songs that were chanted by pagan Arabs during pre–Islamic times. Encircling a stone, they chanted. They sang *tahlīl*, a song for the moon god, and they honored the god on his birthday with hymns. Music could be found in the private, public, and religious life of the Arabs, as there were work songs, war songs, songs of victory and songs of woe. Music and songs resounded around the temples and shrines of the Arabs as it did the temples of Ishtar and Yahweh. Music and song were with the Arabs from the lullaby at the cradle to the elegy at the bier.[27]

Ancient religious ritual was very much alive in Arabia as pilgrims indulged in chanting and hymn singing during *hajj* (pilgrim age). Some fragments of the hymns that were performed and dramatized during the *ḥajj* have been preserved in literature that describes how the Arabs chanted a hymn while encircling the sacrificial stone. Musical rituals were dedicated to Al-Lāt the goddess. Both Umru al-Qais and Labīd, pre–Islamic poets, spoke of "maidens circling a pillar," which would most likely be performed in a dance, accompanied by music and singing.[28]

In ancient Arabia, if a poet appeared in the family, the other nearby tribes would gather together with that family and congratulate them on their good fortune. Feasts would be arranged, women of the tribe would join together in bands, playing lutes, as they did at bridals. This was because a poet was a defense of the honor of them all, a weapon to ward off insults to their good names, and a means of perpetuating their glorious deeds and of establishing their fame forever. At the time, Arabian tribal men fought with words as well as swords. Poetry flew across the desert faster than arrows and found the hearts and bosoms of all those who heard them. Women sang war songs and laments for the slain while playing their tambourines. Singing-girls could be invariably found in the household of every Arab of social standing. It was also the time when music began to extend its ritual and religious function into private entertainment, a tradition that lasted until the beginning of Islam.[29]

Pre-Islamic music derived from the rhythm of the spoken language, and it was little more than unpretentious psalming, varied and embroidered by the singer, male or female, according to the taste, emotion, or effect desired. The oldest form of poetical speech was rhyme without meter, *saj'*, which was defined later as rhymed prose. Out of *saj'* evolved the most ancient of the Arabian meters, known as *rajaz* meter, a measure which is believed to come from the rhythm of everyday desert life in particular, the beat of the steps of a walking camel. The *rajaz* meter was an irregular iambic cadence usually consisting of four or six beats. A poet would write two or three feet to the line, which was a popular tune, the extemporaneous song known as the *ghinā' murtajat*. Untrained minstrels often used a *qadīb* (wand) to mark the beat of the song. At this time, singing was designed to carry the verses, prolonged interminably on a syllable word or hemistich in such a way that the singing of a cantilena of two or three verses might last for hours. The singer demonstrated his talent by the timbre of his voice expressed in mobility and vibrations (the feeling that made it sound or quaver) to please the audience. Sometimes, the singer might prolong the final vowels with a high trill (*tudrī*) and clearly enunciate the syllables (*tartīl*) giving each its due measure and value. The familiar ways of singing well-known in the West, such as singing in unison or in harmony, were quite unknown. The only "harmony" was that supplied by the various instruments of percussion such as the *tabl* (drum), *duff* (tambourine) and the figuration of the melody by means of ornaments in the shape of trills or turns which were called *zawā'id*. Skillful singers could sing antiphonally with others while playing the resounding lute.[30]

In fact, the emergence of Arabic as a dominant literary language, like the European vernaculars many centuries later, came with a musical renaissance that cultivated innovative expressions in music and singing. The center of this emerging music was in Al-Hijaz (a region in the west of present-day Saudi Arabia) and later Mecca. Peripheral to older kingdoms and major empires of the Middle East, Al-Hijaz initially had a minor musical tradition that had not advanced as had the Arab court of Al-Ḥīra (a city of modern Iraq), a contemporary cultural center for musicians and poets. By the close of the sixth century or beginning of the seventh, Al-Hijaz had inherited only a few types of songs such as *nasb* and the *nauḥ*. Poet-minstrel Al-NaĂDr ibn al-Ḥārith (d. 624) introduced several innovations from Al-Ḥīra, one of which was *ghinā'*, a more sophisticated song. He also learned to play a new type of wooden-bellied lute called the *'ūd*, which apparently superseded the old skin-bellied *mizhar*. *Ghinā'* was also a superior and more artistic song than *nasb*, of the old Arabian.[31]

Like the music of late medieval Europe, the emerging music had lasting influence in linguistic history because it separated music from words. In pre–Islamic Arabia, the musical measure of songs was determined by the prosodic feet of the verse, as in Latin liturgical music of the early Middle Ages. The formal sophistication of pre–Islamic poetry reveals that this type of poetic chanting to a simple musical accompaniment had a long history and a well-educated audience. The singer-poet often impressed the audience with an outstanding voice. When Ibn al-Ḥārith introduced the new songs, he became the rival of the Prophet Muhammad for the ear of the public.

Muhammad was initially perceived as a non-singing poet (in the Arabic definition) because he appeared to be another poet-soothsayer (*sha'ir*) or magician (*kāhin*) who possessed a powerful way with words. He preached in the style of the *saj'* (rhymed prose) as did the traditional poets. He was in fact called a *shā'ir majnūn* (a crazy poet, or a poet-soothsayer possessed of a *jinn*, a supernatural being). What made Muhammad original was not his voice but rather his eloquence and his message of revelation articulated with the familiar poetic rhythm.[32] The importance of words (rhymed prose) began to overpower music at a time when the two forms of expression started to depart from each other. As oral tradition (both poetry and prose) was elevated into literary canon, music became the servant of words. This has been a familiar separation in many world civilizations such as in late Medieval Europe and post–Tang China. The only difference is that Arabic transformed from oral to written language while European vernaculars replaced Latin literary tradition.

This apparent competition between forms of delivery of the same language (song or speech, meter or rhyme) has been poorly interpreted by some scholars as Islam's opposition to or condemnation of music. This assumption is understandable in the sense that historians were trying to explain the non-liturgical nature of Islamic worship, as they did not observe singing in the mosque that might parallel the musical rites seen in Judaism and the Christian church. In fact the real reason for this difference lies not in music or attitude towards music but rather in the degrees of maturity of literary language in which various religions defined the forms of worship.[33]

There were variations of the language and singing skills throughout the population of the pre–Islamic Arabian Peninsula, and this diversity might be the reason for the richness of pre–Islamic culture. Nomadic culture was only one of many different pre–Islamic cultures. First, the oldest musical and literary heritage came from the south (Al-Yemen), where several popular musical instruments of Islam were first adopted. For many centuries, the Arabs of Al-Ḥijāz recognized that the best real Arabian music came from Al-Yemen, and Ḥadramī minstrels were considered to be superior.[34] There were two types of singing, the Bedouin and sedentary singing. *Huda* and *nasb* were the first types and were considered simple, naïve and conservative. Their rhythms derived from and reflected the desert life, as they broke the natural, infinite silence and provided comfort for the lonely life of travelers. In the towns and oases, such as Medina, Ta'iif and 'Ukāz, new and more artistic types of music became entertainment. Singing girls served as singers, performers, waitresses, or prostitutes. The songs of the exotic singers were virtuosic and extraordinary. The most famous singers (*qainah*) in Arabia were from Persia or Africa.[35]

Even well before the advance of Islam, music had begun to separate from verse, and the social function of musicians transformed as well. There were different kinds of music and different kinds of singing. *Huda* and *nasib,* favored by the Bedouin nomads, were narrative and nostalgic, presented in repetitive, melodic phrase. They were governed by the prosodic structure of poetry, where melody was enriched by the singer who held long breaths, long notes, proper pronunciation, metrical measurement, and grammatical inflection. The emerging city styles preferred lighter and more varied rhythms and pure musical and vocal presentations. The diversity of musical practice made it possible for music to depart from religious rituals and social function and become performance for entertainment and pleasure. Like in the later period of ancient Mesopotamia, the art began to be associated with brightness and enjoyment. As the word *zahara* meant "to shine brightly," it indicated "brightness." A similar transformation of the function of music did not occur in the West until the early twentieth century, when literature became a mature art.[36]

At the same time, Arabic poetry began to grow into an art form independent from music (or singing), when it had cultivated its own prosody. Unlike European languages, whose literature diversified into prose and poetry (defined by presence or absence of rhyme), Arabic, whose spoken form had already inherited a speaking rhythm, diversified into prose and poetry by presence or absence of meter. In other words, Arabic prose from the very beginning was rhymed (without meter) and poetry had both rhyme and meter because rhyme represented smooth and eloquent speech. These literary genres emerged from an already established and polished speech equipped with both rhyme and rhythm. This is the reason why Arabic poetry is the language of common speakers rather than the artistic language of the cultural elite.[37]

Arabic was the first Semitic language that produced poetry in quantitative measure like the Greek and Latin. However, this quantitative measure occurred in Arabic much more naturally than it did in Latin and Germanic languages. Arabic, by the time of Islam, had already inherited a natural linguistic stress, which made a readily rhythmic foundation of poetic prosody. Its grammatical features had already inherited a speaking rhythm that employed stress and alternation of long and short vowels. With this type of phonetic symmetry, it did not need a cumbersome prosody to force a rhythm into the sound of poetry. The difference between Arabic poetry and prose lies in the degrees of rhythmic repetition rather than the presence of meter. For example, Arabic poetry requires a somewhat higher ratio of long to short syllables than is usual in prose; it never allows more than two short syllables in succession, whereas up to six or more occur in prose. However, generally speaking, poetic meter in Arabic seldom imposes restraint on the normal patterns of speech.[38]

Without an established literary form to imitate (Latin poetry had Greek), Arabic poetic language accumulated piecemeal. It did not begin with an idealistic unity or overall structure, assembled one verse and a few lines at a time for each subject, image, and mood. Several poetic genres evolved with singular and independent themes. Like the early Semitic epic poetry, it gradually became linked and grew into long and coherent form. For example, *qasīda*, the only complete and most dominant pre–Islamic poetic form, did not obtain its coherence until the late part of pre–Islamic poetry. In Medieval Arabic the term *qasida* could be applied to any poem composed in accepted meters of a certain length, perhaps from seven to ten lines.[39]

During the early period on the pre–Islamic Arabian Peninsula, poets did follow set rules of composition in theme or rhythm. They were experimenting with different themes and forms. The poetry that survived from this period mainly consisted of *qit'a*, short poems that highlighted a single theme, and the longer, structurally complex *qasida*. A *qit'a* was addressed to a specific person and expressed eulogy (*marthiya, ritha*), praise (*madih*), or boasting (*fakhr*). The *qasida* was a polythemetatid form in which several parts were joined without transition (*takhallus*) or without apparent reason for their sequence. However, certain forms were more popular among the poets of the Peninsula, and this promoted a sense of standardization.[40]

By the sixth century, the first two sections of *qasida*, the elegiac prelude (*nasīb*) and the description of the camel (*rahīl*), were widely employed by Arab poets. The concluding section that dealt with present intent was less constant. It could include self-praise (*fakhr*), a message to an enemy (*hijā*), or tribute (*madīh*) for a patron, tribal leader or king. By the end of the pre–Islamic period, the three-part structure of the *qasida* was well established and had a higher degree of coherence in its form.[41]

Although varied in thematic arrangement, *qasida* and *qit'a* shared the characteristics of monorhyme and the use of a fixed set of meters based on syllable length. The only difference was that the *qasida*'s overall structure was considerably more complex. Most *qasida* range between about 30 and 100 lines, containing up to thirty syllables each, and divided more or less equally over two hemistiches. Within this structure, the range and arrangement of themes and rhythmic patterns varies considerably.[42] The English word monorhyme reminds one of the sound of French, which is a monotone language with fewer tonal variations, compared with other romantic languages. However, the word monorhyme in reference to Arabic poetry is misleading without qualification. First of all, if read silently, Arabic poetry appears to be quite plain, with a rather unified end rhyme. When it is read in the mind, its lack of intonation creates a false impression, similar to the impression created when academics read and study Chinese Tang poetry as if it is a more familiar form, such as Haiku. The soul of Arabic poetry lies in its sound, its highly dramatized delivery of a variety of music-like modulations of rhythm and tone. Different speakers could change the tempo and gear in performance, and convey a variety of moods and connotations.[43] The only way that a non–Arabic speaker can understand the difference between various delivery forms for an Arabic poem is to imagine a familiar song (with familiar lyrics) performed by different singers using various musical arrangements.

If read silently (by following the superficial monorhyme), Arabic loses its real rhythm. It was composed and meant to be read in cycles. Each cycle contains a cluster of verses to deliver a climactic unity of emotion, theme, and rhythm. Like a musical symphony, it often began with a point of calm, and then it accelerates slowly or quickly to crescendo, finally culminating in a fully expected resolution. A good poet could avoid monotone and tedious rhythmic recurrence and inject emotional apex by manipulating rhythmic cycles. Within this climactic structure, the tension and its resolution recur constantly in the poem, leaving no time to fall into dull monorhythm. In other words, without sound, Arabic poetry is void of bouncing pulse and exciting appeal.[44]

This shared rhythmic cycle in poetry was and remains deeply rooted in Arabic language. After centuries of performance and ritual recitation, Arabic poetry had cultivated a double pattern of anticipation and resolution in the ears and the minds of poets and their audiences. A poet had to compose his lines in pairs because the audience, after hearing the first half of a line, was led to expect the rhyme-syllable of the second half of the line (its metrical twin). The conclusion of the line led the audience to expect another line that followed the same rhyme pattern as the first.[45]

Although relatively close to speech, Arab poetry was an artistic and artificial form distinct from spoken rhythm. Even before it became codified, Arabic poetry employed a set of complicated meters based on syllabic length. The two meters used by the well-known pre–Islamic poets Umru al-Qays, Ṭarafa and Zuhayr, and in Labīd and 'Antara were *ṭawīl* (long) and *kāmil* (perfect). The basic feet in *ṭawīl* were u - - and u—u -, called by the Arabs *fa'ūlun* and *mafā'ilun*. *Kāmil* only had one basic type of foot, u u—u -, called *mutafā'ilun*. The feet are arranged with the permissible alternatives noted directly below the variable syllables. Although the two hemistiches (half-lines) are identical in basic form, variations that occur in one hemistich need not be reflected in the other.[46]

The essential element in Arabic rhyme (*qāfiya*) was the final consonant in the line (*rawīy*), which remained constant throughout the poem for as many as 80–120 lines (often more for *fajaz* poems). The rhymes were usually feminine, such as *sakhīrā, tulīnā, muhīnā; mukhlidī, yadī, 'uwwadī; rijāmuhā, silāmuhā, harāmuhā*. Although Arabic inherited an extraordinary array of rhymes, poets still needed a high degree of technical skill to render a long poem in a single rhyme. The solution was to produce two basic types of rhyme. One was verse-end rhyme in which the *rawiy* alone was the last sound pronounced in reciting each verse. The other was verse-end consonance and assonance in which the *rawiy* was pronounced with a final long-vowel ū/ī/ā. The latter type was the more commonly used.[47]

The simplicity and plasticity of pre–Islamic poetic form gave poets an exceptional degree of freedom as well as manipulative power to compose in a variety of voices, themes, and moods. Arabic poetry was a well developed and refined oral tradition at the time that it became written. Its vivid imagery, sophisticated eloquence and multiple voices provided a rich foundation for its literary poetry. It has long been deemed as the supreme art form among Arabs, one that flourished even at times when other arts were virtually unknown.[48]

Although it had been orally composed, transmitted, and preserved, it only became selected and edited by Muslim scholars during the 8th and 9th centuries. A collection of Arabic poems is usually called a *dīwān*. The early philologists who gathered poems into collections used a variety of organizational categories. Some were named after the tribe under whose protective umbrella the works had been conceived and performed. An example of this is the poems of the Banu Hudhayl. Others were named after their compilers. One of the most cherished was heroism, *hamāsah*, providing the title for a number of collections of which the most renowned was that of the poet Abu Tammām. However, the most favored organizing principle for collections of Arabic poetry had been and remains the gathering of the works of a single poet, *The Dīwān of al-Mutanabbī*, for example.

It was not the practice to give Arabic poems descriptive titles until recently. The majority of collections by early poets were organized in a series of short statements, for example, a recounting of the occasion for which the poem was composed and/or performed, upon the death of a prominent person, or in celebration of a significant event in the life of the community. A preferred mode of sequence for the collected poems was an alphabetical one based on their end-rhymes. The most famous poems were often referred to in this way. Thus, the vagabond-poet Al-Shanfarā's most famous ode is known as "The L-poem of the Arabs" (*lāmiyyat al-Arab*).

Another method of identification is through the opening of the poem. Imru al-Qays' *mu'allaqah* poem is instantly recognizable by its renowned beginning: "Halt, you two companions, and let us weep..." (*qifā nabki*). As the Arabic poetic tradition developed and particular genres came to be recognized as separate entities, the *dīwān* of the poet was often subdivided into categories. Abu Nuwas' collected poetry, for example, contains large separate sections of love poems addressed to males and females (*ghazal*) and wine poems (*khamriyyah*). In addition to the accepted sections on eulogies, lampoons and elegies, there are also others gathered around the themes of hunting, asceticism, and the reprimand. With Abu Tammām's *Dīwān* we find separate sections on eulogies, lampoons, elegies, love, chiding, description, boasting, and asceticism.

The collected poetry contained ample tribal and personal motifs portrayed in a highly personal and lyrical manner. Arabic poetry gave more attention to the lyrical voice of the poet than to its story or subject matter. In other words, the established form had begun to be formalized as a mood setter, which made it possible for poets to move on to an exhibition of eloquence and poetic wording. An example of how different individual sentiments could be expressed in a seemingly highly formalized structure is the comparison of a poem by Durayd ibn-a-imma (d. 630) and another by As-Sanfarā (d. 550).

The first poem was a personal recollection of a raid on an enemy tribe. The raid started well, and the poet's party managed to escape with some booty. On the way home, his tribal cohorts disregarded his good advice about the strength of their well-armored enemy and stopped to divide the spoils. They were overtaken and overrun by a detachment from the offended tribe. Several men, including the poet's brother, died as the result of this foolish mistake.

The first five lines of the poem emphatically assert Durayd's own acumen before proclaiming his tribal loyalty in strikingly jingoistic terms (*awīl/dī*). What is the use to be a wise man, when one is nothing but one of the group (tribe), which decides one's destiny? Another poem expressed an opposite sentiment of a rogue poet who relied not on the backing of his tribe to survive, but on his own wits and hardihood (*awīl/lū*). He preferred to face the world alone and take full responsibility for his actions.

No one serves as a better example of a highly individualized poet in tribal society than Imru' al-Qays, the most renowned of the pre–Islamic Arabic poets. Imru' al-Qays was born in A.D. 526, the youngest son of Hujr, king over the tribes of Asad and Ghutfan in ancient Yemen. His rebellious actions (writing poetry was one of them) against tribal code got him expelled from his kingdom. In exile, he wandered from oasis to oasis, stopping to drink wine, recite poetry, and enjoy the performance of the singing-girls, sometimes lingering for days before packing up to wander again. Ironically, the tribal law that he had rebelled against eventually bound him to spend the rest of his life pursuing vengeance on his enemy for the death of his estranged father. However, his hard traveling life and exceptionally wide range of emotions (with his father, his lover, his friends, and enemies) became an inexhaustible source material for a poem that praises their graces, lambastes their cruelty, and laments their absence, and in so doing explains the longing in his heart.

Between these roles of loyal compiler and discontented rebel of the tribal code lay a wide range of human experiences for other poets to explore. They left to posterity a treasury of love-songs, wine-songs, and hunting-songs. Prominent of course were poems that praised tribes and chieftains and celebrated glorious deeds with occasional elegies on the death of heroes. But there was also praise for the peacemakers.[49]

During the codification process, the early Muslim scholars called any of these single-themed poems on a single theme a *qit'a* piece, as if it was a fragment detached from a larger unit. They reserved the term *qasida* for a three-part ode. An example of this type of ode is a collection called *mu'allaqah* (the suspended odes). The title derived from the legend that they were purportedly written in gold and suspended inside the *ka* (the cubical shrine), which was revered in Mecca even before it became the focus of the Muslim pilgrimage. Some also interpreted the term as the string that ties several themes together.

Through Islamic codification, Arabic poetry became much more formulized and created the model of Arabic poetry for the following centuries.[50] A standard metrical system (*'arūd*) was established to unify the prosody of poetry. This standard remained relatively unchanged from the end of the eighth century until the modern period.

The first part of a *qasida* was known as *nasib* or nostalgic prelude. This was often a memorization or celebration of a lost love. Sometimes what stirred the poet's emotion was an apparition that he took to be the specter of his beloved. More commonly, however, the entire poem started with a situation so conventional and so well understood by the audience that it was not explicitly described: The poet, traveling through the desert with one or two companions, comes upon the traces of an encampment where a woman he loved once dwelt, and he expresses what was known as "weeping over the ruins."

This prelude put both poet and his audience in a place where time was compressed, emotion was frozen and memory lasted forever. Once inside this intimate space, they entered the "abodes of the hearts" that used to be shared by the poet and his loved one and were now also shared by the poet with his audience. In the stillness of these motionless memories, the abodes of the heart have become places of refuge and protection. They are therefore not mere temporal points. They now possess a spacious material dimension. In this private house of emotion and frozen memory lies a very special piece of the past which has nothing to do with finite, historical time, and which has a certain protective quality. This is the realm where flowers become silent gardens of paradise. A poem that began with *nasib* was a guided private tour. The poet invited the readers into his sacred domain of (past) happiness, memory, and longing.[51]

Within the emotion of these memories, tribal enclosures and nightly phantoms are transformed before our eyes into a melancholy garden. Awakening in the morning as if from an ancient dream and then remembering something of that dream, the narcissus sheds its dewy tears of sadness, the same sadness that the poet senses awakening in his heart. It is only then that an equation between the archaic abode and the garden sets in and the metaphor of the poetic instant blends into the symbol of the archetype. "The chill of morning stirred narcissus' lid. A tear of dew first gleamed on it and then rolled down."[52] Thus the "romantic," melancholy garden becomes the place where the memory of ancient abodes may be recaptured. To the Arab poet this scene had nothing to do with nature or earthly paradise. Rather, it served as a background to express his yearning for the scene that had been his native land and that was lost and then remembered as fragrance, color, purity, joy and passion, all sensations and things of beauty.

In the poetry of nostalgia it was characteristic for poets to create images and expression by referring to what had been connoted in ancient poems. This was illustrated by the effectiveness of the proverbial expression *tafarraqu ayadiya Saba'* (they scattered in all directions) from the old Yemeni. This expression was much echoed in the 'Abbasid period, when an antiquarian nostalgia revived. Abu Nuwas, for instance, employed the fullness of his loss in a contemporary Islamic setting by turning to a much more ancient expression of the Bedouin feeling of desolation. His depiction of the place of prayer (*musalla*) read: "Musalla is no more, desolate...." "Those places where once a prosperous life I led, Till youth's down went and gray hair came." "At the hand of fretful time," "they broke apart like ancient Saba's might" as they dispersed and each took a separate way.[53]

The elegiac tone setting of the *nasib* of *qasida* continued to be used even after historical and Qur'anic references became part of the poetic expression in Classical Arabic. The theme of *nasib* became more abstract by shifting the original metaphoric meaning to a functional form of composition. Abu Tammam (788–845) blended the semantic and symbolic connotations of *nasib* with Islamic rites. In his *nasib* he was able to reduce this pre–Islamic convention into functional abstraction by erasing the concrete meanings of words that were normally used in pre–Islamic Arabic and injecting them with new Islamic connotations. In the emerging Islamic idiom, the abode, the garden, the rich soil, the rain, and the mosque became one, as did the question and the prayer, the search and the song. "Perpetual dew surrounds the abode" and "the garden flowers quiver and lull in rich soil." Eventually, a "ruinous abode," over which he stopped in supplication, and its site almost became his "mosque." In grief he sang in searching for both his friends and his song.[54]

Here the "abode" may not be abandoned at all. The poet wishes it well as if still at a distance, remembering. A number of images and questions emerge. Is it a desert or a garden? As long as it evokes memory, it could be both, or which it was could become irrelevant. The poet's traditional "questioning" of the silent ruins was also indirect. It was a call to elicit an echo and a supplication—and thus a prayer; and with his prayer the poet no longer stood before an abode or a ruin but before a mosque, and his prayer was now his quest, which was also his song. All the familiar concrete imagery had left the *nasib* and all that remained was the mood: the feeling of emptiness. The loss and sadness had crystallized and weighed down the hearts of poets.[55]

The conventional tripartite form of the ode provoked diverse interpretations and analysis by both Muslim and Western scholars. Some suggested that the prelude serves as some kind of introduction to establish a rapport with his audience. The poet then complained about the hardships he had endured on his way to his patron, and having thus implied a claim for recompense, he finally launched into his eulogy. The second part depicted the environment, and the third celebrated some of the qualities that a man of the desert needed for survival. If one also takes into account that the tripartite arrangement was a highly prized form but not a must for every poetic outburst, one can see how it suits a special formal and competitive occasion, such as a poetry fair, at which a poet would want to gain the good will of his audience, display the range of his gifts and demonstrate his relevance to the life of his contemporaries.[56]

However, there are deeper and more important reasons for this structure that made them indispensable in Arabic poetry even after the conventional sections that described desert life had been gone for many centuries. The real reason for the lasting relevance of the form of *qasida* lies in its function as a ritual and ceremonial device that had accompanied Arabic poetry, along with its Semitic ancestors, for thousands of years. Poetry has been a dialogue and drama (sometimes highly refined and artistic) rather than merely a form of personal expression. Many Western and Western-trained Arab scholars have been trying to find an organic unity in pre–Islamic and Classical poetry that qualifies as a good literary form in the Western literary sense.[57] They tend to overlook the major difference between the Arabic and Western literature: the degree of maturity as a literary language. As a mature poetry, Arabic had already outgrown the visual and philosophical unity of a literary form that sought to depict an idea or a vision. This was developed by the literary ancestors of Semitic languages, Akkadian, Babylonian, and Hebrew. Arabic poetry had allowed itself to incorporate musical organization into its verbal arts in order to evoke emotion and activate mood. Looking for linear narration or philosophical consistency in Arabic poetry is similar to attempting to locate the musical inspiration for modern jazz within the parameters of classical music, which is a much more structurally rigid form.

Arabic poetry verbalized musical form to cultivate mood. It is on this level that Arabic poetry equates to musical language, which gravitates toward representing and apprehending the specific poetic moods. As mood creation became the very center of poetic composition, visual and thematic consistencies became less relevant. Like in the sonata, a popular form in classical music, each movement of the piece is an independent unit and its sequence of tempi obey no immediately evident logical consistency. In the four-movement sonata or symphony and string quartet that developed in later Romantic Europe, a sonata-allegro movement often was divided into sections, each of which performed specific functions in the musical argument. The introduction was, in most times, slower than the main movement, and it prepared for an upbeat before the main musical argument. The next section, called the exposition, presented the primary thematic material for the movement: one or two themes or theme groups, often in contrasting styles and in opposing keys, connected by a modulating transition. The exposition was followed by an exploration of the harmonic and textural possibilities of the thematic material. This is followed by the recapitulation in the tonic key, and for the recapitulation to complete the musical argument, material that has not been presented in the tonic key is "resolved" by being played, in whole or in part. The movement may conclude with a coda, beyond the final cadence of the recapitulation.[58]

However, unlike the sonata form, which was viewed as a model for musical analysis rather than compositional practice, the *qasida* had been a model of composition for Arabic poetry since the classical period. Compared to music that expresses mood in the speed of the rhythm, *qasida* added more dimensions to the depiction of emotion. It could extend the

curve of mood into lyrical details and express levels of meanings and connotations. It was the same attempt made by Baroque sonata, which had a
binary (A–B) ascending curve to a classical mode that amplified the mood
change by chaining contrasting movements and rhythmic speeds. It began
to sound like *qasida* with alternating changes between fast and slow, sad
and happy, elegiac and heroic. Arabic became an instrument in which a
large and waving curve flow with words was built.[59]

Like musicians of the late Romantic period, when the sonata began
to outgrow its own form after being polished by generations of composers,
Arab poets paid more and more attention to the rhetorical affects of their
words rather than to the structure of the piece. They often were exalted or
condemned on the strength of a single line or a short sequence of lines.
They focused on the balance of themes and the smoothness of transitions.
The length of a line made it possible for them to round off a thought, a
notion, an image, or a fancy. Indeed when, in early Islamic times, prosody
was codified, it was considered a fault if a line could not stand by itself,
in concept as well as grammatical structure. As monorhyme served as a
phonetic structure, the cohesion between lines did not have to be evident.
It became easy to drop some lines, incorporate others, or rearrange the
order. This flexibility gave poets (including the later rectors) the freedom
to amplify or distill imagery as they chose. Sometimes many sententious
lines irrelevant to the theme could be inserted in a poem.[60]

The lack of understanding of Arabic poetry among the Western and
Western-trained Arabic and Persian scholars derived from the fact that
they overlooked the fundamental differences between Arabic and European
languages, from which their poetics emerged. As a unique case in literary
history, Arabic poetry entered into literary history with an impressive corpus of pre–Islamic poems that had firm structure, vivid characterization
and full conventions. The maturity of its form validated a long development, which had no parallel before the later Middle Ages in Western
Europe. A similar development can be found in every literary language
after it outgrew its formative period. In Western literature, what is defined
as mannerism often indicated the beginning of this stage, where the attention of the writers turned to smaller elements (details) of composition and
their approaches became formally and thematically diversified.[61] In this
specific sense, Arabic poetics have not been studied, analyzed, and compared properly with other languages because the level of maturity of Arabic
poetry has gone far beyond that of its European contemporaries.

The refinement of structure only means that poets had to try harder
to be creative and invent something original instead of repeating their natural inheritance. For example, if an English speaker had read and heard

every single possible rhyme in the language and memorized them all (as did the post–Tang Chinese intellectuals), it would be very challenging to compose English verse. Much education and training would be needed to achieve competency. In other words, a poet in a mature language like Arabic had to pay attention to every single rhyme, word, line and image because his audience, who had trained ears for poetry, expected and demanded it. It is the same for Italian opera singers, whose most demanding audience is that in Milan. Even the most prominent tenors can encounter audiences who openly express dissatisfaction if they made a tiny mistake in tone or lyrics. Therefore, Arabic poets had to be able to compose ear-pleasing lines, verses, as well as blocks of verses that combined into long poems.[62]

This high degree of demand for increasingly sophisticated poetic forms forced Arabic poets to invent more diverse forms. Arabic poetry became written and codified in the 8th century by Al-Khalil bin Ahmad (718–786) and has changed little until the modern period. By that time, Arabic poetry had completely separated itself from speech by changing from a rhythm of stress (similar to speech) to one of meter and rhyme. It accumulated considerably more and complex forms compared to the Pre-Islamic period. While maintaining the basic unit of a line (*bayt*) divided into two hemistiches by a caesura, it had to be a syntactic and semantic unit, and the parts could be enjambed with each other.[63] The final consonants of all the second hemistiches were determined and governed by one rhyme-consonant. Now the poetic meter (*wazn*) came to be based on the length of syllables rather than stress. A short syllable is a consonant followed by a short vowel. A long syllable is a vowel followed by either an unvowelled consonant or a long vowel. A nunation sign at the end of a word also makes the final syllable long.

The system of Al-Khalil had fifteen meters that were various combinations of long (—) and short (^) syllables. The patterns were not supposed to be rigidly followed, and two short syllables might be substituted for a long one, etc. Rhyme (*qafiya*) was basically determined by the last consonant of a word. In rhyme-words, nunation was dropped, and sometimes the final vowel. Where the final vowel was *fatha* (short "a"), it must be used consistently each time the rhyme occurred. *Kasra* (short "i") and *damma* (short "u") were interchangeable. If a long vowel preceded the last syllable of a rhyme-word, it also became part of the rhyme. Similarly, *ya* (long "i") and *waw* (long "u") were interchangeable, but *alif* (used as a long "a") was not. Because short vowels were generally considered long when they occurred at the end of a line, the vowels that appeared short in their written form also rhymed with their corresponding long vowels. It was the pronunciation, not the writing, that counted.

During Islamic expansion, the poetic form of Arabic multiplied and magnified as Arabic speakers scattered throughout a vast empire and their language encountered other languages and cultural idioms. Arabic began to be used by different ethnic groups who brought their own vernaculars and expressions. In this substantially extended and widely differing context, Arabic was injected with new blood. By the second half of the eighth century, the gaps had widened substantially between standard Arabic and local vernaculars. Even among Arabic speakers, Bashshār ibn-Burd (714–784) was accused of using "Nabatean jargon," and the next generation recorded jokes built on misunderstandings between desert Arabs, who reportedly still spoke inflected Arabic, and city dwellers, who did not. While non-classical verses began to emerge, the literary establishment did not allow any form of spoken Arabic into the canon.[64]

The codification of literary forms is as old and common as literature itself, Arabian or not. The majority of literary languages had grown into and then surpassed their established forms during various periods of their history. What was unique about Arabic is the multi-lingual environment in which Arabic evolved, transformed, and reinvented itself as its literary identity evolved. Literary Arabic began to assimilate colloquial Arabic and vernacular, non–Arabic languages. In other words, there were simultaneous developments of poetic forms as codification (for cultural and political control) and as deviation that tolerated and adopted local vernaculars. Codification secured the continuity and conformity of Arabic tradition while adaptation provided reinvention and enrichment. This was the main reason that Arabic poetry did not die after its golden age, as did many other ancient literary traditions. It continuously reshaped itself in a variety of new vernacular-based traditions, Arabic and otherwise.

The widening gap between the classical establishment of literary poetry and vernacular poetry was the main dynamic driving the poetic change. Poetic performance constantly channeled and bridged the widening gap, which initiated a variety of combined forms and styles. Scholars have been passionately debating the history of various poetic forms. Most did not come from a specific form because they combined multiple traditions (sometimes more than one language) and multiple forms of the same tradition. Such fusion differed at each time and location because of the local interaction of various expressive forms; the only thing constant was that the organization underlying these variations was open and multi-dimensional. A good illustration of this multifaceted development in literary poetry is observed in the Arabic fusions that occurred in Iran and Spain.

Persian was one cultural tradition that Islamic Arabic encountered during its expansion that already had its own long and continually active literary tradition. Persian poetry gave originality and passion to Arabic literature. Iberian literature provided energy and a sense of resource for Arabic literature at a time when it had begun to decline in the Middle East after centuries of expansion. The characteristics of the languages and the timing of their influences rejuvenated a tiring Arabic.

It is held that there were two Old Iranian languages spoken since the third millennium B.C. The oldest sacrificial liturgy is dated to around the mid–thirteenth to tenth century B.C. It contains songs (*gathas*) of the Zarathustra (poet-priest) in Avestan (which was originally an Eastern Iranian language and became the scriptural language of the Zarathustran religion). Persian literature is rooted by surviving works of Old and Middle Persian.

Old Persian did not descend from Avestan, but rather evolved from a distinct dialect of Ancient Persian. No early sample of it has been found, but significant phonetic differences from Avestan and a much simplified case and verbal system suggest that Old Persian had a long history of development. Old Persian texts date from the 6th to the 4th century and were written in a cuneiform that was a more advanced form than Sumerian and Akkadian. It used a small number of signs and was able to present vowels as well as consonants. Therefore, it had a higher capacity to register spoken language than Semitic. Old Persian had three vowel signs (a, i, u) and thirty-three consonants.[65]

Semitic and Persian literary traditions shared many features, one of which was that their poetry preceded prose because of constant scriptural reorientation. As written languages came and went, oral poetry (including those of regional dialects) lived on in the ears and on the lips of people, poets and their audiences. Music, song, and poetry were evident in the Iranian court before the Islamic conquest. Middle Persian (Pahlavi) script took the Iranian language one step closer to the Semitic form. The Middle Persian spoken between the 3rd century B.C. and 9th century A.D. adopted Aramaic, another Semitic script. However, like the ancient Greeks who embraced Phoenician script, Pahlavi presented more consonants than the Aramaic script and had encountered difficulty with Aramaic's lack of vowel signs. Like pre–Islamic Arabia, pre–Islamic Iran was a culture of rich linguistic and dialectic traditions, yet literature poor. Very few literary works of Achaemenid Persia (559–330 B.C.) survived, but the legacy of Old Persia can be found in many ancient languages outside of Iran. The rich Iranian poetic tradition, like pre–Islamic Arabic poetry, waited centuries for a rich and sophisticated literary language to revive it.[66]

The injection of Arabic script and literature into old Persian culture accomplished the same as it did for the oral poetry of Arabic. It standardized oral and literary expression and revived the ancient oral tradition. After Islamic conquest, the old prestigious form of Middle Iranian (Pahlavi) was replaced by a new standard dialect called Dari in the Iranian court, where many of the poets, protagonists, and patrons of the literature flourished. The Saffarid dynasty (861–1002) was the first of many to officially adopt the new language (A.D. 875). Dari was heavily influenced by the regional dialects of eastern Iran, whereas the earlier Pahlavi standard derived more from the western dialects. This new official dialect became the basis of Standard New Persian. Islam also brought with it the adoption of Arabic script for presenting Persian, Pashto (an eastern Iranian language, spoken in Pakistan and Afghanistan) and Balochi (a northwestern Iranian language spoken in eastern Iran, Pakistan, and southern Afghanistan). All three became written with the addition of a few letters. This development probably occurred sometime during the second half of the 8th century, as the use of Old Middle Persian script began its decline.

Pre-Islamic Iran certainly cultivated its own poetry. The Parthian minstrels (gōsān) enjoyed great fame, and Parthian (pahlavi) was considered to be the language of "royal sessions," such as court entertainment, while Middle Persian (pārsi) was the language of "mobads [priests] and scholars."[67] But there also was a poetry that was contained in the Middle Persian tradition. Records suggest the names of several poets and musicians of the Sasanian court (224–651). This body of work, evident only in minute traces, was probably purely oral. There are, however, remnants left of pre–Islamic poetry within the western Middle Iranian languages.

Middle Persian meter, like the Pahlavi, was governed by stress, with a flexible number of syllables. Like the Akkadian, the Persian poems were generally sung or chanted and were accompanied by musical instrument. The Sasanian court extended generous patronage to its poet-musicians, and Bahram V (r. 420–438) is said to have promoted them to one of the highest social ranks in the courts. The Islamic conquest did not end the minstrel poetry, and it continued particularly in the countryside, where culture was less susceptible to Arabic influence and court formality. Unfortunately, few original Sasanian works have survived. Many were lost in the course of the Muslim invasion and other foreign conquests, and others were lost because of the religious zeal of the Muslim Persians themselves, but mostly because of the change of script from Aramaic to Arabic as standard written language.

It appears that language change did the same thing to Persian poetry that it had done to the Semitic poetic traditions. The sound of poetry altered, and so did its form of presentation. However, the later poetry inherited the metrical principles and sense of verbal balance of the earlier Persian poetry, as did the Arabic from the ancient Semitic. The Pahlavi poetry was written in prose; however, the poetic forms remained recognizable. Like the Arabic, Pahlavi poetry consisted of two hemistiches or was divided into four strophes in both distiches.[68] We can nevertheless recognize that *Draxt ī asūrīg* does not appear to be rhymed, but in other Pahlavi poems rhymes are not infrequent. In *Dārom andarz-ē*, a rhyme in *-ān* appears in the first two hemistiches and, afterwards, at the end of each verse, that is, twice per distich. In *Kay bawād...*, a rhyme likewise (in *-ān*) appears in each verse. In "Hymn to Wisdom," all the distiches, except for the first, end in a comparative in *-tar*. In *Was raft hēm*, the first four distiches have a rhyme in *-ag* and the following four end in the word *xrad*. These rhymes differ from those of classical Persian poetry in that the same word or the same suffix is allowed to rhyme with it.[69]

Rhymes with this same structure and placement appear in almost all the pieces of Arabic or Persian texts. For example, in the hymn of the Karkoy pyre, all the (very short) verses rhymed together (in *ōš*). The same is true of the two poems quoted by Tohfat al-molūk, although the metrics were the same as the classical model. In short, Iranian poetry, with or without Arabic influence, had begun to cultivate its own prosody, distinct from that of Classical Arabic. The poetry of the Sasanian period was unrhymed. Later on, Pahlavi poetic forms developed regular or non-regular repetition of the same syllable or the same word, either at the end of the verses or at the end of the distiches. These rhymed forms continued in popular poetry and also in Persian poems in classical prosody. The prosodic structure of Middle Persian and Parthian was not based on the short or long quantity of the syllables, as in classical Arabic and Persian poetry, but was syllabic. Middle Persian poetry contained a range of variable number of syllables (stressed and unstressed syllables) and its versification was based on stress.[70]

Light syllables are all short syllables, and those long syllables belong to auxiliary words or words that are weak in positions (in prosthesis or anaptyxis). Heavy syllables are all other long syllables. The stresses or beats (ictus) that define the rhythm of a verse always fall on heavy syllables. Analysis of the intact verses of the Manichean hymn cycles supports the following rules. First, the stress often coincides with the accent on the word, but not always. We may suppose that the accent and the stress are characterized by different phonetic properties, for instance the accent by a higher pitch and the stress by intensity or a length. Second, the basic rhythmic unit (foot) is formed by a heavy syllable that carries the stress, preceded by a variable number of heavy and light syllables; but for a given poem the number of heavy syllables per foot is limited. The third, enclitics, are treated in the same way as root words.

It appears that in the two hymn cycles in Parthian (published by Boyce), the verse has four stresses and the foot contains a maximum of three heavy syllables, including the one that bears the stress. The Manichean poem in Parthian M 10, published by Henning (1933) and also analyzed by Lazard (1985 and 2003), has four stresses per verse, but a maximum of two heavy syllables per foot. Lazard also applied these principles to some Pahlavi poems. In the "Hymn to Wisdom" (2001), and *Was raft hēm...* (2002), he found four stresses per verse with a maximum of two heavy syllables per foot. In the *Draxt ī asūrīg* (2003), there were four stresses per verse with a maximum of three heavy syllables per foot.

On this linguistic foundation, classical Persian versification is different from that of pre–Islamic Iran; it is based, as in Arabic versification, on the arrangement of short and long syllables. It was for a long time believed that this quantitative system was borrowed from Arabic poetry. This claim will have to be seriously qualified. In fact, although the principle is the same, the use that is made of it is not the same on both sides. The meters most used in Persian are rare or nonexistent in Arabic, and vice versa. This is not surprising, for, although any system of versification is more or less artificial, it is nevertheless conditioned by the phonological properties of the language. The phonology of Persian scarcely differs from that of Middle Persian (and Parthian), for from Western Middle Persian to New Persian the evolution is minimal. We merely need to take into account the massive borrowing of Arabic words, which increased the proportion of short vowels. Hence the natural rhythms of New Persian ought to be little different from those of Middle Persian (and Parthian). One is thus led to believe that there must be some lineal relationship between pre–Islamic Iranian meters and those of Persian poetry.

Benveniste first expressed this idea: "The originality of the Persians as regards poetic technique consisted of subjecting the syllabic Iranian meter to Arabic quantitative prosody." If we replace "syllabic" by "accentual," this formula preserves its value. This idea has also been expressed by Utas: "The origin of many of the New Persian meters must be sought in earlier Iranian rhythmic structures that were formally adapted to a quantitative structure." Grunebaum has suggested that certain meters used by Arab poets, "the *ramal*, the *mutaqârib*, and perhaps the *khafîf*, may be considered as adaptations of Persian (Pahlavi) meters to Arabic linguistic conditions."[71]

The method is as follows: The accentual meter is coded in a "structural formula" containing all the syllables, required or optional (the latter shown in parentheses), and indicating the stresses. Then one seeks among the usual meters of classical Persian poetry one that has the same number of syllables and in which the long syllables correspond to the stressed syllables of the accentual meter. For example, the meter of the "Hymn to Wisdom" is represented by the following formula (where the capital letters symbolize the syllables bearing the stress): (x) (x) X (x) x X (x) (x) X x X, with the condition that all optional syllables are never simultaneously present or absent. Additionally, as mentioned above, there are no more than two heavy syllables in a foot. It appears that this formula superimposes itself exactly on the structure of the narrative *motaqāreb*; moreover, the stress falls on those syllables where, in the *motaqāreb* meter, the word accents are most frequently placed.[72] Not only do the stresses of the accentual meter correspond to some of the long syllables of the quantitative meter, but also all short syllables of the quantitative meter correspond to some of the optional syllables of the accentual meter.

Lineal relationships between pre–Islamic versification and Persian versification have not been strictly proven. However, considering that all the above-mentioned conditions about the number and nature of the syllables on both sides are fulfilled, it may be thought that the correspondences observed are not possible. It is true that the quantitative meter is always longer than the corresponding accentual meter. But we know that New Persian has more short syllables than Middle Persian does. Moreover, the short syllables of the classical Persian meter are often merely the third mora of an overlong syllable, that is, actually a phantom syllable.

It was not an accident that Persia produced the most eminent poets in Arabic literature during and after the Islamic expansion. As the majority of Persian writers and poets wrote in both Arabic and Persian, the bulk of Persian literature after the Islamic conquest of Persia (A.D. 650) had an Arabic version. After the Abbasids came to power (A.D. 750), the Persians became the scribes and bureaucrats of the Islamic empire and, increasingly, also its writers and poets. They dominated literary circles. Persian poets such as Ferdowsi, Sa'di, Hafiz, Rumi and Omar Khayyam are also known in the West and have influenced the literature of many countries.

The Sufi tradition also produced poetry closely linked to religion. Sufism is a mystical interpretation of Islam and it emphasizes the allegorical nature of language and writing. Many of the works of Sufi poets appear to be simple *ghazal* or *khamriyyah*. Under the guise of the love or wine poem they would contemplate the mortal flesh and attempt to achieve transcendence. Rabia al-Adawiyya, Abd Yazid al-Bistami and Mansur al-Hallaj were some of the most significant Sufi poets, but their poetry and doctrine were considered dangerous. Al-Hallaj was eventually crucified for heresy.

An important aspect of Arabic poetry from the start was its complexity, but court poetry became an art form in itself, known as *badi'*. There were

features such as metaphor, pun, juxtaposing opposites and tricky theological allusions. Bashar ibn Burd was instrumental in developing these com-
plexities, which later poets felt they had to surpass. Although not all writers
enjoyed the baroque style, with argumentative letters on the matter being
sent by Ibn Burd and Ibn Miskawayh, the poetic brinkmanship of *badi'* led
to a certain formality in poetic art, with only the greatest poets' words
shining through the complex structures and wordplay. This can make Arabic
poetry even more difficult to translate than poetry from other languages,
with much of a poet's skill often lost in translation.

Arabic music and poetry reinvented itself in southern Europe where
they interacted with Iberian cultural forms. The *muwashshah-* and *zajal-*
type songs have their roots in the Arab east and in North Africa, but were
developed in Al-Andalus. When the Arabs moved westward into North
Africa they found a music that differed very little from their own. Some
historians even believe that pre–Islamic music in that part of the world
came from the Arabian Peninsula, carried by Arab tribes migrating throughout the centuries to North Africa.

The vitality of the Arabic poetry that flourished in the periphery of
the Islamic kingdom derived from a rich and diverse musical culture. In
Persia and Andalusia, music played an important role in the formation of
poetic forms, while in Arabic courts it had been nothing but a form of
entertainment. An example of the musical activities in western Islamic
countries was the career of Abu 1-Hasan 'Ali Ibn Nafi', nicknamed Ziryab
(789–857). Steeped in the refined music he had learned in Baghdad, he
reached his musical and literary potential in Islamic Spain. He improved
the oud (*Laúd*) by adding a fifth pair of strings and plucking it with an
eagle's beak or quill instead of a wooden pick. Ziryab also dyed four strings
one color to symbolize the Aristotelian humors, and the fifth string another,
to represent the soul. He is said to have created a unique and influential
style of musical performance, and wrote songs that were performed in
Liberia for generations. He was a great influence on Spanish music, and
is considered the founder of the Andalusian music traditions of North
Africa. He also established the first conservatory of music in Cordoba and
later, others in the larger centers of Muslim Spain. By the eleventh century,
Moorish Spain and Portugal became the center for the manufacture of
musical instruments. These goods spread gradually to Provence, influenc-
ing French troubadours and trouvères and eventually reaching the rest of
Europe.

The poetry of *muwashshah* was born in the musical culture of southern
Spain. Muqaddam Ibn Mu afa al-Qabri (a blind poet and singer of Cabra)
was the creator of the *muwashshaha* and its vernacular for *zajal*. During

the 11th and 12th centuries, *muwashshah* and *zajal* verse reached perfection in Moorish Spain. In this period, first under the *tawa'if* (petty states), then the subsequent Almoravid and Almohad dynasties, both of these forms of music and song enjoyed a great popularity and were incorporated into the Arab/Islamic art of entertainment.[73]

As early as the Abbasid period (750–1258), Arab poets began to experiment with strophic poetry, which was imitated in other parts of the Muslim world. They cut the relatively long lines of *qasida* into several segments with internal rhyme (*tarsi'*). They made this practice (which was only used in the opening lines of classical poetry) into a new poetic form called *muzdawij*, in which two or even three internal rhymes were employed (aa, bb, cc or aaa, bbb, ccc, etc.). *Muzdawij* was similar to Latin *sequentia* (sequence) due to its progressive repetition, but it differed in the way that Arabic sequence went back to the same metrical form (Latin sequence introduced a different metrical form). The end result of this innovation in Arabic was *musammat* (string), which is a poem with independent changing rhymes and ends with segments in common rhyme (aaa a / bbb a / ccc a). This new form became popular during the tenth century and is said to be the innovation of a poet who was half Arab and half non–Arab. Musammat developed the longest segmental forms in Persia and Andalusia.[74]

The word *muwashshah* came from the Syriac word *musahta*, and began to appear as early as the 9th or 10th century. The full sense of the word is thought to come from the Syriac word *musahta*, which means "rhythm" or "a psalm verse." As a musical genre, it refers to an ensemble that includes the oud (lute), *kamanja* (spike fiddle), *qanun* (box zither), *darabukkah* (goblet drum), and *daf* (tambourine). It was performed in Syria sometimes as a solo with a few chosen lines of the selected text, or multiple *maqam* rows (scales) and up to three rhythms (*awzān*).[75]

The earliest *muwashshah*, as poetry, appeared in the Levant, where it is believed to have been heavily influenced by the Syriac sacral music. In classical Arabic, it consisted of a multi-lined strophic verse poem, usually consisting of five stanzas, alternating with a refrain with a running rhyme. It was customary to open with one or two lines that matched the second part of the poem in rhyme and meter. In North Africa, poets ignored the strict rules of Arabic meter, while the poets in the East followed them. In Southern Spain, *muwashshah* was written in classical Arabic except the conclusion (called *kharja*), which was in vulgar Arabic or one of the Romance languages found at the Moorish Iberian Peninsula. Similar to the *musammat*, the *muwashshah* consisted of five parts presented in three- to six-line stanzas in a same meter with a recurring rhyme, introduced at the beginning. Each section of the poem is complete or autonomous in itself, engraved by the refrain. It is said that the interwoven rhymes of the *muwashshah* represent the exact auditory-rhythmic counterpart of the interlacing arches in the Great Mosque of Cordoba. It was a disjunct arabesque with many centers of tension, many successive parts, each as important as every other one, only rejoined by a recurring beginning rhyme.[76]

The *zajal* is vernacular verse that developed from the *muwashshaha*, which some believe is the oldest form of the *muwashshah*. It was a spontaneous form of short poem composed from whatever entered a performer's mind. The poet experimented with different themes and wove them in and out of the current of the verse. It was often sung in stanzas, each following a different rhyme. A popular form of entertainment, it was composed entirely in the local tongues of the Iberian Peninsula. *Zajal* reached its zenith under the adventurer and famous Cordovan poet Ibn Quzman (1080–1160), one of the foremost poets of medieval Europe. Quzman used to boast that his *zajal* was sung as far away as the eastern Arab world. He was the greatest composer of this type of poetry, and wrote a book that included 150 *zajals*, which mused on love, wine and the other joys of life.[77]

Zajal, the voice of the ordinary man, survives even today. It is constantly ironic, often tender, at times brutal but always full of good humor. It still heard in the night spots of Lebanon, where the audience is captivated for hours as the performers satirize or praise each other with flowery poetic commentary. With their original and impromptu verse, they elevate or calm the emotions of the audience, as did the Arab *zajal* poets in Moorish Spain centuries earlier.

At first, the *muwashshahat* and *zajal,* both constituting a departure from the tradition represented by classical poetry, existed side by side and often overlapped. However, in the ensuing centuries, because of the longstanding Arab tradition of not writing the vernacular, only some *muwashshahat* and a few *zajals* have survived in written form. Perhaps because of their smooth flow and other literary Arabic qualities, the *muwashshahat* were worthy of preservation. On the other hand, *zajal* remained only transmitted, thus it was influenced by non–Arab speech or divergent Arabic dialects.

Zajal, in the vulgar Arabic and the Romance tongues, was sung by everyone in both Christian and Muslim Spain. Chejne contends that there is a striking similarity between *zajal* and early Spanish and Provençal poetry in rhyme, theme, the number of strophes, the use of a messenger between the lover and beloved and the duty of the lover toward the beloved. He cites as an example Juan Ruiz's *El Libro de Buen Amor*, known as *The Arcipreste de Hita*, in which the author's use of *zajal* is reminiscent of the model created by the Arab Andalusians.

The *kharjas* of the *muwashshahat*, very similar to *zajal*, are believed to be the oldest poetic texts of any vernacular in Europe. Hence, they very well could have been the origin of lyric poetry in Romance literature. It is believed that they gave rise to the 15th century *villancico*, a type of Christian carol to which they bear a close resemblance, and the *coplas* (ballads), still found throughout the Spanish-speaking world.

Those who are familiar with Spanish music assert that it was from the *muwashshahat* and *zajal* that the Spanish *cantigas* developed. In the *Cantigas de Santa Maria* compiled by Alfonso the Wise, the musical form of the *zajal* is clearly evident. Some music chroniclers maintain that the majority of Alfonso's *cantigas* were direct translations of Arab *zajal* verses.

The *cantigas* had an immense impact on the Western medieval world. They not only influenced the songs of Spain, but also gave impetus to the evolution of all European music. Both *muwashshah* and *zajal* poetry is clearly to be found in the early music and song of Europe. For centuries Arab culture exercised a strong influence on the entertainment of the southern part of that continent. E.G. Gómez, writing about Moorish Spain in Islam and the Arab world, indicates that the *muwashshah* verse is probably more interesting to Westerners than to the eastern Arabs (both ancient and modern), who, although attracted by its sensuous qualities, regarded it rather dimly as a cancer in the body of Arab classicism. This appeal to the Western ear, no doubt, helped enormously in its incorporation into European music.

The early Provençal epic poems were modeled on the *zajal*. So strikingly similar in form and content is the poetry of southern Europe to the *zajal* that it cannot be regarded as a coincidence. The first known European poet of courtly love, Prince William, Duke of Aquitaine, is said to have spoken Arabic and is believed to have been familiar with both the *muwashshahat* and *zajal*. His poetry is a direct imitation of the Arabic rather than an independent invention. The rhythm of his early verses is very similar to songs still being recited in North Africa.

In Spain by the early Middle Ages, Arabic poetry diversified into three distinct forms: that written in classical Arabic, that in colloquial Arabic, and that in a mixture of Arabic and Spanish. Andalusian poets found themselves at a crossroads of two languages and two prosodic systems. The Arabic system was based on consonants, although vowels might be involved, while the Romance rhymes were based on the repetition of sound in one or more end syllables of the line. The rhyming factor is often a stressed syllable. What made things more complex was that in classical Arabic and regionally defined vernacular, the Arabic had various rhyme rules.[78]

In tenth century Andalusia, presumably because it was not completely Islamized or Arabized, a small breach was found in the fortified walls of classicism. This innovation was an elaborate kind of strophic poem known as the *muwassa*, composed entirely in the classical language except for the closing line or couplet, which was in a mixture of Arabic and Spanish. What is even more significant is that the *muwassa* was almost certainly derived from a simpler form of folk poetry, the *zajal*, which was entirely in the local vernacular. Although literary history records that the *zajal* appeared later than the *muwassa,* this was because of the persistent reluctance of the writers to record folk texts. Once it broke through the surface of literary history, the *zajal* gained sufficient currency in Spain to earn notoriety for one of its masters, Ibn-Quzmān (c. 1086–1160).[79]

Zajal eventually spread to other parts of the Arab world, the term being sometimes loosely used for all verse compositions in the vernacular. To it were added descriptions of several other non-classical verse forms, including the *mawāliyā* mentioned above. It became customary to refer to these departures from the classical monorhyme as "the seven arts," although they were more numerous, for it was not always the same seven that were included in different collections. The first study of the kind was by a well-established poet in Iraq, Afiyy-ad-Dīn al-illī (1278–c. 1349). Characteristically, he confessed that he had composed a great deal in these various forms during his misguided youth, but had retained only enough of these immature efforts to illustrate his treatise. Some present-day collectors of folk literature are equally apologetic about their efforts.

Following Al-illī, other reputable poets occasionally toyed with non-classical verse forms involving colloquial usage, but these compositions were regarded as curiosities or humorous sallies at best, and were usually excluded from their collected works. This has been true even of major modern poets such as Amadawqī (1868–1932). The latest compilation of his poetry ignores his *zajal* altogether. And in a nine-volume edition of his complete works, two of his *zajal* are relegated to the end of the last volume, long after the focus has moved from his poetry to his prose and to his plays. Moreover, in his introductory volume, the editor says of them and of the poet: "They are not worthy of him, but such is one of the impositions made by an environment in which the colloquial predominates."

Turning oral poetry into written literature was a process that produced a special kind of music: the music of poetry or song in words. There were essentially two methods to verbalize the music: first, to sing without music by creating musical rhythm with words (prosody); second, to compose poetry as if it were music. In this verbal composition, unlike prose that aimed at describing events and classifying concepts, poetry is intended to create a mood and shared emotional space where feelings between the poets and audience could be exchanged.

CHAPTER 3

Rhythm from Poetry,
to Prose, to Speech

This chapter is about how Arabic poetry, the first and the most important form of its literary expression, defined the sound and rhythm of its written and spoken language. To emerge from an ancient oral tradition, to be elevated to literature and to create narratives of precision and abstract logic are the main steps of literary development common to many languages. These steps are not unique to Arabic, because a score of Semitic languages, from Akkadian to Hebrew, have done the same.[1] Several ancient Semitic traditions became highly advanced and polished and had no equal in sophistication among their contemporaries. They have left their evidence in over five thousand years of Middle Eastern history. However, all of these rich literatures eventually lost their sound and uprooted themselves from spoken languages after they became a vehicle of literary expression and abstract reasoning (religion or philosophy). This did not happen to Arabic. Arabic poetry with its various sounds, shapes and colors is very much alive more than a thousand years after its emergence from the Arabian Peninsula.

Keeping the sound and rhythm of Arabic in the ears and on the lips of its speakers while building a refined literature capable of precision and abstraction is what separated Arabic from various ancient Semitic languages. Ancient Semitic languages depended on music and performance to keep poetry alive by making their words heard and dramatized. Arabic relied on the rhythm of its poetry (including verse and prose) to maintain its appeal. A unique process made words sing not only in the ears of speakers but also in their minds, hearts, and memory. This rhythm, initially created by poetry, now became the rhythm of the language itself and resounded in the imagination of its speakers. This chapter focuses on how Arabic created and maintained its poetic rhythm on both literary and non-literary levels by standardizing speech and publicizing poetry.

Arabic had an immediate and intimate relationship with its speakers because of the way in which it had been recited, performed, and heard throughout the centuries. Immediately after the rise of Islam, the pagan songs of Arabia came to serve the new god. During the pilgrimage (*hajj*), praising God in poetry was adapted and began to be accompanied by fife (*shahin*) and drum (*tabl*).[2] As music pervaded poetry and prose, chanting (*talhīn*) of the call to prayer (*adhdān*) became the standard for worship. The Qur'an was naturally easy to sing and lent itself to being chanted because of a prosodic structure that was now cultivated in pre–Islamic poetry. Composed in rhymed prose (*saj'*), the assonance of the Qur'an tempted the voice to use modulated sound when read. As Hadith pointed out, Allah would listen more intently to a man with a beautiful voice reading the Qur'an rather than the voice of a singing-girl. In short, Islam was a literary civilization based on a preference for chanting words rather than singing them because its language inherited a superior capacity to excite, to convince and to persuade. The Arabic words that had been chanted day and night for centuries cultivated an extraordinary capacity to touch and arouse the emotions of the average man. This emotional effect, which was deeply rooted in oral and ritual practice, made Arabic poetry extremely intimate, personal, and constantly present.[3]

At the beginning of Islam, two kinds of verbal delivery competed against each other in various kinds of singing: Qur'anic chanting with melody (*bi-naghma*) and chanting without it (*min ghayr naghma*). The former was highly melismatic and later adopted *maqam* modulation. One of the first chanters of the Qur'an was 'Ubaidallah b. Abi Bakr (fl. 669), whose singing was described as dirge-like and quite different from ordinary melody (*lahn*) in singing (*ghina'*). The distinction between reading aloud and singing appeared to be exaggerated by Islamic legalists who, in their opposition to music, looked upon this singing as improper and so discriminated between "cantillation" (*taghbīr*, "raising the voice") and singing (*ghina'*).[4]

By the ninth century, even the melodies of popular ballads were being used in the Qur'anic chant (*tajwīd*). Despite the violent opposition of the purists to all music, the chanting of the Qur'an became one of the supreme cultural accomplishments of Islam. While prosodic vocalization and punctuation were strictly governed by rules, the chanting itself was not confined to any fixed melodic contour. Therefore, the forms of chanting could be heard in almost as many patterns as there were mosques. For the Muslims, the familiar sound of Qur'anic recitation became the predominant and most immediate means of contact with the Word of God. Heard day and night, on the street, in shops, in mosques, and at homes, the sound of recitation was far more impressive than the pervasive background music of daily life in the Arab world. Qur'anic recitation, a public performance of poetry, persists until today.[5]

The "call to prayer" (*adhdhān*) was initially instituted as a means of summoning the faithful to their religious duties. At first it was merely a simple announcement on the streets, and was performed by *Bilāl*, the first "caller" (*mu'adhdhin*). Then, from the minaret of the mosque came a dirge-like call for chanting of the Qur'an. This way of chanting continued until the tenth century in Egypt. After that, it became the general practice to chant the Qur'an in a melody proper, indistinguishable from ordinary singing (*ghina'*). This singing performance was called *ṭaṭrīb*.

The office of *mu'adhdhin* was initially hereditary, but before long the duties became so onerous that there had to be several callers in each mosque. By the ninth and tenth centuries, these callers took their turns to make the first call, and later they would join in chorus to chant the second call (*iqāma*) for their mosque. *Bilāl* Ibn Rabah or *Bilāl* Al-Habashi (580–640), a Muslim who was born in Mecca and a companion of Muhammad, was the first *muezzin* (caller for praying) chosen by the prophet himself.

Qur'anic recitation had to follow rules of pronunciation, intonation, and caesuras that Muhammad established and was initially recorded in the eighth century. During the post–Islamic centuries, many sets of rules were codified, and ten schools of recitation developed that made Qur'anic recitation a form of art. Qur'anic elocution (*tajwīd*) derived from trilateral root *j-w-d*, meaning to make well, make better, or to improve. The most prevalent among the rules that governed how the Qur'an should be read was the recitation of Imam 'Asim as transmitted by Imam Hafs. Each melodic passage centers on a single tone level, but the melodic contour and melodic passages were largely shaped by the reading rules, creating passages of different lengths whose temporal expansion is defined through caesuras. Skilled readers might read professionally for mosques in various cities.

There were many different schools and styles to chant the Qur'an, from the plain, ingenuous, unaffected chant to highly flowery coloratura. The methods of each school and style carried rigid transmission regulation. This minimized mistakes and carefully preserved intonations, cadence, and punctuation. The script in which the Qur'an was first recorded indicated only the consonantal skeleton of the words. Oral recitation was an essential element to define the form of textual transmission. Exact pronunciation was important and took years to learn. Special schools were established to ensure that no error would creep in, as the traditional chanting methods were handed down from recitor to recitor and from one generation to the next. Gradually, Qur'anic recitation became an elaborate science of expression.[6]

The musicality of the Qur'an derived from its linguistic and literary structure, which combined the characteristics of both poetry and prose. It made literature sound like a rhythmic speech. Unlike classical poetry, the verses of the Qur'an were not restricted by one single rhyme; thus there was more room for flexibility and freedom of expression. The Qur'an did, however, maintain certain aspects of poetry, especially with respect to its use of words with identical numbers of syllables. This "music" of language was more noticeable in short verses such as surat 53 (*al-Najm*) where words of similar length produced prose rhythm ending in the same sound (the long *a*).

1. Wannajmi ith_a_ haw_a_
2. M_a_ dalla _sa_hibukum wam_a_ ghaw_a_
3. Wam_a_ yantiqu AAani alhaw_a_
4. In huwa ill_a_ wahyun yooh_a_
5. AAallamahu shadeedu alquw_a_
6. Thoo mirratin fastaw_a_
7. Wahuwa bil-ofuqi al-aAAl_a_
8. Thumma dana fatadall_a_
9. Fakan_a_ qab_a_ qawsayni aw adn_a_
10. Faawh_a_ il_a_ AAabdihi ma_a_ wh_a_
11. M_a_ kath_a_ba alfu-_a_du m_a_ra_a_
12. Afatum_a_roonahu AAal_a_ m_a_yar_a_

There was another type of internal rhythm inherent in the structure of the single sentence. This appeared when the length of words varied within the same *surat*. A good example of this is *Surat* 19 (*Maryam*), which began with short words and phrases, then changed to longer ones. The rhythm of the various segments was enhanced by the use of two main rhymes throughout the entire *surat*. These rhymes ended either in *nun* or *mim* preceded by either *ya'* or *wa'w*:

1. Kaf-ha-ya-AAayn-sad
2. Thikru rahmati rabbika Aaabdahuzakariyya
3. Ith nada rabbahu nidaankhafiyya
4. Qala rabbi innee wahana alAAathmuminnee washtaAAala arra / su shayban walam akunbiduAAa-ika rabbi shaqiyya
5. Wa-innee khiftu almawaliya min wara-eewakanati imraatee AAaqiran fahab lee min ladunkawaliyya
6. Yarithunee wayarithu min ali yaAAqoobawajAAalhu rabbi radiyya
7. Ya zakariyya innanubashshiruka bighulamin ismuhu yahya lam-najAAal lahu min qablu samiyya

8. Qala rabbi anna yakoonu leeghulamun wakanati imraatee AAaqiran waqadbalaghtu mina alkibari AAitiyya

This musicality of words in speech followed a regular beat. The Qur'an was chanted in an acoustic realm where words and singing, message and sound, combined to carry the significance of the revelation to even higher levels of understanding and emotional appeal. The practitioner of *tajwīd* was required to possess a beautiful and appealing voice, to give emphasis to specific consonants and vowels through elongation. "*N*" and "*m*" were singled out for nasalization (*ghunnah*). As chanting used these techniques to accentuate the assonantal features of passages such as *Surat* 17 (*al-Baqarah*) or the opening *Surat* 97 (*al-Qadr*), it blended the technical repertoire into the rise and fall of traditional chant, and intensified the effect for listeners. The chanting in fact transcended the verbal message.

Once the Qur'an was established and canonized in textual form, the overwhelming bulk of learning devoted to its study was concerned with its written form. However, unlike in the Latin and Hebrew traditions, the oral dimension of Arabic continued to exert its enduring influence on the formation of cultural expression. The ability of a devout Muslim to memorize the entire text and to recite it at will has been and still remains a sign of a complete Islamic education. This education begins at Qur'anic schools around the Muslim world where the text is taught by rote. Recitation and chanting of the Qur'an have been and still are daily occurrences in the Muslim world. In this particular sense, chanting (rather than reading words) became a ritual full of celebration of the sounds of the sacred text. It could be heard and observed several times a day in the mosques and on the streets where the often heavily amplified voice of *lmu'adhdh* filled the air with his elaborate intonations as he summoned the faithful to prayer.

Qur'anic chanting was instrumental in the codification and spread of the Arabic language. The status of the Qur'an as a canonical text served as the basis for the initiation of a series of fields of study that were later to develop into the Islamic sciences and into Arabic literary scholarship. The need to write down the grammar and to clarify the phonology did not come from a general desire for scientific research or abstract learning; rather it emerged from the practical need to teach Muslims to read and hear the Qur'an in absolute accuracy. A tradition has it that the caliph 'Ali (598–661), who was recognized as most knowledgeable in the Qur'an and *Sunna*, initially refused to patronize a guild book for Qur'anic reading until the day that he heard the Qur'an read inaccurately. Mistakes in reading vowels gave the text a false meaning. He changed his mind and decided to compile a book to avoid such errors. He commissioned a scribe to write down every single sound as he chanted the text. He gave strict instruction as how to mark the vowels. He asked the scribe to mark a point over a letter when he pronounced it with an open mouth (*aftahu*); a mark before the letter if he closed his mouth during pronunciation of it (*adummuhu*); and a mark under it if he puckered (*aksuruhu*). Ali also instructed Abu al-aswad al-Du'al (603–688) to prepare a work that would summarize Arabic grammar. This initiative began with a process of codification and debate that greatly expanded during the eighth and ninth centuries among the intellectual communities in the rival Iraqi cities of al-Basrah and al-Kufah.[7]

The process of recording the sound of the utterances in written form required that the alphabetic system be redefined to the point where it could not only clarify the distinctions between sets of similar graphemes but also incorporate symbols for vowels, elisions, and stops. Refinement of recitation was developed by three disciplines: *tajwīd, qira'at* and *tafsīr. Tajwīd*, as mentioned before, was a system that codified the sound of the divine language and accent of Qur'anic recitation in terms of rhythm, timber, textual phrasing, and phonetics. It specified the very basis of reading and identified marks of recitation. *Qira'at* characterized a different text system to be used for recitation and verified various implications of various regulations of the *tajwīd*.

Tafsīr mainly dealt with textual issues. The word *tafsīr* is derived from the root *f-s-r* (to explain, to expound) and it means "explanation" or "interpretation." The word *tafsīr* is used for explanation, interpretation and commentary on the Qur'an including all the efforts to make its text comprehensible, such as proper understanding of it, explanations of its meanings and clarification of its legal and moral implications. In a linguistic sense, *tafsīr* worked its way into building a connection between words, words that had similar meanings, distinct meanings and opposite meanings, and words that had precise and ambiguous meanings and connotations. By doing so, it created a verbal web of Arabic in which words built upon one another according to logical principles. For example, a hierarchy of words was established according to degrees of importance of the words of the Qur'an. The best *tafsīr* was believed to be the explanation of the Qur'an by the words of the Qur'an (in a different textual context); the second best was the explanation of the Qur'an by the words of the Prophet Muhammad, who acted according to his understanding of the words of God. If nothing could be found either in the Qur'an or in the *Sunna* of the Prophet, one had to turn to the reports from the *sahaba* (the companions of Muhammad). If nothing could be found in the Qur'an, the *Sunna* and the reports from the *sahaba*, one had to turn to the reports from the *tabi'in* (Muslims who were born after the death of Muhammad but were students of his companions).

In short, *tafsīr* explained the "outer" (*zahir*) or apparent meanings of the Qur'an while *tajwīd* pursued the inner or concealed meanings of the Qur'an.[8]

With the development of Qur'anic interpretation, Arabic as a literary language expanded rapidly and substantially. The early Qur'an contained many words and phrases that reflected the linguistic and religious environment of the Arabian Peninsula in the pre–Islamic era. These words had to be codified, and their meanings and origins had to be investigated. The search for precedents for the language of the Qur'an gave birth to Arabic lexicography. The principal sources that are believed to have been the foundation of Qur'anic language were the sayings of the pre–Islamic soothsayers lodged in an ornate variety of the language known as *saj'* (rhyming prose) and the highly refined poetry that had been orally transmitted for many generations.[9]

Once the revelations of the Qur'an had been committed to writing, the process of studying and interpreting the text began. Codification was easier, as the issues of the Qur'an carried extensive and explicit rulings in matters such as family law, debt, and inheritance. The Qur'an also had injunctions concerning God's will and the obligation of the Muslims to him. These texts formed the five "pillars" of Islam: the statement of belief (*shahādah*); the five daily prayers (*salāt*); almsgiving (*zakāt*), fasting during the holy month of Ramadān (*sawm*); and pilgrimage to Mecca (*hajj*). Jihad became another obligation, and the individual and community needed to make efforts to spread the word of Islam to other peoples and defend the religion against its opponents.

The more difficult part of the codification rested beyond these well-defined rituals and obligations. There are many topics on which the Qur'an remains silent. Muslim scholars had to resort to another source for guidance, records of the Prophet's own conduct during his lifetime, the *Sunna*. This in turn initiated another process of gathering information, as accounts of Muhammad's actions (Hadith) and sayings were collected and organized by category. As the Hadith accumulated and was compiled and established as an addition to Islamic laws and ethics, a new tradition of textual criticism specific for the Hadith developed. This was designed to validate the authenticity of the Hadith and if it was truthful, who witnessed it, how it was described and scribed. The processes of sifting through accounts and authenticating sources also initiated the search for detailed information on the reliability of individuals, the history of family groups and tribes. Genealogy was thus added to the list of fields with which the Islamic community concerned itself, as scholars investigated the histories of prominent families and their tribal affiliations. Like in Qur'anic interpretation, the

search for authentic Hadith also involved linguistic precedents to the lex-
icon and style of the Qur'an, and pre–Islamic poetry that shared the same
linguistic foundation of the prose. At a later date, the reports that were
believed to be the most reliable were collected into volumes called *Sahīh*
("genuine and correct"). The two most famous collections were those of
al-Bukhārī (d. 870) and Muslim (d. 875). This process of collecting and
sorting the Hadith also marked the initial stages in the tradition of Qur'anic
exegesis (*tafsīr*), since the accounts often included discussions of prob-
lematic passages that had been recorded from earliest times. It was the
great historian Al-Tabarī who was the first to compile a commentary on
the Qur'an that incorporated within it the labors of his predecessors.[10]

The codification of all the sacred texts (the Qur'an and the Hadith)
did not eliminate textual ambiguity and diversity as intended because the
accumulation of exegete literature actually expanded the textual repertoire
from which even more diverse interpretations emerged. The accumulation
of commentaries established a path for further division and contradiction
of opinions and perspectives. Although holding the intention to classify
and unify the reading and understanding of scripture, Muslim scholars discovered that the Qur'an accumulated several levels of meanings. There
were meanings (exegesis) known to scholars, meanings (language) known
by Arabic speakers, meanings (the allowed and forbidden) that believers
could not afford to ignore; and hidden meanings that needed to be interpreted. The Qur'an referred to particular and general issues: the references
particular to Muslims, those particular to polytheists, and those general to
all mankind. The Qur'an also contained accounts about the hearts of the
believers and accounts of what was in the hearts of the unbelievers who
acted against the Islamic faith. There were ambiguous and univocal passages, explained and unexplained passages, and deletions as well as explicit
utterances. There were connective items, abrogating and abrogated verses.
There were similar utterances with many different aspects, and passages
that continued in a different *surat*. There were commandments, laws, ordi-
nances, and parables by which God refers to Himself, parables by which
He refers to unbelievers and idols, and parables by which He refers to this
world, to resurrection and to the world to come.

Multi-leveled reading of the Qur'an and the Hadith texts made it possible to develop contrary opinions among Muslim scholars and eventually
founded divisions of various linguistic and legal schools and political fac-
tions. Just like any other religious texts composed in a formative prose,
the meaning of the Qur'an was not always transparent and explicit. Clarification and commentary of the Qur'an and the Hadith were constantly in
demand as Islamic civilization rapidly expanded around the world. A clear

vision was needed for the newly established Islamic order as the Muslim community that had just converted to Islam was eager to reshape itself according to the commandments of the new religion. However, a poetic language did not make this transition easy, because of its inherited rich and multi-dimensional linguistic capacity. The more language was used to define meanings by juxtaposition, the less it could clarify, unify and restrain meanings.

Muslim leaders and scholars were well aware of the power of the Arabic language (including its power to generate diversity and even dispute) and of the challenges that they faced in the development of a unified canon (or perfect copy) to bind the community. They closed the canonical corpus of the Qur'an only twenty years after the death of the Prophet in an attempt to make the Qur'an a fixed text that could not be modified.[11] However, as soon as the door of the codification closed, the war of competing commentators and readers of the Qur'an began. Muslim scholars differed not only in their Qur'anic readings and interpretations, but also in their approaches to the holy text. For example, textual interpretation was held with respect in Kufa (a prominent center of Qur'anic scholarship in early Islam), whereas in Basra there was a tendency to ridicule the Kufan interpretations because of lack of insight in linguistic matters. There were many Basran reports about Qur'anic readers making mistakes in their grammatical analysis of the Qur'an, and there must have been a general feeling among Basran grammarians that they themselves represented a new approach to the study of speech.

The science of Qur'anic exegesis (*tafsīr*) proper remained one of the pillars of the Islamic sciences. In later commentaries we still find linguistic remarks on the text of the Qur'an, but these no longer represent an independent development within exegesis. Commentators received extensive linguistic training from professional grammarians, and it was from them that they borrowed their technical apparatus for the description of Qur'anic usage. Exegesis explored various directions without losing the connection with its earliest roots and its original aim, which was the elucidation of God's intention. Because of the accumulation of Qur'anic scholarship, commentators usually specialized in one aspect of exegesis. Thus we find commentaries whose main purpose is to discuss textual variants, others that concentrate on the grammatical and syntactic analysis or the analysis of the narrative parts of the text. Still others are mostly interested in the legal aspects of the text.

The distinction between the local traditions of Basra and Kufa was extended by later generations into formal schools. This development occurred at a time when the representatives of the two traditions started to meet each other much more frequently in the new capital of the 'Abbasid Empire in Baghdad. They both felt the need to define their own ways. Representatives of the Basran tradition became far superior to those of Kufa in the development of technical grammar. Consequently, the exegetical approach to linguistics was abandoned by all grammarians and, eventually, the Basran approach prevailed.[12]

It took only a century for the majority of Muslim scholars to realize the limitation of textual research of the Qur'an. Sibawayh (760–796?) was the first to write on Arabic grammar and to explain Arabic grammar from a non–Arabic perspective (he was born in Iran). Much of the impetus for this work came from the desire for non–Arab Muslims to understand the Qur'an properly and thoroughly. The Qur'an, which was composed in a poetic language that even native Arabic speakers had to study with great care in order to comprehend thoroughly, was even more difficult for those who did not grow up speaking it. In addition, as written Arabic did not necessarily mark all pronounced vowel sounds, even native Arabic speakers could mispronounce the Qur'an's text. This created a problem, as the Qur'an was regarded by Muslims as the literal word of God to man. This severe frustration made even the best scholars dejected. It was said that in Baghdad, the 'Abbasid minister Yahya ibn Khalid held a debate on standard Arabic usage between Sibawayh, representing the Basra school, and Kisa'i, the leading scholar of the rival school of Kufa. Sibawayh became so depressed after being misread and misinterpreted that he left his beloved Baghdad and went back to Iran after the contest.[13]

The scholars in Basra focused their research in the structure of language rather than on the structure of the Qur'anic text. They were still active as specialists of Qur'anic exegesis but extended their investigations to general phenomena of Arabic language. This development culminated in the first dictionary, *Kitab al-Ayn*, by Al-Khalil ibn Ahmad al-Farāhīdī (718–786). Since then, there has always been a correlation between Qur'anic scholarship and that of linguistic tradition. Abd-Allāh ibn Abī Ishāq al-Hadramī (d. 735) was the earliest known grammarian of the Arabic language. He compiled a prescriptive grammar that referred to the usage of the Bedouins, who were considered to be the purest Arabic speakers. Two students of Abi Ishaq's were 'Isa ibn Umar al-Thaqafi (d. 767) and Abu 'Amr ibn al-'Alā' (d. 773). Al-Thaqafi had a more prescriptive approach while Al-Ala's was more descriptive. Their differences further evolved to the late division of Arabic grammar into the schools of Kufa and Basra and Qur'anic interpretation.[14]

Al-Khalil was the most famous philologist from Basra. His best known contribution is *Kitab al-'Ayn*, the first dictionary of the Arabic language, the current standard for *Harakat* (vowel marks in Arabic script), and the invention of *al-'arud* (the study of Arabic prosody). Sibawayh, the founder of Arabic grammar, was among his students.[15] The *Kitab al-'Ayn* departed from the established exegete tradition and introduced a radically different concept of lexicography. It aimed at the collection of all roots in language, rather than at just recording rare words from Bedouin poetry. In this book, words were ordered around the permutations of their radicals. In Arabic, as in all Semitic languages, the root consonants of the word carry the semantic load, whereas the vowels and auxiliary consonants provide information about derivational and declensional morphology. For instance, the root *k-t-b* produces the lexical items *kataba* (he wrote), *yaktubu* (he writes), *kutiba* (it was written), *yuktabu* (it is written), *katib* (writer), *maktub* (written), *kitab* (book), plural *kutub* (books); *mukataba* (correspondence), *'aktaba* (he made someone else write), *istaktaba* (he asked someone to write), *takataba* (he corresponded with someone), *maktaba* (library), and so on. In all of these words the radical consonants *k-t-b* convey the notion of "writing," whereas the auxiliary consonants (*m, t, y,* etc.) indicate the morphological categories. To represent the pattern of a word grammarians used a notational device in which the letter */f/* indicated the first radical of a word, the letter /'a/ the second, and the letter /1/ the third. The pattern of *maktaba*, for instance, is *maf'ala*, that of *istaktaba* is *istaf'ala*, and so on.

Al-Khalil's system first assembled words by roots, putting together all of a word's derivates, for example the root *k-t-b*. All roots containing these same consonants were organized in a hierarchy. The root *k-t-b* was entered in one section together with the roots *k-b-t, b-k-t, t-b-k,* and *b-t-k*. This represented a step forward compared to the arrangement of the previous word list, which either followed the order of the text being explained, or arranged words semantically. Although the structure of his book provided assurance that it was very easy to find a word, it remained in fact a cumbersome arrangement. The book made an attempt to organize words at least in an ordering principle, although this did not mean that one could know in advance exactly where a word was to be found. There is no indication that al-Khalil's system was intended to reflect a higher semantic unity between the permutated roots, although some later grammarians looked for such common meanings.[16]

The second remarkable feature of Al-Khalil's arrangement was his linguistic (rather than textual) approach to Qur'anic language, which was manifested in the consonantal categorization. He did not use the normal alphabetical order of the Arabic alphabet, but applied a phonetic criterion and began with the guttural consonants, then the velars, until he reached the bilabials. The reason for this order was his reluctance to start with the element *'alif*, because it is a weak consonant. Actually, in the phonological theory of Arabic grammar the *'alif* has a special status. It is a glide like /y/ and /w/, but unlike these it is never realized on the phonetic level and serves only as an abstract phonological element (represented here as /'/). The long vowels that we distinguish in Arabic were not acknowledged by the Arabic grammarians. They regarded long vowels as combinations of a vowel and a glide (/w/, /y/, /'/), i.e., /uw/, /iy/, /a'/, which are realized as /ū/, /ī/, /ā/. The only difference between /w/, /y/, and *'alif* is that the latter either disappears at the phonetic level, or is realized phonetically as a glottal stop /'/ or as one of the two other glides.

Kitab al-'Ayn usually provided information about some derivations of a root and was illustrated, sometimes, with a quotation from a poem or the Qur'an. The intention of the dictionary was to include all current roots from each combination of radicals, not necessarily all words derived from these roots. Common words were supposed to be known by the native speaker, so the lexicographer did not feel the need to elaborate on them. Primary distinction was made between those roots that were *musta'mal* ("used") and those that were *muhmal* ("neglected"), such as those that were "not occurring in Arabic." When words derived from a root were mentioned, it only demonstrated that the root actually existed in the language.

The development of Arabic linguistic scholarship illustrates how the study and interpretation of a single book (the Qur'an) led to the codification of the entire repertoire of a language. For lexicographers the wish to include all Arabic words increased. Usually they copied all available information from earlier lexicographers and then added their own observations on rare words that they had found in other sources. In this way the dictionaries continually expanded.

Al-'Azhari's (895–980) *Tahdhīb al-lugha the lemma '-sh-q* was already much larger than the original lemma in the *Kitâb al-'ayn*. The chapter on the consonants /'/, /q/, /sh/ found in the *Kitâb al-'ayn* contained the same root under the same heading, but with the addition of *'-q-sh* and *sh-q-'*. The following debate about the additional roots demonstrates how much work and reasoning had been involved in making the additions.

> 'Abu l-'Abbās 'Ahmad ibn Yahyā was asked whether love or passion was more praise worthy. He said: "Love, because passion includes a degree of exaggeration." Ibn al-'A'râbî said: " '*Ushuq* are the men who trim the sets of sweet-smelling plants; when said of a camel *'ushuq* means one that keeps to its mate and does not desire any other." He said: " '*Ashaq* is the lablab-tree; its singular is *'ashaqa*." He said: " '*Ashaq* is also the *arak*-tree. An *'āshiq* 'lover' is called thus because he withers from the intensity of his passion in the same way as the *'ashaqa* [lablabtree] when it is cut."

'Abu 'Ubayd said: "*Imra'a 'ashiq* 'a woman in love,' without the feminine ending -a, and likewise *rajul 'âshiq* 'a man in love.'" I say: The Arabs delete the
feminine ending from the feminine attribute in many words, e.g., [in the expres-
sion] "you regard her as stupid, since she is bakhis 'deficient.'" They also say
imra'a baligh [a nubile woman] when she has reached puberty, and they call a
female slave *khadim* [servant]. In these words the masculine form is the same.
Al-Layth said: "The expression is *'ashiqa* [imperfect], *ya'shaqu* [verbal noun],
'ishq 'to love.'" This is what he said, but *'ashaq* is the verbal noun and *'ishq* is
the noun. Ru'ba said in describing a male and female ass: "and he did not lead her
astray between loathing and passion."[17]

The later Arabic lexicographers inherited this method and incorporated
the entire past scholarship. Ibn Manzur (1233–1311), the author of the *Lisān
al-'Arab* (The Arab Tongue), the best known and most comprehensive dictionaries of the Arabic language, used the *Tahdhīb al-Lugha* as one of his
most important source. The *Lisān al-'Arab*'s 20 volumes followed the
arrangement of the roots. The head words are not arranged by the alphabetical order of the radicals as usually done today in the study of Semitic
languages, but according to the last radical, which makes finding rhyming
endings significantly easier.

The Qur'an's success as the Bible of the Arabic language established
it not only as the authority of religious thinking but also as a literary standard. From here, prose began to emerge and became increasingly important
as a literary form. This took Arabic from the margins of Middle Eastern
literature to the cultural center.[18] Prose became the vehicle for philosophical
and scientific development for Islam. The first generation of Arabic scholars
(by language as well as by education) made substantial contributions to
the development of Islamic culture. First, they entered into passionate and
fruitful discussions about the issues of religion and its philosophy. For
example, Al-Jahiz (781–868) was the first Muslim biologist to develop a
theory on evolution, almost ten centuries before Charles Darwin (1809–
1882) did. His book *Al-Hayawan* (Book of Animals) was an encyclopedia
of seven volumes of anecdotes, poetic descriptions and proverbs describing
over 350 varieties of animals. As the first environmental determinist, he
wrote on the effects of the environment on the likelihood of an animal to
survive, and he first described the struggle for existence. However, unlike
Darwinism, which later developed into a theory opposing the religious
notion of creation, Al-Jahiz attempted to unify nature, God, the natural
world, and social morality through a promotion of eloquence (debate,
Kalam) and reasoning.[19]

As soon as descriptive language provided adequate imagery and
chronological cohorts in writing, a new scholarship of Arabic science
emerged. The best known early Arab scientist was Al-Kindi (801–873). He

wrote at least two hundred and sixty books, mainly concerning geometry, medicine, philosophy, logic, and physics. His influence in the fields of physics, mathematics, medicine, philosophy and music was far-reaching and lasted for several centuries.[20] As the language of science became increasingly specific and abstract through writing, Islamic science flourished in many different directions, including in medicine, mathematics, algebra, physics, and philosophy.[21]

The emergence of Islamic or Arabic science has been portrayed as a result of Greek influence, the fact of which has been well verified. However, the scientific mode of thinking did not have a single origin or belong to any particular language or culture. It simply occurred during certain periods of linguistic evolution for every language in the world, although during this period the subject culture tended to be more open to scientific influence and the achievements of other cultures. The development of Islamic science was a case in point. Interaction between cultures had existed in the ancient Mediterranean for thousands of years before the emergence of Islam. The Arabic Middle East was not ready for science and abstract reasoning until its language developed the capacity to classify, specify, and distill its accumulating knowledge. The large-scale efforts of the Arabic philologists and lexicographers during the eighth and ninth centuries paved the way for the birth of Islamic science. The availability of the Greek material on science and philosophy was translated with great effort by Arab scholars.[22]

While the language of religion (the Qur'an) inspired universal vision and the descriptive language of science, the writing about the life of Muhammad accumulated the vocabulary and narrative framework of biographical literature in Arabic. The genre of *tabaqat* (biographical dictionaries) thus emerged. The narrative language of both geography and history also made it possible for the evolution of historical writing and travel literature. The greatest of all Arabic historians was Ibn Khaldun (1332–1406), whose history *Muqaddimah* focused on society and is a founding text in sociology and economics. After Ibn Khaldun's sweeping historical and sociological account, Arab historians began to concentrate on a smaller scope of history and regional histories such as the history of Mecca and Baghdad.[23]

Narrative style remained one of the most creative innovations of the Qur'an, and it profoundly influenced and enriched the Arabic language. The style of storytelling seen in pre–Islamic poetry was relatively crude and primitive because its subject matter was narrow and limited. The Qur'an, as a religious manifesto that dealt with universal issues, had to substantially widen its formal scope and develop more diverse storytelling techniques. The Qur'an innovated remarkably highly developed narrative presentations. Some of these included beginning a story with a short sum-mary, followed by the details from beginning to end (as in *Surat* 18, *Al-Kahf*), and beginning a story by presenting the conclusions first, describing the lesson to be learned from it, and then telling the story from beginning to end (the story of Moses in *Surat* 28, *Al-Qasas*). Other innovations included the presentation of the story directly without introduction, as in that of Mary following the birth of Jesus (in *Surat* 19, *Maryam*), and the story of King Solomon and the ants (in *Surat* 27, *Al-Naml*). The last, perhaps most innovative, was to present the story through dramatization. This technique gives only a brief introduction signaling the beginning of the scene, fol-lowed by a dramatization of the story with a dialogue among the various characters, as in the story of Abraham and Ismail (in *Surat* 2, *Al-Baqarah*).

The Qur'an uses elements of surprise to dramatize the storytelling. In some cases the anticlimax was kept from the main players and spectators, and was unfolded for both simultaneously towards the end, as in *Surat* 18 (*Al-Kahf*) (in the story of Moses and the scholar). Another use of the ele-ment of surprise reveals the unexpected ending to the audience but conceals it from the characters, who act in total ignorance. The Qur'an commonly uses this technique in situations where satire is intended (satire which is directed at the actors and their behavior) as in the story in *Surat* 68 (*Al-Qalam*). A third technique reveals part of the conclusion to the audience while keeping part of it concealed from both the audience and the charac-ters, as in the story in *Surat* 27 (*al-Naml*). In short, the Qur'an integrated dramatic presentation and plotting (which took Greek, Latin, and English playwrights centuries to craft on the stage) into Arabic prose. It did not take much time for a rich and mature literature to develop dramatic nar-ration and highlight its expression. Arabic, a mature literature in form, had an experience similar to Chinese literature of the thirteenth century and modern English, which developed post-literary dramatic writing.[24]

The structure of Qur'anic narrative displays some well-developed ele-ments of an integrated literary work. One of these is the change of scenery to dramatize the story. For example, readers are presented with a series of scenes, each of which leads to the next, picking up the main thread of the story, in *Surat* 12 (*Yūsuf*). Joseph's life story is told here in twenty-eight scenes, which are organized in a sequence maintaining the organic unity of the entire narrative. All the scenes are in the form of dialogues in which characters who play a role (good or bad, rightly or wrongly) in Joseph's life, tell their versions of the events of the story. These scenes are opposing and contrary insights portraying the experiences, involvement, and personal interests of the characters. These contradictory perceptions and presenta-tions dramatize the story line by repeating details and ideas.

Joseph's story engages the reader with narrative every step of the way, moving effortlessly from one scene to another. The reader is effectively drawn through a coherent series of events (sometimes contradictory), which sustain his curiosity and interest as he learns about Joseph and the life lessons contained in the story. For example, in one scene, one of Joseph's brothers enters the king's court in Egypt where Joseph is the keeper of the storehouse of the land. In this scene, Joseph stipulates to his brothers that they should bring their younger brother to the king's court in order to receive provisions. The next scene portrays the brothers deliberating among themselves. This is followed by a scene in which they have returned to face their father, Jacob. The next scene takes the brothers back to Egypt to confront Joseph. In this sequence, the story is told effortlessly as the drama is unfolded before the eyes of the reader, who certainly knows more about the plot than each of the characters knows. The brothers do not know that Joseph, whom they believed had been thrown into the well, has survived; the father does not know what has happened to Joseph for many years. These diverse perspectives and various levels of awareness are produced in the Qur'an with dialogue. This makes the scenes more vivid and lifelike and allows a variety of conclusions according to one's perspective. This innovative art of dramatic presentation is common to many established literatures in the world, especially in dramatic writing, but it is only in Arabic that it was introduced in its first book of prose.

The Qur'an also set a precedent for the portrayal of literary personae. The depiction of personalities in the various narratives managed to convey to the reader the precise dimensions of these characters and the changes in their emotions and attitudes. This was done through the words and actions of the personalities that were portrayed from various angles. In the story of Moses, for example, the reader is readily able to discern, through Moses' actions, the type of aggressive yet emotionally sensitive person he was meant to be. Conversely, the Qur'an also carefully portrays a calm, peaceful, and patient Abraham in his story. This terse yet detailed and accurate delineation of characters was effected largely through dialogue, which skillfully brought out the characteristics of its personalities. The dialogue, in turn, was rendered even more effective by a very careful choice of words.[25]

The following section of *Surat* 26 (*Al-Shu'arā'*) vividly depicts how Moses was persuaded by God and changed his feelings about his commission as a messenger of God. Initially, Moses felt diffident about speaking against the pharaoh, begging God to send someone else. "O my Lord!" he said, "I do fear that they will accuse me of lying." "My heart would fail me, and my tongue will cleave to my mouth, and they had already accused me of murder." "I am afraid that they would kill me" (12–14). Moses was afraid that his speech would be impeded because he believed that his life was in danger if he took on this task.

Moses was brought to the palace of the pharaoh, as narrated in his personal story in *Surat* 20 (*taha*). While growing up in Egypt he witnessed how Egyptians oppressed his own people. This made him very angry. After he saw an Egyptian smiting an Israelite, he rebelled. He slew the Egyptian and fled to the Sinai Peninsula, where he received the divine commission. But the charge of slaying the Egyptian was facing him. He was also (apparently) irascible. But God's grace made him wise. God's assurance also cured him from impediment in speech and he could stand and speak boldly to the pharaoh. He announced that he was the messenger of God, the Lord of the heavens and the earth, and all in between. When the pharaoh replied, "If you dare to worship any God other than me, I will certainly put you in prison!" and "Cut off both hands and both feet, and I will make you die on the cross!" Moses answered: "I don't care, no matter what, we shall return to our Lord!"[26]

The high quality of Qur'anic prose illustrates how it turned a local poetic tradition into an international media and why it was quickly accepted, embraced, and eventually absorbed in the new countries that converted to Islam. This achievement, comparable to those of Greek and Latin in the past and English and Spanish at the present, has been explained in terms of the work's association with the religion of Islam. However, the real reason behind the spread and the sustaining influence of Islam lies in Arabic, the language in which the Islamic message was and is delivered to millions of converts, as it communicate their needs and cultivates their consciousness. Arabic, which was initially preached as the words of God, became the language of the people because non–Arabic speaking Muslims have decided either to adapt to the new language or modify their native languages according to Arabic. This is because they found that Arabic helped them to see, express, and think about their world more than their native language ever could. By speaking, writing, or imitating Arabic expression, they learn more of wisdom, think more deeply, and express emotions and moods more accurately. The desire on the part of the new converts to identify with the resourceful pioneers of the Arabian Peninsula was yet another factor in their adoption of the language.

Qur'anic prose added immeasurably to the beauty of the Arabic language by introducing new styles, forms of expression, figures of speech, and complex structures. The Qur'an also enriched and expanded the vocabulary of the Arabic language by employing hundreds of words of foreign origin, thus demonstrating the legitimacy of lexical borrowing as a linguistic device. The Qur'an presented Arab scholars with a higher criterion of literary excellence and set new and more detailed standards for literary composition for subsequent generations of scholars. The model that the Qur'an provided, while remaining inimitable, has sharpened the literary skill and kindled the talent of generations of scholars in their attempts to emulate the style and literary excellence of the Qur'an. Within this multi-lingual context, the Arabic language also underwent drastic changes in its structure, content, and status due to its association with Islam.

Among many literary forms that were inspired by Qur'anic prose and the narrative form of the Hadith was the frame tale (called fantasy fiction by some). This type of prose fiction, as the forerunner of fiction writing, framed unrelated tales or episodes in an overarching story that provided a context for storytelling. Although many of the stories derived from non–Arabic sources, such as those from Persia and India, it was literary Arabic that successfully strung them together into collections of short stories or episodes framed into a long tale. *The One Thousand and One Nights* (*Arabian Nights*), easily the best known of all works of Arabic literature, became the model of narrative for the European fiction writers.[27]

It took about four centuries (from the 10th to the 14th century) for the modern versions of the *Arabian Nights* to be written down and reach final form. During the process, the number and type of tales varied from one manuscript to another. Included were fables of animals, fables of *jihad* or propagation of the faith, proverbs, humorous tales, accounts of the wily con-man Ali Zaybaq, and tales about the prankster Juha. Various characters from these tales have become cultural icons in Western culture (Aladdin, Sinbad and Ali Baba). Remnants of Arabian and Persian mythology remained common themes even in modern fantasy (such as genies, bahamuts, magic carpets, magic lamps). However, the most important contribution of Arabic literature to world fiction writing was its innovative narrative structure, the string that hold the pearls together, so to speak, to make a beautiful necklace. Many important works of Western literature adopted this narrative structure: Dante's *Divine Comedy*, Chaucer's *Canterbury Tales*, and Boccaccio's *Decameron*.[28]

Scholars have debated and will continue to debate the origins of episodic fiction as a literary form. These fictions did not come from a single language or single tradition but rather sprouted from a single episode of literary evolution that was shared by almost every literary language, except those did not survive and grow into maturity.[29] Arabic prose wrote the earliest fictional narrative simply because it had been writing episodic stories for centuries before it came to produce standards (of fantasy tales) such as *The Thousand and One Nights*.[30] By the same token, European vernaculars developed their own versions of episodic fictions when their language transformed from formative storytelling and linear narrative to multiple plotting and dramatic presentation. In short, mature literary language often produces more complex narrative forms. Arabic happened to be older and more mature than the majority of the literary languages of medieval Western Europe.

Qur'anic literature and its studies also played an unprecedented role as transmitters and bridges between poetry, prose and speech. It is well known that Qur'an marked the beginning of Arabic prose. However, most people have less knowledge about the significance of Qur'anic prose in the development of Arabic language because the English concept of prose falls short of the exact meaning of Arabic prose in both concept and historical significance. The majority of English words emerged from a pair of opposites, so prose means the opposite of poetry. If poetry has rhyme, prose does not; poetry is meant to be read aloud, prose is to be read silently; poetry is a form somewhere between oral and written presentation, prose belongs to the latter. But in the history of Arabic language, prose is an extension of poetry. It is not only that the Qur'an emerged from a highly developed and polished poetic language, but also that Qur'anic prose inherited many characteristics of pre–Islamic poetry, especially poetic and dramatic delivery and sophisticated rhythm.

The most important function of Qur'anic prose is to bridge the written and spoken language by imposing and advertising an accent-based meter that is close to speaking rhythm. Unlike poetry that followed the rule of syllabic counting and restriction, *saj*'s meter is based on the balance of length of words and linguistic rhythm.[31] Although grammatical codification is common to many languages, Arabic was the only language whose grammatical codification had an extraordinary oral dimension. What the Qur'an codified was much more than grammar or a form of writing. It standardized the sound, the rhythm and the articulation of the Arabic language. As recitation of the Qur'an has been and remains a daily phenomenon, practiced by the faithful, linguistic repetition accomplished much more than the transmission of a religious message. It allowed the short paralleling phrases and repetitive rhyme to become a habit of speaking and model of eloquence. As these features transferred from the purely textual to the acoustic realm, a gradually upgraded spoken language obtained literary quality. In the form of words and chant, message and sound combined to carry the significance of the revelation to even higher levels of understanding and emotional response.

The practitioner of *tajwīd* was required to possess a beautiful voice. Emphasis could be given to specific consonants and vowels through elongation and by singling out "*n*" and "*m*" for nasalization (*ghunnah*). These techniques were used to accentuate the assonantal features of passages such as *Surat* 2 (*Al-Baqarah*), "*summun bukmun 'umyun' fahum la yub-siruna*" and *Surat* 97 (*Al-Qadr*), "*inna anzalnāhufī laylati 1-qadri*," and to blend this technical repertoire into the rise and fall of traditional chant. The effect on the listener transcended that of words alone. This specific chanting technique was very similar to the early Hebrew chanting, which later evolved into melody-driven cantillation. The Babylonian biblical manuscripts from the Geonic period contain no cantillation marks in the current sense, but small Hebrew letters were used to mark significant divisions within a verse. Up to eight different letters are found, depending on the importance of the break and where it occurred in the verse. These correspond roughly to the disjunctives of the Tiberian system. Nothing is known of the musical realization of these marks, but it seems likely that, if any of these signs were associated with a musical motif, the motif was applied not to the individual word but to the whole phrase, ending with the break. A somewhat similar system is used in manuscripts of the Qur'an to guide the reader in fitting the chant to the verse.

This system is reflected in the cantillation practices of the Yemenite Jews, who now use the Tiberian symbols, but that system tends to have musical motifs only for the disjunctives and renders the conjunctives in a monotone. It is notable that the Yemenites have only eight disjunctive motifs, clearly reflecting the Babylonian notation. The same is true of the *Karaite* mode for the *haftarah*. In the *Sephardi haftarah* different disjunctives often have the same or closely similar motifs.

The ritual chanting of the Qur'an clearly has a powerful effect on listeners. As numerous accounts show, that effect will often assume an enhanced form in the rituals of the Sufi community. The gathering of a brotherhood (a *hadrah*) will include not only recitations from the Qur'an but also texts in praise of God (*dhikr*) and mystical poems such as the Burdah of Al-Busrī (d. 1296). It is the heightened intensity brought about by this kind of experience, and in particular in Sufi orders, whose rituals make full use of it, that has led to an uneasy tension between popular practice in many Muslim communities and the orthodox conservative scholars who have always viewed the impact of music on believers with suspicion.[32]

The form of Qur'anic recitation played an increasingly important role as Islam expanded into the non–Arabic-speaking world. As the majority of Muslims did not understand Arabic, Qur'anic language became an abstract religious message rather than a living communication. This is paralleled by the impact of Latin on speakers of European vernaculars. The language of the Qur'an became an expression that its listeners could not understand (they might know the general idea of it but not word for word), but they could sense a oneness of faith as Arabic poetry beat out a perfect measured cadence.[33]

Unlike Hebrew and Latin languages, which lost their sound after ascending to a language of literature and religious ritual, Qur'anic reading and recitation remained a science and an art throughout Islamic history. Ibn al-Jazari (1350–1429) was a distinguished and prolific scholar and ultimate authority in the field of the reading (*qira'at*) of the Qur'an. He learned the art of Qur'anic recitation at an early age and memorized the Qur'an by the age of 13. In Damascus, Al-Jazari founded and headed a school that specialized in Qur'anic science (*Dar al-Qur'an*). He compiled more than ninety works on Qur'anic reading, the Hadith, and Islamic history while traveling around the Middle East.[34]

As the Qur'an was chanted throughout the world, it became a (wordless) music or universal language to deliver messages, as Arabic words were not understood by non–Arabic-speaking Muslims. As an important part of Islamic ritual, music (in notes and/or words) brought a sub-verbal and multimedia type of conformity to Islamic culture that Arabic, as a literary language, could not produce as it ventured into other parts of the world. Musical modulation that accompanied words (in different languages) provided a more universal and more flexible medium to transmit meanings. The best example of the formation and function of this cross-lingual media is the evolution and transplantation of a form of Arabic music, *maqam*.

Arabic *maqam* is the system of melodic modes used in traditional Arabic music. The word *maqam* means place, location or rank. In this specific context, the best English translation for *maqam* is scale or hierarchy (or system) of notes. In Arabic music, a *maqam* is a set of notes with traditions that define relationships between them, habitual patterns, and their melodic development. *Maqāmā* are best defined and understood in the context of the rich repertoire of Arabic music. The nearest equivalent in Western classical music would be a mode (major and minor). Arabic scales are not even-tempered (the difference in pitch between each note is not identical), unlike the chromatic scale used in modern Western music. Instead, 5th notes are tuned based on the 3rd harmonic. The tuning of the remaining notes entirely depends on the *maqam* (modulation). The reasons for this tuning were historically determined by the kinds of musical instruments used in Arabic music. Instead of the organ and piano, which derived their scale from physical dimensions, string instruments such as the *oud* created more varied pitch by vibration. A side effect of not having even-tempered tuning is that the same note (by name) may have a slightly different pitch depending on which *maqam* it is played in, as *maqam* is "a technique of improvisation" that defines the pitches, patterns, and development of a piece of music. This is unique to Arabian art music. There are seventy-two heptatonic tone scales of *maqāmāt*, which are constructed from major, medium, and minor seconds. Each *maqam* is built on a scale, and carries a tradition that defines its habitual phrases, important notes, melodic development and modulation. It also determines the tonic (starting note), the ending note, and the dominant note. It also determines which notes should be emphasized and which should not. Both compositions and improvisations in traditional Arabic music are based on the *maqam* system. *Maqam* can be realized with either vocal or instrumental music, and do not include a rhythmic component.[35]

An essential, decisive factor in *maqam* performance is that each describes the "tonal-spatial factor" or set of musical notes and the relationships between them, including traditional patterns and development of melody, while the rhythmic-temporal component is subjected to no definite organization. A *maqam* does not have a so-called established, regularly recurring bar scheme or an unchanging meter. A certain rhythm does sometimes identify the style of a performer, but this is dependent upon his performance technique. There has never been a universal *maqam* as understood in Western music. The compositional or rather pre-compositional aspect of the *maqam* is the tonal-spatial organization, including the number of tone levels and the improvisational aspect. Together (as understood by Europeans) these form the rhythmic-temporal scheme.

Maqam initially originated in Sassanid Persia (224–651), where modal music was developed by a highly significant court musician, Barbad, the *khosravani*. Persian music made the most important contribution to Arabic music. This might be the reason why many Arabic *maqāmāt* can trace their names to the Persian language, such as *Nikriz, Farahfaza, Suzidil, Suznak, Rast, Sikah* (from *Se-Gah*), *Jiharkah* (from *Chehar-Gah*) and *Nairuz* (from *Nowruz*). The reverse is also true, with Persian Goosheh names taken from Arabic: *Hejaz* (from *Hijaz*), *Hoseyni* (from *Husayni*), *Oshshagh* (from *'Ushshaq*) and *Hodi*. Similarly, many Arabic *maqam* names come from the Turkish *Makam*, Sultani *Yekah, Buselik* and *Bastanikar*, while the following Turkish Makam names trace their origin to Arabic: *Hicâz, Irak, Hüseynî, Sünbüle* and *Uşşakpuselik*.[36]

Arabic *maqam* was based on a musical scale of seven notes that repeat at the octave. Some *maqam* had two or more alternative scales (for example, *Rast, Nahawand* and *Hijaz*). *Maqam* scales in traditional Arabic music were microtonal, not based on a twelve-tone, equally-tempered musical tuning system. Most *maqam* scales included a perfect fifth or a perfect fourth (or both), and all octaves were perfect. The remaining notes in a *maqam* scale might or might not exactly fall on semitones. For this reason *maqam* scales were mostly taught orally, and by extensive listening to traditional Arabic music.

Maqam scales are made up of smaller sets of consecutive notes that have a very recognizable melody and convey a distinctive mood. Such a set is called *jins* (pl. *ajnas*), meaning "gender" or "kind." In most cases, a *jins* is made up of four consecutive notes (tetrachord), although *ajnas* of three consecutive notes (trichord) or five consecutive notes (pentachord) also exist.

Ajnas are the building blocks of a *maqam* scale. A *maqam* scale has a lower (or first) *jins* and an upper (or second) *jins*. In most cases *maqam* are classified into families or branches based on their lower *jins*. The upper *jins* may start on the ending note of the lower *jins* or on the note following. In some cases the upper and lower *ajnas* may overlap. The starting note of the upper *jins* is called the dominant, and is the second most important note in that scale after the tonic. *Maqam* scales often include secondary *ajnas* that start on notes other than the tonic or the dominant. Secondary *ajnas* are highlighted in the course of modulation.

Like modern jazz, *maqam* was a more refined music that combined composition and improvisation. Performers had greater freedom to create various moods. Each *maqam* evokes a specific emotion or set of emotions determined by the tone row and the nucleus. Different *maqāmāt* sharing the same tone row but differing in nucleus create different emotion. *Maqam rast* evokes pride, power, soundness of mind, and masculinity. *Maqam bayati* conveys vitality, joy, and femininity, *Sikah* portrays love, *Saba* expresses sadness and pain while *Hijaz* presents the distant desert.[37]

Emotion is evoked in part through changes in the size of an interval during a *maqam* presentation. *Maqam saba*, for example, contains in its first four notes D, E-quarter-flat, F, and Gb, two medium seconds, one larger (160 cents) and one smaller (140 cents) than a three-quarter tone, and a minor second (95 cents). Further, E-quarter-flat and G-flat may vary slightly, causing a "sad" or "sensitive" mood.[38]

Generally speaking, each *maqam* evokes a different emotion for the listener. At a more basic level, each *jins* conveys a different mood or color. For this reason *maqams* of the same family share a common mood since they start with the same *jins*. There is no consensus on exactly what the mood of each *maqam* or *jins* is. Some references describe *maqam* moods using very vague and subjective terminology (e.g., *maqams* evoking love, femininity, pride or distant desert). However there has not been any serious research using scientific methodology on a diverse sample of listeners (whether Arab or non–Arab) proving that they feel the same emotion when hearing the same *maqam*.

Attempting the same exercise in more recent tonal classical music would mean relating a mood to the major and minor modes. In that case there is a wider consensus that the minor scale is sadder and the major scale is happier. Attempting the same exercise in older modal classical music with Dorian, Phrygian, Lydian and Mixolydian modes would probably produce similar results.

Modulation was a technique used during the melodic development of a *maqam*. In simple terms it means changing from one *maqam* to another (compatible or closely related) *maqam*. This involves using a new musical scale. A long musical piece can modulate over many *maqāmāt* but usually ends with the starting *maqam* (in rare cases the purpose of the modulation is to actually end with a new *maqam*). A more subtle form of modulation within the same *maqam* is to shift the emphasis from one *jins* to another so as to imply a new *maqam*.

Modulation made music more interesting and varied, and is present in almost every *maqam*-based melody. When modulation took place from one *maqam* to another, there are two possible scenarios. One was that the new *maqam* had the same tonic as the original *maqam* (e.g., modulation from *Rast* on C to *Nahawand* on C). The other was that the new *maqam* was based on a note from the original *maqam* other than its tonic (e.g., modulation from *Rast* on C) to *Bayati* on G (*Bayati Nawa*). Modulations that were pleasing to the ear were created by adhering to compatible combinations of *ajnas* and *maqāmāt* long established in traditional Arabic music. Although such combinations were often documented in musical references, most experienced musicians learn them by extensive listening.

The Arabic scales on which *maqāmāt* are built from are not even-tempered, unlike the chromatic scale used in Western classical music. Instead, fifth notes are tuned based on the third harmonic. The tuning of the remaining notes entirely depends on the maqam. The reasons for this tuning are probably historically based on string instruments like the *oud*. A side effect of not having even-tempered tuning is that the same note (by name) may have a slightly different pitch depending on which maqam it is played in.[39]

There is no absolute reference for the Arabic scale. In 1932, the Arabic Music Conference in Cairo established that regional variations existed in the intonation of Arabic *maqāmāt*. Within each region, oral traditions continued and created de facto standards, although these standards converged to some extent with the advent of recording and broadcasting.

The phenomenon that greatly influenced intonation in Arabic music was the introduction of even-tempered instruments (some of which were altered to produce quarter tones), mostly in the second half of the 20th century. The accordion, electric guitar, electric (fretted) bass, piano, guitar, electric keyboard, electric organ and synthesizer were gradually introduced to the Arabic ensemble. The main incentive behind this change was innovation, modernization, and the desire to add harmony to Arabic music.

When Arabic *maqāmāt* are performed on even-tempered instruments, they sound different in subtle ways for the following reasons:

The intonation of the same quarter tone can vary with each *maqam*. For example, the E in *maqam Rast* has a higher tuning than the E in *maqam Bayati*. Even-tempered instruments eliminate these subtle variations, producing dry and rigid quarter tones.

Moreover, the Arabic *maqam* has regional variations. For example, the E in *maqam Rast* has a higher tuning in Aleppo than in Cairo. Even-tempered instruments eliminate these regional variations, reducing the Arabic *maqam* to its base.

Even semitones in the Arabic scale often include microtonal variations. A prime example are the 2nd and 3rd notes in the Hijaz tetrachord, which are played closer together so as to shrink the 1½ tone interval. These variations cannot be performed on even-tempered instruments. In case of harmonic music, microtonal variations are undesirable since they reduce harmony.

The original tuning of *maqam* Hijaz has been lost except in a handful of new recordings, and is replaced with what is called "piano *Hijaz*" (a derogatory term). Equally bad is the "piano *Ajam*," where the 3rd note should be slightly lower and more mellow. *Maqāmāt* such as *Jiharkah* are rarely played on even-tempered instruments, even on ones that have been altered to produce quarter tones.

In conclusion, the new generation of Arabic musicians, singers and listeners is losing touch with the traditional intonation of the 1920s and '30s largely because of the introduction of even-tempered instruments and harmony in Arabic music.

By the time that the *maqam* musical model was adopted by literature, it (now called *maqāmā*, "assemblies") became a skeleton to hold words that could do whatever they pleased. It became an Arabic literary genre of rhymed prose with intervals of poetry in which rhetorical extravagance is dominant. The 10th century author Badī' al-Zaman al-Hamadhānī is said to have invented the form, which was extended by Al-Harīrī of Basra in the next century. Both authors' *maqāmāt* center on trickster figures whose wanderings and exploits in speaking to assemblies of the powerful are conveyed by a narrator. The protagonist is a silver-tongued hustler, a rogue drifter who survives by dazzling onlookers with virtuoso displays of rhetorical acrobatics, which include a mastery of classical Arabic poetry (or of biblical Hebrew poetry and prose in the case of the Hebrew *maqāmāt*), and classical philosophy. Typically, there are 50 unrelated episodes in which the rogue character, often in disguise, tricks the narrator out of his money and leads him into straitened, embarrassing, and even violent circumstances. Despite this serial abuse, the narrator-dupe character continues to seek out the trickster, fascinated by his rhetorical flow.[40]

In the year 1111, Al-Harīrī read his *maqāmāt* to some of men of letters and allowed them write down his words, exchange notes about what they heard, and correct mistakes. This was the common way to publish literature at the time. The manuscript that was created in this conference was brought back to Europe and introduced to different readers and writers who rewrote their versions.[41]

In contrast to the third-person narratives of epic and romances, *maqāmā* stories were first-person accounts. As the protagonist told his story, readers could judge his veracity. This form created various layered expressions, as found in Western theatrical performance. For example, the performer could do or say one thing, and simultaneously reveal other feelings. He could greet a person whom he hated with a smile on his face. This vividly manifested a chasm between appearance and concealed reality. The rhetorical device served to highlight the contrast between highly embellished rhetoric and revealed faulty morality. From this contrast emerged a different character, opposite to the epic and romances: antiheroes. The writer did not intend to teach the reader a moral lesson but rather wished to illustrate how and why characters behaved in certain manners. Thus, fiction became far more interesting than a morality play, as readers had to be prepared for different tricks that might or might not deceive the victim or culminate in a surprise ending.[42]

Each *maqāmā* dealt with a separate topic in each episode, the whole being unified by the characters of the narrator and the traveler, as in Abu'l-Fatb in Al-Hamadhani's (967–1007) *maqāmāt*, Abu Zayd of Saruj in those by the later Al-Harīrī (1054–1122). The story had also departed from geographic and temporal continuity. In one *maqāmāt* the protagonist could be in China and in the next Baghdad, without any explanation in between. In *maqama* narrative, storytelling did not have to be linear and changed narrative perspective by putting words into its character's mouth, providing a distinct view of the described issue.[43]

If in the Qur'an, prose tells the (divine) truth, while pre–Islamic poetry does not, in *maqāmā* the person speaking poetry was often the deceiver.

Manuscripts of al-Harīrī's *maqāmāt*, anecdotes of a roguish wanderer Abu Zayd from Saruj, were frequently illustrated with miniatures. Al-

Harīrī far exceeded the rhetorical stylistics of the genre's innovator, Al-Hamadhani, to such a degree that his *maqāmāt* was used as a textbook for rhetoric and lexicography (the cataloging of rare words from the Bedouin speech of the 7th and 8th centuries) until Early Modern times.

By now the characteristic features of Arabic literary prose writing had prevailed under the Persian influence. The terse, incisive and simple expression of early days had disappeared forever, and it was supplanted by an ornate and elegant style, rich in elaborate similes and replete with rhymes. The whole period was marked by a predominance of humanistic over scientific expressions. Intellectually it was a period of decline that supported a literary proletariat, many of whose members, with no independent means of livelihood, roamed from place to place ready to engage others on linguistic issues and grammatical technicalities or flash their poetical swords over trivial matters with a view to winning favors from wealthy patrons. The *maqāmā* emerged as a preferred medium for these encounters.

This style enabled the authors to display all the brilliance of their erudition, rhetoric, and wit. The *maqāmā* became well-known and highly appreciated as literary works of later times among the Arabs. In particular, Al-Harare's *maqāmāt* were praised highly and remained a favorite in the Muslim world. Finding imitators all over its sphere of influence, including Spain, were the *maqāmā* of the Jewish thinker Al-Harizi (thirteenth century). The influence of *maqāmā* exemplified a literary form that could transcend language and religion and succeed in several cultures for centuries.[44]

The *maqāmā* genre was also adopted in Hebrew. The later Hebrew *maqāmāt* made more significant departures, structurally and stylistically, from the classical Arabic *maqāmāt* of Al-Hamadhānī and Al-Harīrī. Joseph ibn Zabara (end of 12th–beginning of 13th centuries A.D.), a resident of Barcelona and a Catalan speaker, wrote the *Sēfer sha'ashū'īm* (*The Book of Delights*), in which the author, the narrator, and the protagonist are all Ibn Zabara himself, and in which the episodes are arranged in linear, not cyclical, fashion, in a way that anticipates the structure of Spanish picaresque novels such as the anonymous *Lazarillo de Tormes* (1535) and *Guzmán de Alfarache* (1599) by Mateo Alemán.

Arabic music has the ability to uplift listeners from their current state and take them somewhere else on an emotional journey. You can easily find all forms and degrees of *tarab* in all genres and forms of Arabic music. Each one would have a unique characteristic style, sound, and feel. However, out of all the styles, in my opinion Classical Arabic music, or what is also called *Tarab* music (both old and new) allows one to experience *tarab* at its finest. Those who want to understand Arabic music on a deeper level must first understand the concept of *tarab*. The way that *tarab* is expressed in Arabic music is what separates it from many different cultures that share a similar concept in their music. This makes it an intriguing art form that is starting to attract many ears in the West.

Like Western classical music, the most important influence of Arabic music upon literatures of non–Arabic language is much more than its emotional appeal. It is the historical association or even obsession with words which inspired the long-time interaction and mutual influence between words and music. This close relationship between words made it possible for literary expressions to constantly adopt and assimilate musical forms of expression. Literature attempted to be as expressive, individualistic, and emotionally effective as music, yet was more precise and terse in its execution. This association also elevated literary expression from merely a pursuit of meaning, precision, and definition to a rhetorical form and eloquence through which meanings were conveyed and suggested.

In world history, only a few musical traditions evolved into maturity that could exercise cross-lingual influence upon the music and literature of other languages and extend their influence beyond religious ritual. Arabic was one of those languages. To illustrate how and why it happened to Arabic rather than Hebrew or Latin, one has to understand the distinct characteristics of Arabic *maqam* in comparison to Hebrew and Latin cantillation and the way cantillation was codified and transplanted.

Hebrew ritual chanting had a longer history and deeper roots than that of Arabic. Cantillation signs guide the reader in applying a chant to biblical readings. This chant is technically regarded as a ritualized form of speech intonation rather than as a musical exercise (like the singing of metrical hymns). For this reason, Jews always speak of saying or reading a passage rather than of singing it. (In Yiddish the word is *leynen*, "read," derived from Latin *legere*, giving rise to the Jewish-English verb "to leyn.")

The musical value of cantillation signs serves the same function for Jews worldwide, but the specific tunes vary between different communities. The most common tunes are cantillation signs that guide the reader in applying a chant to biblical readings. The most common tunes were Ashkenazic melodies from central and Western Europe (the most common tunes both in Israel and the diaspora), the Jerusalem Sephardic melodies (with relations such as Greek/Turkish/Balkan, Syrian and Egyptian melodies), Yemenite melodies, and two Iraqi melodies.[45] However, unlike the Arabic tradition in which Qur'anic text was marked for reading and recitation, the diversity of biblical cantillation became codified music in which the Bible could be recited and chanted. However, in biblical chanting of the Babylonian period, Hebrew was marked according to grammar and syntax rather than musical tune.

Maqam flourished in North Africa, the Middle East, southern Europe, and central Asia with hundreds of variations geared to its native and local languages and dialects. Music, rather than cantillation melody, became a universal medium because it was free from an entanglement with words. A similar revolution took place in early modern Europe when Christian musical ritual dissyndicated and inspired (separately) a musical tradition and an array of vernaculars in Europe.

To illustrate the historical consequence of the association of music and literature in Arabic and its defining influence on the development and maturity of other languages is to observe what has happened to contemporary music and literature in the West after centuries under the influence of classical music. Classical music did not stop at an accumulated repertoire of compositions and masterpieces of performance similar to the melodic repertoire of Hebrew music in various Jewish communities of the world. Rather, it inspired and generated the emergence of a modern music that established a variety of relationships with modern languages in Europe.

The separation between music and words provided a cultural revolution that made it possible to transplant forms of expression beyond language, similar to the revolution of late Medieval Europe when Latin produced and inspired several European vernacular cultures. The same process had taken place in the Middle East and Islamic countries in south Asia.

Conclusions

Literary Arabic evolved within the context of interaction with non-literary expressions, such as oral language and music. As oral poetry migrated to prose writing, this substantially widened the vision of Arabic and made it possible to tell stories, deliver arguments, express opinions, and eventually to create a world that was depicted in detailed images, organized in specific sequences, and explained in profound logic. Thus, the Qur'an, the first prose writing in Arabic, initiated much more than a religious belief or worldview; it opened the minds and eyes of the Muslim community and provided it with the ability to explore, to create, and to communicate with other linguistic communities.

What distinguished Arabic scholars from those of other ancient traditions was their ability to outgrow exegete tradition and textual interpretation, and expand linguistic study as a part of literary development. This linguistic dimension kept Arabic standing fast on the ground as its poetic imagination and abstract reasoning soared with literary creation. As a result, Arabic civilization spread into the world at large, not simply as literary or religious tradition as did the Latin and Hebrew texts, but also as living utterance, rhythmic sound and cultural performance.

The interaction between literary language and music was a constant dynamic driving the growth and maturity of both music and literature. As musical language matured through composition, recitation, and improvisation, literature followed a similar evolutionary path. Arabic poetry came to express more individualistic and intimate feelings and to present more personal visions and voices. With an inherited, exceptional intimacy with words, Arabic music traveled further than the Arabic language itself. Words, tones, and rhymes were carried by a rhythm shared by music and poetry that could be comprehended by different languages, recited in different songs, and performed as different cultural rituals.

PART TWO

*The Formation
of Arabic Imagery*

Part Two describes the formation, transformation, accumulation and refinement of imagery in Arabic literature. The emergence of Arabic prose marked a new beginning for Arabic literature and Islam provided the ancient Arabic poetry a new voice to sing, new subjects to envisage, and a new devotional life to cultivate. As post-Islamic Arabic vision expanded rapidly with its new religious beliefs and growing vocabularies, its imagery enlarged and it became more varied, precise, and abstract during the classical period. When these fresh images were rendered in the established rhythm of pre-Islamic poetry and articulated in spoken language, they became easily adopted into prose writing. A brand new literary world emerged.

Arabic images that had never been restrained by the vision of the naked eye or limited by philosophy quickly overrode the moral boundaries and closed the gap between God and world and between God and believers. Unlike the early Latin literature where Christian imagination had to accumulate images from scratch and meditate in words alone, the Arabic sense of visual distinction quickly transformed into abstract art forms. It became a pattern of shapes and colors, a pure form of beauty without any concrete figuration. It took several centuries for this broad vision to refocus and fill with detailed imageries that were fluid enough to adapt with changing moods. As imagery acquired more individual variations, the world and God became personal and intimate again to the creative mind.

The best example of this personal and intimate relationship between poet, world and God can be found in Sufi poetic tradition. Sufi poetry cultivated a richly textured vocabulary in Arabic and provided the needed template for the language of the individual soul. This vocabulary created a loving world that no longer needed a concrete image of the relationship between man and God. A love for God and also for one's self juxtaposed into a unified imagery. Sufi images are famous for conveying various levels of meaning. With these interlinked images and connotations, the line between real and unreal, lyrical and mystical, emotional and intellectual, divine and human, natural and supernatural quickly disappeared. In that world, words could signify a lover courting a beloved, a politician addressing his devoted followers, and a believer receiving spiritual wisdom.

Modern Arabic poetry portrays a world of words that change color, shape, and mood according to the feelings of its creator. In contemporary poetry, the richly textured and inclusive language of love has substantially widened from that of Sufi poetic tradition. The subject of love expanded into an increasingly broader horizon, to encompass a nation or a world. Love is mystical, but at the same time very personal and sensual. In this new linguistic context, everyday images such as *a woman who enters my life like a dagger, the eyes of a rabbit* and *innocent as children's bibs* carry the centuries old tradition of Arabic love poetry, updated with modern experience, and echo the rhythm, intonation, and idioms of everyday language.

CHAPTER 4

Imagery of the World:
Poetry and Prose

This chapter depicts the expansion and transformation of Arabic imagery from pre–Islamic poetry, Qur'anic prose, to classical literature. It focuses on how the scope of this repertoire of images evolved through the creativity of Arab and non–Arab writers. It illustrates how the mature and complex pre–Islamic language of poetry expanded in reaction to its ever-changing environment and new challenges, and how this expansion enriched the newborn Arabic literature. After centuries of accumulation and distillation until the rise of Islam, Arabic poetry had become too symbolic, terse and narrow for an urban and international civilization. The imaginative horizon of pre–Islamic Arabic was very limited; its repertoire of vocabulary was suggestive, ambiguous and pregnant with overlapping levels of meanings. Most important of all, the poetic form was compacted and refined to the point that it restrained imagination. Emotional expression was tightly locked by worn-out symbols and allusions, and poetry was gradually losing its vitality and flexibility. Arabic language not only needed to revitalize its poetry, but also had to invent more varied forms of expression.

Prose writing introduced more precise and clear images and expanded the descriptive horizons of the Arabic language. Post-Islamic Arabic also reconstructed the Muslim community according to a simplified division between believers and non-believers. It was a community where one's pious virtue (the relationship with God) and social behavior were regulated by Islamic law. As the Muslim community expanded into more diverse ethnical and cultural territories the law had to be constantly redefined, codified and interpreted. The language of law rapidly cultivated levels of meanings and connotations as legal scholarship evolved and judicial institutions established. The accumulation and enrichment of literary Arabic

115

also paved the way for the development of science and philosophy. It forced the emerging Arabic civilization to grow and mature at an unprecedented speed until it became the most advanced civilization in the medieval world.

The imagery of pre- and early Islamic Arabic painted a world narrow in scope yet refined in expression. Like the Chinese poetry of late medieval period (Song Dynasty), the number of subjects that were described in the Arabic poetry shrank while their portrayal expanded with variety and details. The emotional engagement deepened and became more subtle. Arab poets gave more attention to describing and provoking a certain mood with verbal eloquence rather than specific narrative. They produced a focused poetry with distinct vocabulary and brief ideas in their loosely connected verses. The seemingly simple imagery (such as a ruin that reminded the poet of his beloved) had layers of meaning that activated a sensibility of vision, touch and smell in the minds of readers.[1]

Qasida, the most important poetic form of pre–Islamic poetry, often began with a scene of an abandoned campsite: charred firewood, blackened hearthstones, shards of pottery, shreds of wool, camel dung, traces in the sand from rain trenches and tent pegs. It was a ruin (*atlal*) left by the tribe (often that of the poet's beloved) that reminded the poet of his past emotional loss. These were silent scenes that inspired anguished riffs on love and sorrow. The visual prelude served as an emotional background from which poetry would emerge and express an emotional release. The poet who created the intended mood hoped to invoke a demand for release and designed response from his reader and audience.

With familiar visual cues, the poems were highly personal as remembrance took different forms and created different images. For instance, the sleepless night reminded the poet of his happy moment with his lost love. The ruffled beds evoked the memory of her changing mood and affection; her absence evoked the scene of her departure with her tribal mates in their richly embroidered camel litters; the sorrowful moaning of the dove echoed the hoariness of glances back at lost youth. These themes and sub-themes recurred from poem to poem with slight variants and ritual solemnity. However, each required a new configuration according to a subtle and newly discovered logic of sorrow. Each new realization of loss generated a new poem with its own circumstance, undertone, and personality.

Minute distinctions were conveyed in every different descriptive image, seemingly isolated and yet recollected and chained into a necklace of similes. The beloved's mouth could be compared to wine as fresh as the cold stream, her eyes to the eyes of white onyx, and her grace to that of a gazelle. The evoked images of spring rain, running streams, flowering meadows, and desert animals nursing in idyllic tranquility were overrun by the flow of emotion that changed constantly but refused to be pinned down. All of these mental images and fluid emotions were set to contrast a backdrop of the dry, empty and silent desert. With his beloved gone, the poet was left by himself. He was alone on a journey marked by swarming locusts in the heat, the death call of an owl at night, the wasting away of a camel, and the disorientation and terror of a mirage. As night fell, the solitary rider's image was enveloped by darkness.

The final movement of *qasida* often took the form of a wine song wherein the writer moved away from his lonely journey to boast of a more settled state of mind. A singing girl was presented as consolation for the lost love. The more wine the poet consumed, the more he could proclaim how well he had gotten over his past loss and the more he proclaimed, the more he believed himself. This bacchic antinomy was at the heart of the poem. However, much of the *nasib* was now only remembrance, and denial haunted the poem.[2]

Naqa (female camel) sacrifice often was the dramatic center of the movement of boasting. The *naqa,* as distinct from its more cumbersome male counterpart, was prized in Bedouin society for its versatility. It was swift and it provided sweet milk. Bedouin mothers often washed their infants in its urine. It was even an object of ritual sacrifice. Should it outlive its owner, the *naqa* was tethered to his tomb and left to die. Hence in Labid's *Mu'allaqa* we read, "To the shelter of my tent-ropes comes every forewearied woman / starved as a tomb-tethered camel, her garments tattered and shrunk." Precisely because of *naqa's* symbolic role in the life of the tribe, its proper name was rarely used in the pre–Islamic poetry, but it appeared steadily as with the poet's horse (or *faras*), as a wide array of connotative epithets and synonyms.

In the *naqa*-sacrifice scene, which usually occurs toward the end of the *rahil* (journey) section, the animal was offered up not to any god or spirit but rather to the tribe itself, as a token of cohesiveness and plenitude. Labid (560–661), perhaps the gentlest and most prudent of the pre–Islamic poets, pledged meat to the poor. Imru al-Qays (526–565?) was irreverently playful as he turned the scene into a titillating game of catch as the meat was tossed about by young girls. On the other hand, Tarafa (543–569), the most rascally of the seven pre–Islamic poets, did not sacrifice his own camel but that of an "old stick man," and thereby incurred the wrath of the tribe. It appeared to be a "sacrifice gone wrong," and Tarafa's ensuing boast was tinged with the anxiety of being misrepresented, and of having his reputation tarnished: "Don't make me a man / whose resolve wasn't my own / who could never replace me / or cast my shadow."

The exchanging of boasts and taunts between opposing tribes reflected an ironically common meditation upon the fate and absurdity of humanity and the personal struggles with in tribal society. Beyond the seemingly agitated antagonism there was suspicion that both war and required tribal loyalty were nothing personal at all but rather events guided and predetermined by fate. Fate determined everyone's allotted timing to fight, win, lose and die. As the battle boast intensified, the hierarchy of tribal society and its moral of vengeance began to unravel within. At the moment of death, the poet/warrior looked into the eyes of his slain enemy, where he saw his own reflection.[3]

Among the pre–Islamic poets, Zuhair (520–609) perhaps was the best at presenting *muruwwa* (manliness). Meticulous, clear-voiced, terse, and the most sententious of the seven poets, Zuhair was also called Abid al-Shi'r (the slave to poetry). He wrote his great *qasida* after the cessation of war between the tribes of Abs and Dhubyan (believed to have lasted forty years). As a spokesman for the tribe of Ghatafan, he praised the peacemakers, *Harim* and *Al-Harith*. He described the ritual circling of the Ka'ba and the swearing of the oath "by the Holy House about which circumambulate / men of Koraish and Jurhum." He spoke strongly against the horrors of war, and offered a series of gnomic sayings with balanced and languid movements. Those who keep their promise escape blame, while those who direct their hearts to the calm resting-place of integrity will never stammer in the assemblies of his nation. Those who tremble at all possible causes of death, fall in their way; even though they desired to mount the skies on a scaling-ladder. Those, who continually debase their minds by suffering others to ride over it, and never raise it from so abject a state, will at last repent of their meanness.

Committed to an ethos of tribal survival and moral rectitude, the pre–Islamic poets used *qasida* for celebrate the delicate social fabric of nomadic life. This might explain the darker and more transgressive side of the pre–Islamic poetry. Time and again, particularly in the *rahil*, the poet/warrior presented himself not only as a clan leader but also as a rebel and troublemaker, a reviler, a man on the run or companion to a band of outlaws. When deviance dominated the *qasida*, we have a *su'luk* (*sa'alik*) (brigand) poem. In fact, the very vitality of the *qasida* lies in its incorporation of gangster-like elements. A good example is the life and poetry of Imru al-Qays. He was banished by his royal family for composing verses and lived as a poor fugitive for most of his life. His night journey, "wolf scene," and description of bedding another man's wife portrayed the life of an ancient version of the modern Bohemian poet of the age of rebellions.[4]

Regardless of its rebellious spirit, a profound fatalism lied at the heart of the *qasida*, while the poet's bravado was asserted more often than not while facing death. The poetic boast was a testament to the glorification of the poet-hero, who would conclude his poem by boasting of his lyric and martial prowess. At the end, the poetic memory expressed a personal confession as well as a tribal mythopoeia. Unlike modern poetry, in which oppositions often battle one another, the *qasida*'s fluidity allowed for both an individual and a collective voice to be heard. Like in Labid's poetry, personal bragging was juxtaposed with extravagant praise of the clan.

Islamic expansion substantially widened the worldview of the Arabs, and extended both vertically, like an artist accustomed to painting miniatures given a canvas as large as the eyes could see. In this much grander world, the story of man became more than a history of one hero, one's ancestors, a tribe or the entire desert community. It expanded into the history of man (the human race) as created by God. Therefore, poetry and its poets needed more vocabulary, language skills, and thus were required to play a more significant role. He was no longer the chief speaker of his nomad life, noble representative of his culture, and defender of his justice. He was obliged to defend God, his creator, His divine kingdom on the earth, and justice for the entire universe. Under this heavy obligation, the ancient language of poetry appeared to be extremely inadequate, and its vocabulary was too limited. Arabic language needed new vocabularies to cultivate worldview and new images to portray an ideal vision. It needed a new kind of writing to serve its new God.

The emergence of prose writing rescued poetic language that had, through its long accumulation and elaboration, become stale to the point where imagery and meaning were distilled into fixed associations which imprisoned each other. The language of the Qur'an not only brought an abundance of new words and new images into Arabic, but also re-envisaged the pre–Islamic world, assisting the old language to serve a completely different conceptual purpose. An example of this drastic change in literary imagery was the vivid depiction in the Qur'an in verse 31 of *Surat* 22 (*Hajj*):

> Being true in faith to God, and never assigning partners to Him. If anyone dares to assign partners to God, he would fall from the heaven and be snatched up by birds. As if the wind has swooped (like a bird on its prey) and thrown him into a far away place [The English translation is retrieved from Qur'an Online Project with minor change of wording].

This *surat* illustrates what would happen to a man if he fell from the worship of the One and True God. He would fall from heaven and halfway down be picked up by birds of prey. A fierce blast of wind, the Wrath of God, would come and snatch him away, and then throw him to a place far, far away from any place he could imagined, the hell of those who dared to defy God.

This vivid and terrifying imagery was well-established and articulated in pre–Islamic poetry. The word *tayr* (vultures) was used by Imru' al-Qays to describe what had happened to his tribesmen. They were slaughtered as the carrion birds and vultures gathered, to wait their turns to tear away their eyes and brows. "Their dirty heads were drenched in their own blood."[5] A similar violent death was also envisaged by 'Antara (525–608) as "I left him (my intimate companion) with carrion and vultures circling over" him "like maidens rallying to escort the bride to her chamber." But they would be held up from "dining on his flesh, by a hand or leg that stirred with life!" The carrion birds and vultures following and hovering overhead marching troops, hoping to feast on the bodies of fallen warriors, was a common image in battle scenes of pre–Islamic poetry. Nabighah (535–604) provided one of the most vivid images: a "group of carrion birds and vultures hover over the troops," thirsting for their blood. They were sitting behind the hosts "waiting with greedy eyes" like "old men squatting in black garments."[6]

This was a typical way for Arabic prose to rework the imagery and connotations of pre–Islamic poetry. The expression *khatf al-tayr* clearly meant violent death. However, death now had different associations other than a physical condition in which someone was left to be eaten alive after war. The Qur'an described the fate of the people who shirked in their respect to God: as if they had fallen from the sky to the ground, died, and become the prey of vultures. Therefore, imagery of violent death became associated with religious belief after disassociation from tribal war. The short expression *fa takhtafuhu 't-tayr* did not need to explicitly mention death and falling, because it was used as a catchword to activate an image already stored in the memory of Arabs. Then a reference to any part of that image would bring the entire scene to the mind of listeners and readers, allowing the author to leave unmentioned some of its elements and leave its completion to the listener's imagination.

Brevity of expression depends on the actual capacities of a language and its inventory of catch phrases. Here the connotations of words and expressions merge and convey meanings not made explicit, or, to be more precise, they convey the contextual situation. This is the very heart of brevity, and it is identical to literary eloquence (*al-ijaz huwa al-balaghah*). The Qur'anic succinctness of expression rests on the actual possibilities of the Arabic language, and prose simply extends the link between words and imagery that are inherited in the minds of Arabic speakers since the pre–Islamic period.

The Qur'an has made remarkable contributions to the structure and style of the Arabic language, and it substantially enriched the repertoire of Arabic images by using abundant figures of speech in place of simple words. Arabic poetry allowed the Arabic language to sing to please the ears. Qur'anic prose allowed Arabic to paint and to please the eyes. With extensive use of illustrations, imagery, and metaphor it added beauty, life, and color to plain words of the newborn literature. The preference for figures of speech over plain words, a general trend that permeates the entire Qur'anic text, can be demonstrated in the following passages. This is the typical way in which the Qur'an illustrated the different fortunes of the believer and non-believer at the divine judgment: heaven and hell.

> To those who reject Our signs and treat them with arrogance, the gates of heaven will not open, nor will they enter the garden, unless the camel can pass through the eye of the needle. This is Our reward for those who have sinned.
> For them there is Hell, as a couch [below] and folds and folds of covering above: this is Our requital of those who do wrong.
> But those who believe and do right, no burden do We place on any soul, but that which it can bear, they will be Companions of the Garden, where they will dwell [for ever].
> And we shall remove any lurking sense of injury [pain of past life and its painful memory], from their hearts and rivers shall flow beneath them. They shall say: "Praise be to God, who hath guided us to this [felicity]: never could we have found guidance, had it not been for the guidance of God. Indeed it was the truth, that the messengers of our Lord brought unto us." And they shall hear the cry: "Behold! The garden before you! Ye have inherit its [heaven], for your deeds [of righteousness]."[7]

There were many more figurative narratives to illustrate the same idea of distinct retribution according to moral righteousness:

> The parable of those who reject their Lord is that their works are as ashes on which the wind blows furiously as on a tempestuous day [14: 18].

The lightness and un-substantiality of the ungodly doing is described as ashes, useless rubbish that remains out of the faculties and opportunities that they have misused (by burning them up). The ashes blown about by the wind are envisioned as ungodly works that have no compass, direction, or purpose. The wind that blows the ashes is not ordinary wind. It is the Wrath of God, a furious gale blowing things that have neither internal peace nor external gain. In the scattering of the ashes they lose control even of such things as they might have earned but for their misdeeds. Their whole nature is contaminated. All their wishes go astray. They are carried far, far away from what was on their minds. What did they aim at, and what did they achieve?[8]

The spirit and wisdom of the Qur'an have never been abstract, and were always argued and affirmed with vivid imagery. The Qur'an likens those who worship gods other than Allah to spiders building a web, the spider's house, the flimsiest of houses (29: 41). The horrors of Doomsday are envisioned as the day when every nursing mother will forget her suck-ling-babe, and every pregnant woman will deliver her load. All of mankind is in a drunken riot without drinking (22: 2).

The anthropomorphic style breathes life into every one of the simplest natural phenomena. Dawn is breathing away the darkness (78: 10); the night conceals the sun and veils the day. The wind fecundates and makes the rain fall (15: 22). The sea is likened to ink that, if used and wasted, will not suffice to write the words of God:

> If the ocean were ink with which to write out the words of my Lord, sooner would the ocean be exhausted, even if we added another ocean like it [18: 109].
> If slander is eating another person's flesh, don't speak ill of each other behind their backs, you wouldn't like to eat the flesh of his dead brother, would you? [49: 12].

Qur'anic imagery became a rich source for allusion and citation by writers for generations. When the caliph-poet Ibn al-Mu'tazz (d. 908) wrote his *Kitab al-badf* (*Book of Figures of Speech*) with the purpose of codifying poetic devices, the Qur'an was a principal source for examples of imagery. Qur'anic imagery and allusion appeared not only in religious genres such as poems of asceticism (*zuhdiyyah*) and the inspirational odes of Sufis, but also in the more overtly political poetry, such the odes in praise of the caliphs and their entourages. The quest for forgiveness and the depiction of paradise provide thematic links between the message of the Qur'an and the tradition of love poetry (*ghazal*) that emerged as an independent genre in the early decades of Islam. Early Islamic poets adopted the stock images of love poetry and of wine poetry to provide a symbolic representation of the believer's aspiration for closer contact with the Almighty.[9]

The first human images that Islamic Arabic invented were of the Prophet Muhammad and his community, the Muslims. The revelations of God to Muhammad included a number of different narratives. Some, par-ticularly during the Meccan period, included many rhyming passages replete with colorful imagery that was frequently confused with the dis-course used by soothsayers and other popular preachers. The recording of the revelations in textual form marked the beginning of a lengthy and elab-orate process whereby such a huge amount of information was preserved, sifted, and studied. Among categories of text recorded in this way were some of the earliest samples of Arabic prose.

The oldest and most basic mode by which information was transferred was known in Arabic as the *khabar* (pl. *akhabar*). The distinct characteristic of *akhbar* from the earliest times was that they announce clearly their status as narratives by recording in detail the series of sources through whose mediation the information has become available, working back from the present into the past and finally to the alleged point of origin. This structure (known in Arabic as the *isnad*, "chain of authorities," took a form similar to the following: "X told me that he had heard Y telling a story that he had heard from Z, to the effect that he had been present when the following occurrence happened...." The actual account that follows the chain of authorities is termed the *matn* ("the report itself"). The placing of such information regarding the narrative act and its sources at the beginning of the report is characteristic of a large number of narrative genres in Arabic.

A series of accounts, as much a mirror of the intertribal rivalries of the early stages in the development of the Muslim community as they are a reflection of the spirit of the pre–Islamic era itself, are the *akhbar* known collectively as the *ayyam al-'arab*. These are narratives of the wars and battles in pre–Islamic times when the fighting men of the clan avenged wrongs and resolved their conflicts with other tribes. The War of Basus, for example, set in an atmosphere fraught with tribal rivalries and family tensions, began with the slaying of a prized she-camel and degenerated into a prolonged period of intertribal strife.

Another characteristic mode of expression from the pre–Islamic period was the rhyming utterances of the soothsayers, with terse phraseology and prolific use of parallelism and colorful imagery. This particular style of composition and delivery is found not only in the *sura* (chapters) of the Qur'an but also in a variety of examples of composition from early Islamic history. There were testaments (*wasaya*), proverbs, sermons, and orations (*khutab*). Along with the extant examples of early legal texts, treaties, and the beginnings of official chancery documents, they form part of the recorded legacy of the early period in the development of the Muslim community in the seventh century.

When the third caliph, 'Uthman ibn 'Affan (r. 644–656), declared a single version of the revelations to Muhammad to be the only authorized Qur'an, he may have resolved the issue of the canon of the central source of divine guidance for his community, but there remained numerous other areas of conduct and belief on which the Qur'an was silent. Faced with these many situations, the community resorted to reports on what the Prophet had said and done. By the end of the seventh century it was clear that, in order to disambiguate the sources for the code of belief and behavior for the Muslim community in a number of areas, it was necessary to make a record of the statements and actions of Muhammad during his lifetime. The movement thus set in motion provided Arabic literature with two important types of text that were to have a significant influence on the development of a tradition of prose discourse: the Hadith, a report of a statement by Muhammad on a particular issue or occasion, and the *Sirah,* the record of the Prophet's life.

When the collection of accounts concerning the life and conduct of the Prophet was organized into a hierarchy, the *isnad* segment of each account (described above) now assumed an increased significance. It provided religious scholars with the evidence needed to check the authenticity of a report. The Hadith accounts themselves vary widely in both length and degree of elaboration. Among the lengthier ones were those that elaborated on references found in the Qur'an. The slander Hadith (*hadith al-ifk*), for example, provided considerable detail on the incident in which the Prophet's wife, 'Ahah, the daughter of Abu Bakr (later to become the first caliph), was slandered. The account dwelled on her emotions as the events unfold and on the tensions that inevitably arose between Muhammad and his loyal companion until the entire issue was resolved.

The process of compiling the vast collection of reports that make up the Hadith collections (the second major source on matters of doctrine and behavior, after the Qur'an itself) occurred in several stages, each employing different principles. The first stage (at the end of the seventh century) involved the collection of materials preserved by companions and followers of the Prophet (named *Suhuf,* sing. *Sahfahi*). By the mid–eighth century, collections were being organized by category (*musannaf*). The best-known example is *Al-Muwatta'* by Mālik ibn Anas (d. 770), the founder of one of the four major schools of Islamic law. However, this mode of compiling such a large corpus of materials did not address the increasing problem regarding Hadith of dubious authenticity. By the end of the eighth century, scholars were beginning to pay closer attention to the issues raised by the *isnad*: the type of compilations that they produced, and arranged according to the names of the Prophet's companions (who served as the source of the account), was termed *musnad* (from the same verbal root as *isnad*). One of the most famous examples of this kind of Hadith collection is from another founder of a school of law, Ahmad ibn Hanbal (d. 855), whose *Al-Musnad* consists of some 30,000 Hadith. By the ninth century, the science of Hadith scholarship had refined a critical process that permitted the compilation of the two most famous collections, those of Al-Bukhari (d. 870) and Muslim ibn al-HajJāj (d. 875). The combined collection of their works called *Al-Jami al-sahih* ("authentic or correct collection") was the Hadith that conformed with criteria of the most authenticated reports.[10]

Accounts of Muhammad's life were among the best Arabic writing during the early Islamic period. Under the title *Al-sirah al-nabawiyyah* (*The Biography of the Prophet*) numerous works were compiled. The most famous work to appear under this title was that of Muhammad ibn Ishaq

(704–767?), as edited by Ibn Hisham (d. c. 833). The biography focused on Muhammad's life, with accounts of his contacts with family, companions, and adversaries, descriptions of battles and negotiations, and citations of correspondence. The collections (and segments of larger works) comprised a mixture of anecdotes, battle narratives, miraculous tales, and poetry. Also included were elaboration on incidents, tales concerning the lives of prophets that were mentioned in the Qur'an, and discussion of the genealogy of Arabian tribes.[11]

Arabic biography and history writing went far beyond the achievement of Christian hagiography. Arab writers created a "scientific" foundation of the religious history. In fact, from the "scientific" writing about Muhammad, a secular historiography emerged. The implication of this method went far beyond any writer's expectation. First, it cultivated an identity based on religious belief by creating history for the Muslim community, incorporating all Arabs, Bedouins, and Iranians into one large Muslim community. Second, recording the words of God and his prophet established a hierarchy of words whose authority and binding power were maintained by a legal system.

The writing of the life and teachings of Muhammad marked the beginning of narrative tradition and history writing in the Arabic language. *Ilm ar-Rijal* ("science of biography") emerged and was applied to the codification of the life of the prophet, Muhammad, and then to the lives of the four Rightly Guided Caliphs. The writer had to search for *isnad* to validate stories and events. *Isnad* originally meant support and referred to a list of authorities upon which the narrative was based, and it traced the chain of transmission that led to the written texts. It was like a medieval version of the research footnotes of modern non-fiction writing. The researcher or non-fiction writer had the obligation to look for reliable sources and sort out facts from accusations and bias from evidence. The "science of Hadith" was the process by which Muslim scholars evaluated the source and content of Hadith, the second most important document of Islam. They classified the source of Hadith into *sahih* (correct), *Hasan* (good) and *da'if* (weak) and established the standard of integrity of the writings. This method later applied to various kinds of research and writing and came to be called "science of biography," "science of hadith" and "Isnad" (chain of transmission).[12]

History writing reached its greatest scholarly level in the hands of Ibn Khaldun (1332–1406), who has been considered the forerunner of modern historiography and sociology. The study of Ibn Khaldun's life and the chronology of his writings illustrate the steady widening of Arabic language, perspective and worldview. He wrote his first book at the age of nineteen. *Lubabu l-Muhassal,* a commentary on the Islamic theology of Fakhr al-Din al-Razi, was written under the supervision of his Tunisian teacher. His book on Sufism, *Sifa'u l-Sa'il,* was written around 1373 in Fes, Morocco. While at the court of Muhammad V, sultan of Granada, Ibn Khaldun composed a work on logic, *'allaqa li-l-Sultan.* So far, his writing career did not show any difference from that of a traditional Muslim scholar of his time. His writing on history started out as a history of Berbers with a long title, *Book of Lessons, Record of Beginnings and Events in the History of the Arabs and Berbers and Their Powerful Contemporaries.* It contained two volumes of detailed history of the Berber peoples and the Maghreb based on his own research and observation. However, by the time he completed the book, it became a "universal history," which consisted of seven volumes. The first volume, *Muqaddimah* (*Introduction*), was a book of historiography. It can also read as a book of sociology as it deals with politics, urban life, economics, and knowledge.

As he was writing himself out of the rigid domain of history (as past facts), Ibn Khaldun went out on a tangent about some of his most original observations about human conditions. *'Asabiyyah* was the new concept that Ibn Khaldun coined to describe the group solidarity underlying social and political behavior. He illustrated how kinship feelings, which could be intensified and enlarged by a political and religious ideology, drove social and political changes. This feeling of belonging could carry a social group to power but also undermine it when this feeling of belonging shifted, replacing an old establishment with a new group. Civilization rose and declined in the same fashion, according to Ibn Khaldun. When a society became a great civilization (the dominant culture in its region), its high point was followed by a period of decay. This means that the next cohesive group that conquered the diminished civilization was, by comparison, a group of barbarians. Once the barbarians solidified their control over the conquered society, they became attracted to the more refined aspects of the conquered civilization, such as literacy and arts. They learned to appropriate such cultural practices and became assimilated by them. Eventually, the former barbarians were conquered by a new set of barbarians, who repeated the process.

Ibn Khaldun refined the scientific method of history writing several centuries before the modern concept of historiography ever emerged, and he also coined his specific terminology for this "new science" of history. He was also the first scholar to articulate the role of the state and its politics and ideologies in imposing bias upon historical writing. He was the first scholar to recognize the historical distance between the time in which history occurred and the time in which it was written, and he proposed a critical standing towards historical data. Based on this critical distance, he promoted critical study of historical records and necessary rules for truth comparison.[13]

However, to identify Ibn Khaldun's idea of historiography as social science is a mistake, as modern social science ignores the linguistic and cultural distinctions between Arabic and English or German. The Arabic concept of science, *'alm*, inherited different connotations from those of modern sciences. First of all, Arabic science within the context of medieval Islamic civilization was distinct but not contrary to religion. In Medieval Arabic, history was a philosophical science, a method to study the past. The distance that Ibn Khaldun created in Arabic was much narrower or shallower than the gap that exists in German or English between history (science) and religion, a conceptual gap that has existed in Western Europe and North America since the Enlightenment. Ibn Khaldun's science of history was more scientific only in comparison to the uncritical acceptance of historical data when history was written and read. In other words, to recognize the distance between culture and political conditions of history as it occurred and the history that was being written did not lead to the English concept of objectivity of modern social science. Ibn Khaldun recognized the limitations of historians without claiming universal validity for his own words, as do the modern social sciences. Ibn Khaldun still believed his God, while modern historians are playing God in the name of "objectivity."

What Ibn Khaldun proposed in his writing was to abstract rational principles and underlying logic from historical phenomena. He did not stop at knowing what had happened but was also interested in why it happened. Through comparison of data, he made original observations about the historical role of state, communication, propaganda and systematic bias. It can be regarded as the earliest attempt made by any historian to discover a pattern in the changes that occur in man's political and social organization. Rational in its approach, analytical in its method, encyclopedic in detail, it represented an almost complete departure from traditional historiography, discarding conventional concepts and clichés and seeking, beyond the mere chronicle of events, an explanation, and hence a philosophy of history.[14]

Abstraction of language and deepening of observation and logical thinking did not occur in history writing alone. It was more prominent in the field of Islamic law and jurisprudence. Islamic law did not become a legal system, in the modern sense of the word, until many years after Muhammad's death. Qur'anic messages that contained legal matters were confusing and fragmentary at the best. Another reason why the Qur'an alone could not be used as a code of law was that its language was too terse and sometimes abrupt; it did not deliver a clear line of thought and argument, a very important aspect of legal presentation.

Sharia (Islamic law) was gradually cultivated by the writings of Islamic scholars during the early centuries of Islam. As divine expression, the specific rulings of *Sharia* had to derive from the exact wordings of either the Qur'an or the Hadith and constituted a system of duties that are incumbent upon a Muslim by virtue of his religious belief. Islamic law covered all aspects of life, from stately matters such as politics and foreign relations to many issues of daily living. The Qur'an and *Sunnah* contained laws of inheritance, marriage, and restitution for injuries and murder, and defined punishments for five specific crimes: unlawful intercourse, false accusation of unlawful intercourse, consumption of alcohol, theft, and highway robbery. There were rules for fasting, charity, and prayer. However, these prescriptions and prohibitions were described in broad and general terms, and when applied to specific legal cases, their precise wording and lack of flexibility made it a challenge to adopt to practical variations. Islamic scholars spent centuries to elaborate systems of law on the basis of these rules and their interpretations.[15]

The consequence of centuries of scholarly writing in order to classify, elaborate, and interpret Qur'anic rulings was legal Arabic, distinct from the languages of poetry and prose. Clarity was the main achievement of legal Arabic, which tightened conceptual boundaries between words and their associations. It began with making necessary distinctions by defining the exact meaning of a word, then safeguarding the boundary by excluding the possibility of contamination and fluidity of meaning. To eliminate overlapping words, legal Arabic established conceptual boundaries and specific relationships among similar words. To exclude verbal contradictions, it built a hierarchy that granted certain words more arbitrary and overriding capacity. With these changes, Islamic legal theorists took Islamic law from a collection of sporadic rules found in religious texts to a coherent system specific enough to draw judgment and flexible enough to adopt complex legal practice. According to Islamic legal theory, law had four fundamental roots which were given precedence in the following order: the Qur'an, the *Sunnah* (the practice of Muhammad), the consensus of the Muslim jurists (*ijma*), and analogical reasoning (*qiyas*).[16]

As the Qur'an and Hadith were silent about some important issues, Muslim jurists (*fuqaha*) attempted to arrive at legal conclusions by other means. For example, Sunni jurists accepted and used analogy (*qiyas*) and historical consensus of the community (*ijma*) as rules of law. The rulings that were produced through these additional methods constituted a wider array of law than the *Sharia*, and they were called *fiqh*. *Fiqh* covered two main areas, rules concerning actions (*'amaliyya*) and those concerning the circumstances surrounding actions (wadia'). Unlike rulings of the *Sharia, fiqh* was not regarded as sacred, and the schools of thought have different views on its details, without viewing other conclusions as sacrilegious. This division of interpretation in more detailed issues formed different schools of legal thought (*adh'hab*). Each school had its distinct ideas and interpretations of law and was further divided into several areas built into another hierarchy according to degrees of certainty obligations (*fardh*), recommendation (*mustahabb*), permissions (*mubah*), disrecommendation (*makrooh*), and prohibition (*haraam*). The rules concerning the circumstances comprised: condition (*shart*), cause (*sabab*), preventer (*mani*), permitted/enforced (*rukhsah, azeemah*), valid/corrupt/invalid (*sahih, faasid, batil*) and on time/debt/repeat (*adaa, qadaa, i'ada*).

There were also different approaches to the methodology used in *fiqh* to derive law from the Islamic sources. The main accepted Sunni schools were Hanafi, Maliki, Shafi'I, and Hanbali. The *Shi'a fiqh* was called *Jafari figh* (also called the twelver), and there were many minor schools of law. Each school of thought had its place in legal history because it contributed to the general repertoire of legal language. Although the importance and the degrees of influence of these ideas varied from time to time, the combination (not exclusion) of these became the ultimate source of future laws.[17]

As legal Arabic explored the principles of Islamic law, another branch of Arabic began to explore the coherence and logic of the world and beyond. The first Muslim scholar in this pursuit was Al-Kindi (801–873). Unlike Islamic jurisprudence, which was deeply rooted in Arabic and pre–Islamic customary law, Arabic philosophy had great input from Greek. Arabic philosophy began with where Greek philosophers ended and went far beyond. Al-Kindi's first task was to oversee the translation of Greek philosophical works into Arabic, a mission supported by the House of Wisdom, an institute of translation and learning patronized by the Abbasid Caliphs. Through translation, he built a complete arsenal of philosophical vocabulary by borrowing from the Greeks. This philosophical vocabulary in standard Arabic was instrumental for the later development of Arab philosophy without which the work of philosophers such as Al-Farabi, Avicenna, and Al-Ghazali might not have been possible.[18]

Although Greek philosophical language provided clarity and precision that formative Arabic needed, it was a struggle for Al-Kindi to reconcile two different languages with various conceptual boundaries. Greek philosophical terms were less fluid and tighter than those of Arabic, such as for some crucial concepts of philosophy (reason, philosophy, and its relationship with religion). Although his philosophy was not always original, and was even considered clumsy by some, he successfully established a dialogue between two languages and philosophical traditions and incorporated Aristotelian and neo–Platonist thought into an Islamic philosophical framework. This dialogue continued for the next centuries between two distinct philosophical traditions, until it became heated debate as they moved further away from each other. However, Al-Kindi provided the linguistic bridge that made the debate and controversy possible.[19]

When Arabic encountered Greek, it was possible to think as Al-Kindi, who believed that prophecy and philosophy were two different paths to truth. He described the difference between philosopher and prophet in an interesting way. The philosopher had to endure a long period of training and meditation to arrive at the truth in his own mind, while the prophet had God to reveal the truth to him. Bestowed by God, divine prophecy was more clear and comprehensive, so the prophet had a better ability to express the truth to ordinary people than did the philosopher. Al-Kindi might sound overly simplified and naïve to modern ears, but his writings reflected the linguistic distinctiveness of Arabic and Greek of the ninth century. In Arabic, universal truth (as perceived in philosophical Greek) was one and the same as it was recorded in the Qur'an and *Sunnah*. At the time, Arabic had yet to cultivate an abstract and specialized language for philosophers. So knowledge and reasoning were called wisdom and could be taught and conveyed to any who listened and read.[20]

This situation changed after the generation of Al-Kindi, when Arabic developed its philosophical language based on the debate between *Falsafa* (philosophy in Arabic) and *Kalam* (theological dialectic). They both cultivated specialized language for philosophical and theological discourses, as did the scholars of jurisprudence, who had their own language distinct from that of legal practitioners. However, the language of early philosophers laid a conceptual foundation upon which philosophy and theology could interact, dispute and influence one another. For example, Al-Kindi adopted a naturalistic view of prophetic vision, arguing that, through the faculty of imagination as conceived in Aristotelian philosophy, certain pure and well-prepared souls were able to receive information about future events. He did not attribute such vision to revelation from God, but instead explained that imagination enabled a man with a purified soul to receive divine vision. Gray areas or inconsistencies such as this became the field wherein constant philosophical debate in Arabic germinated, thus continuing the effort of classification and clarification.

While Al-Kindi attempted to mediate Greek and Arabic philosophical thinking, Al-Farabi (872–950) spent his life pursuing the unification of theory and practice, and philosophy and religion. Despite his contribution to many different philosophical disciplines and traditions, Al-Farabi was a more coherent philosopher than Al-Kindi was. His great service to Islamic philosophy was to continue Al-Kindi's work and illustrate how Greek philosophy could be adopted to answer questions that still puzzled Muslims. He had the vision to realize that philosophy had ended in other parts of the world but had a real chance for new life in Islam. He was a step ahead of Al-Kindi in believing that the religion of Islam needed a philosophy because human reason was superior to revelation. He had nothing against divine truth but based his argument upon the various ways in which religion and philosophy could both communicate truth. Religion provided truth in a symbolic form to non-philosophers who were not able to comprehend pure philosophy.

Al-Farabi's writing was mainly devoted to politics and state order. Like Plato, he believed that a philosopher, the most perfect kind of man, should rule the state, leaving God to rule the universe. He believed that the contemporary political upheavals were due to the absence of a philosopher leader. However, in contrast to Plato's philosopher-king, he believed that the best state should be ruled by the prophet-imam.[21]

By the time of Ibn Sina (Avicenna, 980–1037), philosophical Arabic had evolved to a point where religion and philosophy could be combined into a coherent and comprehensive system. The philosophy of Ibn Sina, one of the most significant philosophers in the Islamic tradition and arguably the most influential philosopher of the pre-modern world, created a space for God in philosophy as the Necessary Existence. This argument provided the foundation for his theories of soul, intellect and cosmos. He was the first Islamic philosopher to refuse to apologize for his attempt to forge peace between philosophy and religion. He rejected Neoplatonic epistemology and the theory of pre-existent soul, although he adopted some key aspects such as an emanationist cosmology. Avicennan metaphysics became the foundation for discussions of Islamic philosophy and philosophical theology.

Ibn Sina wrote extensively on early Islamic philosophy, especially the subjects of logic, ethics, and metaphysics. Most of his works were written in Arabic, the de facto scientific language of the time in the Middle East, and some were written in the Persian. Ibn Sina's commentaries often corrected Aristotle, encouraging a lively debate in the spirit of *ijtihad* (personal effort to make decision). With Avicenna's successful reconciliation of Aristotelianism and Neoplatonism along with Kalam, Avicennism eventually became the leading school of Islamic philosophy by the 12th century. Ibn Sina became a dominant central authority on Islamic philosophy.[22]

His idea of the nature of the soul and the distinction between existence and essence became very influential in medieval Europe because it was the same issue that troubled Christian minds for centuries. Arabic was the only language at the time that possessed the degree of maturity and subtlety to construct a conceptual unity by leveling the gap between the divine and the human. These were the same issues European scholars wrestled with for centuries because of the linguistic re-orientations (Hebrew, Greek, Latin, and European vernaculars). Ibn Sina's psychology and theory of knowledge influenced William of Auvergne, bishop of Paris, and Albertus Magnus, while his metaphysics had an impact on the thought of Thomas Aquinas. However, his increasing influence appeared to be in modern times when the West began to pursue the knowledge of human psychology.[23]

Linguistic subtlety eventually made it possible for Islamic philosophy to surpass the Greek tradition of speculate thinking through the writings of Al-Ghazali (1058–1111) and Ibn Rushd (Averroes, 1126–1198). The Arabic in which Al-Ghazali and Ibn Rushd wrote was different from that of Al-Kindi and Al-Farabi, as Arabic concepts had completely replaced Greek concepts and connotations in philosophical, scientific and legal writing. Philosophical Arabic differed from philosophical Greek (and French, German and English during the modern period) in the following ways. First, it became a philosophical and scientific mode of expression, but was not totally uprooted from concrete, metaphorical and poetic idioms. For example, the language of philosophers had departed from literary and religious expression, especially compared to that of Al-Kindi's time. However, it still shared many concepts and connotations with the language of religion and poetry from which Arabic originally derived. Second, because of the shared repertoire of verbal resources, religious, scientific, and philosophical arguments often went back and forth among these disciplines without apology. Third, Arabic, a mature and diverse literary tradition, had the capacity to explore deeper human thoughts and emotions. This was not possible in the languages of Western Europe until modern times. In this specific sense, while the West discovered psychology in the early modern period, Arabic had been depicting and exploring the inner being of humanity for centuries.

The implication of these linguistic differences did not lead to the construction of an Arabic philosophy distinct from Greek philosophy. Rather, it became a discourse and ongoing debate among different schools of thought in Arabic whose arguments, based on various shades of meaning and connotations, derived from the Greek that had been constantly redefined in Arabic. In other words, the Arabic discourse had less and less to do with Greek philosophy than with the evolution of philosophical, religious, and legal Arabic. Islamic philosophy had completely assimilated Greek philosophy and integrated the latter into the Arabic discourse of *kalam* and Islamic theology.[24]

Al-Ghazali's book *The Incoherence of the Philosophers* (*Tahafut al-Falasifa*) marked a major transition in Islamic philosophy, bringing to a head the conflict between *kalam* (speculative theology) and *falsafa* (philosophy). He condemned certain Arab philosophers who had been so impressed by "high sounding names such as Socrates, Hippocrates, Plato, Aristotle and their likes" that they became imitators of Greek philosophy. Without thoughts of their own, these philosophers used Greek philosophy to rationalize their disregard for the rituals and obligations of their Islamic belief. *Tahafut* was to illustrate the incoherence of the philosopher's beliefs and the contradictions of their metaphysical statements.

However, Al-Ghazali's discourse was not a philosophical one between religion and natural philosophy as it was in Western Europe during early modern period. The discourse in Arabic was about the definition of philosophy and the connotation of God as pre-existing eternally. Arabic theologians, even the most conservative, were not against science, because the Arabic notion of philosophy included scientific principles, such as those of mathematics, astronomical science and logic. In fact, Al-Ghazali, while discussing astronomy, firmly expressed his support for a scientific methodology based on demonstration and mathematics. After describing the scientific facts of the solar eclipse resulting from the Moon coming between the Sun and Earth and the lunar eclipse resulting from the Earth coming between the Sun and Moon, he wrote: "Whosoever thought that to engage in a disputation for refuting such a [scientific] theory was a religious duty would harm religion and weakens it. For these [scientific] matters that were rested on demonstrations, geometrical and arithmetical, left no room for doubt." Therefore, in his mind, it was fatal for religion to fight against science, and religion should leave experimental science alone.

His quarrel with philosophy was a philosophical statement in Arabic that was contrary to Islamic doctrine as it claimed that the world was eternal (as it went against God's will and act of creation). He pointed out that philosophers could not demonstrate the creation of the world by God, or the spiritual substance of the human soul. In particular, he argued that philosophers become infidels on three issues: the eternity of the world, the impossibility of God's knowledge of particulars, and the denial of bodily resurrection and mortality of the individual souls. Al-Ghazali stressed the fact that it was God who created the linkage among the phenomena. In God there was an Essence (*haqiqah*), and this Essence was equivalent to his Existence, namely that God was free from non-being and privation.

God was able to overturn the rules of natural eventualities and submitted the functioning of nature to completely new laws.[25]

Al-Ghazali found his logical certainty in God; his opponent, Ibn Rushd, found his in philosophy. Their discourse followed the traditional Arabic method of debate by challenging and redefining the meanings of the basic concepts in order to achieve logical consistency. Ibn Rushd's most important original philosophical work was *The Incoherence of the Incoherence* (*Tahafut al-tahafut*), in which he defended Aristotelian philosophy against Al-Ghazali's claims in his *The Incoherence of the Philosophers* (*Tahafut al-falasifa*). Al-Ghazali argued that Aristotelianism, especially as presented in the writings of Ibn Sina, was self-contradictory and an affront to the teachings of Islam. Ibn Rushd's rebuttal was a two-part argument. First, Ibn Sina's interpretation of Aristotle departed from the original meaning of the Greek philosophy, and therefore, second, Al-Ghazali's arguments were mistaken because he was aiming at the wrong target.

Like most Arabic philosophers, Ibn Rushd's works were spread over 20,000 pages covering a variety of different subjects, including early Islamic philosophy, logic in philosophy, medicine, mathematics, astronomy, Arabic grammar and Islamic theology, law, and jurisprudence. He wrote commentaries on most of the surviving works of Aristotle; however, these were based not on Greek originals, but rather on Arabic translations. This could be the reason for Ibn Rushd's free reinterpretation of many Aristotle ideas: he was not restrained by the boundaries of the Greek originals. He offered some new interpretations of philosophy, law and physics. He turned Aristotelian ideas into an Arabic enterprise. Ibn Rushd completely redefined Aristotle's philosophy by making him speak Arabic. Like Al-Ghazali, who forced philosophers admit that their concept of God was contrary to that of Islam, Ibn Rushd reinterpreted Aristotle by putting his own words into Aristotle's mouth. For Arab philosophers, agreement and disagreement were employed in philosophical discourse to create intriguing works of language.[26]

The debate between Al-Ghazali and Ibn Rushd happened to take place during the last few generations before philosophy as a discipline completely disappeared from Islamic discourse. The fact that Al-Ghazali's ideas became the mainstream for Islamic theology while philosophy declined used to be interpreted as the victory of religion (of Islam) over Greek or Western philosophy. In fact, the victory of Islam lies in Arabic literary language, which had the capacity to assimilate Greek philosophical terms and integrated them into Arabic rational thinking. Religious thought became rationalized and philosophized. This process of assimilation was quite similar to Latin philosophy during the later Middle Ages, when philosophy could not be distinguished from Christian theology. By the same token, modern Islamic philosophy never evolved into an independent thought (without the entanglement with religion or politics), contrary to the relatively clear divisions between religion and philosophy, religion and science in Western Europe.[27]

The distinct path through which Islamic thinking traveled was determined by its medium, literary Arabic, which carried a religious evolution and scientific revolution without the linguistic reorientation that occurred in Western Europe. During linguistic reorientation, religion used its own language (Latin) for centuries. The languages of science and religion were influenced by many vernaculars throughout Europe. Without the re-orientation, Arabic speculative thinking evolved sharing a common repertoire of words and basic assumptions with traditional religious thought. Emerging as a branch of theology, rationalism in many ways could not separate itself or make a clean break from the mainstream theology.

The rationalization of Islamic thought began before the introduction of Greek philosophical terms and ideas. As the rationalization of ideas often came after verbal classification, the development of Islamic philosophy was well underway when Greek philosophy began to be translated. Greek input accelerated (rather than caused) the existing rational tendency in Islam. The first systematic attempt to build a rational foundation of Islam was made by the Mu'tazilah school, a speculative theology that emerged during Umayyad and flourished in the cities of Basra and Baghdad during the 8th to 10th centuries. The adherents of the Mu'tazili school are best known for their assertion that, because of the perfect unity and eternal nature of Allah, the Qur'an must therefore have been created, as it could not be co-eternal with God. From this premise, the Mu'tazili school of Kalam proceeded to posit that the injunctions of God were accessible to rational thought and inquiry because knowledge was derived from reason, and reason was the final arbiter in distinguishing right from wrong. Therefore, sacred precedent was not an effective means of determining what was just, as what was obligatory in religion was only obligatory by virtue of reason.[28]

The emergence of the Mu'tazilis movement reflected the ways in which Islamic ideas took their original form. Meditation on words, first the words of the Qur'an and words of Hadith, then interpretations of the sacred texts by leading intellectuals, generated volumes of reasoning. In a way, Arabic *Kalam* (speech, word) had much wider and more active connotation than the word as used in Greek philosophical tradition because it meant more than word as written or divinely given. It also meant a continued argumentation that could generate more words and more diverse reasoning. In the views of early Mu'tazilis, the speech of God and that of man came from the same genus as human speech. At the time, there was not any separation or unbridgeable gap between the words of God and those of man. The difference between the divine and human speech was defined by 'Abd al-Jabbar's (935–1025) argument that acting immorally or unwisely stems from need and deficiency. One acts in a repugnant way when one does not know the ugliness of one's deeds because of a lack of knowledge, or when one knows, but has some material or psychological need. Since God is absolutely self-sufficient (from the cosmological "proof" of His existence), all-knowing, and all-powerful, He is categorically free from any type of need and, consequently, He never does anything that is ridiculous, unwise, ugly, or evil.[29]

The Mu'tazilis had a theory regarding reason, divine revelation, and the relationship between them based on arguments about speech. They celebrated the power of reason and human intellectual power. To them, it was the human intellect that guided a man to know God, His attributes, and the very basics of morality. Once this foundational knowledge was attained and one ascertained the truth of Islam and the divine origins of the Qur'an, the intellect then interacted with scripture such that both reason and revelation would come together to be the main source of guidance and knowledge for believers.[30]

'Abd al-Jabbar's student Al-Ash'ari (d. A.D. 935), the head of the Basran school of Mu'tazilis rebelled against Mu'tazila. In taking this step he capitalized on popular discontent with the excessive rationalism of the Mu'tazilites, which had been steadily gaining ground since their loss of official patronage half a century earlier. After his conversion, Al-Ash'ari continued to use the dialectic method in theology but insisted that reason must be subservient to revelation. It is not possible to discuss Al-Ash'ari's successors in detail here, but it should be noted that from the second half of the twelfth century onwards, the movement adopted the language and concepts of the Islamic philosophers whose views they sought to refute. Ash'arite's separation between the eternal speech of God and the created words of the Qur'an was the earliest attempt to set up a barrier between God's will and human knowledgeability of it, which later germinated into Islamic mysticism championed by some of the most significant thinkers of the later Ash'arites, such as Al-Ghazali and Fakhr al-Din al-Razi (1149–1209).[31]

The mystic turn of Islamic theology was not contrary to the development of Islamic science because it was actually conditioned by the cultivation of the established linguistic capacity in Arabic. One of the important linguistic differences between Arabic and Latin was Arabic's increasing repertoire of concrete (non-abstract) and technical vocabulary. This did occur in Europe but in vernaculars, such as French, English and Italian, rather than Latin. The language of observation, description, and experiment that was conceptually connected to abstract language of theories provided the linguistic foundation of scientific method; empirical, experimental science; and quantitative research.

Arabic produced a scientific revolution several centuries before Western Europe. Most importantly, Arabic science expanded simultaneously in both theory and practice. There was a gap of centuries between Greek scientific theories and European experiment. Between the 8th and 13th centuries, science was practiced on a unprecedented scale.[32]

Like the European science of the early modern period, Muslim science derived from curiosity and study of religion, and the problems that presented in Qur'anic script. For example, Al-Hasan ibn al-Haytham (Alhazen, 965–1040), who made significant contributions to physics, optics and mathematics, was a devout Muslim. For him, the pursuit of God and the true knowledge of science were one and the same. Based on his Islamic faith, he doubted and criticized the findings of Greek science. In his *Al-Shukūk 'alā Batlamyūs* (*Doubts Concerning Ptolemy*), Alhazen criticized many of Ptolemy's works, including the *Almagest*, *Planetary Hypotheses*, and *Optics*, pointing out various contradictions he found in these works. He considered that some of the mathematical devices Ptolemy introduced into astronomy, especially the equant, failed to satisfy the physical requirement of uniform circular motion, and wrote a scathing critique of the physical reality of Ptolemy's astronomical system, noting the absurdity of relating actual physical motions to imaginary mathematical points, lines and circles. Alhazen criticized Ptolemy's model on empirical, observational and experimental grounds by saying that if a man were to imagine a circle in the heavens with planets moving in it, this did not cause the specific motion of the planets.[33]

The reason Arab scientists could override Greek science lay in their ability to demonstrate their theories, observe further detail and adjust their theories accordingly. Alhazen was among the first scientists to pioneer quantitative research as experiment, and he helped shift the emphasis from abstract theorizing to systematic and repeatable experimentation, followed by careful criticism of premises and inferences. As Alhazen put it, God did not prevent the scientist from error and had not safeguarded science from man's shortcomings and faults. Therefore, religion for the Muslims was a general inspiration that set up the goals of their inquiries and motivated their efforts. But scientists still had to work hard to reveal the endless secrets of the world that God had created. For example, it is known that certain advances made by medieval Muslim astronomers, geographers and mathematicians were motivated by problems presented in Islamic scripture. Examples are Al-Khwarizmi's (780–850) development of algebra in order to solve Islamic inheritance laws; and developments in astronomy, geography, spherical geometry and spherical trigonometry in order to determine the direction of the Qibla, the times of Salah prayers, and the dates of the Islamic calendar.[34]

The increased use of dissection in Islamic medicine during the 12th and 13th centuries was influenced by the writings of the Islamic theologian Al-Ghazali, who encouraged the study of anatomy and the use of dissections as a method of gaining knowledge of God's creation. In Al-Bukhari's and Muslim's collection of *sahih* Hadith it is said: "There is no disease that Allah has created, except that He also has created its treatment" (7–71:582). This culminated in the work of Ibn al-Nafis (1213–1288), who discovered pulmonary circulation in 1242 and used his discovery as evidence for the orthodox Islamic doctrine of bodily resurrection. Ibn al-Nafis also used Islamic scripture as justification for his rejection of wine as self-medication. Criticisms against alchemy and astrology were also motivated by religion, as orthodox Islamic theologians viewed the beliefs of alchemists and astrologers as superstitious.[35]

Fakhr al-Din al-Razi (1149–1209) redefined the conception of physics and the physical world and opened the door for a new Islamic cosmology. He criticized the Aristotelian geocentric notion of the Earth's centrality within the universe, and explored the concept of the existence of a multi-universe. His theory was based on the Qur'anic verse, "All praise belongs to God, Lord of the Worlds."

> It is established by evidence that beyond this world there was a void without a terminal limit [*khala' la nihayata laha*]. It had been established and validated that God Most High had power over all contingent beings [*al-mumkinat*]. Therefore He had the power [*qadir*] to create worlds beyond this world. Each one of those worlds was bigger than this world; it had the same things that this world had: the throne [*al-arsh*], the chair [*al-kursiyy*], the heavens [*al-samawat*], the earth [*al-ard*], the sun [*al-shams*] and the moon [*al-qamar*].

He pointed out that the arguments of the philosophers who believed in the uniqueness of this world were weak and flimsy arguments founded upon feeble premises.

This criticism arose from Fakhr al-Din's affirmation of atomism, as advocated by the Ash'ari school of Islamic theology, which entailed the existence of vacant space in which the atoms move, combine and separate. He discussed more extensively the issue of the void, the empty spaces between stars and constellations in the universe, which contained very few or no stars. He argued that there was an infinite outer space beyond the known world, and that God had the power to fill the vacuum with an infinite number of universes.[36]

Cosmology was studied comprehensively in the Muslim world. There are exactly seven verses in the Qur'an that specify that there are seven heavens. One verse says that each heaven or sky has its own order (law). Another verse mentioned similar earths with the seven heavens.

Astronomy was one of the oldest sciences that had been practiced in ancient Mesopotamia. Unlike the Babylonians, Greeks, and Indians, who had developed elaborate systems of mathematical astronomical study, the pre–Islamic Arabs relied entirely on empirical observations. These observations were based on the rising and setting of particular stars. This area of astronomical study was known as *anwa*. *Anwa* continued to be developed by the Arabs after Islam. Islamic astronomers added mathematical methods to their empirical observations.[37]

The rise of Islam and the need to accurately locate the *qibla* (direction to Makkah) inspired more study in astronomy. Arab scientists had researched the subject since the early half of the eighth century. They began with the assimilation and consolidation of earlier Hellenistic, Indian and Sassanid astronomical findings. The first astronomical texts that were translated into Arabic were from India and Persia. The most notable of the texts was *Zij al-Sindhind*, an 8th-century Indian astronomical work that was written under the supervision of an Indian astronomer who visited the court of caliph Al-Mansur in 770. Another translated text was the *Zij al-Shah*, a collection of astronomical tables (based on Indian parameters) compiled in Sassanid Persia over two centuries. Fragments of texts from this period indicate that Arabs adopted the sine function (inherited from India) in place of the chords of arc used in Greek trigonometry.[38]

Before Arab scholars invented their own astronomical theory, the Ptolemaic system was accepted and contributed to the development of Arabic investigation. The first major Muslim work of astronomy was *Zij al-Sindhind* by Al-Khwarizmi (780–850), a Persian mathematician, astronomer and geographer who was a scholar in the House of Wisdom in Baghdad. The work contained tables for the movements of the sun, the moon and the five planets known at the time. The work was significant as it introduced Ptolemaic concepts into Islamic sciences. This work also marked a turning point in Islamic astronomy. Ever since, Muslim astronomers adopted an approach primarily based on research, translating works of others and learning already-discovered knowledge. Al-Khwarizmi's work marked the beginning of nontraditional methods of astronomical study and calculations.

In 850, Al-Farghani (9th century) wrote *Kitab fi Jawani* (*A Compendium of the Science of Stars*). While giving a primary summary of Ptolemic cosmography the book also corrected Ptolemy based on findings of earlier Arab astronomers. Al-Farghani provided revised values for the obliquity of the ecliptic, the processional movement of the apogees of the sun and the moon, and the circumference of the earth. This was probably the first attempt since the time of Eratosthenes (276–194 B.C.) to measure the length of a degree. Although there are no surviving eyewitness accounts of the experiment, later sources have shown how it was conducted. Two locations were identified whose latitudes, determined astronomically, differed by one degree. A north-south baseline connecting them was carefully laid out by sighting along pegs, and the length of that baseline was measured. In the experiment in which Al-Farghani took part, two pairs of locations were actually chosen, one pair in northern Iraq, on the plain of Sinjar, and the other near Kufah. These areas appeared to be as flat and featureless as possible. The results were then compared, and the length of a degree established as 56⅔ miles. Al-Farghani subsequently wrote a thin yet very influential book on astronomy; a number of copies of this Arabic text survive. The title was *Compendium of the Science of the Stars and Celestial Motions*. This book was twice translated into Latin in Spain during the Middle Ages, was widely circulated in Europe and remained a standard authority almost to the time of Galileo; it was first printed in 1493, the same year that Columbus returned from his first voyage.[39]

During the period between 825 and 1025 a distinctive Arabic system of astronomy flourished. The period began as the Muslim astronomers began questioning the framework of the Ptolemaic system of astronomy. These criticisms, however, remained within the geocentric framework and followed Ptolemy's astronomical paradigm. This effort has been described as "a reformist project intended to consolidate Ptolemaic astronomy by bringing it into line with its own principles."[40] Between 1025 and 1028, Ibn al-Haytham wrote his *Al-Shuku ala Batlamyus* (*Doubts on Ptolemy*). While maintaining the physical reality of the geocentric model, he criticized elements of the Ptolemaic models. Many astronomers took up the challenge posed in this work, to develop alternate models that resolved these difficulties. In 1070, Abu Ubayd al-Jūzjānī (980–1037), a student of Ibn Sīnā, published *Tarik al-Aflak* (*The Arrangement of the Spheres*). Jūzjānī expressed his abiding interest in astronomy and his difficulty in comprehending the equant and the components of motion in latitude (inclination, twisting, and slant of the epicycle). He turned to Ibn Sīnā for guidance and was told: "I came to understand the problem after great effort and much toil and I will not teach it to anybody. Apply yourself to it and it may be revealed to you as it was revealed to me." Jūzjānī was skeptical of Ibn Sīnā's claim, for he states: "I suspect I was the first to achieve an understanding of these problems." Jūzjānī's issue with the equant was that "we know that the motions of celestial bodies cannot be nonuniform, so that they are at times faster and at times slower. Jūzjānī proposed to solve the equant problem with a model in which all spheres (the deferent, the epicycle, and a secondary epicycle) moved at uniform speeds around their centers. However, the model is unworkable.

The significance of Jūzjānī's critique of the equant lay not in his unworkable solution but rather in the fact that his contribution was independent of the critique of the equant in the work of his elder contemporary Ibn al-Haytham. These represented the earliest known critiques of Ptolemy's equant hypothesis, which ultimately led to alternative models formulated by Naṣīr al-Dīn al-Ṭūsī and others (sometimes referred to as the Marāgha School) regarding planetary motion that did not resort to the equant. While Ibn al-Haytham's critique seems to have been more influential, the Marāgha astronomers were aware of Jūzjānī's contribution. There had been widespread discussion about the same issues that troubled Jūzjānī among Arabic scholars on both sides of Mediterranean.[41]

Ibn Ahmad al-Biruni (973–1048) was regarded as one of the greatest scholars of the medieval Islamic era and was well-versed in physics, mathematics, and astronomy. He wrote 95 books about astronomy, representing more than a half of his lifetime's work. Biruni wrote an extensive commentary on Indian astronomy in the *Kitab ta'rikh al-Hind* (*The History of India*) in which he claims to have resolved the matter of Earth's rotation in his work *Miftah-ilm-alhai'a* (*The Key to Astronomy*), which did not survive. Biruni repeatedly attacked Aristotle's celestial physics: he argued by simple experiment that vacuum must exist. He was amazed by the weakness of Aristotle's argument against elliptical orbits on the basis that they would have created vacuum. In his major extant astronomical work, the *Mas'ud Canon*, he regards heliocentric and geocentric hypotheses as mathematically equivalent but heliocentrism as physically impossible. Yet he approved the theory that the earth rotated on its axis. He utilized his observational data to disprove Ptolemy's immobile solar apogee. More recently, Biruni's eclipse data was used by Dunthorne in 1749 to help determine the acceleration of the moon, and his observational data has entered the larger astronomical historical record and is still used today in geophysics and astronomy.[42]

Muslims also combined the disciplines of medicine and astrology by linking the curative properties of herbs with specific zodiacal signs and planets. Mars, for instance, was considered hot and dry and so ruled plants with a hot or pungent taste, such as hellebore, tobacco and mustard. These beliefs were adopted by European herbalists such as Culpeper right up until the development of modern medicine. They also developed a system called Arabic parts, by which the difference between the ascendant and each planet of the zodiac was calculated. This new position then became a "part" of some kind. For example, the "part of fortune" is found by taking the difference between the sun and the ascendant and adding it to the moon. If the "part" thus calculated was in the 10th House in Libra, for instance, it suggested that money could be made from some kind of partnership.[43]

Another notable astrologer and astronomer was Qutb al-Din al Shirazi (1236–1311). He wrote critiques of Ptolemy's *Almagest* and produced two prominent works on astronomy: *The Limit of Accomplishment Concerning Knowledge of the Heavens* in 1281 and *The Royal Present* in 1284, both of which commented upon and improved on Ptolemy's work, particularly in the field of planetary motion. Al-Shirazi was also the first person to give the correct scientific explanation for the formation of a rainbow.

Mathematics was another area of Arabic scientific experimentation, and it flourished under the caliphate established across the Middle East, the Iberian Peninsula and Southern Asia. The most important contribution of Islamic mathematicians was the development of algebra after combining Indian and Babylonian material with Greek geometry. Al-Khwarizmi (800–847) was considered the father of modern algebra. He wrote the first book that designated algebra as a separate discipline: Al-*Kitab al-jabra wa'l-muqabalah* (*The Book of Completion and Balancing*). The word *al-jabra* means "restoration," referring to the transposition of subtracted terms to the other side of the equation or adding equal terms to both sides of the equation to eliminate negative terms. The word *muqabalah* means "balancing," referring to the reduction of positive terms by subtracting equal amounts from both sides of the equation.[44]

It was only through mathematics that Arabic became a true global language, in which logic and verbal expressions were elevated (or reduced) to symbols (such as x, y or z) for numbers in order to solve mathematical problems. It is to Al-Khwarizmi that Arabic owes the widespread use of Arabic numbers, positional notation in base 10, and the free use of irrational numbers. These innovations provided not only a method of calculation, but also an abstract way to represent relationships and their underlying logic in simple and precise terms that were versatile and variable.

Further developments in algebra were made by Al-Karaji (953–1029). In his treatise *Al-Fakhri*, he extended the methodology to incorporate integer powers and integer roots of unknown quantities. Something close to a proof by mathematical induction appears in a book written by him around

A.D. 1000 that verified the binomial theorem, Pascal's triangle, and the sum of integral cubes. A historian of mathematics, Al-Karaji was praised as "the first who introduced the theory of algebraic calculus." Also in the 10th century, Abul Wafa translated the works of Diophantus into Arabic. Ibn al-Haytham was the first mathematician to derive the formula for the sum of the fourth powers, using a method that readily determined the general formula for the sum of any integral powers. He performed an integration in order to find the volume of a paraboloid, and was able to generalize his result for the integrals of polynomials up to the fourth degree. He came close to finding a general formula for the integrals of polynomials, but he was not concerned with any polynomials higher than the fourth degree.[45]

Omar Khayyám (1038–1123) wrote *Explanations of the Difficulties in the Postulates in Euclid's Elements*. The book consists of several sections on the parallel postulate (book 1), on the Euclidean definition of ratios and the Anthyphairetic ratio (modern continued fractions) (book 2), and on the multiplication of ratios (book 3). The first section is a treatise containing some propositions and lemmas concerning the parallel postulate. This could be considered the first treatment of the parallels axiom, which was not based on *petitio principii* but on more intuitive postulates. Khayyám refuted the previous attempts by other Greek and Persian mathematicians to prove the proposition. He also refuted the use of motion in geometry and therefore dismissed the attempt by Ibn Haytham as well. In a sense, he made the first attempt at formulating a non–Euclidean postulate as an alternative to the parallel postulate. This philosophical view of mathematics had a significant impact on Khayyám's celebrated approach and method in geometric algebra and in particular in solving cubic equations. In this case, his solution was not a direct path to a numerical solution but rather made use of line segments. In this regard Khayyám's work could be considered the first systematic study of cubic equations and the first exact method of solving them.[46]

Regarding more general equations, he stated that the solution of cubic equations required the use of conic sections, and that they could not be solved by ruler and compass methods. A proof of this impossibility was plausible only 750 years after Khayyám died. It wasn't until 600 years later that Giordano Vitale made an advance on Khayyám in his book *Euclide restituo* (1680, 1686), in which he used the quadrilateral to prove that if three points are equidistant on the base AB and the summit CD, then AB and CD are everywhere equidistant. Saccheri himself based the whole of his long, heroic, and ultimately flawed proof of the parallel postulate around the quadrilateral and its three cases, proving many theorems about its properties along the way.

In the 13th century, Nasir al-Din al-Tusi (1201–1274) developed a novel approach to the investigation of cubic equations, one that entailed finding the point at which a cubic polynomial obtains its maximum value. He made advances in spherical trigonometry and wrote an influential work on Euclid's parallel postulate. Al-Tusi was the first to write a work on trigonometry that was independent of astronomy, in his *Treatise on the Quadrilateral*. It was in the works of Al-Tusi that trigonometry achieved the status of an independent branch of pure mathematics distinct from astronomy, to which it had been linked for so long.

Conclusions

As Arabic evolved from poetry to prose, from oral to literary language, from the language of literature to that of law, science, and philosophy, its vision rapidly expanded from a narrow world of tribal man to the entire world and universe. When Islam advanced across the continents, Arabic embraced and assimilated the lands, the people, their languages and their worlds. Arabic became the home of world civilizations.

An increasing number of Western scholars, orientalists and otherwise, have been debating how much Arabic and Islamic civilization have influenced the modern cultures of Western Europe. The reason for this debate is the fact that more and more scholars, especially historians, have discovered that many literary forms and ideas that we called modern were in fact present in the medieval Islamic world. Does this mean that modern European culture, poetry, narrative, historiography, science, sociology, and even psychology originated in the Middle East?

Not necessarily so, because the ideas did not come from a single origin but rather sprouted during the evolution of language, as thought acquired a means of expression and creation. The reason why medieval Islam cultivated many ideas that are considered modern to Western Europe was because Arabic language was a much older and established literary language compared to European vernaculars. For example, Ibn Khaldun's theory of history attracted the attention of Western scholars only when English, French, and German began to develop abstract concepts and ideas during the eighteenth and nineteenth centuries. Only during the last couple of decades have Western scholars begun to pay attention to the mystical side of Islam and appreciate Sufi poetry. In short, everything has to do with time; specifically, the timing of literary evolution in each specific language.

CHAPTER 5

Imagery of the Universe:
Arts and Literature

This chapter focuses on the widening and deepening of Arabic vision through visual abstraction and sharpened variations. This process is seen and analyzed in terms of creating artistic and architectural patterning without figurative images as Arabic prose was building general and abstract vocabulary for religious, philosophical and legal writing. The non-verbal expression is demonstrated here in Islamic arts and architecture that projected a grand vision with increasingly sophisticated decorative motifs. These images embodied a majestic and penetrating unity; seemingly anti-image yet open to increasingly detailed and refined individual creativity. They portrayed a universe beyond its appearance, free from the lens of the naked eye, that was defined not only by line and shape but also by rhythm, the same rhythm that is heard in Arabic poetry, seen by gazing at a mosaic and felt by meditating on a piece of calligraphy. Arabic became one of the very few languages in the world that could envision rhythm without imagery, provoke thinking without words and activate emotion without definite meaning. Arabic visual language, like its literary counterpart, possessed the ability to communicate and induce emotions with its sound and flowing line.

Unlike most historical studies that interpret Islamic arts in terms of religion and/or philosophy, this chapter sees Islamic arts as one of many forms of expression. This visual expression interacted with the development of literary language, and inspired and enriched its literary vision. Rather than being a slave to serve codified meanings (religious, scientific or philosophical), the abstract form of expression is portrayed as preconditioned, inspired, and envisioned by worldviews in Arabic. It attempts to demonstrate the distinctive development of visual expression in specific periods of Islamic civilization in terms of specific evolutionary phases of the Arabic language. It explores variant meanings that are expressed in both words and arts. For example, the recreation and transfiguration of Byzantine arts and architecture and the invention of uniquely Islamic forms are narrated as a part of a widening and focusing of Arabic imagery that was manifested in prose writing as well as artistic and architectural expression. The emergence of *muqarnas*, a three-dimensional architectural form, is portrayed as a part of an expansion and refinement of Arabic vision that is manifested both in increasingly personal religious poetry and in more creative visual forms in architecture, art and calligraphy.[1]

Like Arabic literary language, grown in the rich soil of ancient Semitic literature, Arabic art forms inherited a wealth of visual vocabulary that had been articulated in the Middle East through the ancient civilizations of the Greeks, Romans, Persians, and Byzantines. After the Islamic conquest, and unlike the spoken voice of the region, which had been mostly replaced by the emerging Arabic language, the old images remained to be seen and touched by the new conquering culture and naturally served as constant inspiration for the emerging Islamic arts. In a seemingly miraculous birth of Islamic art occurring only a century after Muhammad's death, a complex visual language appeared in architecture and ornamental art from Arabia, a land of relative poverty of visual expression. The accelerated formation and development of Islamic art have been described as super-saturation and final crystallization driven by the expansion of a new religion assimilating the existing art forms of the ancient Middle East. Islam provided a much-needed unity to reproduce and re-canonize the unevenly inherited Greco-Roman and indigenous Semitic and non–Semitic arts and craftsmanship.[2]

The history of development of architecture has always been closely geared to literary development in both Western and Eastern civilizations. However, the degrees of refinement of the given literary language and its environment of artistic expression (the available and accumulated artistic vocabulary at the time and place where certain literature emerged) determined what types of visual language a literary language would adopt, conceptualize and crystallize. At the time when Islam began to emerge, it inherited its contemporary visual language accumulated by Byzantine art and architecture, which represented a much more developed visual language compared to that of the classic Roman. Byzantine art had outgrown the form based on natural imitation and developed an internal dimension. Emerging cultures germinating from a mature poetic tradition, such as Arabic and Russian three centuries later, were more likely to be drawn to the more complex and refined Byzantine form.[3]

The architectural form that Arabic/Islamic architecture inherited from the Middle East was not as formative as the early Roman construction. Until the beginning of Justinian, most church buildings were basilicas, a timber roofed halls with or without aisles, originating from the second or third century B.C. in Italy. The theme had developed variations such as galleries, apses, multiple aisles, narthices, and atria. They were simply designed to adopt new functions. New architectural vocabulary, capitals, colonnades, arcades, mosaic and vaults began to emerge over time. Prior to the pendentive development, the device of corbelling or the use of the squinch in corners of a room had been employed. Pendentives were commonly used in Orthodox churches, with a drum with windows often inserted between the pendentives and the dome. The pendentives were originally used in the Roman dome, initially in the 2nd to 3rd centuries A.D. It took several centuries for the form to completely develop into the 6th century Hagia Sophia at Constantinople. The diameter of Hagia Sophia's central dome was unsurpassed until the completion of the Renaissance cathedral of Florence.[4]

Hagia Sophia is one of the greatest surviving examples of Byzantine architecture. Of great artistic value was its decorated interior with mosaics and marble pillars and coverings. It was to remain the world's largest cathedral for the next ten centuries, until the completion of the cathedral in Seville in Spain. Sophia was the first complex building with a vast interior. The nave is covered by a central dome, which at its maximum is 55.6 m from floor level and rests on an arcade of 40 arched windows. At the western entrance side and eastern liturgical side, there are arched openings extended by half domes that are identical in diameter to the central dome, carried on smaller semi-domed exedras. A hierarchy of dome-headed elements was built up to create a vast, oblong interior crowned by the central dome, with a clear span of 76.2 m.

The dome of Hagia Sophia was carried on four concave triangular pendentives, which served as a transition from the circular base of the dome to the rectangular base below. These were reinforced with buttresses during Ottoman times, under the guidance of the architect Mimar Sinan. The weight of the dome remained a problem for most of the building's existence. The original dome collapsed entirely in 558; in 563 a new dome, slightly taller than the original, was built including ribbing. Larger sections of the second dome collapsed as well, in two portions. The present dome consists of two sections at the north and south that date from the 562 reconstruction. The north section covers 8 ribs of the entire dome's 40, while the south section includes 6 ribs.

Forty windows were around base of the dome, and they made Hagia Sophia famous for the mystical quality of light that reflects everywhere in the interior of the nave. This exceptional light, which gave the dome the appearance of hovering above the nave, was made possible by the special design with ribs that extend from the top of the dome down to the base to form a scalloped shell shape. These ribs allowed the weight of the dome to flow between the windows, down the pendentives, and ultimately to the foundation.[5]

The Hagia Sophia and other Byzantine buildings exhibited enormous architectural craftsmanship. This attention to detail was apparent even in smaller buildings. The largest columns of granite were about 20 meters high and at least 1.5 meters in diameter. The largest, weighing well over 70 tons, used to build Hagia Sophia were disassembled from Baalbek, Lebanon, and shipped to Constantinople for the construction. Semitic artists and craftsmen contributed to the construction of Byzantine architecture long before the Islamic movement. Although historians have and will continue to debate how to define the architectural revival of the Mediterranean region (Graeco-Roman or Byzantine) the fact remains that there was a continuing architectural tradition and craftsmanship in the region that later was assimilated into the formation of Islamic architecture.

The first Islamic city (*medina*) was defined and built by the Prophet Muhammad. Rashidun Caliphate (632–661) was the first state to build Islamic architecture and use Islamic forts and administration systems (*Dar al-Imara*). It provided the foundation for future Islamic cities. The first garrison town of Islam was *khitat* in Kufa, Basra, Fustat and Qayrawan.[6]

The Muslim conquests found two cities on their way to ancient Mesopotamia to shelter their troops: Basra (636), near the mouth of two rivers, and Kufa (637–638) on the Euphrates, where the desert met cultivated plain. It held the first free-standing mosque that Muslims built during their conquest. It was simply a space fenced with reeds. It later was replaced by a building of sun-dried bricks (*labin*) with a thatch *'ushb* (roof) during the third quarter of the seventh century.[7]

The mosque 'Amr ibn al-'As at Fustat is said to be the oldest mosque in Egypt and even Africa. In 641, the army, led by Caliph 'Amr, was on its way to conquer Alexandria, the capital city of Egypt. Although impressed by Alexandria, 'Amr decided to look for a new location for his Islamic nation for security reasons. He needed a place in the center of Egypt that could not be easily reached by water. One day he pitched his tent near the site of the battle of Babylon, about a quarter of a mile northeast of the fort. Next morning, as the men began to pull down the tents and pack them for the journey, they found that a dove had nested on one of the tents and had laid eggs. 'Amr ordered that the tent be kept standing in the plain of Babylon while the army marched away. In this unusual incident 'Amr saw a divine sign. He decided that Muslims should build their city where the dove had nested. As 'Amr's tent was to be the focal point of the city, the city was called Fustat (tent). The first structure to be built was the mosque, which later became famous as the Mosque of 'Amr ibn al-'As. Over time, Fustat was extended to include the old town of Babylon. It grew to become a bustling city and the commercial center of Egypt.[8]

The original layout of the Mosque of 'Amr was a simple rectangle (29 × 17 meters). It was a low shed with columns made of split palm tree trunks, stones and mud bricks, covered by a roof of wood and palm leaves (not much more "modern" than Mohammad's house/mosque). The floor was gravel. Inside the building the orientation toward Mecca was not noted by a concave niche like it would be in all later mosques. Instead, four columns were used to indicate the direction of Mecca; they were inserted on the *qibla* wall. It was large enough to provide prayer space for Amr's army, but had no other adornments or minarets.

The mosque was completely rebuilt in 673 by Mu'awiya (602–680), the first Umayyad Caliph, who added four minarets to each of the mosque's corners, doubling its size. The addition of these minarets allowed the call to prayer to be heard from every corner and taken up by other nearby mosques. Its size was doubled again at the end of the seventh century, and a concave prayer niche was added to replace the flat one in 711. About a hundred years later, seven new aisles were built, parallel to the wall of the *qibla*. Each aisle had an arcade of columns, with the last column in each row attached to the wall by means of a wooden architrave carved with a frieze. It expanded twice to the size of 120 by 112 meters. The minarets were rebuilt during the early Fatimad period. However, the only part of the old structure of the mosque that can still be seen are some of the architraves, which were added during the reconstruction in 827.[9]

The Dome of the Rock in Jerusalem was completed in 691, and it is the earliest remaining Islamic monument. The major characteristics of the Dome of the Rock appeared to be Christian during late antiquity, a style similar to that of the great Christian sanctuaries in Jerusalem. Most of the construction technique used in building the Dome derived from Byzantine church architecture: the arches on piers and columns with wooden domes, grilled windows, stone and brick masonry and the carefully thought-out and intricate system of proportion. The decoration also reflected an artistic theme of Byzantine origin: the crowns and the jewels. Compared to early Roman Christian architecture, Byzantine buildings increased in geometric complexity. Brick and plaster were used in addition to stone in the decoration of important public structures, classical orders were used more freely, mosaics replaced carved decoration, complex domes rested upon massive piers, and windows filtered light through thin sheets of alabaster to softly illuminate interiors. Most of the surviving structures are sacred in nature, with secular buildings mostly known only through contemporaneous descriptions.

The Dome of the Rock, as the first Islamic architecture, departed from the Byzantine themes and model techniques in several ways. The first was the nature of its decoration. The mosaic decoration on a huge area of about 280 square meters did not contain a single image of man or beast, which was deliberately inconsistent with the Byzantine vocabulary at the time. The mosaic was completely ornamental or abstract as seen in later Islamic buildings. Trees, leaves, flowers, and fruits were portrayed in both realistic and artificial manners and a mixture of jewels, crowns, and breastplates were portrayed, the remnants of Christian, Jewish, and Sassanian motifs.

The second was its inscription, a trademark of Islamic art running below the ceiling of the octagons. The inscription was both decorative and symbolic. It served as a border for the rest of the ornamentation and it contained carefully selected Qur'anic passages concerning Christianity. Alongside classical motifs the mosaics also had palmettos, wings, and composite flowers.

The mosaic of the Dome of the Rock introduced Islamic decorative principles of non-realistic portrayal of natural shapes and artificial combination of realistic images. This tendency was going to develop further and cultivate more and more abstract and refined forms. Muslim artists would not hesitate to transform the trunk of a tree into a bejeweled box. They would completely ignore the restraints of classical naturalism and combine images freely as they saw fit. Although using very few designs (mainly the acanthus scroll, the garland, the vine scroll, the tree, and the rosette), they were able to fill the entire building with brilliant variations without exact repetition. Each variation within a theme represented an individual interpretation of some general principle of the design.

The Dome of the Rock established a new relationship between architecture and decoration. Until the pre–Islamic period, Classical principles of decoration, especially ornamental decoration, had been the dominant feature of Mediterranean architecture and arts. Decorative art had been a servant of architecture to emphasize parts of the latter and seldom suppressed the essential values of construction. The builders of the Dome changed this established relationship. They hid almost all of their clearly defined, classically based structure with brilliant marble and mosaic. The most striking was one of the soffits of the arches of the octagon, where three bands of design spread over the entire surface. The composition of the decoration was asymmetrical with various widths of bands. Only one motif continued on to the vertical surface of the spandrel to emphasize one curve of the arch against the other arch. The inherited motifs were not discarded, and they were selectively used to decorate the areas provided by the architecture: tall trees to decorate high rectangular surfaces and scrolls for square spaces. These inherited motifs were also organized and reconstructed into an Arabic textile design. An expensive shell around the structure, which reminded one of the language of Ma'aba in Mecca, covered the outside with multicolored textile hangings and was filled inside with a huge number of images and treasures. It represented a formative stage of the creation of pure geometric shape.[10]

The concept and original shape of a mosque was Arabic in origin: *masjid*, meaning a place where one prostrates one's self (in front of God). *Masjid* later became a holy building, *masjid Allah* (God's sanctuary) and *masjid al-Haram* (a place forbidden for but Muslims). The general concept of *masjid* as a place of worship had its first material and visual realization in Muhammad's house in Madina, where he prayed and lived. As the empire extended, it became impossible to combine worship and dwelling, but the idea of the combination remained. Early mosques were usually set next to the governor's palace and included within their boundaries a small structure serving as the treasury of the Muslim community (examples survived in Damascus and Hama, Syria). They remained not only the religious buildings but also the main social and political centers as implied by the name of *al-masjid al-jami'*(congregational mosque). This was further established as typological architecture by early buildings at Madina, Jerusalem, Damascus, Basra, Kufa, and Wasit. As Islam successfully expanded, mosques began to incorporate non–Arabic shapes and structures such as Persian *apadanas* (large halls with many columns) or Egyptian temples, just to accommodate the increasingly large population of believers and their religious activities.[11]

However, practical needs alone would not automatically lead to architectural creativity. Without Byzantine visual language, it would have taken Muslims many more centuries to develop Islamic architecture from Muhammad's *zulla*, a shelter made of palm tree trunks with a roof of palm leaves and mud, to the magnificent masterpieces that we know today. Islamic architecture took the formal innovation begun by the Byzantine artists and reinvented it in a distinctive form. During the process of this reinvention, Islam's concentration on geometric patterns drew attention away from the physical world to one of pure form, poised tension and dynamic equilibrium. Ironically, this type of imagery is now used by modern atomic physics to confirm the essential mathematical and geometric patterns occurring in nature.

The reason that Islamic architecture took geometrical form as the foundation of visual presentation many centuries before Western Europe did (in the modernism of the twentieth century) is consistent with the early maturity of the Arabic language. Arabic expression was no longer looking for inspiration from national forms; rather, it became able to recognize and comprehend the essential relationships that lie beneath the visual surface of the world. The significance from the Islamic standpoint is that, to trace the origins of creation, the direction to search is not backwards but inwards. In other words, as the intuitive mind of an individual seeks sources and reasons for its existence it is led inward and away from the three-dimensional world toward fewer and more comprehensive ideas and principles. Muslim artists had different goals in minds, to project their inner wisdom and harmony in concrete visible forms instead of imitating beauty perceived in nature.[12]

The best way to illustrate the evolution of Byzantine architecture into Islamic architecture is to investigate the specific decorative forms of Islamic building and illustrate how the representations of the mosaic were transformed. The fantastic trees, plants, fruits, jewels, chalices and crowns gradually departed from uniformity throughout a building and exclusively focused on the inner face of the octagonal colonnade and of the drum. As Christian churches began to be converted to mosques, the scenes from the Old or New Testaments or devotional images of Christ, the Virgin or saints disappeared. As symbolic arts were transferred from one religion to another and from one language to another, they naturally became abstracted. For example, when symbols changed from Christianity to Islam, they became emptied of their specific meanings. As a result, instead of glorifying a particular God, they came to represent a sense of holiness, an abstraction of divinity.[13]

Although the Dome of the Rock had many Islamic features such as the strengthened support for the cupola and extended inner space, the interior seemed to be more Byzantine and Roman than Islamic. As Islam had not established its own architectural style, it had to adopt the methods of Byzantine arts, its workmanship, and its architectural tradition. The floor plan reflected the synthesis of circles and squares, movement and repose, time and space. Heavenly and earthly spheres were shared by Byzantine and Islamic theologies. To claim its Islamic origin and primacy over its religious rival (Christianity), Qur'anic inscription was installed on a mosaic frieze on the walls of the building. There was a rounded, continuous arcade over a row of alternating pillars and columns, and the walls were embellished with splendid gold-based glass mosaics. It had patterns of trees, grapevines, and crowns that illustrated an early stage of Islamic art before it developed geometric arabesque.[14]

A further step into abstraction was illustrated on Mshatta, the façade of a winter residence south of Amman, Jordan. Built at the end of the Umayyad (661–750), it departed from the classical and Byzantine form and represented a much more varied and lively design. For example, the zigzag shape was a new static element supporting the roof. It took on a dynamic and rhythmic decorative role. Mshatta was not yet an Islamic art but it initiated a tendency to combine different plans of decor and large reliefs of zigzag molding. Decorative triangles and geometrical rosettes were superimposed on the facets of bastion towers and later became a general trademark of Islamic art.[15]

The most celebrated Umayyad desert complex in Jordan was centered on the bathhouse at Qasr 'Amra, a diminutive structure nestled in a broad depression about 85 kilometers east of Amman. Though the limestone and basalt building was not particularly impressive from the outside, 'Amra's interior walls and ceilings displayed a dazzling array of painted frescos from the mid–eighth century, with less well-preserved fragments of mosaics, carved stone and marble cladding. The fresco art is important not only for the information it provides about the culture and tastes of the notables who built these complexes; it also shows the Umayyad dynasty's clear links with both the classical and Byzantine traditions it had inherited, as well as demonstrating contemporary cultural influences from Mesopotamia, Persia and other Asian civilizations.

'Amra marked the transition from Byzantine to Arabic expression. It is thought to have been built during the reign of the Caliph Walid I (705–715), builder of the great Umayyad Mosque in Damascus, although some scholars believe it may be the work of his uncle, Walid II (743–744). The complex comprised the baths, an attached audience hall and domestic rooms. It had a hydraulic system (all within a walled area) and a small, square, fort-like residential building (*caravanserai*) and nearby watchtower in the hills to the northwest, where the staff and troops of 'Amra's patron probably lived. There were also traces of what some scholars believe to be an ancient dam, and enclosure walls that delineated an agricultural area of some 62 acres. It was a remarkable eighth century water system that had a 40-meter circular well, and remains of the *saqiya* (water-lifting apparatus). Even the circle marks made by the animal that drove the water mill (to raise the water and send it through ceramic pipes to the baths or the adjacent outdoor tank) remained visible.

The walls and ceilings of the spacious, rectangular, three-aisled audience hall were covered in relatively well-preserved frescos. They depicted a variety of scenes that were typical Umayyad decoration: hunting scenes, bathing scenes, and the famous Fresco of the Six Kings. There were Greek and Arabic inscriptions under busts of Caesar (as the Byzantine emperor was then called); the Sassanian king Kisra; Roderic, the last Visigoth king of Spain, who was killed by Walid I in 711; the Negus of Abyssinia; and two other busts thought to depict the emperor of China and the king of the Turks. The audience hall also had frescos of Victory, attended by servants and flanked by peacocks, heavy-set wrestlers, flying angels, pacing lions, dancers and musicians. There were also an enthroned Byzantine emperor, saluki hounds energetically chasing some hapless onagers, and a lion attacking a horse. Three female figures personify Poetry, History and Philosophy, as described in the accompanying Greek inscriptions, and 32 individual panels depict craftsmen in various stages of the construction process, including blacksmiths, carpenters, and masons.

The bath was typical of the period and consisted of a changing room (apodyterium), a warm room (tepidarium), with its raised floor to allow warm air to circulate beneath the bathers, and a hot room (calidarium) close to the furnace. The frescos in the bath displayed a wide variety of motifs and styles, including three busts thought to represent the three ages of humankind—childhood, youth and old age—and pastoral scenes reminiscent of those in Byzantine mosaics of churches in the region several centuries before and during the Umayyad era.

The dome above the hot room was considered to be 'Amra's most pleasing combination of architecture and art. The Dome of Heaven was painted with the constellations of the Northern Hemisphere accompanied by the signs of the zodiac. It is believed to be the earliest surviving attempt to represent the vault of heaven on a hemispherical, rather than a flat surface, as had been frequently done by preceding civilizations. As a key monument of Arabic art, it marked a transitional phrase between Byzantine imagery and newly discovered Arabic inspiration.[16]

New Arabic concepts and architectural plans were developed and put into practice in both religious and secular buildings. The "Arab plan," with court and hypostyle prayer hall, became a dominant functional type. Located near Jericho in the Jordan Valley, Khirbat al-Mafjar was and remains one of the most highly sophisticated Umayyad palaces in the region for its elaborate mosaics, stucco carvings and overall sculptural magnificence. Built mainly of sandstone highlighted at times with baked brick, the complex encompassed three main areas: a two-storied palace, a mosque accompanied by a small courtyard, and a bath with an audience hall (throne room), all of which were enclosed by an outer wall. To the east, bordering the length of the site, extended a forecourt with a centrally featured fountain. The main gate of the compound was centrally located on the southern façade of the palace and was flanked by two buttress towers at either edge of the front of the structure. The palace itself featured a central courtyard in which two pathways guided a visitor to either the side forecourt to the east or to a small courtyard to the north.

The excavation of Khirbat al-Mafjar uncovered some of the most stunning artwork of the early Islamic period. Khirbat al-Mafjar was one exceptional example of the settlement of marginal lands by the early Muslims employing the bounty from their conquests. An aqueduct brought water from springs to irrigate about 150 acres of gardens enclosed in a long boundary wall. The principal building held the great hall and bath, a reception hall not unlike the Sassanian palace at Firuzabad in Iran. It is not difficult to imagine the mosaics and see Persian carpets spread over the hall floors. Perhaps the most extraordinary element is the ceremonial entryway. The porch exhibits a high central niche carrying a standing figure with a sword on two lions, very likely the caliphate patron himself, Hisham. The palace is more typical of Umayyad residences, wonderfully decorated with stuccoes and frescoes.

The plan of the palatial complex reveals the height of sophistication reached during late Umayyad architecture. The whole design scheme was incorporated in a rectangular enclosure protected by strong walls supported by circular towers at equal intervals. There was a domestic section and the palace proper, a two-story structure occupying the southern side of the complex. It had a symmetrical plan ordered around a large courtyard which contained a succession of rooms that were arranged in pairs along the eastern and western sides. At the eastern end, the center rooms were transformed into an entrance hall connecting with the porch.

At the opposite side of the courtyard was a single room of barrel vault of brick. At the center of the southern enclosure was a rectangular structure composed of five equal rooms. The central room had a niche (*mihrab*) in the southern wall, behind which was a square minaret. This was a domestic mosque and was most likely reserved for the household of the prince. At the northern end of the domestic section there was a large room equal in size to the five rooms of the southern wall. In the center of this room were the remains of six piers which may have provided the support for six arcades of two arches each, which in their turn must have supported the vaults of the roof. In the cloister of the west side was a double-landing staircase leading down to a sunken court preceding a vaulted crypt lit by triple windows. This was the so-called *serdab* (literally "cold water" in Persian), a room for keeping cool on summer days.

Next to the north was another section containing the main mosque and its courtyard. The mosque, occupying the eastern side, was made of a large room of two aisles raised by eight piers arranged parallel to the *mihrab* wall (*qibla*). At the back was a small section in the form of a narthex accessed by three doors. The third section encompassed one of the largest and most magnificent baths found in the Muslim world. A richly decorated porch approached the structure from the west. The most significant feature of the porch was a statue of the caliph standing over a platform of two symmetrical lions fitted in a concave above the center of the portal. The design of the hall showed that Al-Walid II indeed lived in a lavish and luxurious style. The bath's main room, the frigidarium, was a hall of generous proportions carried on sixteen composite piers supporting the domes and barrel vaults. The bath was believed to have been adequately lit by clerestory windows as in a Byzantine building. The other important feature was the presence of the so-called exedrae, semicircular apses flanked by a pair of engaged columns that were inserted in the four external walls. These exedrae were crowned with semi-domes. This theme was also reflected in the lobed corners of the pier plans. The center of the bath was crowned by a great dome rising above the eight surrounding vaults, which in turn rose higher than the apsidal walls. The huge space was subdivided into three functional sections.

An oblong pool, about 20 meters in length, was set along the southern side of the bath, and was approached by steps in the western corner indicating that it might have been for the private access of the prince. Behind these was a hall that had a ceremonial function, which may also have served for banquets, a hypothesis confirmed by a picture of a knife, gourd, and leaf depicted in a mosaic at its focal point. The *diwan* (the audience hall) was richly decorated and was located in the area of the palace where the caliph could separate himself from political pressures by meeting his advisors in a relaxing atmosphere. He also could screen his visitors by keeping them away from the entrance of the palace.

The bath proper was situated behind the ceremonial hall and was connected with the hot and cold rooms through doors in its northern wall. Excavations revealed the existence of two cold rooms that were next to the frigidarium and were equipped with benches all around the walls. There were also two hot rooms (furnaces) facing each other and connected through a door. The most peculiar of these was the second room on the north side of the first furnace. It was a circular chamber made of eight horseshoe-shaped apses with semi-domes. The furnace was placed under the niche accessible only from the exterior. The hot air was carried up the walls by a connection of short pottery pipes hidden by marble paneling.

Khirbat al-Mafjar is renowned for the mosaics and stucco carvings that adorn the audience hall and bathhouse. Geometrically decorated mosaics of the highest standard cover the floor of the bathhouse. In the audience hall, another famous mosaic panel displays an apple tree providing cover on its right side for two gazelles that chew at its foliage while to the left a lion is shown attacking another gazelle from behind.[17]

The Great Mosque of Damascus was the first monumental work of architecture in Islamic history. The building served as a central gathering point after Mecca to consolidate Muslims in their faith so that they could continue to rule the surrounding territories under the Umayyad Caliphate. This Umayyad mosque, which was built at the site of the temple of the thunderstorm and rain god, Hadad-Ramman, was erected by the Aramaean state Aram-Damascus (from the late 12th century to 734 B.C.). After the Romans came in A.D. 64, the Temple of Hadad-Ramman continued to serve in its primary role as a temple to worship the storm and rain god, but for the Latin God of thunder, Zeus (Jupiter). The temple was expanded yet preserved its Semitic design. An image of the god stood in the cellar in the center of the courtyard. There was one tower at each of the courtyard's four corners. The towers were used for rituals of ancient Semitic religious traditions where sacrifices were made on high places. The Roman temple combined the pagan gods affiliated with heaven that were worshiped in the region (such as Hadad, Ba'al-Shamin and Dushara) into the "supreme-heavenly-astral Zeus." The Temple of Jupiter would attain further additions during the early period of Roman rule of the city, mostly initiated by high priests who collected contributions from the wealthy citizens of Damascus.[18]

By the 4th-century A.D., the temple was renovated for its size and appearance. It was separated from the city by two sets of walls. The first, wider wall spanned a wide area that included a market, and the second wall surrounded the actual sanctuary of Jupiter. It was the largest temple in Roman Syria. Towards the end of the 4th century, the Temple of Jupiter was converted into the Cathedral of Saint John by the Christian Byzantine emperor Theodosius I. After the Muslim conquest in 634, the sixth Umayyad caliph, Al-Walid I, commissioned the construction of a mosque on the site of the Byzantine cathedral in 706. The construction of the mosque completely altered the layout of the building. The new house of worship was meant to serve as a large congregational mosque for the citizens of Damascus and as a tribute to the city. It was completed in 715.[19]

It consisted of a courtyard surrounded on three sides by porticoes on piers alternating with two columns. The fourth side is the *qibla* (direction of Kaaba) facade. It had three wide aisles, parallel to the southern wall, cut in the center by a perpendicular (axial) nave over whose second bay rose a high dome. The aisles had large monolithic columns taken from older buildings, surmounted by capitals, impost blocks, and arches. Above the arches an additional small arcade lifted the gabled roof even higher. In the *qibla* wall were four niches known as *mihrabs* (semicircular niches), symmetrically arranged with the central one located precisely in the middle of the axial nave. Just as in the Dome of the Rock, practically all the elements of construction derived from the traditional architecture of Syria, but there were two innovations, the floor plan and the introduction of the *mihrab*.[20]

The layout of the mosque was a 97 m × 156 m rectangle with the *sahn* (courtyard) on the northern side. The *sahn* was punctuated by three major elements: the ablution fountain, covered with a dome that was supported by columns; the Khazne Dome on the western side, supported by eight Corinthian columns; and the Zein al-Abidin Dome on the eastern side, also supported by eight columns. Alternating stone columns and piers with one pier between every two columns supported the *riwaq* (arcade) surrounding the *sahn*. Three *riwaqs*, parallel to the *qibla*, were supported by two rows of stone Corinthian columns. Each *riwaq* had two levels, the first with large semicircular arches and the second with double arches.

The exterior walls of the mosque were built in the Roman period when the building functioned as a temple. Four defense towers were built at each corner, but only the two southern ones remained when Al-Walid began his project. These towers were used as foundations to erect the eastern and western minarets. Then a third square minaret tower known as the Arus Minaret (The Minaret of the Bride) was built near the northern gate. The lower part of this minaret is still in its original form, but the middle part is an Ayyubid addition built after the fire of 1174. The eastern minaret, Eesa Minaret (Minaret of Jesus), is also a pastiche of different architectural styles that correspond to changing political environments. It has a Mamluk lower part and an Ottoman top due to its renovation after the earthquake of 1759. The western minaret is the most articulated; its stone carvings and inscriptions record its restorations in 1488 and after Timur's conquest in 1401.

The two main materials used for cladding were *fusayfusa'a* mosaic and marble. The *fusayfusa'a* fragments were mixed with colored glass particles and others of glass covered with gold and silver leaf. In addition, bits of stone and marble were included to create a unique reflective material that highlighted its geometric and floral patterns. The *fusayfusa'a* was originally used to cover the top parts of the walls on both the interior and exterior sides in the *haram*, *riwaqs,* and the arches and undersides of the vaults. The painted patterns formed scenic panels that symbolized the magnificent natural landscapes of Damascus. The Barada River flowed alongside the great Umayyad palaces and orchards of fruit-bearing trees that were thought to be an image of heaven. Heavily veined marble was used to clad the lower parts of the walls, as it is a stronger, more enduring material than the mother-of-pearl mosaics. The veins of the marble were used to create patterns because of the way that the panels were joined and attached to the walls. Nothing is left of these panels except for small holes where the marble masons attached them to the walls. A highly ornate band of carved marble separated these materials on the walls. The vegetation-inspired designs were known as the "great golden vines" because of their resemblance to the intertwined grape vines that were common in the Classical (Roman and Byzantine) periods. Some fragments of this famous band still remain today in the mosque. Additional ornamentation included the Ottoman blue clay tiles that replaced the missing marble panels in the *sahn*.[21]

The vegetal mosaic of Damascus reminds one of the Dome of the Rock except that they are more realistic in their depiction of specific plants and include fewer mixtures of forms from different origins. The scope of its painting was massive. On the façade of the axial nave and some of the spandrels of the northern and western porticoes, buildings of all types appear in the foliage. In the richly framed panel on the wall of the western portico, a large composition depicts a number of small rivers flowing into a body of water along which stand splendid tall trees that provide a frame for a series of small buildings. Small houses are clustered around a church; vast piazzas are surrounded by porticoes, and stately palaces on the banks of a river illustrate a variety of styles that are realistic, fantastic and composed from unrelated elements.[22]

While these images invited various scholarly interpretations, they definitely do not belong to mainstream Islamic arts. The first sign of change in style was seen in Iraq, the site of the second Islamic kingdom, in the Abbasid caliphs. Compared to Syria, Egypt, and Jerusalem, the ancient inheritance of Iraq was almost purely Sumerian and Semitic. It represented the original home of the Sufi fraction of Islam, nurtured in its timeless poetic tradition. The mosque of Samarra was built in 836, after it became the capital city of the Abbasid caliphs. It was replaced in 849–852 by a new mosque built on a grand scale, which for a long time was the largest mosque of the Islamic world. It continued to be used until the end of the 11th century.

Abbasid mosques were mainly decorated very soberly. At Samarra there was almost no applied ornament, and in the mosque of Ibn Tulun stucco was used only to emphasize the major architectural lines. The majority of decoration developed within identifiable frames, most commonly in long bands, but sometimes in simple rectangles or polygons. Its typical feature was the vine leaf, its parts always sharply outlined, with four deeply sunken eyes and often with incised veins. These were the same motifs used in Umayyad except for more striking special contrast. Gradually the deep grooves between motifs (leafs or flowers) were covered by small notches and dots, and the outline was simplified into an almost abstract shape. Although not as appealing as the naturalist motifs at the Dome of Damascus or the façade of Mshatta, the new abstract shape, which acquired its significance only in relation to other units of decoration, was peculiarly appealing because of its symmetrically arranged patterns that constantly contrasted inner tension and movement with the rigidity of geometric borders.

Abbasid architecture introduced many original forms to Islamic arts. *Muqarnas* had enduring implications for centuries to come. The brick mausoleum of Imam Dur (1085) incorporated the first Iraqi *muqarnas* dome. Bastions projected from the four corners to support this square structure. Its exterior was plain with layered sections on each façade of geometrically patterned, raised brick near the top of the structure. The inner chamber was also square, featuring a domed room with four corner niches that formed the support for the octagonal structure from which the five-tiered *muqarnas* dome climbs. The dome concluded at a great height with a small, fluted cupola. The tomb's interior was adorned with stucco ornamentation.[23]

Compared to the earlier decorative form, *muqarnas* had freer lines and evoked endless rhythmic repetitions of curved lines with spiral endings that at times included additional notches, slits, or pearl borders. More importantly, the line became beveled to meet the surface obliquely, giving the wall surface a strongly plastic quality. This abstract and almost three-dimensional style could erase the traditional boundaries between themes, motifs, and traditional geometric vegetal or animal themes and their background. The background had disappeared and the entire surface of the wall became ornament. In short, the main characteristics of this new style were repetition, beveling, abstract themes, total covering and symmetry. It was the first instance of a more sophisticated art experience that later was called *muqarnas*. This will be analyzed in detail later in the chapter.[24]

The Samarra style of mosque was carried to Egypt by Ahmad ibn Tulun (835–884), the governor of Egypt of Abbasid and later the independent ruler of Egypt. Ibn Tulun founded his own capital, Al-Qatta'i, north of the previous capital Fustat, and built a new mosque to replace the old Mosque of 'Amr. The Mosque of Ibn Tulun was built entirely of well-fired red brick faced in carved stucco. It had *ziyadas* and a roof supported by arcades on piers. The mosque was constructed around a courtyard, with one covered hall on each of the four sides. The largest hall was on the side of the *qibla*. The original mosque had its ablution fountain (*sabil*) in the area between the inner and outer walls. A distinctive *sabil* with a high drum dome was added in the central courtyard at the end of the thirteenth century.

Historians have been debating the date of construction of the famous spiral minaret of the Ibn Tulun Mosque. It featured a helical outer staircase similar to that of the famous minaret in Samarra. Legend has it that ibn Tulun himself designed the structure. However, many architectural features of the building suggest otherwise. The ablution fountain and dome were built on the site of the *fawwara* (fountain) and destroyed by fire in 986. The *fawwara*, which was purely decorative, was housed in a pavilion comprising a dome carried on gilded marble columns. The original ablution facilities and a clinic were housed in the *ziyada* for hygienic reasons.[25]

The Fatimid architecture followed Tulunid techniques and used similar materials, but also developed those of their own. In Cairo, their first congregational mosque was the Al-Azhar mosque (969–973). Among the architectural innovations applied to the building was the first use of dressed stone, instead of brick. The façade's various motifs were carved in the stone to replace the previous simple façades, similar to those in the mosques of 'Amr and Ibn Tulun. The pride of Fatimid architecture was its attractive and beautiful ornament. Decorated Kufic inscriptions and stucco ornament attained a high standard in their beautiful motifs, balanced distribution and varied designs. They were most highly developed in *mihrabs,* and they formed borders for arches and windows. Egyptian craftsmanship was not confined to stucco decoration alone; it also excelled in the art of wood carving. Doors of *minbars*, movable *mihabs* and wooden tie-beams all bore witness to the great skill of the period.

Al-Azhar became the spiritual center for Ismaili Shia with its adjacent institution of higher learning, Al-Azhar University. The original structure of the mosque was 85 × 69 meters and comprised three arcades situated around a courtyard. The original prayer hall was built in a hypostyle, five aisles deep to the southeast of the courtyard measuring 79 × 23 meters. The marble columns supporting the four arcades that made up the prayer hall were reused from sites extant at different times in Egyptian history.

There were originally three domes, but none of them have survived Al-Azhar's constant renovations. The original *mihrab* has a semi-dome with a marble column on either side. Stucco decorations were a prominent feature of the mosque. The *mihrab* had two sets of Qur'anic verses inscribed in the conch; these were the only surviving pieces of decoration that was dated to the Fatimids. Five keel-shaped arches were supported by cylindrical columns. Above each arch was a large circular inscribed stucco decoration, and above each column was a large inscribed stucco decoration that mirrored the shape of the arch and columns. It appeared that *muqarnas* had been established and widely spread in Egypt, and its decoration can be seen in several minarets and wall decorations.

For political reasons, the Mosque of Al-Azhar lost its prestige with the later Sunni caliphates. In the 12th century, Sultan Saladin, the founder of the staunchly Sunni Ayyubid Dynasty (1170–1250), converted Al-Azhar to a Shafi'ite Sunni center of learning. The Mamluk Sultanate (1250–1517) made restorations and additions to the mosque, overseeing a rapid expansion of its educational programs. Among the restorations was a modification of the *mihrab*, with the installation of polychrome marble facing.[26]

The Madrasa Gawhariyya, built in 1440, contained the tomb of Gawhar al-Qanaqba'i, a Sudanese eunuch who became treasurer to the sultan of Egypt. The floor of the *madrasa* was marble and the walls were lined with cupboards, decoratively inlaid with ebony, ivory, and nacre. The tomb chamber was covered with a small *arabesque* dome. The minaret of Qaytbay, built in 1483, had three balconies, supported by *muqarnas* that provided a smooth transition from a flat surface to a curved one. The first shaft was octagonal, decorated with keel-arched panels on each side, with a cluster of three columns separating each panel. Above the shaft was the second octagonal shaft, which was separated from the first by a balcony and decorated with plaiting. A second balcony, which separated this shaft from the final cylindrical shaft, was decorated with four arches. Above this was the third balcony, crowned by the finial top of the minaret. The minaret is thought to have been built earlier as Fatimid-era brick is apparent, suggesting that the minaret had been rebuilt several times.

The Bab al-Gindi (Gate of Qaytbay) was built in 1495 directly across the courtyard from the entrance of the Bab al-Muzayinīn. This gate led to the court of the prayer hall. The double finial minaret was built in 1509 by Qansah al-Ghuri. It was an ornate carved stone octagonal minaret with a carved stone railing around the central balconies. Above the second balcony the minaret split into two rectangular shafts, each tipped by railing and a bulb-shaped finial.[27]

The reign of the Mamluks (1250–1517) witnessed a breathtaking flowering of Islamic art. Compared to previous periods, the Mamluk architectural designs in Cairo were more diverse and individualistic because they were mainly sponsored by wealthy individuals who erected their own memorials according to their personal tastes. All of the sponsors of the mosques of Baibars, Al-Nasir Muhammad, Faraj, Al-Mu'ayyad, Barsbay, Qaitbay and Al-Ghawri preferred to build several mosques instead of focusing on one colossal monument. They decorated each dome and minaret with distinct patterns as symbols of commemoration and worship. Patterns carved on domes ranged from ribs and zigzags to floral and geometric star designs. The best example of this stylistic diversity was the four domes of the funeral complex of Sultan Barsbay. The dome of Barsbay's own mausoleum was made of three distinct levels of patterns, with eight-pointed, seven-pointed and six-pointed stars arranged from the bottom up. The north dome, the Janibak, had a row of halves of twelve-pointed stars radiating from the base of the dome and ten-pointed stars above them, positioned in a zigzag pattern. The eastern dome had eight-pointed stars supporting and seven-pointed stars towards the top. It showed a much higher degree of consistency in form and harmony. The period of Qa'itbay (r. 1468–96) introduced new ideas in dome building and decoration. Instead of beginning from the bottom, the geometrical pattern moved from apex to base. Thus the dome of Ba'itbay consisted of a pattern of sixteen-pointed stars at the top center of the dome, covering the upper half of the space, with the lines continuing to form a row of irregular seven-pointed stars. The bottom part was decorated with halves of twelve-pointed stars. The pattern covered the entire space to conceal any apparent irregularities.[28]

The Mamluk sultans competed with each other in the construction of mosques, schools, mausoleums, *sabils*, palaces and *wikalas*. Muslim architecture in Egypt began to establish itself during this period, gaining a special individuality that laid down its own standards and characteristics, as demonstrated in the floor plan of mosques, dignified façades and huge and beautiful portals. Stucco work was used with increasing skill and variation as decoration. Gradually, marble began to replace stucco. *Mihrabs* and dadoes were made with marble of different colors and in beautiful designs, distinguished by careful craftsmanship and harmony of color. At the same time, woodworking was developed and refined quickly. Decoration with ivory inlay work, ebony and *zarnashan* appeared side by side with fine carving on *minbars*, doors and windows. The design of wooden ceilings underwent a great development and refinement with richly gilded decoration. Progress in metal work was also evident in the copper-plated doors, showing skill in the engraving, piercing and inlaying of copper.

The Mamluk period produced superb domes and minarets. Domes were built of stone instead of brick. Their substructure took various forms, and faience was introduced for decorating their drums. The decoration of the external surface of domes varied from ribbing to chevrons, until they reached a high standard in the days of the Circassian Mamluks (1382–1517), when they were ornamented with geometrical and arabesque designs. Minarets, keeping pace with domes, rose gloriously to a great height, attracting attention with their remarkable beauty. The upper caps of some of them were covered with tiles of faience, apparent in the minarets of the Khanqa of Baybars al-Gashankir and the mosque of An-Nasir Muhammad at the Citadel. Sometimes the middle storey was decorated with marble inlay as seen in the minarets of the mosques of Barquq and the Qadi-Yahya. Decoration increased in variety and richness towards the beginning of the sixteenth century. The cruciform-plan *madrasas* also evolved during this period. They were composed of an open *sahn* (courtyard), surrounded by four *iwans* (rectangular halls). Mausoleums for the founders were annexed near these *madrasas*, while *sabils* (water fountains) and *kuttabs* (schools) were annexed to some of them. Towards the end of the period, *madrasas* (schools) were built to a smaller scale, compared with earlier periods, and their *sahns* were covered with highly decorated wooden roofs.[29]

Like its poetry, Iran possessed a rich repertoire of visual vocabulary that drew upon over 3,000 years of architectural development from various civilizations of the Iranian plateau. Islam initiated a new wave of remarkable religious buildings in which the arts of stucco, mosaic, and calligraphy evolved. Post-Islamic architecture drew ideas from its pre–Islamic predecessor, and had geometrical and repetitive forms, as well as surfaces that were richly decorated with glazed tiles, carved stucco, patterned brickwork, floral motifs, and scripture. The dome structure of *muqarnas* was utilized to construct the ceilings of the brick buildings. To place a circular brick dome on a square-plan building, squinch arches needed to be inserted into the four corners of the room in order to create an octagonal shape that approximated a circle. As a way of aesthetically unifying the horizontal layers formed by the continuation of these squinch arches, *muqarnas*, which link a square room to a circular dome, are thought to have developed from Persian brick architecture predating the Seljuk Empire. The wall patterns in 11th century Iranian tombs faithfully reproduced the image of decorated squinch arches. The lower section of the wall patterns illustrated a square room and the upper part a circular dome, with a complex succession of small arches between the two.

Persian architecture from the 15th through 17th centuries was the pinnacle of post–Islamic architectural achievement. Various buildings such as mosques, mausoleums, bazaars, bridges and palaces have survived from this period. Safavid Isfahan tried to achieve grandeur in scale; Isfahan's Naghsh-i Jahan Square was the sixth largest square worldwide. The great mosques of Khorasan, Isfahan and Tabriz each used local geometry, local materials and local building methods to express, each in its own way, the order, harmony and unity of Islamic architecture. Persian architecture often revealed complex geometrical relationships, a studied hierarchy of form and ornament, and great depths of symbolic meaning.

Persian artists also built the most impressive dome in the Islamic world. The Sassanid Empire initiated the construction of the first large-scale domes in Persia, with such royal buildings as the Palace of Ardashir and Ghal'eh Dokhtar. After the Muslim conquest, the Persian style became a major influence on Muslim societies and the dome also became a feature of Muslim architecture.

The innovations of dome building in the Il-Khanate period made it possible for the Persians to construct much taller buildings. These changes later paved the way for Safavid architecture. The pinnacle of Il-Khanate architecture was reached with the construction of the Soltaniyeh Dome (1302–1312) in Zanjan, which measures 50 m in height and 25 m in diameter, the 3rd largest and the tallest masonry dome ever erected.

The renaissance in Persian mosque and dome building came during the Safavid dynasty, when Shah Abbas, in 1598, initiated the reconstruction of Isfahan, with Naqsh-e Jahan Square as the centerpiece of his new capital. Architecturally these works borrowed heavily from Il-Khanate designs, but artistically they elevated the designs to a new level. What distinguished Persian domes from domes created in the Christian world or the Ottoman and Mughal empires was the use of colorful tiles that covered the exterior of the domes much like the interior. Dozens of these were erected in Isfahan, and the distinct blue shape dominated the skyline of the city. Reflecting the light of the sun, these domes looked like glittering turquoise gems and could be seen from miles away by travelers following the Silk Road through Persia.

This very distinct style of Iranian architecture was inherited from the Seljuq dynasty (11th to 14th centuries), who for centuries had used it in their mosque building, but it was perfected during the Safavids (1501–1722) when they invented the *haft- rangi* (seven-color style of tile burning), a process that enabled them to apply more colors to each tile, creating richer patterns that were more pleasing to the eye. Persians favored gold, white and turquoise patterns on a dark blue background. The extensive inscription bands of calligraphy and arabesque on most of the major buildings were carefully planned and executed by Ali Reza Abbasi, who was appointed head of the royal library and master calligrapher at the Shah's court in 1598, while Shaykh Bahai oversaw the construction projects. Reaching 53 meters in height, the dome of Masjed-e Shah (Shah Mosque) became the tallest in the city when it was finished in 1629. It was built as a double-shelled dome, spanning 14 m between the two layers and resting on an octagonal, domed chamber.[30]

Islamic art and architecture in Andalusia developed their own characteristics and styles like in Iran. The construction of the Great Mosque at

Cordoba (Mezquita), which began in 785, marked the beginning of Islamic architecture in the Iberian Peninsula and North Africa. The site was originally a pagan temple, then a Visigothic Christian church, before the Umayyad Moors converted the building into a mosque. The Mezquita is regarded as the one of the most accomplished monuments of Islamic architecture and is most noted for its arcaded hypostyle hall, with 856 columns of jasper, onyx, marble, and granite. These were made from pieces of the Roman temple that had occupied the site previously, as well as other destroyed Roman buildings, such as the Mérida amphitheatre. The Moorish builders introduced double arches that allowed higher ceilings than would otherwise have been possible with relatively low columns. The double arches consisted of a lower horseshoe arch and an upper semicircular arch. The famous alternating red and white voussoirs of the arches were inspired by those in the Dome of the Rock and also resemble those of the Aachen Cathedral, which were built at almost the same time. A centrally located honeycombed dome had blue tiles decorated with stars.

The mosque also had richly gilded prayer niches, and its *mihrab* (prayer niche in the *qibla* wall) was a masterpiece of geometric and flowing floral designs. Other prominent features were an open courtyard surrounded by arcades, screens of wood, minarets, colorful mosaics, and windows of colored glass. The walls of the mosque had Qur'anic inscriptions. Like earlier Islamic mosques, it had a rectangular prayer hall with aisles arranged perpendicular to the *qibla*. The prayer hall was large in size, flat, with timber ceilings held up by horseshoe-shaped arches. These arches, described as countless pillars, are believed to portray rows of palm trees in the oases of Syria, the homeland of the exiled Umayyad rulers who came to Europe to escape Abbasid execution. Until the eleventh century, the courtyard was unpaved earth with citrus and palm trees irrigated at first by rainwater cisterns and later by aqueduct. Excavation indicates that the trees were planted in a pattern with surface irrigation channels. Cordoba became the political and legal center of the Islamic kingdom in Spain.

Moorish architecture, which began in Cordoba, reached its peak with the construction of the Alhambra, the magnificent palace/fortress of Granada, with its open and breezy interior spaces adorned in red, blue, and gold. The walls were decorated with stylized foliage motifs, Arabic inscriptions, and arabesque design work, with walls covered in glazed tile. Other smaller examples such as the Bab Mardum in Toledo, or the caliphate city of Medina Azahara, survived. Moorish architecture has its roots deeply established in the Arab tradition of architecture and design established during the era of the first caliphate of the Umayyad in the Levant, circa A.D. 660. In Damascus there are very well preserved examples of fine Arab

Islamic design and geometric, including the carmen, which is the typical Damascene house, opening on the inside with a fountain as the house's centerpiece.

Even after the completion of the Reconquista, Islamic influence had a lasting impact on the architecture of Spain. In particular, medieval Spaniards used the Mudéjar style. One of the best examples of the Moors' lasting impact on Spanish architecture is the Alcázar of Seville. The square lattice pattern of surface decoration in Cordoba also reached its apex in Alhambra Palace. The decorations within the palaces typified the remains of the Moorish dominion within Spain and ushered in the last great period of Andalusian art in Granada. Since then, artists repeatedly reproduced the same forms and trends until they developed a new style during the Nasrid Dynasty. The Nasrids freely adopted and integrated all the stylistic elements that had accumulated during the eight centuries of Muslim rule in the Peninsula. They included the Caliphate horseshoe arch, the Almohad *sebka* (a grid of rhombuses), the Almoravid palm, and unique combinations of them, as well as innovations such as stilted arches and *muqarnas*. Like in the Alhambra, columns, honeycombed domes (with thousands of tiny cells), walls decorated with arabesques and calligraphy, and *muqarnas* appeared in chambers and the interiors of many Andalusian palaces.[31]

The arabesque, a form of artistic decoration consisting of surface stylings based on rhythmic linear patterns of scrolling and interlacing foliage tendrils, was very popular in Islamic architecture from the 9th century on, and was adopted by European decorative art during the Renaissance. Islamic arabesques derived from the Late Antique and Byzantine types of scrolling vegetal decoration, and were relatively unchanged in early Islamic art. The plants most often used were stylized versions of the acanthus, with its emphasis on leafy forms, and the vine, with an equal emphasis on twining stems. These forms evolved into a distinctive Islamic type by the 11th century. Thereafter it was used very widely across the Islamic world as local variants in Arab and non–Arab areas were assimilated, and it continued to develop further through regional enrichment. In the process of development the plant forms became increasingly simplified and stylized.[32]

As early as in the art of Samarra (Abbasid period), the relatively natural tendencies in decorative arts gave way to an abstract form of ornamentation known as spiraloid form. In these abstract forms, ornamental art almost shed natural forms and presented only distant likenesses to the plants from which they originally derived. Now only rhythmic patterns remained, representing movement and rhythm. Although almost unrecognizable as natural objects, the movement was conveyed with contracting and expanding lines and waves having different degrees of consonance. The designs were not symmetrical, but did have a certain repetition and balance. This art allowed rhythm, normally only heard, to be visual through the spiral undulations of lines. Compared to its Greco-Roman contemporaries, which embraced a naturalistic form, arabesque interlacing had a geometrical complexity and rhythmic quality that escaped the Roman arts. The shape of arabesque often is built on one or several regular figures inscribed in a circle, then developed according to the principle of the star polygon, meaning that the proportions inherent to the basic figure are repeated in each and every level of development.[33]

There were two modes to arabesque art. The first recalled the principles that govern the order of the world. These principles were manifested in the bare basics of what made objects structurally sound and visually beautiful. In the first mode, each repeating geometric form had a built-in symbolism ascribed to it. For example, the square, with its four equilateral sides, was symbolic of the equally important elements of nature: earth, air, fire and water. Without any one of the four, the physical world, represented by a circle inscribed in the square, would collapse upon itself and cease to exist. The second mode was based upon the flowing nature of plant forms, the rhythm of movement or the life of the universe itself. This mode represented natural evolution. With shape and movement of nature as illustrated in the two modes, an art that combined them into one would be the highest form of arabesque beauty. This combination is Arabic calligraphy. The reason calligraphy became the highest form of Islamic art is that it not only presents the words of God, but also illustrates the essence of the universe, its shape and rhythm as well as its voice (God's words). The coming together of these three forms creates the arabesque, and this is a reflection of unity arising from diversity (a basic tenet of Islam).

At first glance, there was great similarity between arabesque artwork from very different geographic and linguistic regions. In fact, the similarities are so pronounced that it is sometimes difficult for experts to tell where a given style of arabesque comes from. The reason for this is that Arabic language after the classical period has absorbed the language of precision and technology that was distilled from science and mathematics and that was required to construct arabesque artwork. Thanks to the poetic side of Arabic, a universal and precise vision could be easily seen through the eyes of individual artists. Therefore, for most Muslims, the best artwork that could be created by man for use in the mosque was artwork that displayed the underlying order and unity of God's nature and a glimpse of the spiritual world, the place where the only true reality exists.[34]

The evolution of Arabic calligraphy progressed in a similar fashion to that of the arts. Its emphasis began with geometric shape and proportion, then incorporated rhythmic movement and harmony. The earliest Arabic calligraphy shared the geometric form of Islamic arts. Kufic, a script consisting of straight lines and angles, was a cleaner, more geometric style, with a very visible rhythm and a stress on horizontal lines. It originally did not have consonant pointing to distinguish, for example, *b, t,* and *th.* It is still employed in Islamic regions, although it has undergone a number of alterations and often displays regional variations. The difference between the Kufic script used in the Arabian Peninsula and that employed in North African states is very marked. Sometimes, vowels were noted as red dots; consonants were distinguished with small dashes to make the texts more readable. A number of Qur'ans written in this style have been found in the mosque at Kairouan, in Tunisia. Kufic writing also appears on ancient coins.[35]

The Maghribi script and its Andalusi variant became less rigid versions of Kufic, with more curves. For the writing of Qur'ans and other documents, Kufic was eventually replaced by the cursive scripts. It remained in use for decorative purposes: In "Flowering Kufi," slender geometric lettering was associated with stylized vegetal elements. In "Geometric Kufi," the letters are arranged in complex, two-dimensional geometric patterns (for example, filling a square). This aims at decoration rather than readability. Naskh script appeared in an Egyptian Qur'an from the 14th–15th centuries. Cursive styles of calligraphy appeared during the 10th century. They were easier to write and read and soon replaced the earlier geometric style, except for decorative purposes.

The canonical "six cursive scripts" (*al-aqlam al-sittah*) were pioneered by the Persian Ibn Muqla Shirazi (d. 939) and were reformed and refined by Ibn al-Bawwab (d. 1022) by developing a system of proportional measurement so that each letter could be measured by its height and width in dots. Yaqut al-Musta'simi (d. 1298) refined the six scripts set down by Ibn al-Bawwab by giving the letter shapes new dimension by emphasizing the slanted cut of the pen. He also further systematized the method of proportional measurement with dots.[36]

The straight, angular forms of Kufic were replaced in the new script by curved and oblique lines. *Tulut* (*thuluth*) was a more monumental and energetic writing style, with elongated verticals. It was used by Mamluks in mosque decorations during the 14th–15th centuries. With some slight changes, *tulut* was used to write the headings of *sura* (Qur'anic chapters). Some of the oldest copies of the Qur'an were written in *tulut*. Later copies were written in a combination of *tulut* and either *Naskhi* or *Muhakkak,* while after the 15th century *Naskhi* came to be used exclusively. More

Qur'anic texts have been written in *Naskh* than in all the other scripts combined. *Naskh* appealed particularly to the ordinary person because the script was relatively easy to read and write. It is usually written with short horizontal stems and with almost equal vertical depth above and below the medial line. The curves are full and deep, the uprights straight and vertical, and the words generally well spaced.

Naskh or *naskhi* was a simple cursive writing that was used in correspondence before the calligraphers started using it for Qur'an writing. It is slender and supple, without any particular emphasis, and highly readable. It remains among the most widespread styles. The most famous calligrapher of this genre was Hâfiz Osman, an Ottoman calligrapher who lived during the 17th century. *Naskh* is the basis of modern Arabic print.

Islamic Mosque calligraphy can be found in and out of mosques, typically in combination with arabesque motifs. Arabesque is a form of Islamic art known for its repetitive geometric forms creating beautiful decorations. These geometric shapes often include Arabic calligraphy written on walls and ceilings inside and outside of mosques. The subject of these writings can be derived from different sources in Islam. It can be derived from the written words of the Qur'an or from the oral traditions relating to the words and deeds of the Islamic Prophet Muhammad.

There is a beautiful harmony between the inscriptions and the functions of the mosque. Specific *surahs* (chapters) or *ayats* (verses) from the Qur'an are inscribed in accordance with functions of specific architectural elements. For example, on the domes you can find the *Nour ayat* (the divine stress on light) written. Above the main entrance you find verses related to the entrances to paradise. On the windows the divine names of Allah are inscribed so that reflection of the sun rays through those windows reminds the believer that Allah manifests Himself upon the universe in all high qualities.[37]

Among the most important contributions of non–Arabic architecture to the Islamic tradition was the addition of brilliant colors. The Persian poet Nizami Ganjavi (1141–1209) was the first person to add more colors into the established palette of Arabic hues, which was limited to green, white, black, and gold, colors that were closely associated with religious meanings. The green is used in the decoration of mosques, bindings of Qur'ans, silken covers for the graves of Sufi saints, and in the flags of various Muslim countries. For the Arabs, green symbolizes nature and life. They envision paradise as green and its inhabitants as clothed in green silk garments. White symbolizes purity and peace. Muslims wear white while attending Friday prayers and *hajj* (pilgrimage). Black means mourning and reminds believers of their religious martyrs. Persian poetry, architecture and illustrative arts brought color from heaven to earth and to everyday life. In his *Haft Paykar* (*Love, Color and the Universe*), Nizami used seven colors to structure his classic poem. The central theme of the book was the tale of the Sassanian prince Bahram Gur, who had seven pavilions built in seven colors for his seven brides. He visited them one by one on each of the seven days of the week, wearing the appropriate color. Other than being a bedazzling exploration of the pleasure of love, the poem portrayed seven stages of human life, the seven aspects of destiny, or the seven stages of the mystical path.[38]

From here, color was liberated from the domain of philosophy and religion (as symbols of abstract meanings), and became alive. Color became visible and touchable as it played a crucial role in the surface design of architecture, metal-works, enameling on metals and glass, especially the glazes used by potters and textile works. In architecture, colorful decorations in the form of tiles, glass mosaics or painted walls and ceilings were mostly found inside buildings. There appeared to be regional differences in the use and display of color in the Islamic world. In India builders and patrons used natural red sandstone for their buildings. In Iran, where the buff-colored brick did not afford the same kind of opportunity, they were forced to incorporate colors in other ways, as in colorful tile decorations. Finally, the passion for color was extended from buildings to lavishly colorful gardens.

The Islamic garden turned nature into a captured and beautified space full of colors, details and patterns. Only during this stage of maturity could visual art produce so many concrete, fresh, and stylish images of an idea as old as paradise. The underlying theme of the Islamic garden is the concept of the *chahar-bagh* or four-fold garden. Classically, the *chahar-bagh* is constructed around a central pool or fountain, with four streams flowing from it, representing the four main elements of life. The Prophet Muhammad, describing his miraculous journey to heaven, mentions four rivers: flowing with wine, milk, honey and water. The number four has an inherent symbolism reflecting the natural world. The symbolism of an Islamic garden represents a universal theme, the understanding of nature and the universe.[39]

This concept, which was deeply rooted in religions for thousands of years, finally came to life in the hands of Islamic designers and architects. Like the Qur'anic scriptures on the walls of mosques that provide verbal meanings of the buildings, Qur'anic uses of the garden as an analogy for paradise significantly influences garden design. Traditionally, an Islamic garden is a cool place of rest and reflection, and a reminder of paradise. The Qur'an has many references to gardens, and the garden is used as an earthly analogue for the life in paradise that is promised to believers:

Allah has promised to the believers gardens beneath which rivers flow, wherein they abide eternally, and pleasant dwellings in gardens of perpetual residence; but approval from Allah is greater. It is that which is the great attainment [Qur'an 9.72].

Paradise (*janna*) promised the pious and devout streams of water that would not go rank and rivers of milk whose taste would not change, rivers of delectable wine, streams of pure honey, fruits of every kind, and forgiveness from the lord.[40]

The literary images of paradise described in the Qur'an did not automatically result in inspirations in garden design and building. During the first four centuries of Islam, hardly any consciously designed gardens (with four quadrants and four water channels) were built to imitate the paradise scene. The gardens that were built were void of religious meaning. As Islamic civilization evolved, its ideas and concepts began to be realized in artistic forms, such as architecture and visual art. Like the mosques, which developed from functional buildings to monuments demonstrating a builder's ideas, viewpoints and artistic capacities, the Islamic garden projected the Muslim vision of the universe. In other words, an Islamic garden had little to do with nature (wild or enclosed) in the English sense of the word, although water, trees and plants were its components. The Islamic garden, more like the Chinese and Japanese classical garden, projected a sense of order, balance and rhythm that were much grander and deeper than the natural world visible to the naked eyes.

Unlike the English concept of enclosed (or artificial) nature, where human eyes and hands impose control, the Islamic garden was designed by and projected a divine order that Muslims believe to be God given and shared by man and nature. Abstract arts and design were the typical means to present this sense of order, balance, and rhythm (of the universe). Geometry, symmetry, shape, surface, proportion, and movement of lines all reflected a natural process, an inherent organization. This sense of balance was revealed in the design of the garden, which often was divided into four large green areas surrounding a centrally located palace or pavilion. This stood in complete contrast to a courtyard within a palace, dwelling, fort, mosque or *madrasa*. There were trees, flowers and/or grass in the garden while the surface of a courtyard was predominantly hard, made of stone, marble, or mosaic. The contrast often was softened by water. The buildings, walls, arcades, axial pathways, steps, straight canals, and parterres were in complete contrast to the background bushes, shrubs, and flowers hanging on the edges of support structures.[41]

Like many other civilizations, Arabic literature developed a rich symbolic relationship with water, as projected in Islamic architecture, especially its garden designs. Water was the symbolic center and basis of garden design. It divided a garden into intended shapes and it flowed through narrow canals, implying the passage or flow of time. Since paradise had to overflow with water, fountains, tanks, and canals in Islamic gardens always flowed over the rim. Water was also used imaginatively in the garden plan, and it creatively contributed to architecture and landscape. Pools often contained fish, ducks, and water plants. Water tanks led to fountains that delighted both the eyes and ears. The falling spray of water generated ever-expanding ripples so that when looking at the basin one wondered if the water was motionless or the marble was rippling. In short, water was used as an element of design to contrast with the stability and stillness of the architecture.

The water's edge was one of the most attractive areas in the Islamic garden. Although canals had hard edges, the sides of the pools often extended over the surrounding ground with elaborately carved edges. The water in the pools was normally shallow; but when deliberately left murky, it appeared to be infinite. The reflection on the pool of still water introduced light and the illusion of space, while the passing cloud symbolized transience. The pool of shallow water could also be strewn with rose petals, or bore candles set adrift on tiny rafts to provide a sense of peaceful beauty and profound satisfaction.[42]

In the gardens of Moorish Spain, fountains were everywhere. Large pools were included in the designs of gardens in the Arabic Middle East, Iran and India. The layout of the gardens was strictly geometric, confined by walls of masonry or hedges. The geometric shape was also confirmed by irrigating parterres. The gardens were small in size. Even the large ones were partitioned into small and linked enclosures. Andalusian gardens were urban and well attended, as they were filled with fragrant flowers and seemed to be covered by a floral rug. In the flat sites of Cordova and Seville the garden was considered to be an outdoor room, an extension of the building. High walls of white stuccoed masonry cast a welcome shadow.

Conclusions

The world that Arabic created had been substantially widened both in scope and depth with the evolution and accumulation of its descriptive forms. From the small world of a desert tribal community to the Islamic nations and to the universe that created by God, this leap of faith was carried each step of the way by Arabic reading, writing, and painting. Words did not only paint a larger world, they also penetrated beyond it as Arabic became further distilled into more abstract forms. Arabic became able to

describe visions beyond what was seen by the naked eye: the logic underlying natural evolution, principles that governed the movement of the universe and social conditions, and most importantly the divine wisdom that
made life comprehensible.

The abstraction of language is not unique to Arabic. Almost every
language in the world encountered a classical period through internal evolution or external influence. What was unique in the Middle East was that
Arabic, because of its deep rooting in poetry and ritual and linguistic performance, managed to keep its feet on the ground. The multitude and diversity did amount to a gap between the seen and unseen, abstract and concrete
and between written and spoken. Arabic vision remained unified and free.

CHAPTER 6

Imagery of Man and His Feelings

This chapter is a brief history of the evolution of Arabic imagery of man (a general and collective concept of human) and his feelings. It traces the creation and transformation of ideal images in terms of the accumulation of the vocabulary of love. Without a language reorientation, as seen in medieval Europe, language of love in Arabic enjoyed a remarkable continuity that is rarely found in world literature. This vocabulary has been used to express love, friendship, affection, and worship to ideal images both human and divine. This language of love (for man, woman or God) also shared a similar pattern of formation and transfiguration. In the process, images (ideal and concrete, of worship and worshiper) were constantly redefined in literature, especially in poetry. For example, the primal concept of Godhead that Arabic inherited from ancient Semitic began with a notion of God as opposite to man. Descriptive language evolved in hymns, God gradually retained many images. So did the concept of man as it was transfigured by the accumulation of a diverse language of praying and ritual of worship. When God was revealed in various faces, sought in various signs, worshipped in various objects of worship, and pursued in the visible and invisible, he appeared different to every pair of eyes gazing upon him. Each of his believers could find and unite with Him on his own personal terms. Increasingly personalized poetry would create a variably perceived Divine that was communicated in a highly individualized language to each and every writer, reader, and believer.

Man began to cultivate a concept of individuality only after a culture had developed a language of love capable of perceptual and emotional sensibility. This linguistic evolution took place in many cultures at different stages, the later medieval period in Western Europe and the post–Tang period in China, for example. The language of love was not a stranger to the Middle East even before the emergence of Arabic and Islam. Akkadian love poetry followed Sumerian prototypes. The ancient Mesopotamians began their love affair with Inanna when they sang to her in prayers and hymns. At the time, Istar was the "lady of heaven" who was in charge of love and sexual attraction. An Old Babylonian hymn, composed for King Amiditana (1683–1647 B.C.), represented love in a rather coarse language with poor and limited imagery. It was that the goddess was "clothed with love and joy, and adorned with seduction, grace and sex-appeal." She was described having "honey-sweet lips" and "vibrant mouth." Her eyes were "shining and bright" and she gave "life, power, and protection" wherever she looked. She "subdued the four corners of the world."[1]

Without a more abstract word for love or affection, the face of the Divine retained clumsy images from the standard Sumerian epithets of the goddess. As a personification of beauty, love and charm, she was illustrated with the word *inbu*, taken from horticultural terminology. *Inbu* (Akkadian) derived from the Sumerian word *bilga* (fruit), which extended its meaning to refer to male ancestors and symbolized a connection to human sexual intercourse. The Akkadian word *kuzbu* was the closest to the Sumerian word *hi-li* (sex appeal and irresistible attraction); voluptuousness and orgasm were also the common renditions of the story of God.[2]

Similar to the Greek mythologies, whose language became less violent and vulgar over time, the Babylonian tale of love was much less graphic, even though some Sumerian verbal remnants remained. King Amiditana (1683–1647 B.C.) was the lover of the goddess Innana, but his sex appeal was not mentioned. His praise and love for her were a part of his pious duty. He was subject to her command. Thus, the tone of love was altogether formal, polite and distanced. He demonstrated his love for the goddess by sacrifice and prayer, hoping to be rewarded with military success (dominion around the world) and long life.

The relationship between the ruler and the gods was described in a manner quite different from the royal hymns of the Ur III/Isin-Larsa period. Old Babylonian royal inscriptions generally emphasized the humanity of the king rather than his claims to divine status. The gods did indeed recognize the king as their representative, but he was also qualified as an able administrator and purveyor of earthly justice. Rather than blurring the distinctions between king and gods, as in the Ur III royal hymns, the Babylonian royal ideology highlighted the gulf between them. All the mythological trappings of kinship between ruler and the gods disappeared from the texts. There was no more of the king's divine birth, of him being suckled by the mother-goddesses. The symbolic sexual union between ruler and the goddess also lost currency, because, like the metaphors of divine kinship, it contradicted the spirit of this separation and the sense of propriety concerning gods' affairs.[3]

Istar was not the only goddess who was associated with sexuality. Little is known about the origins of Nannâ (or Nanaya), who appeared in Sumerian texts from the Ur III period onwards. She received offerings at the portals of the Giparu at Uruk during the Neo-Sumerian period. She was a daughter of An, and like Inanna, a sister of Utu. She was also a manifestation of the planet Venus. There was a royal hymn to Išbi-Erra of Isin, which described the relationship between Inanna and Nannâ (Sin in Akkadian), her lover who was available at her command. In an Old Babylonian royal hymn composed for Samsuiluna (1749–1712 B.C., the son and successor of Hammurabi), Inanna was described in terms of the sun and the moon of her people. Her shadow was filled with splendor and she was rich of fertility, glory, sweetness and sex appeal and full of joy, laughter and love.[4]

Divine love affairs now were portrayed in less vulgar terms, focusing more on the couple's desire for each other and the reflection of love and sex rather than the sexual act itself. "She fills his heart with happiness." "Your love-making is sweet and your erotic ability was sated with honey." "He was thirsting for her as he did for water."[5] In contrast to the Sumerian love-dialogues, where the king himself was the lover, and where the lovers were described in detailed imagery of love-making, this was a composite text, where the king was clearly dissociated from the amorous preoccupation of the divine couple, the deities Nannâ and Muati. Their dialogue was a collage of hackneyed erotic phrases, a rather formal recitation, which was interspersed with references to the king who was seeking the blessings of the goddess. This was not a personal love-poem in a modern sense, but rather a specially commissioned text, dedicated to the statue of the goddess. As personal feelings were not expressed in divine dialogue, the language of love became a passionate exchange between gods and goddesses, when divine marriage ceremonies between Nabû and Nannâ were celebrated in Babylon during the first millennium. The love and sexual relationship of Nannâ, an Istar-type goddess, and her consort Muati became a divine affair. Unlike the Sumerian ruler, who dedicated himself to satisfying the erotic demands of his goddess, the Babylonian king abdicated this task to another god, who was more capable of providing the goddess with sensual enjoyment. The Babylonian literature said that the "robust" (*šamha*, actually "voluptuous," "potent") Muati would be equal to the task. The king, however, still expected the blessings that the goddess usually bestowed on her lover; but now her new husband, Muati, interceded for him and asked his spouse "to let him live forever," a favor that Nannâ alone could grant.[6]

The language of love and passionate speech remained mainly among the immortals and within the context of divine marriage. The love of mortals for the goddess was described as a burning heart and lust crying out in agitation; they would "reminisce on their former bliss" and "the marriage they had experienced in the now ruined temple." Although on rare occasions, the Babylon texts seemed to continue the address to the male lover, providing more details about intimacy and the act of love-making, such as "The beating of your heats is joyful music," and "Rise and let me make love to you!," this love affair became a ritual form without any personal meaning. It became a part of ritual performance in which quoted, passionate speech formed a part of the composition of the ceremonial performance.[7]

There were striking similarities between Akkadian and Sumerian love songs in tone and imagery. They both used the first-person plural suffix "our" for the women's parts. (Some scholars suggested that this could imply her sharing them with her lover.) This was presented as a female voice of seduction, calling from her perfumed bed. The noticeable difference from the Sumerian poems was in the directness of her speech and details of description. Only in bridal songs did the young woman speak of her own genitals, where she pointed out the visible signs of nudity ("now our parts have grown hair ... now our breasts stand up").[8] However, in Akkadian love-songs, the male lover sometimes described the vulva as being as sweet as honey or beer, but even in the most intimate situations the woman did not talk of her bodily parts except in poetic allusions. The whole tenor of the Babylonian fragment had none of the intense intimacy of the Sumerian courtly love poem. When the setting was no longer a tête-à-tête between human lovers, but rather a symbolic act of a divine couple, the nuances and subtleties disappeared and the language became correspondingly stronger. They magically created and activated vivid imagery of divine lovemaking.

The development distinction between Sumerian and Babylonian love poetry was similar to that between Latin classical poetry and the early Troubadour poetry in France. For example, the poetry of Guillem IX, duke of Aquitaine, was rather direct and earthy in contrast to that of Ovid. The erotic poetry in Akkadian was popular and much admired in the old scribal center of Kiš, which was active throughout the preceding Isin-Larsa period. However, unlike in Provence, there was not a great development of courtly poetry in post–Old Babylonian poetry, although there was a tendency to write Akkadian love-songs, to some extent imitating Sumerian court poetry. The reason was that the Akkadian disappeared as a popular language, and it gradually became replaced by other regional vernaculars and literatures while its written form was still used. Even after the Greek invasion under Alexander the Great in the 4th century B.C., Akkadian was still a contender as a written language; but like Latin, spoken Akkadian was likely extinct by this time, or at least rarely used.[9]

The linguistic reorientation of ancient Mesopotamia (from Akkadian to mushrooming regional vernaculars) put an end to the abstraction tendency of the language of love, which evolved from Sumerian to Akkadian literatures. Emerging vernaculars breathed new life into the expression of feelings in Semitic languages. Similar to what happened in late medieval Western Europe where vernaculars spread the words of love from the church into villages, cities and the streets, a highly personal and sensitive poetry of feelings emerged and was cultivated in pre–Islamic poetry. The ancient gods gradually became forgotten as the voice of hymns diminished, the memory of their myth was lost, and temples of worship were abandoned after new and diverse deities were cultivated in various regional languages. Thus, the authority and royalty of gods and goddesses was transformed to human authorities such as tribal kings and chiefs, while poets took different roles as the leaders and lips of the community.

Ancient Arabic emerged from diverse cultural and regional societies. The South Arabians had an ancient, settled civilization, while the northern Arabs were nomads and dwellers in oases, dependent on caravan trade routes and the pastoral use of an arid expanse of parched semi-desert. The nomadic tribes had neither architecture (only the tent, with three hearthstones in front of it) nor pictorial art, except rock drawings. However, music was played on the lyre and similar sophisticated stringed instruments, and verses were chanted at social functions. In the company of flute and tambourine their seemingly wild desert life was organized by tribal social convention. Here men were measured by the qualities of their personality rather than their relationships with gods. They had to be loyal to their tribal community and do everything that they could to defend its interests and pride. However, the awareness of honor went beyond social and collective codes; it was engraved in man's character that had been cultivated by the sound and rhythm of poetry for generations. An ideal man had to be honorable (*sharaf*), generous and hospitable (*karam*), and give succor (*najdah*) to the weak (women and children). His manhood should be judged by his prowess, bravery or even personal sacrifice in tribal war to defend its honor.

Swords and words were vehicles of social mobility in tribal Arabia, where persons from lower social and ethnical backgrounds could distinguish themselves as heroes. For example, Antara Ibn Shaddad (525–608), one of the most renowned pre–Islamic poets, was the son of Shaddad, a well-respected member of the Arabian tribe of Banu Abs; his mother was Zabibah, an Ethiopian slave. Initially both his father and his tribe neglected

Antara as he was growing up in servitude. He was considered one of the "Arab crows" (*Al-aghribah al-'Arab*) because of his jet-black complexion. Antara eventually gained attention and respect for himself by his remarkable personal qualities and courage in battlefield, and he became an accomplished poet and a mighty warrior. He earned his freedom after a tribe invaded Banu Abs when his father promised, "Defend your tribe and you are free." Antara fought many great tribal wars and eventually died as a hero for the cause.

Antarah's poetry is well preserved, and often presented chivalrous values, courage and heroism in war, as well as his love for Abla, his cousin. He was immortalized when one of his poems was included in the *Hanged Poems*. The poetry's historical and cultural importance derives from its detailed descriptions of battles, armor, weapons, horses, the desert and other themes from his time.[10]

His boast, running to over thirty lines, reads as a danse macabre, a grim display of courage that devolves into unconstrained bloodletting. And yet it was precisely here, "as the whirl of death / dragged champion after champion down," and the poet was facing the flying arrows and swards, that he abandoned for a moment all posturing and deflected his helpless anguish onto his poetry. As he pushed his spear into his enemy's breast and clothed him in blood, he saw tears in his eyes. "Had he known how to speak he would have protested. Had he known to use words, he would have spoken to me now." These closing lines forced a powerful image of life and death in the minds of readers.

Antara's poetry provided vivid imagery of the Arabian hero, especially his extremely diverse personalities and fluid emotions. He was gentle and mild by nature when his rights were not violated. He loved his life and his woman; he often gazed at and dreamed of her naked and exquisite neck and he wept at her absence. When he was injured, however, his resentment became firm and bitter as coloquintida to the taste of the aggressor. The enemy had sought his blood, the blood of his kinsmen, who never had wronged them; he had to go to war for sweet revenge. He put himself as a shield between his loved one and hostile spears; he well recognized the danger at the place where he fixed his foot, which was too narrow to admit a companion. "Go on, Antara!" the exulting warriors cried. Against the coming tide of the enemy he pressed forward. With a nimble and double-handed stroke, he prevented the enemy's attack. He rapidly struck him to the heart with an Indian scimitar, with the blade of bright water, till streams of blood gushed out of the wound. He defied war's terrors by silencing his enemies. He left them dead like sacrificed victims, to the lions of the forest and ravenous vultures hovering over their heads. "Well done," his kinsmen cheered. His wounded pride healed and his anger dispersed and he felt like he was on the top of the world.

The cruelty of war affected women poets differently than it did men. Women's poetic expertise was to lament for the dead and express grief in moving metaphors and similes. Al-Khansa' (575–646) was considered by many the best Arabic poetesses. Her life was full of tragedies and a chain of wounds that never healed, as she lost not only her brothers, but also her four sons in war. Her elegy for her brother Sakr made her well-known even before Islam as she won competitions for poetic performance. Her elegy (*al-ritha'*) "Lament of Sakr" expressed her grief in vivid metaphors: as if time had gnawed at her, bit and cut her. The lost of her brother had wounded and harmed her so badly that for years she still saw the riders, the broad swords and grey spears, which turned faces deathly white and cut bodies. Yes, her tribe won the war and the praise of people, but her brother was dead and gone forever. She herself melted into tears that flowed endless and would never dry. She would weep for his death as long as there were mountain peaks, watered earth, and morning clouds.

Unlike the elegiac tradition of the western language that mainly depicted characterizations of the departed, Arabic elegy focused on the experience of suffering and expression of the emotion of the mourner, which made the poetry moving and effective. In her elegy for Sakr, Al-Khansa' presented only one image of Sakr; the spear point whose bright shape lights up the night. She promised that she would cry for him and mourn as long as the dove sang and the stars shined. She would never forgive the enemies who killed him. Poetry here became an act, a performance in public by a group of women during pre–Islamic or early Islamic periods. The intensity of the expression attempted to matched the finality of death and turn mourning into a heroic deed, as heroic as the death of men in the battle.[11]

Al-Khansa' was a contemporary of Muhammad, who often came to her recital performances and listened to her poetry. In 629 she converted to Islam and sent her four sons to the war of Islamic conquest with her words: "Remember the great merit of fighting to defend your faith. Recite the verses of Qur'an about patience in the midst of distress. Tomorrow morning, rise from your bed hale and hearty and join the battle with fearless courage. Go into the midst of the thickest battle, encounter the boldest enemy and die as martyrs if you have to." They joined the war with fearless courage, with the words of their mother ringing in their ears. They plunged themselves heroically into the battle and put many enemies to the sword. They were killed one after the other. When the news of the death of her sons reached her, she asked the messenger about the outcome of the battle.

When she was told that the Muslims had won, she thanked God for the martyrdom of her sons, and asked, "Who dies, if Islam lives?"

She found new meaning in her sacrifice: for Allah and Islam. Now, she no longer shed tears or lamented the blind twist of fate. Pagan imageries in her verses had disappeared. Her suffering from the loss of her sons was more serene and congruent with her new faith. However, her poetry still sang with the same poignant immediacy and touching emotions.

When she saw the dead bodies of her sons, she did not weep. She burst into an elegy: "My sons, I have borne you with pain and brought you up with great care. You have fallen today for the cause of Islam. Who says you are dead? No, you are very much alive. You are alive with honor." When Al-Khansa' returned to Madina, Caliph Omar Bin al Khattab went to her house to express his condolence over the death of her sons. She merely said: "Please congratulate me, commander of the faithful. I am proud to be the mother of martyrs."

The passion to die for glory in the battlefields came with the same passion for life. The warrior/poet lived for the moments of pleasure that might not be there tomorrow. He enjoyed music, wine and the company of singing girls. He loved his woman as a companion, the only warmth in a cold and cruel life; he remembered her as white as a star, in her striped gown or her saffron robe with widely open collar showing her tender skin. As a lonely traveler with no luggage or invitation, he enjoyed the faces that lit up like novas, the smiles that mirrored marigolds and the joy in shortening a cloudy day, lying with a well-fleshed lady under a firmly pitched tent.[12]

No early Islamic poet has ever injected more fresh blood into the stream of love poetry of Arabic than Abu-Nuwas (756–814) did. He used new words, unconventional (often un–Islamic) topics such as wine and self-indulgence, and vernacular expressions to reinvent the language of love. The imagery of Abu Nuwas was rooted in pre–Islamic poetry, and his composition was grammatically sound and based on the old Arab traditions of layered textual allusions. His themes and imagery, however, were drawn from urban life, not the desert. He was particularly known for his poems on wine and exotic pleasure. His verse was laced with humor and irony, reflecting the genial yet cynical outlook of the poet whose life was caught in contemporary politics although all he had ever been interested in was poetry and personal happiness.[13]

Abu Nuwas was outspoken, blunt and heedless of consequence. He had exhausted the expression of lover's grievance and turned the entire horizon of speech inside out. His imagination was absolutely free and boundless; it could shatter all strictures of decorum and derail all complacency in ways that were either scandalously graphic or almost imperceptibly slight. This was how he described one of his personal divines: idealized man and lover. He was a gazelle whose eyes dealt out among the people their allotted time. Even the mystic prophet Khidr would answered his prayer and ransom himself for him. "If we were ever to deny God we would worship him instead. I don't need anything else in life except that the darkness of night envelop us, him and me. When he appeared, I thought that I saw the crescent moon walking."[14]

However, the poetry of Abu Nuwas was still two and a half centuries a way from the poetry of Rumi (1207–1273), a Sufi poet who embraced God and united with Him with his poetry. At the moment, Abu Nuwas simply established a subject of love (and worship) and created a game between the subject and its worshiper in which the relationship remained fluid and volatile at times. His subject of love was an idealized and perfected human image that could be admired, pursued, dominated and even abused. The act of love, therefore, could be tender, loving, sensitive, or cruel, which evoke longing, suffering, doubt, fear (of being scorned), and resentment (after rejection). Unlike the pre–Islamic poetry that mainly focused on sorrow, Abu Nuwas portrayed a mosaic of feelings that could be calmed, stirred or agitated by a glance of the eye, a touch of a finger or the utterance of a word.[15]

In order to understand the complexity and historical significance of Abu Nuwas' language of love, one has to comprehend what he had inherited from ancient and pre–Islamic love poetry. By the Abbasid period (the middle of the eighth century), Arabic love poetry had developed in two or three principal forms, newly detached from a complex multi-themed and ritualized pre–Islamic ode (*qasida*). Two independent genres, *'udhri* (chaste or platonic) love poetry and *ibahi* (sensual or erotic) love poetry, began to evolve in the seventh century. They both remained quite dependent on a common stock of descriptive imagery and certain standard motifs (for instance, those of the bestiary of love: the gazelle-like aspects of the paramour). *'Udhri* took its name from the *Banu 'Udhra,* an Arab tribe from a valley in the northern Hijaz most associated with this kind of expression, while the *Ibahi* in Arabic simply meant "permissive."[16]

'Udhri poetry proper, which was essentially a phenomenon of the desert, was relatively short-lived, unlike the idealistic and unattainable love of medieval Europe. Courtly love did have a far-reaching influence through the ages upon Arabic classical poetry, but it was far from being the most dominant tendency of Arabic love poetry during and after the classical period. *Ibahi* poetry, associated mainly with the Meccan dissolute 'Umar ibn Abi Rabi'a (d. 712), was a poetry of seduction that originated

from Arabian Bedouin context, and had not yet become entirely urbanized. There had been some precedents for the intensity of *'udhri* poetry in pre–Islamic Arabia. The influence of Islam could be felt in the language and imagery of the new genre (assimilating religious practice into a quasi-spiritual enterprise), reflected significantly in its changed perspectives of time and reality. The *'udhri* poet was an introspective individual; he had an individual view of the world, which he observed through the prism of his love and suffering. The outer world, according to the way he viewed its landscape and fauna, was internalized in psychological harmony with him. The poet devoted himself faithfully and exclusively to the one beloved.

When love was blighted by time and separation, the pre–Islamic poet tended to "cut the ropes of affection" (to cut losses in a heroic posture); the *'udhri* poet, by contrast, projected his love into the future opened up by the new religion: toward death and what lay beyond. The *ibahi* poet too had precedents for some essential features in early and late pre–Islamic verse. The philandering 'Umar ibn Abi Rabi'a modeled himself partly on Imru'al-Qays. 'Umar's animated poem, in which he described a nocturnal visit to his beloved's tribe (stealing into her tent, spending the night and oversleeping, and having to escape the encampment at dawn draped in a woman's robes, trailing them behind him to erase his tracks), expanded upon a short passage in Imru'al-Qays' poetry. Abu Nuwas inherited this essential dichotomy of love poetry, and he combined the characteristics of both *udhri* and *ibahi* expressions.[17]

Abu Nuwas did not invent the image of wine, which was rooted in pre- and early Islamic poetry. As early as the first half of the seventh century, the motif of wine (*khamr*) appeared in *nasib* of the *qasida* to console the poet's despondent love. It was used either as a fleeting description of the beloved, or as a boast of hedonistic pleasure directly addressing the beloved. The poets attempted to console despondent love in a vaunting manner. However, the image of the beloved and the wine motif were simply juxtaposed and static, without a narrative focal point. There was not any contrast of emotions or feminine imagery in the descriptive topics of the wine. In this sense, the wine simply dissipated rather than condensed the emotions. The poem of Abu Dhu'ayb al-Hubhali (d. 649), a forerunner of the *'udhri* poetry, represented a depth of emotion that was rarely seen in pre–Islamic poetry. His expression of love was spirited and went beyond the monochrome austerity of the usual pre–Islamic poetry. Wine became an object of sanctification and pilgrimage as he described and celebrated a love that threatened to kill the poet.

Another example was the poetry of 'Umar ibn Abi Rabi'a, who was one of the inventors of *ghazal* (love poetry). Not a specific form of poetry, *ghazal* was defined as a poetic expression of love, specifically an illicit and unattainable love. The love was always viewed as something that would complete a human being, and if attained would lift him into the ranks of the wise, or will bring satisfaction to the soul of the poet. In this genre, love was a rather broad concept; it might or not have an explicit element of sexual desire in it. As an abstract love, it could be directed to either a man or a woman, and it also could be spiritual, which made it possible to apply to the love to God. The *ghazal* was always written from the point of view of the unrequited lover whose beloved was portrayed as unattainable. Most often either the beloved did not return the poet's love or returned it without sincerity, or else the societal circumstances did not allow it. The lover was aware of and resigned to this fate but continued loving nonetheless. The lyrical impetus of the poem that derived from this tension did not demand long elaboration and consistency of thought, but it took years and years of distillation. Representations of the lover's powerlessness to resist his feelings often included lyrically exaggerated violence. The beloved's power to captivate the speaker could be portrayed in extended metaphors about the "arrows of his eyes," or by referring to the beloved as an assassin or a killer of the soul of the lover. In style and content it was a genre that proved capable of an extraordinary variety of expression around its central themes of love and separation. Abi Rabi'a often depicted a dialogue of himself with his own heart.[18]

The treatment of wine survived into the poetry of Al-Akhṭal (640–710), the Umayyad court poet, and also was used by early Abbasid poets. Their images of wine were sharpened and intensified but they remained within the pre–Islamic tradition.

Abu Nuwas celebrated wine by juxtaposing elements of *nasib* and *ghazal* into single poems of a composite but cohesive texture. In his tighter structure the wine motif illustrated the contrast of emotions and also carried the narrative of seduction. Thus, the new perspectives of love affected wine poetry as well as *ghazal*. A sense of the future certainly had a growing role to play in the rebellious Bacchism of the Umayyad and 'Abbasid periods. As Islam added a temporal dimension to the inspiration of these poets, it also brought a new tension, for both love and wine were set against the strictest of religious cautions. Both the love poet and the wine poet came to defy Islam, either by assimilating its imagery or by adopting a rebellious stance.

The most significant developments of Umayyad love poetry were represented by Abi Rabi'a and the *'udhri* poets. Their poems combined erotic narrative and descriptive images (both male and female) with dialogue in which a hedonistic episode was followed and prefaced by what came close to a motif of censure. For example, the lover's eyes had already slain the poet and left him drunk before the attack of the wine and the taste of wine in lover's mouth revived the dead poet, indicating complete harmony between the effect of love and that of the wine. The poetry of Al-Walid b. Yazid (d. 744) particularly marked the point where Abu Nuwas inherited from this poetic tradition. Al-Walid had consciously developed the imagery and language of both *ghazal* and *khamriyah* so that they became in certain respects interchangeable. His language was light and lyrical, and his mood was consistently one of incitement.[19]

Al-Walid's initial imperatives also set a keynote after which the brief depictions of wine, women or men, and song followed. In the poetry of wine, love and wine existed side by side without the contrived contrast of emotions. "If I am unlucky in love, I would have the advantage of having once fasted and prayed!" "I call upon God to be my witness, I desire music, song and like to drink wine and to bite the cheeks of nubile youths." This was how Al-Walid channeled his various passions into a humorous counter-testament of religious faith. In a similar sentiment and attitude, Abū Nuwas adopted the structure and yet gave wine poetry (*khamriyyāt*) relative complexity. Abu Nuwas simply juxtaposed love, wine, and women or men in one sentence: "I love the song, the drinking, the intimacy of women and the Lord of the Suras."[20]

Abu Nuwas further assimilated religious language in a variance of exotic interpretation to warp the idealistic tone into poetic lyricism. His description of love was idealistic and sensual at the same time. For example, among the motifs rendered bland with repetition was that of the beloved depicted as the full or crescent moon and the sun (one and the only like God) and as beauty inscribed upon his forehead: the true love; there was no comely one other than him. "Sweet one! Love for you possesses me; I cannot have two hearts: one preoccupied, the other one blithe." Sometime the failure of human language to describe the sacred subject of love was portrayed as if the tongue were flagging. Here the inability to delineate was meant to evoke not human failing but a quasi-numinous ineffability: the poet contemplated a divine darling who produced ethereal light. Therefore, human failure to grasp godly perfection despite being captivated by an image was illustrated by poetic inability.[21]

Unlike religious and scientific prose, Arabic poetry flourished with the use of contrary tones, moods, and dramatic play of various seemingly incoherent elements. Abu Nuwas' originality within this repertoire could be surreal, at once intense and amusing, and had both earnest and playful aspects. He would announce that he saw the sun walking about on Friday night while the people were stirred and collapsed to the ground in terror, assuming that the Apocalypse was coming. His expression of profound feeling, although alluring, could be enigmatic; no more so than when he stole a look into his sweetheart's face and glimpsed his own. Was it the beauty of a burnished complexion that was suggested? Or the threats of violence, a spying glance being caught and returned at the poet's expense? Abu Nuwas' poetry was replete with kaleidoscopic contrasts. It gave a sense of apparently endless variety: moods and themes coiled around each other in diverse, sometimes antithetical configurations, managed with either abrupt or discreet transitions.

While Nuwas produced risqué but beautiful poems, many of which pushed the limit of what was acceptable under Islam, others produced more conventional and religious poetry. The works of Sufi poets, which appeared to be simple ghazal or *khamriyah* (wine poetry) continued Abu Nuwas' attempt to combine emotional experience under the guise of love or wine and pursuit of divine. (In the context of poetic evolution, the language that pursued God or the perfect woman or man was one and the same, at least initially.) However, unlike bacchist poetry, which defied Islamic morality and its rules of conduct, Sufi poetry attempted to contemplate the mortal flesh to achieve transcendence. However, their works, like Nuwas' unconventional behavior, were initially considered heretical or dangerous.[22]

If Abu Nuwas represented a sensitive side of poetic sentiment, the poetry of Al-Mutanabbi (915–965) championed the traditional man and his chivalry as inherited from the pre–Islamic Arabic poetry. Al-Mutanabbi's best topics were courage, bravery (in battlefields) and the philosophy of life. He did in fact excel in all that was expected of a poet in his day. He composed love poetry and he praised rich and powerful rulers. But two things distinguished him from other poets: his verse had a rhythmic sweep that is not easily accounted for by the standard scansion, and a powerful personality shines through even when he deals with impersonal themes. He did not have an amiable personality; he was one whose ambition puffed his ego and sharpened his mouth. It was life's cruelty that he was destined to sing the praises of wielders of power—rabbits who happened to be kings—many of whom he despised.[23]

With this inflated ego, his love poetry addressed women in a different tone. He was more a picker in the arena of love than a beggar. He even mildly protested against the fact that every eloquent poet of his time had to be enslaved by love and expected to plead for the favors of beautiful women. For a proud man like himself, he needed to include a love theme as a prelude to a hero's journey that would test his mettle. In an early poem, Al-Mutanabbi described in extravagant terms the beauty of his beloved and then went on to expound his own valor. "My lifeblood is in your hands, do whatever you please, to abate its torment or else increase it, or put it to death," he said to the beloved. "You can't drink someone's blood only if the blood of a bunch of grapes. Pour this to me, then, my soul would be ransom for your eyes. All my possessions of my entire life, my whitened hair, my self-abasement, my emaciation and my tears are witnesses to my passion." For whatever the response from this plea, he was vowed to live proudly or else die honorably amid the thrusting lances and the fluttering pennants, for spearheads, the best for dispelling rage or quenching the thirst of rancorous breasts.[24]

The best-known of Al-Mutanabbi's compositions were panegyrics for men who wielded various degrees of authority. Unlike 'Antara, Al-Mutanabbi was not a warrior; perhaps the only way in which he could obtain glory was to gain the favor of the glorious rulers who could get with swords what he could never get in words. However, he was not a permissive follower, as he always declared that his station was higher than the sun or the moon, especially the subject of his praise. His best years, from 948 to 957, during which he wrote his greatest and most famous poems, were spent in the service of Sayf-ad-Dawla (916–967), the founder of the Amdani dynasty at Northern Syria. Sayf-ad-Dawla was a hero and prince that Al-Mutanabbi had never and would never be. He often engaged in border battles with the Byzantine Empire while maintaining a brilliant court that attracted many of the leading intellects and artistic talents of the day. Al-Mutanabbi was abundantly rewarded with money, but he remained a supplicant. Like a delinquent schoolboy he had to plead illness when he failed to deliver a poem that had been expected of him, and he had to take part in drinking parties that he heartily disliked. But his panegyrics resounded far and wide, and he seldom failed to embed in them a few lines singing his own praises as a doughty warrior and a supreme poet. In a poem declaimed on the occasion of a religious feast, Al-Mutanabbi praised his master Sayf-ad-Dawla: "You surpass all others in judgment and wisdom and you outrank them in virtue, status, and lineage. Your good deeds are so subtle for ordinary minds to perceive who concede only what is clear." He begged him: "Fortified my wrist wields a sword with your favor, my wrist wields a sword that lops off many heads while still in its sheath." He told him: "Nothing am I but a lance, which you carry: It adorns on parade and strikes terror when pointed."

His comparison of himself to a lance was particularly felicitous, as the occasion was marked by a military parade, but the lines that followed could scarcely have won him many friends. Eventually, he roused animosities among so many that he had to depart in haste. Al-Mutanabbi's next destination was Egypt, and his next patron was the exact opposite of all that Al-Mutanabbi admired in Sayf-ad-Dawla. This was Abu al-Misk Kāfūr (905–968) the vizier of the Ikshīdid dynasty. Kāfūr was originally an African slave belonging to the founder of the Ikshīdid dynasty, Muhammad ibn Tughj. Muhammad recognized Kāfūr's talent, made him tutor to his children, and promoted him to an officer. Kāfūr showed outstanding military abilities in the campaigns in Syria and the Hejaz. On his deathbed Muhammad appointed Kāfūr guardian of one of his two sons, and thus Kāfūr became the real ruler of Egypt during the reign of Unujur (946–961) and his brother and successor, 'Ali (961–966). Kāfūr ruled in his own name thereafter, but soon after his death in 968, Ikshīdid power in Egypt was overturned by the Fatimids.

Kāfūr was an able ruler, but the fact that he accomplished his purposes without spectacular feats of arms did not catch Al-Mutanabbi's imagination. More importantly, Kāfūr recognized Al-Mutanabbi's political ambition and considered it a threat. He made sure that Al-Mutanabbi could not get what he wanted. Al-Mutanabbi was angry and claimed that the poems he had composed in Kāfūr's praise were meant to be ironic. After four years, which Al-Mutanabbi claimed he spent as a virtual prisoner in Egypt, he managed to leave. As soon as he was out of Kāfūr's reach he composed a vitriolic satire in which he dwelt rancorously not only on his former patron's ethnical background, but also on the physiological features of eunuchs.[25]

In Al-Mutanabbi's poetry one witnessed a transformation of the poetic persona of the Arabic language. With increasingly lavish imagery and reckless audacity of imagination, he turned panegyrics of his patrons from a means to gain support or livelihood into self-validation and promotion. Not only did he manage to capture the attention of Arab audience and their rulers with short abrupt verses, which are still quoted today, he also enjoyed a broad sphere of admirers and exercised more lasting influence than did their patrons. Openly swollen with pride from his supremacy as a poet, Al-Mutanabbi often sang his own praises with well known sentences such as, "The desert knows me well, the night and the mounted men, the battle and the sword, the paper and the pen." For him, time was but a reciter of his necklace-like poems: when he strung them together, ages would recite them. He believed that his poetry could move a tone-deaf man and make him sing with a trill. He told his patrons, reward me for all the poems you hear, for it is my poems that bring all your eulogists. Ignore the voice of others because only mine is the one that soars and is being copied and echoed.

Al-Mutanabbi's pride often bordered on arrogance, which was the foundation of much of his brilliant writings. In a sense, Al-Mutanabbi was a very controversial figure of his time. His poetry achieved much success with its opulently metaphorical and skillfully attacking or slyly praising *qasida*. His subject matters always bring to mind the time-honored and accepted Arab intrinsic values of reliability, respect, companionship, courage, and gallantry. During Al-Mutanabbi's lifetime and till the present day, his poetry attracted and attracts a great deal of interest. As with many controversial figures in history, the censure he received at times gave him popularity and opened the doors of his patrons in the cultural centers of the Arab world in the tenth century. Finally he achieved with his words what his patrons did in deeds.[26]

By the beginning of the 11th century, Arabic had cultivated many human images of perfection: those of man (of characters), woman (of beauty and seduction), and rulers (of wealth and power). In the words of writers they became present in vision, acts, and sound. Most important of all, Arabic poetry had found a medium to communicate with these idealized persona and built a verbal path to pursue them. However, gaps remained between human and divine images, between ideal and reality, between divine and profane, and between beloved and lover. How could they find and touch each other without contradictions or barriers? Sufi literature, which began to emerge at this time, was going to fill these gaps and make the divine unity possible as a part of human experience and reality.[27]

The language to depict an invisible subject (love and devotion) and to invoke feeling in the audience was cultivated by poetry. It took Arabic many centuries to refine and polish the image, theme, mood and diction of love that eventually provided the basic medium for early Sufi poetry. The language of Arabic spirituality began with *nasib,* the first part of pre–Islamic *qasida. Nasib* was a remembrance of a lost love, which was triggered by an abandoned campsite, the parting of the beloved, and recalling of the secret experience between the poet and the beloved. Through meditation on the empty site (the ruin), the poet envisioned the lost love affair. It was never a whole story or complete picture, but pieces, isolated snapshots, a faint song, languor in the eyes, a wide smile, a draught of wine, a cold wind, a back slope, night rain and white flowers. The poet kept holding on to the images, hoping to see more, and his gaze followed the parting of the beloved until she disappeared from the horizon of sandscape. It was not a song, but an inner whisper of memory that was just loud enough to bruise the heart and senses.

The unattainable love (seen but impossible to reach, remembered but not present) was initially heightened into a mad vision in which the poet could see and feel things that were not there. Both love madness and perishing imagery later became the key Sufi motifs. The motifs were combined by Sufis with the bewilderment of reason on contact with ultimate reality and in annihilation of the human in mystical union with God. Through this prism, God sees, hears, walks, and touches while saying, "Glory to me," in Sufi poetry. It reminded one of the familiar story of Layla and Majnun in which Majnun (a man driven lovesick) sees and calls everything (including mountains, rivers, and wild animals) "Layla." He even replies "Layla" when asked what his name is. In this specific sense, words in poetry could make poets as well as readers envision anything, including God. The idea that God is everywhere one turns and looks first appeared in the Qur'an (2:115): Whichever way you turn, there is the Face of God. However, to know that God is everywhere is one thing and to actually be able to see Him with one's own eyes is quite another. Sufi poetry provided the vehicle to transform an idea to imagery visible to Muslims.

Sufi poetry first emerged from two pieces of ancient land fertile with poetry even before Arabic or any modern language was spoken: Iraq and Greater Persia, including ancient Khorazan, which was the medieval name of northwestern Afghanistan, and also parts of today's Tajikstan and Uzbekistan. Although the ancient deities were forgotten and temples became ruins, the imaginative capacity that was cultivated by poetic rituals remained and was transmitted from language to language and from generation to generation. Like any of the great religions of the world, whose inner dimension could be explored only through a mature poetry, Sufi poetry in Arabic and the Persian emerged as Islam became mature in its scriptural meditation and religious (ritual) experience.[28]

Rābia al-Basrī (717–801) was one of the earliest Sufi mystics whose poetry was recorded by later Sufis. In her poetry, she created a higher concept of a divine that should be worshiped not out of fear or hope (for reward) but for love alone. She was the one who expressed feeling of intimacy with God, and of his constant presence as her lover in her heart. In her poetry, Sufi became a way of worship and a way of life. The identification of God with the beloved became the ground for a personal relationship with God for Sufi worshipers.[29] The dream that Al-Mutanabbi wished and pursued in his entire life, to be a *wali* (saint or spiritual leader of Muslims) was realized by some the most distinguished Sufi poets. Unlike the Roman Catholic Church, which had an ecclesiastical hierarchy to canonize sainthood, Islam had never had a system to cultivate its saints. The word *wali*, which was used as "saint" in Islam, was derived from the Qur'an (2: 257): God was the *wali* of whoever believes and he takes them from darkness to light. Also: the *walis* of God have neither fear nor grief (10: 62). At the time, *wali* meant "protector, protected friends, and ally" where God, Muslim community and its leaders did not inherit a conceptual gap. This was because in the Arabic of the seventh century, *wali* referred to a patron or guardian of the community. As God declared that he was the protector or friend of the *wali*, he meant that he was the ally of the Muslim community. It was only during the ninth century that *wali* became a title for select Muslims who were believed to possess God-given spiritual power (*barakah*), which was verified by their ability to personally reach God and perform miracles (*karamat*).

The language of love for God was further invented and elaborated by Abu Sa'id Kharraz (d. 899), one of the well-known members of the Sufi circle in Baghdad at the middle of the ninth century. In his book *The Book of Truthfulness* (*Kitab al-Sidq*) he described the feeling and reaction of the God-seeker as he was rendering God's recollection into a perpetual act: he gained a quick understanding, his thoughts became clear, and light lodged in his heart. The love of God lurked deeply hidden in his inmost heart, cleaving his mind and never leaving it. Kharraz gave more detailed depiction of the Sufi intimacy with God in his five epistles, which survived in a single manuscript, *The Book of Light* (*Kitab al-Diya'a*). He portrayed the moment when people were face to face with the essence of divine reality (*'ayn al-'ayn*) and became possessed by an absolute confoundment of spirit (*ahl tayhuhiyya wa-hayruriyya*).[30]

Abu al-Husayn al-Nuri (d. 907–8) provided more vivid imagery of God's presence in the heart of Sufis in his book *Stations of the Hearts* (*maqāmāt al-gulub*). God built a house inside the believer called the heart. Then he sent a mighty wind into the house to clean all the doubt, idolatry, and hypocrisy; he sent rain to the house so all kinds of plants could grow, such as trust, hope, and love. Then he placed a couch of unity at the center of the house and covered it with a rug of contentment; he planted a tree of knowledge opposite to the couch with roots in the heart and branches in the sky. God also opened a door to the Garden of His mercy and sowed there various fragrant herbs of praise, glorification and commemoration. He let the water of guidance shower the plan through a river of kindness. He hung a lamp of grace high on the door and lighted it with oil of purity. Then he locked the door to keep out the wicked. He held onto the key and did not trust any creature with it. He said, this is my treasure on my earth. This is my home of unity on earth.

Al-Nuri spent most of his life in Baghdad and had nicknames such as "prince of the hearts" (*amir al-gulub*) and "the Moon of Sufis" because his enlightening teachings. Al-Nuri was called by his caliph to explain his statement, "I love God and He loves me," because the official preacher did not like the talk of passionate love for God. Al-Nuri replied that he heard God saying it (he quoted verses of Qur'an): He loves them and they love

Him (Qur'an 5: 59). He also told that passionate love (*'ishq*) was not greater than serene love (*mahabba*), except that the passionate lover (*'ashiq*) was kept away, while the serene love enjoy his lover (*muhabb*).[31]

Sufism would have remained a faction of religious ritual instead a system of thoughts and practice if the later Sufi writers had not produce abundant writing to cultivate a theory of worship. One of the most important of the early scholars was Junayd of Baghdad (830–910). Among many of Junayd's contributions to Sufism was his set of basic ideas dealing with a progression that led one to "annihilate" oneself (*fana*) in order to be in a closer union with the Divine. As he put it, people needed to relinquish natural desires, to wipe out human attributes, and to discard selfish motives, so as to cultivate spiritual qualities and to devote themselves to true knowledge. This started with the practice of renunciation (*zuhd*) and continued with withdrawal from society, intensive concentration on devotion (*ibadat*) and remembrance (*dhikr*) of God, sincerity (*ikhlas*) and contemplation (*muraqaba*) respectively; contemplation produces *fana*. This type of "semantic struggle" recreated the experience of trial (*bala*) that was key in Junayd's writings. This enabled people to enter into the state of *fana*. Junayd divided the state of *fana* into three parts. The first was the passing away from one's attributes through the effort of constantly opposing one's ego-self (*nafs*); the second was passing away from one's sense of accomplishment; and the third was passing away from the vision of the reality. Once that has been attained, a person would be in the state of remaining (*baqa*), through which one was able to find God—or rather, have God find him or her. Reaching *baqa* was not an easy thing to do, though; getting through the three stages required strict discipline and patience.[32] Within this civil (rather than political and institutional) structure of sainthood, the majority of recognized Islamic saints were poets who excelled in writing love poetry to God. Many Sufi saints lived through their writings and attained reputation and influence far beyond that of state-sponsored scholars and politicians. Shaykh Umar Ibn al-Farid (1181–1235), whose verses were considered by many to be the pinnacle of Arabic mystical poetry, was one of the best examples. Ibn al-Farid was a master of Arabic poetic tradition and composed in quatrain, *ghazal*, *qasida* and *khamriyah*. His lyrical and complex poetry was highly regarded and admired. The Sultan al-Malik al-Kamil (r. 1218–1238) was so impressed by his writing that he sent a gift of money to him. Unlike the Abbasid court poets, Al-Farid declined the gift (and other similar gifts from amirs of the court) because he refused to be tainted by money or power.

Al-Farid's sanctity was closely tied to his beautiful poetry, which expressed his love for God and depicted the way to unite with Him. Al-Farid's

Wine Ode (*Al-Khamriyah*) was a beautiful meditation on the "wine" of divine bliss. The invisible God was portrayed like the sun in a moon glass decorated with stars; the memory of the Divine was like the fragrance of the wine, a breath, hidden in the heart and mind of the believer. The fragrance of the divine wine alone could intoxicate man without drinking, cure the sick and revive the dead. *The Poem of the Sufi Way* (*Al-Ta'iyah al-Kubra*), perhaps the longest mystical poem composed in Arabic, was a profound exploration of spiritual experience along the Sufi Path. Both poems transformed the love of woman and of wine to an intimate Sufi view of life and devotion to God.[33]

Umar was born in Syria to the family of a knowledgeable scholar who gave his son a good foundation in belles letters. Ibn al-Farid began to go on extended spiritual retreats among the oases, specifically the oasis outside of Cairo, starting in his youth. However, as he felt that he was not making deep enough spiritual progress, he abandoned his spiritual wanderings and entered a school of Islamic law. One day Ibn al-Farid saw a greengrocer performing the ritual Muslim ablutions outside the door of the school, but the man was doing them out of the prescribed order. When Ibn al-Farid tried to correct him, the greengrocer looked at him and told him that he could not learn anything in Egypt. You will be enlightened only in the Hijaz, in Mecca, he said.

Umar was stunned by this statement, and realized that this seemingly simple-minded greengrocer was not an ordinary man. But he argued that he couldn't possibly make the trip to Mecca right away. Then the man gave Ibn al-Farid a vision of Mecca at the very moment and on the spot. Ibn al-Farid was so transfixed by this visual experience that he left immediately for Mecca. In his own words, "Then as I entered it, enlightenment came to me wave after wave and never left me." Al-Farid ended up staying in Mecca for fifteen years. He eventually returned to Cairo when he heard his mentor the greengrocer calling him back to attend his funeral. He came back and wished him farewell at his deathbed.

Upon Ibn al-Farid's return to Cairo, he was treated as a saint. He would hold teaching sessions with judges, viziers and other leaders of the city. While walking down the street, people would come up to him and crowd around him, seeking spiritual blessings (*barakah*) and trying to kiss his hand. He became a scholar of Muslim law, a teacher of the Hadith, and a teacher of Arabic poetry. Like many Sufi saints, Ibn al-Farid's worship was physical as well as poetic. During the later part of his life, he was known to enter into spiritual raptures (*jadhabat*), a common practice in Sufism. It was said that when a mystical state overcame him, his face would increase in beauty and brightness. Sweat would pour from his body and collect on the ground beneath his feet, which was a result of jumping and dancing. During the ritual, Ibn al-Farid claimed to see many things happen that could be considered to be out of this world. He described a lion kneeling down before him, asking him to ride. He also wrote about seeing a man descending a mountain, floating without using his feet. He claimed that a "great green bird" came down at the funeral of the greengrocer and "gobbled up his corpse." He also depicted his meeting and conversation with Mohammed in a dream. It was said that his ecstasies or trances sometimes lasted ten consecutive days without eating, drinking, moving, speaking or hearing outside noises. He would alternately stand, sit, lie on his side or "throw himself down on his side." When he came to, his first words would be a dictation of the verse God had given him.[34]

A similar journey, from begging, seeing, to embracing God was also described by Ibn 'Arabi (1165–1240), a Sufi from Andalusian Spain. He wrote over 350 works including the *Fusus al-Hikam*, an exposition of the inner meaning of the wisdom of the prophets in the Judaic, Christian, and Islamic religions. His *Futuhat al-Makkiyya*, a vast encyclopedia of spiritual knowledge that unites and distinguishes the three strands of tradition, reason and mystical insight was a "spiritual resume" of Islam, covering the whole 560-year period from the beginning of the Islamic era to his own birth. In his *Diwan and Tarjuman al-Ashwaq* he wrote some of the finest poetry in the Arabic language. These extensive writings provide a beautiful exposition of the unity of being, the single and indivisible reality, that simultaneously transcends and is manifested in all the images of the world. Ibn 'Arabi illustrated how man, in perfection, was the complete image of this reality and how those who truly knew their essential selves would know God. Ibn 'Arabi gave expression to the teachings and insights of the generations of Sufis after him. This accumulated knowledge recorded for the first time, systematically and in detail, the vast repertoire of Sufi experiences and oral tradition, by drawing on a treasury of technical terms and symbols greatly enriched by centuries.[35]

Like many of his follow Sufis, Ibn 'Arabi's writing was deeply rooted in Arabic love poetry, and it began with a familiar tone of a desperate lover addressing an unattainable beloved: "I have called you so often," but you haven't "heard me," "you haven't smelled" me after I made myself fragrant; "you haven't tasted me," "savorous food." "Why? Why, you do not see me?" However, this time, the lover's faith was no longer blind; he could see marvelous scenes under the influence of his poetic meditation. He could see a "sea of sand as fluid as water." There were "stones, both large and small, that attracted one another like iron and a magnet. As the stones came together and joined, they formed a ship." The "stone vessel with two hulls"

had two sides, behind which were raised two enormous columns higher
than a man's head. The rear of the ship was at the same level as the sea,
and was "open to the sea without a single grain of sand coming inside."[36]

Beyond this typical example of a miracle (*aja'b*), 'Arabi deliberately
constructed the story by borrowing key terms from a specific Arabic literature. *Bahr* (sea) was the word commonly used for the ocean, but it was
also the word that, in the language of Arabic poetry, denoted the meter of
a poem. *Ramal*, which ordinarily referred to sand, was the name for one
of the sixteen meters in classical Arabic prosody. From this point of view,
the story of the stone vessels sailing over a sea of sand was beyond physical
image and it had nothing to do with the dream state of a delirious mind.
The vessel (*safina*) in fact represented the *qasida*, the classical Arabic
poetry. The inseparable (*magnefed*) stones are *kalimat*, the words that,
when joined together, form the verses that, when arranged together, make
up the poem. The two sides of the boat were the hemistiches of each line
of verse, while the two columns referred to the two "pillars" (*watid*) of
Arabic meter. Thus, with slightly encrypted language, Ibn 'Arabi indicated
that poetry is the privileged way to "travel" in the *'alam al-khayal*, whose
haqa'iq (spiritual realities) it carried, although spiritual realities, by their
very nature, were supraformal.

On this stone vessel (poetry), Sufi poets went on a journey, one they
believed man had been on ever since God created him. By now, however,
for the Sufis the journey was no longer a collective one, the traditional
way as described by early Sufis such as Abû Nasr al-Sarraj or Qushairy,
nor was it based on the relationship of a *shaykh* and a student. Beyond the
simplified language of paradise/hell or love/hate, Sufi poetry had cultivated
a vast vocabulary for highly personalized spiritual experiences. The richness and diversity of Sufi poetry made it possible for an individual worshiper to take an individual journey to pursue his beloved. The journey
took one of various levels/stations of the mystical experience through various ways (*maratib*). The seeker of divine love had to progress step by
step, finding his own way to unite with God.

The path to God varied with each and every worshiper because the
relationship of the man to the Divine Presence was an individually defined
situation, which occurred directly and without any intermediary. In other
words, God loved Man in pre-eternity, and since the love of Man for God
was also ultimately from God, there was originally a possibility of a direct
relationship to God through the heart of Man. However, God related to
each man in different ways because of the nature of each person's heart.
These specific conditions of hearts were believed to be the foundation of
the relationship of the Divine to the human and vice versa. Each person

might come to recognize the Divine according to his own nature, and the Divine also recognized each person according to these forms that were carried within each heart.

From a psychological perspective, the manifestations of God formed an entirely different Divine form for the person's innermost consciousness. Metaphysically, this relationship to the Divine occurred at the level of the Oneness (*wahidiyya*) and not at that of the Uniqueness (*ahadoyyah*); the manifestations witnessed by the seeker were thus those of his own *rabb* and not of Allah. Accordingly, such recognition of the Divine was limited to the *rabb al-khas* (the particular Lord). Each person knows Him according to the form that he desires and loves, and to the extent of his ideals and readiness to see (*istidad*). In other words, the manifestation of divine reality, which was impossible to see through the eyes of an individual human, was seen only according to personally perceivable level or station as put in poetry: in each heart God kept a different secret, and to each heart He told a different secret. To know his God-defined secret, each person had to experience God in his own way.

The mystical journey was the form of practice of the Sufi way (*tariqa*). Every person who felt awakened and had begun to marvel at Being (*hayrah*) accordingly felt called to follow the way of the transcendent. And this was only the beginning. The Sufi learned first to know himself, since an insight gained without knowledge of who he was could not be a true witnessing of the Divine. For this the adept sought a *shaykh* (or was "called" by the *shaykh*) who could help him to change his inner structure by means of re-education, to conform to the Unseen and to develop the taste (*zauq*) required for the long journey. It began with love, with which the steps of journey would be counted and by which he would find the strength to continue on the way. The deeper he swam in this ocean, the greater became his yearning for realization of the Holy. This in turn would precipitate more love. Regardless of which of the ways he took, whether by the degrees (*maratib*) or by direct and immediate inrush (*warid*) of the Divine, the eye of the heart (*'ayn al-qalb*) now saw the contours of that which was sought, and made it possible for him to have a relationship with the Highest.

Ibn 'Arabî's legacy provided a detailed description of the Way, which was like a map of the inner journey through the beautiful names of God and their manifestations (*tajalli*) in existence. These were signs and milestones for the particular seeker, by which he was led to step from one station (*maqāmā*) to the next. When the seeker had reached the point at which he could enjoy the Divine Gentleness (*lutf*) in its totality, he became worthy to appear before the throne of the All-Compassionate (*sarir ar-rahman*), in obliteration (*mahw*) and veiled from himself, such that no trace of existence remained in him. This was the highest point that he could reach. Then the All-Compassionate would endow him with the name of the living (*hayy*) and he would be returned to existence. From this moment he remained forever in this state of *baqa'* (subsistence).[37]

Poetry was the vehicle for the mystic journey. To deepen his love for God, the seeker had to keep prayer and *dhikr* (remembering the words of God) as constant companions and repeat the divine names until they became internalized in his own being. Only when these became a part of him did the seeker arrive in a position to undergo the process of realization of the Divine insight. The love then lended the seeker a deep feeling of security and closeness to God, without which the seeker would loose his way. In this way, words massaged, activated and eventually enlightened the mind.[38] Sufi was the first religious order that succeeded to embody language (words) into the human body and divine into its persona. Other religions did it either through physical or ideological connections. The Sufi order began its human divination through traditional religious linkages (saints, their disciples, and brotherhood) as did Judaism, Christianity and Buddhism. However, Sufi teachings eventually cultivated sacred identity by words alone. Derived from the historical panegyric tradition of poetry, which associated the Prophet Muhammad with God, Sufis elevated verbal divination to a new height.

They applied a method of derivation of a certain meaning from each and every letter of a word (*ishtiqaq kabir*). Therefore, the name of Muhammad or any personal name that they attempt to divinate would consist of a number of words. Muhammad would be glory (*majid*), mercy, (*rahma*), kingdom (*mulk*), and everlasting (*dawam*), based on **mhmd**. The elaboration of the symbolic characteristics of the name of Muhammad was undertaken by many Muslim scholars during the early Islamic period. However, Sufis turned this method into a science. Mansul al-Hallaj (858–922) was the first Sufi to take on the symbolic meaning of Muhammad by letters. He pointed out that the shape of the letters from which the name of Muhammad consisted shared the shape with a human figure. Ibn 'Arabi continued to argue that **mim** represented the head, the world of the supreme sovereignty (*'alam al-malakut al-'ala*) and general intellect (*al-'agl al-'akbar*). The breast and arms under the *ha* represented the number of the angels who carry the throne. The second **mim** represented the stomach, which was the world of the kingdom. The hips, the legs and the feet were from the *dal*, which was the stable composition by means of eternal writ. Many Sufi scholars kept reworking the same symbolic meanings derived from letters of names for the next centuries.[39]

Poetry not only worshipped religious leaders and politicians, it also divined the poets themselves. The divine quests transformed the believers as well as their spiritual leaders. They reinvented their attitudes and knowledge through learning and meditation. Brand new personality and moral characteristics began to radiate out of their characters. This radiance of wisdom affected and was perceived by people around them. For example, in the year 608, Ibn 'Arabi visited Baghdad, the city of Sufi saints. 'Arabi met with the famous Sufi Shihabuddin Suharwardi (d. 632). In this meeting, they stayed together for a while; they both sat with lowered heads and departed without exchanging a single word. Later Ibn 'Arabi explained the silence. He (Suharwardi) was impregnated with the Sunna from tip to toe, while Suharwardi commented about Ibn 'Arabi: "He was an ocean of essential truths [*bahr al-haqaiq*]."[40]

For the majority of Sufi scholars, the self-divination did not come as an intended result of composition but as a consequence of the lifelong pursuit of unity with God. In a historical sense, the distance (or conceptual gap) between the subject of worship and the worshiper was naturally narrowed down by the efforts of generations of poets. A popular metaphor of sight and its mirror can illuminate the evolution of this relationship. As a poet put it in a compact verses: "I am a sight to see," and "You [God] are the mirror of the glance" and "the axis of time.... Encompassed in you is what is dispersed throughout time." The *you* that is the mirror of the glance (the glance being, by definition, a momentary act) was also called the axis of time, holding within itself all that time had dispersed. Similarly, these verses formed a momentary poetic glance within the expression of Arabic love poetry through which the Sufi understandings of mystical states of consciousness had kept unfolding over several centuries. The journey in poetic language (the stone vessel) changed the lives and characters on it. As the Sufi seeker was pursuing divine unity, he himself disappeared while his poetry became a ghost dialogue between a speaker and hearer (you and I). As the space between two voices and two persons diminished, it became a monologue. There is "nothing like me, I am one."[41]

Sufi poetry cultivated a richly textured vocabulary in Arabic and provided the needed template of the language of soul, in which individual and universal, worshipers and worshiped could interflow and be transfigured freely. Sufi poetry transfigured love from that for another to one of both God and self; they juxtaposed the two in one unified image. Arabic love for the Divine went much further than the Latin notion of man's passionate and yet uncontainable love for God. It was virtually impossible to draw a clear line in Nizami's poetry between the mystical and the erotic, between the sacred and the profane.[42]

This inclusive yet sensitive love survived into the modern period. It was revived in the hands of modern poets such as Nizar Qabbani (1923–1998). For him, love was something mystical, but at the same time very personal and sensual. However, his concept of love had substantially broadened. In his early poems, he combined the erotic depiction of attractive women with the chauvinist attitudes of men towards women. Later he also portrayed the complex relationships between men. In the 1950s, Qabbani was, with 'Abd al-Wahhab al-Bayyati, among the pioneers who started to use the simple language of everyday speech in verse, such as, "Who are you, a woman entering my life like a dagger?" You are "mild as the eyes of a rabbit"; "innocent as children's bibs and devouring like words?" *Qasa'id min Nizar Qabbani* (1956) was his most outstanding early collection, in which he assumed a female persona in three poems, "Pregnant," "A Letter from a Spiteful Lady," and "The Vessels of Pus." Qabbani's poems continue the sixteen-centuries-old tradition of Arabic love poetry, but they were updated with modern experiences and echo the rhythm, intonation, and idioms of everyday language.

During the 1960s, he devoted his love poetry to his country and the Arab world with the same passion. He told the world that he had written love poetry to his country: "You have transformed me / from a poet of love and yearning / to a poet writing with a knife." In a poem written immediately the June defeat, Qabbani expressed his frustration and despair towards the politics of Arab countries: "My master Sultan, / You have lost the war twice / because half of our people have no tongues." "What is the worth of a voiceless people?" His words spoke of dictatorship with bitter lines: "O Sultan, my master," "my clothes are ripped and torn" because "your dogs with claws are allowed to tear me." He labeled the betrayal of an Egyptian politician as an agent of Israel who was "mad" and who had "raped" Egypt. His abundant love poetry became a major source of hope that the human heart could finally transcend pain and fear and dare to assert its capacity to summon joy and engage passion. His poetry brought freedom from tension, liberation from gloom, and a refreshing release of laughter and gaiety. It proudly proclaimed a new reverence for the body and it washed away the traditional embarrassment, now many centuries old, that was linked to woman's physical passion.

Iraqi poets redirected their love to their country and the Arab world and became the political and social spokesmen of their time. Political, social and national issues in turn rejuvenated Arabic poetry, in its diction, style, and emotion.[43] For example, Zahawi's poem is cast in the framework of a dream, although that is only revealed in the closing verses. The poet dreams he is dead and buried, and describes his encounter with Munkar and Nakeer, two angels whose duty it is to interrogate the dead by asking a series of specific questions. From a theological perspective, Munkar and Nakeer can be seen as superfluous, as doubtless their interrogative roles have no effect on the final state of bliss or punishment, which is already determined for the dead. Their roles in the poem, however, as with other characters from the Qur'an, are pivotal to Zahawi's portrayal of a highly superficial and mythologized Islam, to which the poet was obviously exposed. This is primarily evident in the conversations that take place between Zahawi and the angels, who bombard the poet with a barrage of questions that are explicitly concerned with the intricate details of Islamic practices. Gradually, Zahawi starts to become impatient with the irrelevance of the questions, and begins to enumerate his accomplishments in his lifetime, like his ceaseless promotion of humanist ideals and his support for women's rights. Yet verses that illustrate Zahawi's egoism are as abundant as those that typify his self-pity. The general temper of the poem is that of an elitist irony, where intellectualism is victimized, religious superstition is prevalent, and revolution against the inhabitants of paradise is the only recourse.

The satirical zenith of the poem lies in Zahawi's description of paradise, once he is taken there by the two angels to give him a glimpse of the absolute ecstasy that he has been denied. The description is highly dependant on Qur'anic imagery but not devoid of Zahawi's humorous tone in listing the inventory of scrumptious food items and vintage wines that are provided for the inhabitants of heaven, not to mention the overt sexuality of the holy maidens, as well as the divinity and youthful beauty of the *ghulman* boy servants, which implies an acceptable homoeroticism in the afterlife. Zahawi's description of hell, on the other hand, while continuing to borrow from the similes of the Qur'an, serves as the ontological dimension of the poem, with the poet employing a concise, yet forceful style in order to express his philosophy of rationalism, and his passionate belief in the ideal of reason.

While in hell, Zahawi is met by Leila, a character with recurring roles in many of the poet's other works, who symbolizes persecuted womanhood and alludes to the oppressed state of the nation. Also, traces of his appreciation of Sufi philosophy can be read in a number of verses, specifically those that narrate Mansur al-Hallaj's post-martyrdom self-elegy. Zahawi is then met by a number of notable poets, scientists, and philosophers, who have contributed to the development of humankind: Socrates, Dante, Shakespeare, Umar al-Khayyam, Mutanabbi, Ibn Sina, Voltaire, and Darwin, to name a few. After a few scattered conversations that the poet holds with the characters, a triumphant revolt against the angels is planned and led by poet Abu al-'Ala' al-Ma'arri, despite his blindness. The ironic sequel to the vividly illustrated revolt is a deliberately designed anticlimax that reveals itself as the abrupt awakening of Zahawi from a bad dream, one which he blames on his indulgence of watercress before going to sleep.[44]

Muhammad Mahdi al-Jawahiri (1899–1997) was no doubt the greatest Iraqi poet of his time.

Like Sufi poetry, modern Arabic poetry created a universe made of words, in which every word regardless what it means has an active and animated life. The sea, like a little boy, dreams; night, like woman, gets pregnant. The house grows old, the earth writes, the season tells; days, clouds, fire and voice live and die. Every Arabic word, including abstract words, has a face, a body, and a pair of hands, and it could speak, act and transform before the very eyes of its readers. Time has eyelashes; the life (of a person) looks, signs, and light up like lanterns; she also stares, ponders and holds one's hands to the future. The physics (nature in an abstract sense) of things walks the abbeys, tall as the wind. He comes alive when stone becomes a lake and shadows a city; he carried a continent and moved the sea; he borrows the shoes of night and waits for what never comes. He also peels human beings as an onion.[45]

CHAPTER 7

The World in Arabic Fiction

Literary Arabic took a path of evolution distinct from that of English and other European languages because of its rich poetic tradition and refined literary sensibility, which were cultivated by an advanced literature. Before the majority of European literary languages began to mature (during the modern period) Arabic had reached its creative apex (in the pre-modern period) and began to retract after producing some of the best lyrical poetry of the world and large volumes of prose literature in a wide range of subjects. Arabic imagination had gone to the moon, traveled through the space and came back to the earth, leaving a universe full of ideas, images, allusions, and symbols. Thus, modern Arabic literature was facing a challenge different from that of formative languages, which just started to search for ways to build their universe of words. Arabic writers had to learn to deal with the heavy burden of the past and build a new life with old words, imagery and symbols.

Modern Arabic writers had different kinds of audiences and readers whose pride and sensibility were highly attuned by words and whose emotions were exceptionally fluid. Unfortunately, modern life was not kind to the Arabs of the nineteenth and twentieth century, whose daily reality was slipping farther and farther away from the ideals that their words had built in volumes. The bottom line was the question of how to write about a low life, a life that had fallen off from the heyday of collective memory with a highly sophisticated language of rich repertoire of symbols; how to mediate between a glorious past and high opinion of oneself and a depressive life full of poverty, corruption and war that one was trying to escape. New ideas needed to be imagined and conceptualized into a literature that was as attractive and moving as that in the past. Life had to be celebrated and love had to be freely expressed, and words had to be able to make readers laugh, cry, sing, and/or be entertained as they had done for centuries.

The main challenge of Arabic narrative was to bridge two ends of the literary expression: high moral ideals and universal symbols on the one hand and the everyday lives and personal feelings of common men on the other. As has often happened in history, human failure and even misery always generate the most brilliant literature. The turbulent life in the modern Middle East, which was filled with sharp contrast and emotional roller coasters, provided fertile soil and demanding tests for Arabic writers. This was the reason why they produced some of the best fiction and poetry in the modern world.

Arabic narrative began during the pre–Islamic period when stories were told about battles, kings, heroes, paupers, traveler, and lovers as well as their colorful adventures. However, as it emerged from poetry, a highly formulated and refined language, early Arabic prose inherited many characteristics of pre- and early Islamic poetry: its meter, rhyme and economy of words. During this early period, *khabar* (news) became the most common form of narrative, with a condensed and terse style. Later, two most important developments occurred in Arabic storytelling: complexity in structure and fluidity in presentation. Unlike poetry, which became shorter and more compact in form and closer to spoken language, narrative prose gradually gained scope and depth.[1]

The first written narrative of Arabic language was Hadith, which depicted the life events of the Prophet Muhammad. However, due to its religious and political significance, it had been heavily edited and scrutinized because it claimed to be a piece of history rather than literature. Everything Muhammad had said and done had to be verified to make sure that it was consistent with the memories of his companions. In addition, Arabic narrative that freshly emerged from a poetic language tended to be more suggestive than descriptive. It often focused on creating an atmosphere surrounding the beloved and worshiped hero than portraying the image of the hero himself. Thus the activities of Muhammad came to be portrayed in a manner that illustrated his character rather than giving a specific description of his life story. For example, he was shown as praying with a small child or avoiding waking up a sleeping cat. These all suggested a sense of intimacy and friendliness in his presence.[2]

It was in the Umayyad period (661–750) that prose writing gained more importance, although it remained the poor cousin to poetry for the next centuries. A storyteller was designated for every major mosque (*al-Masjid al-Jami'*) to preach to the populace. Moreover, storytellers were sent to accompany soldiers in the battlefield of Islamic conquests. During the 'Abbasid caliphate (750–1258), storytelling developed an immensely wide range of types and styles. The most important two types of storytellers were eloquent scholars who used stories for preaching and teaching, and professional storytellers who made a living entertaining the public. The best known story was *Kalila wa Dimna*, which Ibn al-Muqffa' (721–756) translated from Persian literature.[3]

Kalila wa Dimna was considered by some the first masterpiece of prose narrative in Arabic. It was originally composed in Sanskrit as the *Panchatantra* in India around A.D. 300 and was later translated into a collection of animal fables in Middle Persian. For the first time, writing was done for the purpose of storytelling rather than as religious, political or didactical rhetoric. It was also constructed in the form of a conversation between a teacher and student, and between a storyteller and his audience. In the context of formative Arabic, the work was created for a live performance, and it was not written down until five centuries after Al-Muqffa's death. As it aimed at an oral presentation, the stories were told in simple diction and plain syntactical structure. The events were arranged by narrators, who provided a beginning and end to each performance. In short, it was a work marked by formative and performative language free from religious and political meanings and rhetorical functions.[4]

The translation of *Kalila* was instrumental in opening innovative avenues in Arabic prose narrative. The introduction of episodic narrative paved the way for later authors of *maqāmā* (assemblies), such as Badi al-Zaman al-Hamadhani (969–1007) and the original inventor Al-Harīrī (1054–1122). Al-Harīrī's *Maqāmāt* consisted of a series of fifty seemingly independent episodes narrated by an unreliable and sometimes inconsistent narrator, who was also the main character in each narration. In every episode, the narrator encountered an eloquent rogue, usually with a shabby appearance. The rogue might appear as a young boy, an old man, a drifter, or a sheikh. In the course of each narrative, the rogue dazzled the narrator with his eloquence and relieved him of his money and/or property. The relationship between narrator and character was an inversion of the student/teacher roles played by the lion and the jackals in *Kalila*. In the former, the characters narrated tales of the short-sightedness and gullibility of others. In Al-Harīrī's *Maqāmāt*, the teacher/rogue consistently deceived the student/narrator.[5]

The episodic structure of the *maqāmā* (assemblies) was derived from an oral narrative contrary to more linear works such as the Byzantine novels, which had many centuries of literary tradition. Badi al-Zaman al-Hamadhani was said to compose his narration publicly as oral improvisation. The *maqāmā* continued to be performed as a traditional form of scholarly reading, even after it was canonized as a written literary form by Al-Harīrī. For instance, the earliest manuscript of *maqāmā* recorded thirty public readings, the primary means of transmission of the work at the time. The tradition of *maqāmā* combined aspects of the picaresque that were demonstrated in the relationship between narrative, the characters and their surroundings.[6]

Al-Jahiz's (776–868?) *Al-Bukhala* (*The Book of Misers*) illustrated his ability to observe and depict details in human conditions. His precise portrayal and description were unprecedented in Arabic narrative.[7] The following section from the "Tale of Harithi" demonstrates that Arabic narrative combined the language of poetry with descriptive precision of prose to create vivid and provocative human images.[8]

> You prepared a good meal, which contains an abundance of food. It is very expensive. You have spent lavishly on a baker, a cook, a roaster, and a confection maker. Now, you don't have an enemy to annoy, a friend to please, a stranger to befriend, and a visitor to invite home, people who should be grateful (for your generosity).... You don't want to do that because you will realize they are not what you think. As soon as your eyes are off them and you turn your back, they will gobble all the foods, shared out, or even steal from you. It would be worthwhile for you and better than eating alone, and will save the food for yourself, if you invite someone whose presence will benefit you. He will make good conversation to entertain you and make your mealtime pleasant. He will be grateful and tell all his friends about his gratitude to you for years to come.
>
> Why on earth would you let someone share your personal table if he is ungrateful, does not even thank you, or did thank you but did not do it in a proper manner? If he could not even tell the difference between foods that curb hunger from delicious food, and a good meal from the bad?
> ....
> I can put up with a guest or an uninvited person who is accompanying him, but I can tolerate neither a glutton who stuffs meat into his mouth nor a *Jardabil* [person who eats with a wrong hand] who claps his hands over meat to hold it when he cuts it. I found it easier to deal with an uninvited guest in a drinking party than someone who just showed up and gobble everything in front of him.... If I have to share food with somebody, I would prefer someone who does not take all the brain (of poultry) to himself, ignoring me, or snatch the egg off *baqila* [a dish of beans], someone who does not bolt down the chicken liver, race to get the brain of the *sullaha* [bird], grab the kid's kidneys, quickly swallow the stork's stomach, tear at the haunch of the lamb, fillet the stomach of *shisan* [fish], eye the sheep's head, seize the chicken breast, push ahead to run for the young chicken's wingtips.

The narrative inherited a portion of poetic parallelism and had excessive wording. However, it appeared to have gained precision and sharpness in description. The development of this initial narrative came in the form of speech, which was able to portray vivid human images and personalities. At this stage of linguistic development, the art of storytelling for the Arabic writers focused on a good plot that was delivered in a good speech (*nishwar*).[9]

Arabic prose at this period used many metaphors (*isti'ara*) and similes (*tashbih*). There was an obvious balance of sentence against sentence, phrase against phrase, and word against word. Again, there were recognized subdivisions, depending partly on whether similar or contrasting meanings were involved. Among the terms used were *isdiwa*j and *tibaq*. The device called *jinas* was the use of two or more words from the same or similar roots, producing an effect akin to a combination of alliteration and assonance.[10]

With this new technique and vocabulary, Arabic narrative continued to develop by widening its depiction of various characters and themes. There were stories about lovers and political chaos. Consistent with Qur'anic and Hadith literature, narrative often had a tone of morality and self-discipline.

By the time of the *One Thousand and One Nights*, all of the established forms of literature had been adopted in fictional writing: poetry, prose, and proverbs. There was an abundance of poetry in which characters spoke in verse or recited poetry in various settings. They recited poetry to express their feelings as if they were performing monologues to an audience. For example, poetry was used in praising the God and royalty, pleading to God for mercy and forgiveness, lamenting wrong decisions or bad luck, providing riddles, laying questions or challenges, or expressing feelings of happiness, sorrow, anxiety, surprise or anger. Poetry appeared to be the most useful when it described mixed emotions battling each other, as in the description of Queen Bodour when she saw the ring of Prince Qamar al-Zaman that was delivered by the servant announcing his arrival. She was overwhelmed by joy and began to chant: I am "so happy that I am crying," "Oh tearing eyes, you cry with joy and cry in sadness" (Tale 203). The prince responded with his verse to express his feeling of happiness (Tale 205).

Like Arabic poetry, the *One Thousand and One Nights* was a string of pearls, each of which could be picked up and would shine on its own. Many pearls were shining, dramatic writings that vividly presented a play unfolding in front of the eyes of its readers, who were witnessing a drama without a stage. One of the examples was the "Tale of the Three Apples" (also called "The Tale of the Murdered Young Woman"). In this murder mystery, a caliph (the king) discovered a chest, which, when opened, contained the body of a young woman. He ordered his vizier, Giafar, to find the murderer in three days or he himself would be executed.

The vizier Giafar returned home in the greatest distress. "Alas!" he thought, "How is it possible, in so large and vast a city like Bagdad, to find a murderer, who no doubt has committed this crime secretly and alone, and now has possibly fled the city?"

He ordered police officers and justice to make a strict search for the criminal. They sent out their underlings, and exerted themselves personally in this affair. But all their diligence came to nothing; they could discover no traces that might lead to the murderer's capture. The vizier concluded that, unless heaven interposed in his favor, he could not solve this murder. His death was inevitable.

On the third day, an officer of the caliphate came to the house of the unhappy minister, and summoned him to his master. The vizier obeyed, and when the caliph demanded of him the murderer, he replied, with tears in his eyes, "O Commander of the Faithful, I have found no one who could give me any intelligence concerning him."

The caliph reproached Giafar in the bitterest words, and commanded that he should be hanged before the gates of the palace, together with forty of the Barmecides.

While the executioners were preparing the gibbets, and the officers went to seize the forty Barmecides at their different houses, a public crier was ordered by the caliph to proclaim, in all the quarters of the city, that whoever wished to have the satisfaction of seeing the execution of the grand vizier Giafar, and forty of his family, the Barmecides, was to repair to the square before the palace.

When everything was ready, the judge placed the grand vizier and the forty Barmecides each under the gibbet that was destined for him, and cords were fastened round the neck of the prisoners. The people who crowded the square could not behold such a spectacle without feeling pity and shedding tears, for the vizier Giafar and his relations the Barmecides were much loved for their probity and liberality, not only in Bagdad, but throughout the whole empire of the caliph.

Everything was ready for the execution of the caliph's cruel order, and the next moment would have seen the death of some of the worthy inhabitants of the city, when a young man, of comely appearance and well dressed, pressed through the crowd till he reached the grand vizier. He kissed Giafar's hand, and exclaimed, "Sovereign vizier, chief of the emirs of this court, the refuge of the poor! You are not guilty of the crime for which you are going to suffer. Let me expiate the death of the lady who was thrown into the Tigris. I am her murderer! I alone ought to be punished!"

Although this speech created great joy in the vizier, he nevertheless felt pity for the youth, whose countenance, far from expressing guilt, indicated nobility of soul. He was going to reply, when an old man, who had also pushed through the crowd, came up and said to the vizier, "My lord, do not believe what this young man has said to you. I alone am the person that killed the lady! I alone am worthy of punishment. In the name of God I conjure you not to confound the innocent with the guilty."

"O my master," interrupted the young man, addressing himself to the vizier, "I assure you that it was I who committed this wicked action, and that no person in the world is my accomplice."

"Alas! My son," resumed the old man, "despair has led you hither, and you wish to anticipate your destiny. As for me, I have lived for a long time in this world, let me sacrifice my life to save yours. My lord," he continued, addressing the vizier, "I repeat it, I am the criminal, sentence me to death, and let justice be served."

The contest between the old man and the youth obliged the vizier to bring them before the caliph, with the permission of the commanding officer of justice, who was happy to have an opportunity of obliging him.

When he came into the presence of the sovereign, he kissed the ground seven times, and then spoke these words, "Commander of the Faithful, I bring to you this old man and this youth, each of whom accuses himself as the murderer of the lady."

This dramatic visualization was typical of the narrative of the *One Thousand and One Nights*, in which characters or scenes were presented with an abundance of descriptive detail, mimetic gestures and vividly recorded dialogue. It was like presenting a scene on a stage imaginatively to an audience.[11]

Another example of this dramatization was the story of "The Lover Who Pretended to Be a Thief." The governor of Basra Khalid one day confronted a man of a family who had caught a handsome young man breaking into his home. He accused the young man of theft, and the prisoner fully cooperated and willingly confessed the crime. In the eyes of Khalid, the young man appeared to be too well-spoken and good mannered to be a thief. He suspected that the youth was concealing the truth. As the young man insisted on admitting the guilt of stealing, the governor had no choice but to comply with the law, which was to cut his hands off in public.

In the morning everybody, each man and woman, in Basra came to see the youth's hand cut off; no one would miss the action of punishment. Khalid came riding up and with him the Basran dignitaries. Then he summoned the judges and called for the young man to be brought. So he approached, stumbling in his chains. Everyone at the scene was weeping for him. Voice of women in the crowd rose up in lamentation.

The judge ordered the women to be silenced and he asked him: "These people believe that you have entered their home and stole their possessions. Perhaps you stole an amount less than the quantity that made this punishment necessary by law?" "No, on the contrary, I have stolen precisely the amount necessary for this punishment." He asked again, "Maybe you are co-owner of some of these possessions with them?" He replied, "No, on the contrary, these things are entirely theirs and I have no legal claim to any of them."

At this moment Khalid became angry. He came over to the young man and struck his face with whip and recited the verses loudly: "Man wishes to be given his desire and God refused to give all save what He desires." He called up the butcher, who would be the one to cut off the young man's hand. The butcher came with a knife. He stretched his hands and put the knife on the top of them.

At this moment suddenly a young woman rushed forward from a group of women. She screamed and threw herself upon him. She drew back her veil to reveal her face, which was as beautiful as the moon, and raised the outcry of the people. Now the beloved is willing to sacrifice her reputation and secret love to save her lover from punishment.[12]

The plots of many stories of the *One Thousand and One Nights* were built on a contradiction between what appeared to be inevitable and what was actually happened. It had little to do with fate or destiny but everything to do with the writer, who played games with the assumptions of the audience/reader and manipulated them to create attention to the story.[13] If this technique adopted reverse logic, the foreshadowing took advantage of a linear logical to prepare the reader for the progress of the narrative. It contained repeated references to some character or object that appeared insignificant when first mentioned but reappeared later to intrude suddenly in the narrative. The tale of "The Three Apples" was one of the most noticeable examples. The clue for the murder mystery was dropped earlier to prepare the reader for the happy ending. Another early foreshadowing technique was formal patterning, where the organization of the events, actions and gestures constituted a narrative and gave shape to a story; when done well, formal patterning allowed the audience the pleasure of discerning and anticipating the structure of the plot as it unfolded. This technique would become commonplace in modern fiction writing, but it was employed in the *One Thousand and One Nights* many centuries earlier.[14]

The first attempt to combine Arabic literary tradition with contemporary life was made by Syrian and Lebanese writers during the nineteenth century. Nasif al-Yaziji (1800–1871) made an effort to revive Arabic traditional narrative *maqāmā* and wrote his modern narrative in *maqāmā* style (*majma' al-Bahrayn*). Salim al-Bustani (d. 1884) laid foundation of historical novel in Arabic as his novels were published in the periodical *Al-Jinan*. They dealt with the history of the Middle East from Arab conquest of Syria after the death of Muhammad to the beginning of the twentieth century. In 1864, Francis Marrash (1836–1873) published *Ghabat al-haqq* (*The Forest of Justice*), which was an allegorical novel written as a dialogue about ideas of peace, freedom and equality. Through this work, Marrash became the first Arab writer to reflect the optimism and the humanistic view of 18th century Europe. This view projected the hope that education, science and technology would resolve such problems of humanity as slavery, religious discrimination, illiteracy, disease, poverty, and war, and it gave utterance to his hope for brotherhood and equality among peoples. In 1872, he published *Durr al-sadaf*, a novel in which he described the contemporary Lebanese society and its customs.[15]

Between the years 1898 and 1902 Muhammad Ibrahim al-Muwaylihi (1858–1930) serialized his narrative work *Hadith 'Isa ibn Hisham* (*Isa ibn Hisham's Account*). He used the *maqāmā* form with its rhyming prose, episodic structure, and highly rhetorical style to depict the story of an Egyptian pasha of Turkish origin. The pasha came back to life after being dead for many years to witness the astounding social changes that had taken place in Egypt, especially in Westernized Cairo.

Hadith 'Isa ibn Hisham was a modern novel that took contemporary Egypt and its people as a subject and scrutinized them in an intense and humorous manner. However, his modern world was narrated by a neoclassical style of revived *maqāmā*. The narrator, a writer named 'Isa ibn Hisham, met the dead pasha in a dream, and chatted with him about many relevant social, political, and cultural topics, explained to him the many changes in Egypt in the last few decades, and tried to justify the ludicrous incongruities of his compatriots. After many episodes, some of which were very funny, the story of 'Isa and his dream stopped abruptly without ever reaching a conclusion. The writing of this work was substantially more developed compared to the previous attempts of modern writers, and it became a classic and a model for the Egyptian novel as a modern genre.[16]

As in other earlier literary works of the period, Al-Muwaylihi reserved a big section of his book for serious and elaborate discussions of the positive and negative characteristics of both European and Arab civilizations. These strained and poorly motivated debates definitely harm the structure of this work and prevented it from achieving the status of one of the truly great novels in Arabic literature. Were it not for the author's wit and humor, and his lexical abilities and stylistic skills, *Hadith 'Isa ibn Hisham* would not have become so popular, and would not have taken its place in the canon of classical literature in Egypt.

Hafiz Ibrahim's (1872–1932) *Ibrahim's Layali Satih* (*The Nights of Satih*, 1906) was modeled after *Hadith 'Isa ibn Hisham*. Ibrahim made use of encounters between his narrator and a variety of contemporary Egyptians to comment on current political issues. This poorly structured narrative work consisted of seven essays that were encompassed by a clumsy framing story which, like its model, had no logical ending. Ibrahim created a few artificial and unconvincing incidents only to be used as a springboard for discussing serious social, political, and philosophical issues, such as the abolition of the veil, the establishment of universities and specialized schools, pollution, and the judicial immunity granted to Westerners living in Egypt. The author's highly rhetorical style, which resembled that of the *maqāmā*, his inclusion of lengthy prose and verse quotations, as well as many independent essays and anecdotes, made the book even more fragmentary, and it eventually had to be regarded merely as a shallow precursor to the more serious novelistic attempts that occurred later.[17]

Jurji Zaydan (1861–1914) decided to write for the mass of the population rather than the cultural elite. He wrote twenty-three historical novels dealing with crucial phases in Arab history, attempting to imbue the common Arabic-speaking population with knowledge of their own history. To make history interesting and entertaining, his novels usually revolved around a love story that was filled with adventure and intrigues, and ended with happiness ever after. Zaydan researched all the historical facts and yet "wrote down" to his readers' level of interests and understanding. He constructed each of his novels in an almost identical frame yet with different topics and timelines. He then would imagine a romance between fictitious characters and a mystery of some sort to weave into the historical facts in order to engage the readers. His plots were often weak and linear, relying mostly on convenient coincidences to drive the love story and mystery. His characters were unsophisticated and often one-dimensional without any information about their background, point of view, or social status. Their character traits and personalities were described in the first instance, but never developed throughout the story. The plain and straightforward style derived not so much from his lack of skills as from his commitment to educate, inform, and enlighten the majority of Egyptian populace ninety percent of which was illiterate.[18]

As most historians and literary critics of Arabic literature who are writing in English are Western-trained, they inevitably judge Arabic novels against the yardstick of English or French novels. They often miss the most important and distinctive character of the Arabic novel: its rhetoric tendency and moral or political tone. Arab writers rarely wrote just stories, as most English writer insisted was the case for their fiction writing. They wrote to express themselves, their worldviews, social ideas, and sentiments and they were not shy about it. As Mahfouz put it, readers always find politics in all of his writings. As the very axis of their thinking, Arabic novelists always had a political or ideological theme, inherited from traditional Arabic narrative. Just like *maqāmā*, which was a display of incredible stylistic feast by a complete master of Arabic language, writing represents who they are as human beings and intellectuals. This is the ultimate reason why *maqāmā* had been the preferred mode of literary expression ever since the post-classical period.[19] In this specific sense, for the Arabic novel, it is not about whether there was a moral or political message but rather about how the author delivers the message through skillful storytelling. It is rather concerned with whether the ideas are seamlessly woven into the story lines and expressed in an engaging and moving manner or disjoined and simplistically written by writers who had high opinions and low creative talent.

It took many generations of Arabic writers to polish the narrative combining rich literary tradition and tangible contemporary life. It began with two separate streams of writing: the elite and popular writing for different readerships. During the nineteenth century, Egyptian novels were written by theologians, linguists, intellectuals, and poets and related to old Arabic literary forms such as *qasas* and *maqāmā*. Authors of traditional narratives did not pay much attention to either plot or characters. Instead, they dealt mainly with cultural, political, historical, and philosophical questions, clung to conventional issues and conservative topics, and used a highly ornamental and rhetorical prose (which relied heavily on internal or end rhyme). On the contrary, the innovative writers and translators used a much simpler style and were more interested in narrating suspenseful events, placing dramatic characters at the center of their works. They dealt with themes and motifs that were unfamiliar to their traditional compatriots, such as free love, adultery, and women's emancipation. It is obvious from their writings that the first group was mainly interested in educating and enlightening their readers, while the second group was aiming primarily at entertaining their readers and capturing the mass market. It took a long time for these two ends to mingle into one in the works of a single writer and single piece of work.

It took Arabic fiction several decades to find a narrative language that integrated the styles and techniques inherited from the traditional storyteller with those of modern fiction. This was accomplished gradually in several steps. Arabic writers initially introduced the reading public to their own cultural and historical heritage as a subject through historical novels that focused on events and simple stories, as did Zaydan and others. Then, modern fiction began to depict contemporary life and its pressing social and national issues. Eventually, Arabic writers attempted to cultivate a popular taste for high and sophisticated forms, which was enjoyed by less than 10 percent of its citizens for centuries. It was an effort working its way simultaneous from two ends: dealing with everyday issues and clear language (writing down) to the level of the majority, and assimilating vernacular and regional dialects into the literary canon (writing up).

The first Arabic fiction in English concept was *Zaynab* (1913) by Muhammad Husayn Haykel (1888–1956). The story described contemporary Egyptian life and featured dialogue in the vernacular. For the first time, an Egyptian novel told an unglamorous story of a young peasant girl named Zaynab and the three men who at one time or another strove for her affections. At the end, none of them could have a life with his or her true love. Egypt had to wait for more than a decade for another modern novel to be published. During the 1920s most writers turned to short stories, except Teha Husayin (1889–1973).[20]

Arabic developed mature first-person narrative before the modern period. Biographic narrative of Muhammad's life evolved into autobiography beginning from Sufi lives, such as Al-Ghazali's *Al-Munqid mina al-Dalal (Deliverance from Error and Mystical Union with the Almighty)*.[21] Taha Husayn's (1889–1973) *Al-Ayam, (The Days)*, his famous autobiography, made a major contribution to the development of prose literature. Husayn's third-person narrative gave the traditional narrative mode of autobiography a touch of gentle irony by the sense of detachment from his protagonist. Each memory was given its appropriate emotional atmosphere in which his silent sorrow could be read within his mind and deeply felt. His moving and graceful storytelling flew so easily that it sharply contrasted with the forceful rhetoric morality plays that were so commonly produced in the Arabic literature of the early twentieth century. It was no accident that it has remained one of the most enduring masterpieces in a modern Arabic prose literature.[22]

Like Taha Husayn, many writers' first attempt to write a novel initiated from their own life stories. Ibrahim Mazini (1889–1949) was one of them. He published his first novel, *Ibrahim al-Katib*, in 1931. It was a disjointed account of the love of a man for three different kinds of women: a nurse, his cousin, and his real love, whom he was not allowed to marry. Although the novel did not have the same success as did *Zaynab* or the same literary claim as did *Al-Ayam*, it showed Mazini's skill in creating vignettes of characters and provided some amusing moments.[23]

A novel that successfully portrayed an Egyptian family life within the restricted environment of traditional culture was Tawfiq al-Hakim's (1898–1987) *Awdat al-ruh (Return of the Spirit, 1933)*. It was story of a patriotic young Egyptian and his extended family ending with events surrounding the 1919 revolution. Muhsin was a young student living with his relatives in Cairo. All of the male members of the family were fascinated by the charm of the daughter of a neighbor, Saniyyah, while Zannūbah, the spinster of the family, spent all her money and time to become beautiful in order to attract the attention of men and to find a husband. While the potential of this mixture of characters was well exploited in the first part of the book, the atmosphere was shifted when Muhsin returned to his parents' country estate for a vacation. This allowed Al-Hakim to elaborate on the theme, which provided the novel with its title: Egypt's awareness of its ancient heritage. However, to tie the traditional idea of eternal Egypt and its reaction to foreign occupation and nationalist revolution to a realistic portrayal of everyday life in the first part of the novel was less successful, and the forced fusion made the work lose a sense of balance. However, the dramatic role of dialogue in character portrayal that had been convincingly demonstrated in Al-Hakim's novel paved the way for the emergence of the Arabic novel in its full maturity.[24]

Tawfiq al-Hakim succeeded in creating one of the most memorable works of early modern Arabic fiction, *Yawmiyyāt nāib fī al-aryāf* (*Diary of a Public Prosecutor in the Provinces*, 1937). It was an Egyptian comedy of errors, which took the form of the journal of a young public prosecutor posted to a village in rural Egypt. Imbued with the ideals of a European education, he encountered a world of poverty and ignorance where an imported legal system, both alien and incomprehensible, was applied to the beliefs and customs of rural Egypt. The vivid picture of country life was filtered through the vision of an outsider. The chronology was intertwined with the story of Rim, the stunning village beauty who was initially thought to be involved in a murder, but then disappeared only to be discovered, towards the end of the story, as a corpse in a canal. It was a story that was told in sophisticated mix of irony and description, both touching and savagely funny.[25]

The effort to modernize the Arabic language and to combine traditional symbolism, modern issues and high literary form did not witness consistent success until the works of Naguib Mahfouz (1911–2006). Mahfouz was the first novelist to successfully widen traditional symbolism to include modern issues and bring new perception into Egyptian contemporary life experience. He discovered deeper meanings in modern life by exploring the inner world of his characters.[26]

Mahfouz was regarded one of the most influential Arabic authors. He published over 50 novels and over 350 short stories during a career of over 70 years. Mahfouz's writing began with an ambitious plan to cover the entire history of Egypt in a project of 30 books, a plan similar to but grander than that of Zaydan. Mahfouz's early works were a part of this plan: *Abath*

Al-Aqdar (*Khufu's Wisdom*) (1939), *Rhadopis* (*Rhadopis of Nubia*) (1943), and *Kifah Tibah* (*Thebes at War*) (1944) were historical novels. However, after the third volume, Mahfouz decided to shift his subject from the past to the present, the contemporary psychological impact of social change on ordinary people. From that time on, tradition became a form and vehicle (rather than a subject) to depict the social conditions of modern Egypt and to express his ideas about socialism, religion and sexuality, which were forbidden topics at the time.

Mahfouz's central work in the 1950s was the *Cairo Trilogy*, a monumental work of 1,500 pages, which the author completed before the July Revolution. The novels were titled with street names such as Palace Walk, Palace of Desire, and Sugar Street. Mahfouz set the story in the parts of Cairo where he had grown up. They depicted the life of the patriarch El-Sayyed Ahmed Abdel Gawad and his family over three generations, from World War I to the 1950s, when King Farouk I was overthrown. Mahfouz ceased to write for some years after finishing the trilogy. Disappointed in the Nasser régime, he started publishing again in 1959, now prolifically pouring out novels, short stories, journalism, memoirs, essays, and screenplays.

The Children in the Alley (1959), one of Mahfouz's best known works, bluntly expressed his ideas about world religions and their relationships. It portrayed the patriarch Gebelawi and his children, average Egyptians living the lives of Cain and Abel, Moses, Jesus, and Mohammed. Gebelawi had built a mansion in an oasis in the middle of a barren desert; his estate became the scene of a family feud, which continued for generations. Whenever someone was depressed, suffering or humiliated, he would point to the mansion at the top of the alley leading to the desert, and say sadly, "That is our ancestor's house, we are all his children, and we have a right to his property. Why are we starving? What have we done?" The story referred to the related history of the three monotheistic Abrahamic religions (Judaism, Christianity, and Islam), allegorized against the setting of an imaginary 19th century Cairene neighborhood. Gebelawi symbolized religion in general while the first four sections retold the stories of Adam (*Adham*): how he was favored by Gebelawi over the latter's other sons, including Satan/Iblis (*Idris*), Moses (*Gabal*), Jesus (*Rifa'a*), and Muhammad (*Qasim*). Families of each son settled in different parts of the alley, metaphors for Judaism, Christianity and Islam, which spread to different parts of the world. The protagonist of the book's fifth section is Arafa, who represented modern science and, significantly, came after all prophets. All the followers of the established families claimed Arafa as one of their own, as modern religions attempted to interpret science in their own terms. In the 1960s, Mahfouz further developed this theme, that humanity was moving further away from God, in his other novels. In *The Thief and the Dogs* (1961) he depicted the dark thought and deed of a revolutionary anarchist (the thief), who had been released from prison and planned revenge against the people who had betrayed him.[27]

In the 1960s and 1970s Mahfouz developed a form of multiple first-person narrative to construct his novels and to use interior monologues. *Miramar* (1967) was set in 1960s Alexandria with an attractive servant girl, Zohra. The story followed the interactions of the residents of the pension, his Greek mistress Mariana, and her servant. As each character in turn fought for Zohra's affections or allegiance, tension and jealousies arose. The story was retold four times from the perspective of a different resident each time, allowing the reader to understand the intricacies of post-revolutionary Egyptian life. The character Zohra symbolized the ideal modern Egyptian or Egypt. She was hard working and honest but uneducated, and constantly being pulled by different forces. Among those pulling her and Egypt were Europeans, Egyptian nationalists, the wealthy upper class, the Abdel Nasser regime and its followers, and the Muslim Brotherhood.[28]

Tharthara Fawq Al-Nīle (*Adrift on the Nile*) (1966) was one of his most popular novels. The story criticized the decadence of Egyptian society during the Nasser era, narrated through the eyes and consciousness of its main character, Anīs Zaki. The story was set on a houseboat, a symbol of detachment from the world of the city, society and its problems, a means of retreat from the alienation of modern life itself. The boat was moored to the land, which constituted the venue of a crushing and disillusioning reality. The symbol of water, the river on which the boat floated, allowed for a lulling sense of detachment from the unpleasant aspects of the life of Zaki which was forced to confront every day in his office. It was from this environment that he escaped to his houseboat, wafted by the cool evening breezes, and to the circle of companions who joined him in the evening for encounters with drugs and sex. The symbolism implicit in this escape was further underlined by 'Amm 'Abduh, the houseboat's general factotum. He was a huge man who arranged all the necessary equipment for the evening parties: procuring girls for Anīs Zaki and the company, in addition, who also served as imam for a local group of Muslims. Although silent at most times, he was the houseboat, because he was the ropes and lanterns. If for a single moment he did not do his job, the boat would sink or be carried away by the tide.

The group that came to the houseboat was from a variety of professions: a lawyer, a university-graduated feminist, a short story writer, a civil servant, an art critic and a celebrated film actor. The one person who provided a distinct angle to view the activities on the houseboat was the girlfriend of the actor, Samarah. As she was introduced to the group one by one at her first visit, she was shocked and amazed at the blatant way in which the company indulged in illegal activities.

"Aren't you scared of the police?" she asked.

"We're scared of the police," replied 'Alī al-Sayyid, "not to mention the army, the English, the Americans, the overt and the covert. By now it's gone so far that nothing can scare us."

"But the door's wide open!"

"'Amm 'Abduh's outside. He can keep intruders out."

"Don't worry, gorgeous," Rajab said with a smile, "the government's so preoccupied with building things, and it doesn't have any time to bother us."

"Why don't you give this brand of fortitude a try?" asked Mustafa Rashid, offering her the hashish pipe.[29]

It took the group a while to assimilate the new girl, whose impressions and criticism of the group were expressed by the main character, who took and read her diary. Her premonition came to reality when the group piled into a car for a crazy ride in the desert at night. They knocked down and killed a peasant on the road but drove away without stopping to face the consequences. The incident shattered their collective illusions and forced them back to the harsh reality that they had been trying to escape. On the night that Zaki was arrested, the group met in an entirely different atmosphere; it was tense. Samarah insisted that they should go to the police, whereas everyone else was afraid of being exposed. Eventually none of them could muster enough dignity and courage to face the responsibilities.[30]

While Mahfouz portrayed the imagery of death (both in physical and spiritual sense) in life, Ghassan Kanafani (1936–1972) and Palestinian writers accumulated a repertoire of stories of survival (the constant struggle against death). Mahfouz criticized the moral decadence of Egyptian society and hung his hopes on the evolution of human spirit. On the contrary, the Palestinians promoted courage and hope for a hopeless political situation. They represented different sides of the same spirit in Arabic, which had triumphed, been defeated, suffered, struggled, died, and been reborn. It will continue to reinvent itself with the increasingly widened and diversified repertoire of expressions.

No modern Arab novelist has been able to project the tragedy of the Palestinian people in fiction with greater impact than Ghassan Kanafani has. Of all his works of fiction, *Rijāl fī al-shams* (*Men in the Sun*) (1963) was undoubtedly the most famous. The story was about three Palestinian refugees who attempted to travel from the refugee camps in Lebanon to Kuwait, where they hoped to find work as laborers in the oil boom. The three men each arranged with a clerk at a local store to be smuggled to Kuwait by a driver. The men were treated gruffly and humiliated in the process. Once the travel deal was finalized, they found that they had to ride in the back of a truck across the desert on their way to Kuwait. At several checkpoints, the men hid in a large, empty water tank in the stifling mid–day heat as the driver arranged paperwork to get through. After the last checkpoint, within easy driving distance of the travelers' ultimate goal of Kuwait, the driver finally opened the tank to let the men out only to find they had died. Khanafani's excellent use of imagery and brilliant plot construction made the impact of the symbolism very clear and powerful, sometimes too forceful for the sensibility of the readers.[31] Khanafani's second novel, *Ma tabaqqa la kum* (*All That's Left to You*), was considered one of the earliest and most successful modernist experiments in Arabic fiction. Like Mahfouz, he adopted multiple narrators, two of which were inanimate objects. It was the story of a young man, Hamid, who was separated from his mother after they both fled to different areas. Hamid tried desperately to find his mother but he became lost in the desert, crossing paths with an Israeli soldier. He was compelled to desert his original plan of looking for his mother and had to confront his enemy instead. He died before locating his mother. In death he was reunited with his lost land, and the very act of confronting his fears constitutes a symbolic victory. The vivid descriptions of Hamid's unremitting anger and shame for the tragedy that fell on his people symbolized the Palestinian attachment to land and family.

Khanafani made some interesting experiments to develop and clarify his imagery. The five heroes of this novel, Hamid, Maryam, Zakariyyā, Time and the Desert, did not move in parallel or conflicting directions from the beginning. Rather, they intersected in a manner that was so compact that they all seemed to consist of just two separate threads. This juxtaposition also affected both time and place, to such an extent that there was no specific dividing line between places that were far apart or between different time frames, and occasionally between time and place at one and the same time. However, the juxtaposition did not deny the time that played a pivotal role in narration. The events took place over an interval of some eighteen hours, mostly during the night. In addition to generous episodes of flashback, time was represented in two objects that told time: a wall clock whose ticking punctuated the life of those who lived in the Palestinian home which was the major focus of the action, and a watch which Hamid eventually discarded as useless on his journey across the desert at night. The earth as a symbol was another example. Like in *Men Under the Sun*, when Abu Qays was lying on the ground and felt the heartbeat of the earth beneath him, in *All That's Left to You*, Hamid threw himself to the ground "and felt it like a virgin trembling beneath him, as a beam of light silently and softly swept across the folds of sand." In another telling juxtaposition, the beats of the earth beneath Hamid's prostrate body find themselves associated with the fetus inside his sister's womb. Even the desert and time emerged as characters through whose mouths Khanafani spoke. The story was steeped in a powerful symbolism. Place and time, represented by the passing of the hours and the relentless heat of daytime sun, became active contributors to the plot of the story.[32]

Al-Tayyib Salih's (1928–2009) *Season of Migration to the North* (1969) was considered by many the most important Arabic novel of the 20th century. It was one of the distinguished novels dealing with cultural contact, confrontation, and their impact on humanity. The contrast between different cultures that was perceived by the Arab intellectuals returning to the Middle East after spending sometime in Europe had been a common theme. Their experience and the impact of the European cultures have been written about since the nineteenth century. What was refreshing about Salih's work was the penetrating complexity with which he explored the theme, the construction of narrative form and the use of imagery. Instead of a superficial and orientalist portrayal of the story of West v. East, Europe v. Africa, the story had many layers, each of which invited different interpretations.

The young narrator returned to his native Sudanese village on the banks of the Nile after seven years in England to pursue his education. On his arrival home, he encountered a strange new villager named Mustafa Sayd. Mustafa initially appeared to be aloof and distant, and exhibited none of the curiosity about life in Europe that the other villagers did. The narrator found out later that Mustafa had good knowledge of English literature and became curious about his past and especially his experience in England. As the narrator asked Mustafa about his past, he was very reluctant to tell. He simply told him, "I am no Othello, Othello was a lie." Struck by his mystery and fascinated by his past experience of European education that might be similar to his own, the narrator decided to investigate. He discovered that Mustafa used to be a precocious student who had a distinguished career in Sudan, Cairo, and eventually England as a scholar and teacher. He also learned that Mustafa had a violent, hateful and complex relationship with his perceived identity as an Arab African in the eyes of the English.

Mustafa's troubled past in Europe and in particular his love affairs with many British women formed the center storyline of the novel. The

Mustafa in England was a person who was perceived and therefore acted, compelled or chosen, according to the imagery of Europeans about Black Africa. In the process, he became that image: an Arab African man, exotic and savage, an image that led to his self-destruction. Like the young narrator, Mustafa used to be a student who had a mind that was as sharp as a knife. He had a successful career in England as well as being a shark in the social scene. With his acute intelligence, he realized the difference between who he was and who he was perceived and expected to be in the minds of the white English. He decided to manipulate the English illusion about the exotic African man and turned it to his advantage in social encounters. Instead of being a victim, as commonly assumed for a person from a British colony, Mustafa was a warrior and conqueror, "the invader who came from the South (means the East)" to defeat the English with deep seated anger and hatred. He also had the vision that in the process, he "would never make a safe return from the icy battlefield of the North (means the West)." His English experience transformed him from intelligent to insane and from a scholar to a murderer. He lost his own humanity, African, Arab, or otherwise.

He manipulated the English perception of the African man and turned it into his weapon to destroy the white English. About his homeland, dark Africa, he told British women what they wanted to hear: tropical climes, cruel sun, purple horizons to seduce them. He told them lies about deserts of golden suns and jungles where non-existent animals called out to one another. Pretending to be the exotic lover, he became an invader into their hearts and expressed his anger though cold and loveless sexual acts. He eventually went insane from his own lies and hatred. He killed his English wife and drove two more women to suicide. As he wished to confess his crimes and take the punishment of law, the same misunderstanding that made him do what he did in the social scene saved his life. He was let off with a reduced sentence. His defense lawyer argued in the court that the girls (English women) were killed not by Mustafa, but by the germs of a deadly disease that had assailed the people of the colony a thousand years ago. As cruelty and hatred were the European disease, Mustafa was less responsible for his crimes.

To his discomfort and fear, the narrator discovered that Mustafa had awakened in him great anger and despair, as if Mustafa were his doppelganger. The stories of Mustafa's past life in England, and the repercussions on the village around him, took their toll on the narrator, who was driven to the very edge of sanity. In the final chapter, the narrator was floating in the Nile precariously between life and death; he made a decision not to drown and rid himself of Mustafa's lingering presence, and to be his own person.

The story was about the perception and misconception between Arabs and the Europeans. However, unlike the writers before him, Al-Tayyib Salih conveyed these misunderstanding at the broadest cultural level in concrete imagery in a highly personal and honest tone. The main imagery was of two rooms of Mustafa's, symbolizing two sides of his personality and heritage. In Sudan, Mustafa set up an English scholar's study, filled with books and memorabilia, perfect in every pedantic detail, but a place isolated from the life and experience of the countrymen of his homeland. In London, on the other hand, he established a room that served as a grotesque parody of the worst excesses of European notions (or fantasies) concerning the exotic Oriental: a place of fatal couplings, steeped in deception. The author himself has commented on this dimension when he notes: "I had in mind the idea that the relationship between the Arab world and west European civilization ... was based on illusions both on our part and theirs."[33]

In this novel, for the first time, two cultures with their own illusions about themselves and about other cultures were woven into the life and consciousness of a single person, with its various incidents, love or lust partners, marriages, and murders that reflected the turbulent coexistence and clashes. The author not only succeeded in handling the complex time frame of the narrative with great skill, but also managed to sprinkle into the various sections a number of clues, which can recalled later and be made on a purely realistic level between the characters. The narrative constantly shifted between past, present, and occasionally future throughout the work. For example, the following: "I had loafed around the streets of Cairo, visited the opera, gone to the theatre, and once I had swum across the Nile. Nothing whatsoever had happened except that the waterskin had distended further, the bowstring had become tauter. The arrow will shoot forth towards other unknown horizons." This process of switching between the different time frames, not to mention the levels of narrative and symbol, was most effective in showing the way in which the tension implicit in the memories of the past constantly impinges upon the present in the consciousness of Mustafa and the narrator.[34]

Mustafa's relationships with all the female participants represented the evolution of the character within various cultural environments and demonstrated how transplantation brought out different sides of his personality. As a young person traveled to Europe he uprooted himself from his native country, where he was an African Arab as reality, and transplanted himself into the illusionary double that had been living in the imagination of Europeans. In order to succeed in England, he was compelled to act the part designed for him (a black man in a white society) by the illusion of the host culture. As a brilliant man acting his part too well, he lost himself and eventually became the illusion. He was a somewhat "normal" teenager who was brought up by an emotionally detached mother and was hungry for affection. Even his Oedipal feelings towards the wife of the British school teacher would have been replaced (as for millions of youngsters of his age) by his love of his Sudanese wife and "mother of his children" if he had not gone to England. However, living in a foreign land where he had to act (to succeed as he did in school) according to the expectations of the society, he was forced to play a part. He did very well to play the illusion in white women's minds, maybe too well. He lost his humanity. His relationship with a fourth English woman pushed him off the edge of his illusion. She steadfastly refused to succumb to the mysterious and vicious allures that Mustafa had so craftily set up to dangle in front of his victims. By this time, Mustafa would have done anything to maintain his part, which had become the foundation of his existence in Europe. He married her hoping to remain in control. As she continued her own outrageous conduct, she activated the deeply seated anger within him. It turned to hatred, not just for her, but for himself too. Mustafa admitted later, "I was the pirate sailor and Jean Morris the shore of destruction." He had to kill her to save himself, his sailing career, which was the part that he had to play in this foreign land and the imagination of its inhabitants.

This highly personal struggle was so well constructed that it attempted to convince the reader by the words of Mustafa, "I am a desert of thirst. I am no Othello." A brilliant career and scholarly achievement obviously did not satisfy that thirst because to conquer, to defeat, and to equalize became his lifeline, like water. Although Mustafa found the argument of his defense lawyer, which portrayed him as a victim of the political struggle between two worlds, unpalatable and hypocritical, he had to surrender to it because it managed to secure him a relatively light prison sentence of seven years for his wife's murder. He had the opportunity to do some traveling, eventually to his native Sudan, and settle in a village on the Nile. However, he did not belong to Africa anymore. Facing different kinds of expectations and social environments, Mustafa had to construct his suicide to escape.[35]

During the late 1980 and 1990s, Arabic writers began to experiment with new narrative forms as they began to get rid of two restraining burdens of the past, native literary tradition and the Western influence. The Arabic novel came into its own as an art form with or without a political message. The novels were not anti-tradition, anti-modern, anti–West or formless, but simply claimed the authority to reproduce the totality of all these established forms to serve the new purpose of creativity. What Arab writers had learned during the past decades remained visible in the experiential works, such as episodical framework, realistic depiction, usage of dialogue, stream of consciousness, imagery and time as narrative form and multidimensional characterization. However, they reconstructed them in much lesser linear and deeper narratives.[36]

Elias Khoury's (b. 1948) novel *The Little Mountain* (1977) presented a leap in terms of formal complexity in fictional writing. It was about a fifteen-year civil war in Lebanon. It was composed in five chapters, every one of which was represented by a very different voice. Each was an examination of the explosion of hope, love, life, and death that surrounded the chaos of war. The story was told from the perspectives of three characters: a Joint Force fighter; a distressed civil servant; and an idealistic young man, part fighter, part intellectual. The first chapter was about the change from peace to war. It began with a collection of imagery of the Little Mountain suburb prior to the war. A violent scene interrupted the peace when a group of solders marched into a house to look for a young man and harass his mother. It was a short scene depicted in short and sharp sentences to create a sense of urgency in contrast to the calm atmosphere of a community before it was torn down by war. The second chapter was the war story told by a Christian fighter. There was not any personal history about why he entered the war except that he was content with his choice. The entire country was in war and chaos; people still had to live and deal with death every day. The narrator was able to relate horrific events in a matter-of-fact tone, calm and collected and unsentimental. While fighting to stay alive, he still wanted to have slices of life between deaths: to talk with friends, love pretty girls and be happy when he could.

While the first two chapters were about physical war and actual fighters, the remaining three chapters were more introspective and analytical. They were about the feelings and thoughts of more intelligent characters about war. Although as citizens they did not have to fight every day, war had even greater and more terrifying impacts on their lives. Bombshells whistled as though they were coming out of their ears. They could not sleep in or out of their beds because bombs were falling and people were dying outside of their front doors. This story of war was illustrated through the eyes of five people who lived through it and had to cope with it. *Little Mountain* was not about plot or characters so much as a place and its people living, more specifically surviving, in its warzone environment.[37]

In this book one can find many techniques inherited from Arabic literature up to Khoury's time from episodic narration, multi-level storytelling, interior monologue, at times approaching a stream of consciousness, and elements of colloquial Arabic. The use of dialect forms added to the credibility and immediacy of the narrative voice. Although the use of dialogue was relatively common in modern Arabic literature, Khoury was the first to write an entire novel in the form of a one-sided conversation. His book *Gate of the Sun* was a touching story composed entirely in a monologue. The main character, Khalil, went to visit his friend Yunes, who was a Palestinian freedom fighter who fell into a coma after injury. The "discussion" gradually revealed the history of a friendship where nothing was withheld. The two men "discuss" everything and nothing, but always they return, with respect and wonder, to the women in their lives. Early on, Khalil recalled that the novelist Khanafani had interviewed Yunes but had decided not to write about him because "he was looking for mythic stories, and yours was just the story of a man in love. Where would be the symbolism in this love that had no place to root itself? How did you expect he would believe the story of your love for your wife? Is a man's love for his wife really worth writing about?"

Unlike in *Little Mountain* where the location was depicted only in scattered images, the love story of *Gate of the Sun* rooted itself in Bab al-Shams (gate of the sun), a cave where Yunes and his wife, Nahilah, met secretly over the decades of their marriage. Bab al-Shams was where they made love, shared meals and discussed their children. It was also the scene of Nahilah's loving exposure of Yunes's self-delusion, an inspired monologue that chastened and enlightened him. The cave was the novel. At one point, Khalil explained this to Yunes: "We've made a shelter out of words, a country out of words, and women out of words."

Historical events were not absent from Khoury's fiction; in fact, they covered a wide range of history. But he confined them to the conversation between Khalil and Yunes. Speaking about the Holocaust, Khalil told his friend: "You and I and every human being on the face of the planet should have known and not stood by in silence, should have prevented that beast from destroying its victims in that barbaric, unprecedented manner. Not because the victims were Jews but because their death meant the death of humanity within us." On the murder of Israeli athletes at the Munich Olympics, Khalil told Yunes: "I know what you think of that kind of operation, and I know you were one of the few who dared take a stand against the hijacking of airplanes, the operations abroad and the killing of civilians." On Palestinian identity before 1948, Khalil admitted to Yunes: "Palestine was the cities—Haifa, Jaffa, Jerusalem and Acre. In them we could feel something called Palestine. The villages were like all villages.... The truth is that those who occupied Palestine made us discover the country as we were losing it." Asking why the Palestinians fled their land, Khalil demanded: "Tell me about that blackness. I don't want the usual song about the betrayal by the Arab armies in the '48 war—I've had enough of armies. What did you do? Why are you here and they're there?"[38]

Khoury said that his aim in *Gate of the Sun* was to write a great love story. Dr. Khaleel, a paramedic in the makeshift Galilee hospital in Beirut's Shatila refugee camp, kept vigil by the bedside of Yunis, a comatose Palestinian resistance fighter of his father's generation. Khoury was astonished that no Palestinian novelist had ever written a novel about love. For Khoury, Yunis was heroic because he crossed the border for love, not for a country (Palestine). He also believed that creating and closing borders was one of the most stupid ideas of modern times. Yet, counter to what Khoury saw as a tendency in Palestinian literature—particularly poetry—to extol heroes in the service of the cause, his novel questioned the notions of heroism and martyrdom. This led to a painful honesty about humiliation and defeat. As he put it, "I am writing about human beings, not heroes. I don't feel literature can serve any cause. Art was to serve art. Writing was to travel towards discovering others; it's a way to listen to and love them." As Khoury's writing was about life, love, fear, and humiliation, it went beyond physical borders and politics. In one scene, a refugee encounters the Jewish woman who now lived in her house and who had her own painful history. Khoury wrote, instead of for the Palestinian cause, to contest the dominant national ideology, and his way to contest it was to write stories contrary to history, which he believed always was written and would be written by winners.

Little Mountain was one of the most lyrical novels ever written in Arabic; it was a story as well as a song: the words were short, piercing, repeated, and chanted. The narrative was carried by words, as well as by the atmosphere that they created and the rhythm they took. It was a story of the unbearable pain of war yet tuned into a beautiful music of words. It could only be done in Arabic.

Conclusions

Arabic literature had cultivated mature narrative forms before the modern period. Unlike the narrative of the modern European languages, which was created by formative vernaculars, Arab writers had to transform the inherited repertoire of traditional narration into a modern framework. Once transformed, Arabic narrative cultivated an incomparable command of language and imagery and created increasingly varied and individualized visions of the world punctuated with social commitment and personal convictions.

The main achievement of modern Arabic fiction lies in its ability to use imagery for rhetorical rather than descriptive purposes. Instead of painting a world in front of their readers, the Arabic modern fiction writers created personal visions through the eyes of their characters. For example, imagery was used in order to heighten the impact of the cultural interactions and social confrontations found in this novel: murders, infatuations, loveless sex. These symbolic enactments of cultural tensions were portrayed through images of violence and penetration. The bow and arrow, the climbing of the mountain peak, the driving of the tent-peg into the soil, all these were employed to describe character's callous and defiant posture, brilliant yet cold. As images gradually became internalized and carried more emotional weight in narration, fiction began to obtain the capacity of poetry.

Conclusion

The aim of this book is to initiate a multi-disciplinary and non–Western centered approach to the understanding of Arabic literary language.

Arabic, like many non–European languages, has been studied and analyzed based upon established Western literary and cultural theories. These theories have failed to acknowledge Arabic as a literary language that combines a rich poetic heritage, an extremely sensitive readership, and a literary refinement that is almost alien to English speakers. Therefore this book encroaches upon the familiar boundaries of literature, language (as speech), theatre, and music, and it defies the Western dichotomies of literature/society, language/reality, form/formless, and modern/post-modern. It illustrates that one of the most important features of Arabic expression is its exceptional diversity, which derived from its long term accumulation of various forms of sub-literary and literary expressions that contributed to the maturity and refinement of the Arabic language. As the language evolved, Arabic retained its old heritage as it adopted the new. This allowed for the constant expansion of the scope and ability of literary Arabic to enrich itself.

Literary Arabic attained a formal complexity that European languages did not see until later times. Therefore, a judgment on Arabic based upon the theories of European languages is improper. However, the history of Arabic language may provide a way for scholars to analyze and comprehend contemporary and emerging tendencies in English and other European languages.

In Arabic, the distinction and relationship between form and content differ from those in Western literatures. Formalism became prominent during the pre–Islamic and early Islamic periods. English formalism did not emerge until the pre-modern period. Spanish, Italian and French formalism initiated during the late Renaissance and Baroque.

In the Arabic world, the influence of mature poetics and inherited literary sensibility of its readership have never allowed the art of composition to be separated from its content. By the same token, the act and art of writing has always been central to storytelling. Traditions, with their distinct forms and shapes, can be rewritten, reimagined, and redefined. To understand Arabic is to appreciate its form of expression, a form which has enormous power to activate the minds and emotions of its speakers.

Chapter Notes

Part One

1. Abbott, 1957, 1967; Brockelmann, 1982, 6–7; Chejne, 1969, 69–70; Gilliot, 2006, 41–58; Diakonoff, 1988, 24–30, 63, 81; Owens, 2006, 8–13.
2. Rubio, 2005, 321–323; 2007, 7–8; Englund, 1998, 81; Braun, 2002, 8–35; Galpin, 2011, 13–37; Sendrey, 1969, 262–275; Norborg, 1995, 1–126; Qassim, 1980, 5–12, 103–144; Rimmer, 1969, 1–36; Woolly, 1934, 249–273.
3. Cross, 1973, 3–43, 112–144; Gordon and De Moor, 2005, 45–70; Heidel, 1963, 1–16; Levine, 33–56; Sáenz-Badillos, 1993, 1–24, 45–49; Werner, 1976, 1–36; 1984, 73–126.
4. Aitkon, 1990, 4–24; Der Meer and De Moor, 1988, 1–61; De Moor and Watson, 1993, 186–234; Liebhaber, 2010, 163–182; Pardee, 1984, 121–137; Pardee, 1988, xv–21; Reiner, 1985, ix–3; Sasson and Kramer, 1983, 1–353; W.G.E. Watson, 1994, 15–44.

Chapter 1

1. Braun, 2002, 47–188; Duchesne-Guillemin, 1980, 5–26; 1984, 1–26; Farmer, 1939, [PAGES]; Farmer, 1957a, 228–254; Galpin, 1937, 1–37; Kilmer, 2007, 24–37; Sendrey, 1964, 244–266; 1969, 13–26; 1974, 62–66.
2. Clayton, 1992, 141–155; Galpin, 1939, 1; Woolley, 1934, 127; Wu and Dalley, 159–165.
3. Farmer, 1957a, 231–233; Galpin, 1939, 2–3.
4. Galpin, 1939, 6–7.
5. Duchesne-Guillemin, 1981, 287–297.
6. Galpin, 1939, 5–12.
7. Gross, 2012; Krispijn, 2008c, 125–150; Lawergren, 2008, 121–132.
8. Galpin, 1939, 13–14, 39, 54, 61.
9. A.R. George, 1999, 51–58; Alain George, 2003, 67–68; Sharif, 1999, 128–137.
10. Rimmer, 1969, 19.
11. Hickman, 1988, 114–147; Lawergren, 2008, 83–88.

12. Galpin, 1939, 26–27, 55–57.
13. Woolley, 1934, 1: 249–273, 2: 258–259; Cheng, 2009, 163–178.
14. Galpin, 1939, 27–28.
15. Farmer, 1957a, 231–232; Galpin, 1939, 6–10.
16. Farmer, 1957a, 231–238; Kramer and Maier, 1989, 1–21; Black, Green, and Richard, 1989, 173–174; Rogers, 1998, 9–28.
17. Galpin, 1939, 53–55; Farmer, 1957a, 232–233.
18. Langdon, 1909, xi–x, 70–71; Langdon, 1913, viii–xli, Langdon, 1927, v.
19. Farmer, 1957, 231–234; Langdon, 1913, l; Langdon, 1921a, 169–191; 1927, 48–53; Cumming, 2007, 74–76.
20. Farmer, 1957, 236–237.
21. Deutscher, 2007, 20–21; Michalowski, 2008, 33–45; Van de Mieroop, 2007, 4–6, 68–70; Woods, 2006, 91–120.
22. Madhloom, 1967, 76–79; Madhloom, 1968, 45–51; Madhloom, 1969, 43–49; Thompson, 1929, 103–148; Thompson and Hutchinson, 1931, 79–112; 1932, 55–116; 1933, 71–186.
23. Gadd, 1972, 36–40; Galpin, 1929, v–vii; 1937, 2–7.
24. Collon, 2008, 47–65; Farmer, 1957, 237; Lukenbill, 1924, 2: 11–12.
25. Roaf, 2004, 191; Van de Mieroop, 2006, 263.
26. Dalley, 1989, 50–135, 233–281.
27. Reade, 2009, 97–101.
28. Galpin, 1937, 62; Langdon, 1913, xix; 1973, 176; Farmer, 1957, 235.
29. Langdon, 1913, 70–73; Farmer, 1957, 234–235.
30. Mendelsohn, 1955, 129.
31. Mendelsohn, 1955, 129–130.
32. Burgh, 2006, 106–145; Hesk, 1994, 41–42; Hockyer, 2004, 5–8; Steiner, 157–175.
33. Shiloah, 1992, 87–130; Schwadron, 1983, 284–306.
34. Jacobsen, 1997, xiii–xiv.
35. Civil and Rubio, 1999, 254–266; Gelb,

1960, 258–271; Thomason, 2001, 17; Woods, 2006, 92–99.

36. Rubio, 2005, 33–66; 2007a, 89–90.

37. Alster, 1972, 1992b, 23–69; Veldhuis, 1990, 27–44; Ferrara, 1995, 81–117; Michalowski, 1981, 1–18; Black, 1998, 8–13.

38. Rubio, 2009, 34–42; Woods, 2006, 91–120.

39. Hall, 1985, 227.

40. Black, 1998, 12–15; Mindlin, Geller, and Wansbrough, eds., 1987, 1–12, 77–102; Michalowski, 1981, 1–18; 1996, 179–195.

41. Black, 1998, 14–19.

42. Lambert, 1960, 6.

43. Black, 2004, xxii–xxiii.

44. A.R. George, 1999, 51–58; 2000, 2: 101–208; Tigay, 1982, 3–13, 23–54.

45. Black, 2004, xxiv–xxv.

46. Galpin, 1939, 60–61; Klein, 1982, 295–306.

47. Buttner, 2006, 3–22.

48. S. Smith, 1932, 295–308; Galpin, 1939, 62.

49. Langdon, 1921b, 12–13; Galpin, 1939, 64–65.

50. Berlin, 1985, 1–17, 53–59; Kugel, 1981, 1–16; 1984, 107–117; Geller, 1979, 3–15; 1982, 6–12; O'Connor, 1980a, 24–37; Segert, 1979, 729–738; Segert, 1983, 295–306, 697–708; Gu, 2011, 53–86.

51. Kugel, 1981, 8.

52. West, 1997; Dalley, 1989, 39–135; Annus and Lenzi, 2010.

53. Quoted in West, 1997, 175. I have made minor change to the English version to make it read better.

54. *The Epic of Gilgameš*, Old Babylonian Version, Tablet II, lines 1–38, read by Antoine Cavigneaux, Oriental Studies London, http://www.soas.ac.uk/baplar/recordings/the-epic-of-gilgame-old-babylonian-version-tablet-ii-lines-1-38-read-by-antoine-cavigneaux.html.

55. Foster, 1975, 14–15; Kugel, 1981, 25.

56. Lambert, 1960, 33–34. I have made minor changes in the English version.

57. Lambert, 1960, 139–147.

58. Nicholson, 1930, 74; Beeston, 1974, 134–146.

59. M.S. Smith, 1997, 181–196; Berlin, 1983b, 7–16; Der Meer and De Moor, 1988, 1–61; Rainey, 1971, 151–164.

60. De Moor, 1987, 119–139; Der Meer and De Moor, 1988, 1–3.

61. Berlin, 1983, 7–16; S. Parker, 1989, 7–98; Parder, 1981, 116; Dobbs-Allsopp, 2001a, 219–239; 2001b, 370–395; Geller, 1979; Le-Mon, 2005, 375–394; Segert, 1979, 729–738; 1983a, 295–306; Sivan and Yona, 1998, 399–407; W.G.E. Watson, 1982a, 311–312; 1988, 181–187.

62. S. Parker, 1974, 283–294; 2000, 228–231; W.G.E. Watson, 1999, 165–194.

63. Avishur, 1974, 508–525; 1975, 13–47; 1994, 67–71; Margulis, 1970, 332–346; Pardee, 1988, 6–29, 168–201.

64. Kugel, 1981, 25–27.

65. Alter, 2011, 12–13; Blau, 1998, 308–332; Hetzron, 1987, 654–663; Isaksson, 1989–1990, 54–70; Rainey, 1971, 151–164.

66. Alter, 1983a, 71–101; 1984, 615–637; 1985, 4–6, 6–7; John Hobbin, personal web site, http://ancienthebrewpoetry.typepad.com/about.html, posted March 9, 2012.

67. Alter, 2007, xx; Van der Lugt, 2006, 28–34, 445–489, 446–448.

68. Cross and Freedman, 1997, 31–45; Polak, 2001, 2–31; I. Young, 1998, 74–83.

69. Alter, 2007, xx–xxi, Fokkelman, 2001, 37–40.

70. Alter, 1985, 14–15; Hurvitz, 1972, 130–52; 2003, 281–285.

71. Coogan, 2009, 370; Cross, 1973, 100–122; Cross and Freedman, 1997, 9–14; Rosenbaum, 1977, 132–148; Naudé, 2000, 46–71; Rosenberg, 1987, 105–106, 184–206.

72. Albright, 1922, 284–285; 1936, 26–31.

73. Rabin, 1981, 117–136.

74. Alter, 1985, 12–15.

75. Alter, 1985, 15–24.

76. Auffret, 1977; Avishur, 1974, 1977; Chatman, 1960, 1971, 1973; Berlin, 1978, 1982, 1983; Bronznickin, 1979; Fokkelman, 2001, 60–61; Geller, 1979, 1982, 1983; P.J. Miller, 1980a, 1980b, 1983; Pardee, 1988, 8–13.

77. Cross, 2000, 145–146.

78. Fokkelman, 2001, 61–63.

79. Nebes and Stain, 2003, 454–487; Kogan and Korotayev, 1997, 157–183.

Chapter 2

1. Albright, 1932, 15–20; 1948, 6–22; Bachra, 2001, 9–16; Beeston et al., 1983, 1; Abu-Deeb, 1975, 148–184; Agha, 2007, 107–127; Sáenz-Badillos, 1993, 3–14, 29–49, 170–171.

2. Woodard, 2008, 365–390; Hetzron, 1977, 59–63; Versteegh, 1997, 9–36.

3. Segert, 1985, 13–38; Danielas and Bright, 1996, 92–93; Healey, 1990, 20–48; Schniedewind and Hunt, 2007, 20–45.

4. Segert, 1985, 19–20; De Moor, 1987, 7–10; Diringer, 1968, 210–220; Healey, 1990, 197–258; Dietrich, Loretz and Sanmartin, 1995.

5. Albright, 1966, 1–8, 29–33; Colless, 1990, 1991, 1998, 26–46; Darnell and Dobbs-Allsopp, 2005; G.J. Hamilton, 2006.

6. Cross, 1979, 97–111; Ginsberg, 1970, 102–124; Healey, 1990, 201–224; Naveh, 1982, 15–51; Quakenin and Bacon, 1999, 11–34.

7. Healey, 1990, 49–56.

8. Daniels and Bright, 1996, 93–95; Jensen,

1969, 118–123; Coulmas, 2004, 137–178; Hock and Joseph, 1996, 71–87; Markoe, 2000, 108–114.

9. Abbott, 1939, 9–14; Grundler, 1993, 7–28, 231–236; Ryckmans, 2001, 223–235.

10. Beeston, 1981, 178–186; 1984; Korotayev, 1995.

11. Van Soldt, 1991, 519–520; 1995, 183; Cooper, 1999, 74–5; Rensburg, 2003, 71–77.

12. Driver, 1936, 151; Kutscher, 1976, 1977; Saenz-Badillos, 1993, 50–55.

13. Schniedewind, 2004, 35–47; Dalley, 1998, 57–66; Millard, 1987; Niditch, 1996; Young, 1998.

14. Rabin, 1979.

15. Kutscher, 1976, 41.

16. Stevenson, 1962; Kutscher, 1957, 1971a, 1977b, 1982.

17. Dearman, 1989; Mykytiuk, 2004, 95–110, 265–277; Hoffman, 24–34; Herr, 1978, 26–29; Gibson, 1971, 72; Naveh, 1982, 101.

18. Kutscher, 1971a; Rabin and Yadin, 1958; Saenz-Badillos, 1993, 166–167.

19. Baklava, 1984; Batten, 2003; Bellhop and Hare, 1997; Blab, 1988; Stetkevych, 1993, 3–54; Kennedy, 1997; Sperl, 1989; Weipert, 2002; Mumayiz, 2006; Sumi, 2004.

20. Avazini, 2006; Beeston et al., 1983, 1–3; Korotayev, A. 1995; Stein, 2002, 4–5; 2004.

21. Beeston, 1983, 2–4.

22. Hoyland, 2001, 201–208; Versteegh, 1997, 12–18.

23. Beeston et al., 1983, 10–15; Beeston, 1984; 1992, 2: 223–226; Stein, 2005b, 181–199.

24. Haydar, 1989, 159–212.

25. R. Allen, 2000, 71–72.

26. Farmer, 1929, 6–7; Shilhoah, 1995, 6–8.

27. Farmer, 1929, 16–18; Touma, 1996, 4–7, 76.

28. Nicholson, 1969, 73; Stetkevych, 1993, 3–54.

29. Nicholson, 1969, 71–73.

30. Farmer, 1929, 3–14; Farmer, 1988, 134–142; Nicholson, 1969, 74–75; Termanini, 2004; Touma, 1996, 4–5.

31. Farmer, 1929, 15–18; Power, 2005, 9; Maafouf, 2002, Touma, 1996, 5–6.

32. Allen, 1998, Farmer, 1929, 18–21.

33. Farmer, 1929, 22–36; Saoud, 2004, 2–3; Mahdi, 2002, 28; Touma, 1996, 4–6.

34. Kogan and Korotayev, 1997, 157–183; Nebes and Stein, 2003, 454–487; Korotayev, 1995, 4–5.

35. Touma, 1996, 2–3; Farmer, 1957, 423; Shiloah, 1995, 6.

36. Shiloah, 1995, 7–8, 11–16.

37. Allen, 1998, 104; Cantarino, 1975, 41.

38. Angoujard, 6–7; Bateson, 1970, 30–32; Weil, 667–677; Blachere, 1960, 225–236; Moscati, 1964, Yushmanov, 1961, 3–5; Ver-

steegh, 1997a, 26–35; Zwetller, 1978, 110–134; Holes, 16–17.

39. Jacobi, 1996, 26–27.

40. Jacobi, 1996, 21.

41. Jacobi, 1996, 23.

42. Starkey, 2006, 11.

43. Jayyusi, 1996, 7–8.

44. Jayyusi, 1977, 565–573, 594–595; Jayyusi, 1996, 8–9.

45. Scheindlin, 1974, 174–175.

46. Arberry, 1957; Bateson, 1970, 22–24; Nicholson, 1956, 75–78; Grunebaum, 1955, 32; 1969, 281–300; 1942, 147–153; 1944, 121–141; 1973, 212–215.

47. Nicholson, 1956, 77; Zwettler, 1978, 103–104.

48. Jayyusi, 1996, 1–20; Cachia, 2002, 1–5; Gunther, 2005, 15; R. Allen, 2002, 65–66.

49. S.P. Stetkevych, 2010, 4–5.

50. Allen, 1998, 126; Cachia, 2002, 4; J. Stetkevych, 1993, 50–58.

51. J. Stetkevych, 1989, 5.

52. Quoted in J. Stetkevych, 1989, 12.

53. Quoted in Stetkevych, 1989, 13.

54. Quoted in J. Stetkevych, 1989, 15–16.

55. J. Stetkevych, 1989, 16.

56. Cachia, 2002, 5–8; Johnstone, 1972, 90–95.

57. Jaroslav Stetkevych, 1993b, 9–49; Toorawa, 1997, 759–762.

58. Rosen, 1988, 1–12; Caplin, 2000, 17–34; Hepokoski and Darcy, 2006, 14–22.

59. J. Stetkevych, 1993, 16–25.

60. Abu-Deeb, 1975, 148–184; Cachia, 2002, 10; Hillman, 1971, 11–21; 1972, 1–10; 1976; Van Gelder, 1982; Von Grunebaum, 1961, 97–101; Lewis, 1993, 142–156; Montgomery, 1997, 33–36; Scheindlin, 1974, 31–36.

61. Curtius, 1979, 71–73.

62. Schiendlin, 1974, 174–175.

63. Van Gelder, 1982, 35–56.

64. Zwartjez, 1997, 125–126.

65. Beekes, 1988, xxi–xxii, 1–4; Browne, 2009, 78–80; Gershevitch, 2008, 3–12; Humbach, 1991, 1–22; Skjærvo, 2006a; 2006b, 13–15; Boyce, 1984, 134–144.

66. Arbarry, 1953, 200; Browne, 2009, 1: 12–19, 83–85; Farhat, 2004, 2–4.

67. Boyce, 1954, 1–12; Lazard, 1971, 361–62, 385.

68. Boyce, 1954, 1–13; 1957, 45–52; Henning, 1950, 641–648.

69. Elwell-Sutton, 1975, 75–97.

70. Benveniste, 1930, 193–225; 1932a, 245–93; 1932b, 337–80; Boyce, 1954, 46–47; De Blois, 2000, 82–95; Henning, 1950, 641–648.

71. Benveniste, 1930, 193–225; 1932a, 245–93; 1932b, 337–80; Grunebaum, 1955, 18; Utas, 1994, 140.

72. Rypka, 1936, 200–201; cf. Lazard, 1994, 87.

73. Jayyusi, 1992–94, ii: 117; Reynold, 2000, 60–82.
74. Monroe, 1974, 22–23; Van Grunebaum, 121–141; Zwartjez, 1997, 24–26.
75. Touma, 1996, 83.
76. Armistead, 2003, 3–19; Fish Compton, 1976, 6; Monroe, 1975, 341–350; Abu Haidar, 2001, 107–112, 181–234.
77. Gorton, 1975, 1–29.
78. Twartjez, 1997, 125–159.
79. Jones, 1991b; Jones and Hitchcock, 1991.

Chapter 3

1. Lewis, 2001, 6–7.
2. Farmer, 1957, 437–438; 1965, 88–93.
3. Racy, 2003, 5–6; Shiloah, 1995, 16; Touma, 1996, 13, 149.
4. Nelson, 2001, 157–187; Marcus, 2007, 13–14.
5. Farmer, 1929, 22–23; 1957, 439; Nelson, 2001, 5–31; Saoud, 2004, 3–4; Touma, 1996, 153–154.
6. Bukhari, 2008, 1: 578; Sells, 1999, 2–3.
7. Haywood, 1965, 11–12.
8. Rippin, 1988, 13–30; 1999, 29–37.
9. Haywood, 1965, 11–19.
10. Berg, 2000, 1–6; Brown, 2004, 1–37; 2007, 3–19; Hallaq, 1999, 75–90; Melchert, 1997, 1–31; Musa, 2008, 9–24.
11. A'zami, 2003, 85–96; McAuliffe, 2006a, 41–78.
12. Versteegh, 1997b, 4–5.
13. Sibawayh, 1988, 7–12; Touati and Cochrane, 2010, 51.
14. Nassir, 1993, Sibawayh, 1988, 3–12; Broemeling, 2011, 255–257.
15. Carter, 1994, 3–4; Nassir, 1993; Ryding, 1998, 1–15; Sibawayh, 1988, 7–12.
16. Versteegh, 1997b, 24–26.
17. Quoted by Versteegh, 1997b, 29–30.
18. Serjaent, 1983. 114–153; Latham, 1983, 154–179.
19. Craig, 1979, 1994, 92–116; Mansur, 1977, 15–17, 49–50, 93–95; Contadini, 2012, 3–6; Fakhry, 1997, 15–21.
20. Corbin, 1993; Adamson, 2005, 32–51; Gutas, 1998, Lindberg, 18–32; Klain-Frank, 2001, 172–167.
21. Turner, 1997, 36–61; Sabra, 2000, 215–257; Huff, 2003, 47–87; Masood, 2009, 47–52, 105–111, 173–175.
22. Ahmad, 2003, 5–7; Dallal, 158–160; Fakhry, 2004, chapter 1.
23. G. Makdisi, 1986, 173–85; C. Robinson, 2003, 3–4; Ya'qubi, 1969.
24. Badawi, 7–30, Gu, 2011, 180–208.
25. M. Mir, 1992, 1–22; M.M.J. Fischer and M. Abedi, 1990, 120–156.
26. Qur'an, trans. Abdulla Yusu Ali, http://

al-quran.info/. I have made minor changes in the English version to make it less formal.
27. Wacks, 2007, 12–13; Marzolph, 2006, 21–82; Makdisi and Nussbaum, 2008, 1–24.
28. Borges, 1999, 92–93; Muhawi, 2005, 323–337; Mack, 2009, ix–xxiii.
29. Drory, 2000a, 1–10; 2000b, 190–210; Katsumata, 2002, 117–37.
30. Pinault, 1992, 1–11.
31. Stewart, 1990, 101–139.
32. R. Allen, 2000, 61–62.
33. Fischer and Abedi, 1990, 120.
34. Semaan, 1968, 34–35; Nelson, 2001, 88–89; Brockett, 1988, 33–45; Ibn al-Jazari, 2007, 14–27.
35. Touma, 1996, 38–40.
36. Farhat, 2004, 2–3; Lawergren, 1988, 31–45; 1993, 55–76.
37. Touma, 1996, 41–43; Rasmussen, 2010, 100–103.
38. Touma, 1996, 45.
39. Touma, 1993, 41–45.
40. Monroe, 2001, 1–3; Hameen-Anttila, 2002.
41. Monroe, 2001, 2–3.
42. Drory, 2000a, 14–15.
43. Drory, 20002, 14–16; Monroe, 1983; 2001, 6–7, 65.
44. Wacks, 2007, 1–25; Monroe, 2001; Drory, 2000a, 14–15; Katsumata, 2002, 117–37; Wacks, 2003, 68–89.
45. Jacobson, 2002, 1–2, 7–8; Werner, 1984, 1–24.

Chapter 4

1. Stetkevych, 2009, 55–78; Abu-Deeb, 1975, 148–184; 1976, 3–69; Haydar, 1977, 227–262, 1978, 51–82.
2. Stetkevych, 1993a, xi–xii, 3–54.
3. Sells, 1989, 4–7.
4. Stetkevych, 1993a, 87–160, 241–286.
5. Abu al-Fadl Ibrahim, 1990a, 100.
6. Abu al-Fadl Ibrahim, 1990b, 22–23; Ahlwardt, 2008, 51.
7. Surat 40–43, Qur'an Online Project, http://al-quran.info/. I have made minor changes in the English version.
8. Qur'an Online Project, 257, accessed May 30, 2012.
9. R. Allen, 2002, 61–62.
10. J.A.C. Brown, 2007, 77–98; Musa, 2008, 31–68.
11. Robinson, 2003, 15–27; Donner, 1998, 132–133.
12. Katib, 1983, 154–179; Abul Rauf, 1983, 271–288; Abbott, 1983, 289–298.
13. Akhtar, 1997; Enan, 2007, 106–117; Ibn Khaldun, 2005, x, 11–14; Lewis, 2006, 376–380; D. Weiss, 1995, 29–37.
14. Ibn Khaldun, 2005, ix–x.

15. J. Weiss, 66–108, 140–169; Hallaq, 1999, 3–10, 2005, 19–24, 35–76; Paret, 1983, 204–205, 221.
16. Gu, 2006, 135–157; Hallaq, 1985–1986, 93–95; 1993, 48; 2004, 270–302; Mas, 1998, 113–128.
17. Momen, 1985, 184–207; Sachedina, 1988, 58–118.
18. Adamson, 2005, 32–51; 2007, 3–20; Corbin, 1993, 154–155; Nasr, 2006, 137–138.
19. D. Black, 1990, 168–171; Klein-Frank, 2001, 155–167.
20. Corbin, 1993, 156; Adamson, 2005, 47; Gutas, 1998, 61–74.
21. Fakhry, 2002, 6–15; Mahdi, 1001, 131–135.
22. Gutas, 1988, 79–86; Bertolacci, 2006, 37–64.
23. Bertolacci, 2011, 197–224; Burrell, 1986, 35–50; Elkaisy-Friemuth, 2006, 74–118; Bizri, 2000, 219–250; 2001, 753–778; 2003, 67–89; Heath, 1992, 3–18.
24. Peters, 1968, 57–134, 185–214; Griffel, 2009, 6–8.
25. Bello, 1989, 6–8, 111–125; Griffel, 2009, 98–110.
26. R. Glassner, 2009, 1–9, 62–108; Kemal, 2003, 222–288; Leaman, 1998, 15–41.
27. Griffel, 2009, 5–6.
28. Martin and Woodward, 1997, 10–18; Wolfson, 1976, 3–42; J.R.T.M. Peters, 1976, 1–15.
29. Campanini, 76–81; Wolfson, 1976, 1–12; J.R.T.M. Peters, 1976, 293–312.
30. Hourani, 2007, 67–68; Grunebaum, 1962, 1–17.
31. Gimaret, 1990; Leaman, 1985, 123–65; Hourani, 2007, 67–97, 118–123; Griffel, 2009, 5–6.
32. Dallal, 2010, 12–13; Turner, 1997, 270; Sabra, 1996, 3–30.
33. Hazen, 1990, 8–10; Linderberg, 1967, 321–341; Linderberg, 1976, 33–57; Sabra, 1978, 117–131; 1998, 288–330.
34. Ahmad, 1995, 395–403; Granz, 319–391; Qadir, 1990, 183–190; Saliba, 1994, 60–75, Saliba, 2007, chapter 4.
35. Fancy, 2006, 49–59, 232–3; Saliba, 1994, 60–69; Savage-Smith, 1995, 67–110.
36. Iskenderoglu, 2002, 62–79.
37. Dallal, 1999, 162; Saliba, 1994, 245–256; Savage-Smith, 1985, 15–21.
38. Dallal, 1999, 162–171; 2010, 29–31; King, 2005, xvii.
39. Lunde, 1992; Sabra, 1971, 541–545.
40. Dallal, 2010, 32; 1999, 163–171.
41. Sabra, 1998, 322; Saliba, 1994, 85–112, 291–305.
42. Biruni, 2004, 120–236; 2001, 2: 277–278; Stephenson, 2009, 45, 457, 488–499.
43. King, 167–169; Dallal, 2010, 171–172.

44. Boyer, 1989, 229–230; Rashed, 1994, 11–12.
45. Katz, 1995, 163–74.
46. Amir-Moez, 1962, 269–271; Katz, 1998, 270; Rozenfield, 1988, 64–65.

Chapter 5

1. Tabbaa, 2001, 4–6; Necipoglu, 1995, 1–23; Heinrichs, 1997, 175–184.
2. Grabar, 1973, 45–74.
3. Shvidkovskii and Shorban, 2007, 9–12; Thomas, 2007, 17–28.
4. Rasch, 1985, 129–135; Heinle and Schlaich, 1996, 30–32; Krautheimer, 1986, 201–204; Alchermes, 2005, 343–375.
5. Mainstone, 1997, 90–93; Swainson, 2005; Krautheimer, 1986, 205–237.
6. Sayyad, 1991, 43–76; Akbar, 1990, 22–32; Kubiak, 1987, 58–75; Campo, 1991, 48–73; Luz, 1997, 27–54; Preziosi, 1991, 3–11.
7. Cresell, 1989, 91–216; Wheatly, 2001, 43; Kennedy, 1985, 3–27; Stronge, 1900, 5–7.
8. Akbar, 1990, 22–32; Berhens-Abouseif, 1989, 3: 47–50; Kubiak, 1987, 58–75.
9. Sayyad, 1991, 43–76; Sheehan, 2010, 4–15.
10. Ettinghausen and Grabar, 2001, 19–20; Hamdani and Faris, 1938, 14–17, 26–28; Grabar, 1973, 48–67; 1996, 64–84; Rosen-Ayalon, 1989, 4–8, 25–27, 46–49.
11. Grabar, 1973, 104–106; Hillenbraud, 1994, 39–42; Jairazbhoy, 1962, 1–23; Sezgin, 2007, 2010, 4: 1–187.
12. Critchlow, 1976, 8; Kuban, 1974, 1–2.
13. Grabar, 1973, 61–62; Ettinghauser and Grabar, 2001, 19–20; Bloom and Blair, 1997, 21–56.
14. Burchardt, 2009, 13–27; Bloom and Blair, 1997, 23–95; Ettinghausen and Grabar, 2001, 3–4; Grabar, 1973, 65–74; 1996, 2006b.
15. Burchardt, 2009, 17–19; Grabar, 1987, 243–247.
16. Baker, 1980, 22–25; Grabar, 2001, 40–42; Khouri, 1990, 33.
17. Baer, 1999, 32–41; Behrens-Abouseif, 1997, 11–18; Hamilton and Grabar, 1959, 257; Hamilton, 1969, 61–67; 1978, 126–138; Creswell and Allan, 1989, 179–199; Hillenbraud, 1994, 381–392; Yeomans, 2000, 39–40.
18. Barns, 2005, 62–72.
19. Flood, 2001, 114–121; Barns, 2005, 139–190.
20. Ettinghausen and Grabar, 2001, 22–23; Serjeant, 1959, 439–452.
21. Flood, 1997, 2001; Grafman and Rosen-Ayalon, 1999; Shalem, 1994.
22. Ettinghausen and Grabar, 2001, 26.
23. Michell, 1978, 251; Ettinghausen and Grabar, 1987, 296–297.
24. Ettinghausen and Grabar, 2001, 57–59;

Tabbaa, 2001, 74–78, 88, 112–115; Canby, 2005, 20–21.

25. Behrens-Abouseif, 1989, 55; Swelim, 1994; Williams, 2002, 46–49.

26. Alatas, 2006, 112–132.

27. Rabbat, 1996, 45–64; Bloom, 1988a, 21–28; Creswell, 1959, 253–254; Yeomans, 2006, 56.

28. Behrens-Abouseif, 1989, 9–26; Bloom and Blair, 2009, 152.

29. Behrens-Abouseif, 2008, 71–89; Behrens-Abouseif, 1992, 72–73.

30. Savory, 1980, 155–156; Bier, 1986, 1–6; O'Kane, 1995, 85–92; Pope, 1971, 1–16; Canby, 2009, 30–36.

31. Chejine, 1974, 364–366; Hillenbrand, 1992, 112–128; Irwin, 2004, 4–6; Ruggles, 2008, 152; Touma, 2001, 103–136.

32. Tabbaa, 2001, 75–88; Canby, 2005, 26–27.

33. Burchhardt, 2009, 64–8.

34. Ettinghausen and Grabar, 2001, 66.

35. Blair, 2006; Alain George, 2003, 1–15; 2010, 13–20; Mansour and Allan, 2011, 17–22; Burckhardt, 2009, 52–57.

36. Alain George, 2010, chapter 4; 2003, 11–14.

37. Schimmel, 1984, 37–63; 1992, 1–14.

38. Nizami, 1995, 1: 107–132, 2: 39–40.

39. Ruggle, 2008, 3–12.

40. Qur'an, 47: 15, quoted in Ruggles, 2008, 89.

41. Lehrman, 1980, 34–40, 48–49.

42. Lehrman, 1980, 36–37.

Chapter 6

1. Leick, 1994, 180–181.

2. B. Foster, 2001, 9–11; A.R. George, 2000, 1: 8; Kovacs, 1989, 9.

3. Kienast, 1990, 100; Leick, 1994, 182.

4. Hall, 1985, 227; Hallo, 1966, 243; Green, 1992, 232.

5. Lambert, 1966, 53–6.

6. Leick, 1994, 184–185.

7. Lambert, 1966, 52.

8. T. Jacobsen, 1987, 18.

9. Buccellati, 1997, 69–99; A. George, 2007, 31–71.

10. Richmond, 1978.

11. Arberry, 1965, 38–39; Beard, 2008, 25–26.

12. Ahlwardt, 2008, 32–35; Arberry, 1964, 56–58.

13. Kennedy, 2005, 5–25.

14. Kennedy, 2005, 42–48.

15. Kennedy, 2005, 15–17.

16. Grunbaum, 1952, 233–238; Farrin, 2010, 1–24; Kennedy, 2005, 3–134; Sells, 2000, 2–17.

17. Kennedy, 2005, 33–36.

18. Abu Rabi'a, 1977; Jacobi, 1985, 1–17; Jayyusi, 2006, 49; Kennedy, 1997, 19–20; L. Werner, 2001, 38–45.

19. Abu Rabi'a, 1977, 1: 148–151; Von Grunebaum, 1948, 160–204; R. Jacobi, 1992, 109–119; 1994, 145–161; Kennedy, 1007, 23–25.

20. Kennedy, 1997, 24–27.

21. Kennedy, 2005, 33–36.

22. Karamustafa, 2007, 11–13.

23. Cashia, 2005, 56–57.

24. Cashia, 2005, 58–59.

25. Cashia, 2005, 62–63.

26. Cashia, 2005, 62–66; Larkin, 2008, 128–129.

27. Chittick, 1987, 378–409; 1989, 1–4; Sells and Ernst, 1996, 56–74.

28. Sells, 1996a, 21–22.

29. M. Smith, 1984, 20–30; Jamal, 2009, 5–7; Sells, 1996a, 20–21.

30. Karamustafa, 2007, 7–8.

31. Karamustafa, 2007, 11–14.

32. Ansari, 1983, 33–56; Sells, 1996a, 21–25.

33. Ibn al-Farid, 2001, 46–50; O'Kane and Redtke, 2003, 1–6; Homerin, 2004, 1–14; Homerin, 2011, 1–14.

34. Homerin, 2001a, 33–54; 2001b, 41–51; Homerin, 2011, 31–48; Jayyusi, 2006, 45.

35. Addas, 1993, 2–5; 2000, 3–5; Austin, 1971, 48; Ibn 'Arabi, 2002–2004.

36. Ibn 'Arabi, 2002–2004, 1: 129, Corbin, 1969, 174.

37. Addas, 1993, 33–73; Corbin, 1969, 73–74; Addas, 2000, 1–10.

38. Chittick, 1994b, 70–111; 1996, 974–523; Sells, 1994b, 70–78.

39. Huda, 2003, 83–108.

40. Ohlander, 2008, 79–80.

41. Abou-Bakr, 1992, 40–57; Alvarez, 2005, 1–32; 2009, 35–62; Sells, 2009, xi–xix.

42. Sells, 1996a, 2–3, 19–20.

43. Jayyusi, 1977, 182–186.

44. Jayyusi, 1987, 109; Badawi, 1975, 53.

45. Adunis, 2010, 12–14, 23–24; Jayyusi, 1987, 138–140, 411–412.

Chapter 7

1. Jayyusi, 2010, 2–4, 37–70; Khalifa, 2010, 5; Haywood, 1965, 19.

2. Berg, 2000, 8–9; Speight, 2000, 265–271; Zubaidi, 1983, 322–343.

3. Jayyusi, 2010, 318–345; Khalifa, 2010, 5–6.

4. Beeston, 1971, 1–12; De Blois, 1990, 1–23; Latham, 1990, 48–77; Wacks, 2003, 178–189.

5. Hariri, 1980; Grabar, 2006c, 93–150, 167–186.

6. R. Allen, 1992a, 180–181; Drory, 2001, 191–193; Wacks, 2003, 185–188.

7. Jayyusi, 2010, 305–17; Serjeant, 2000, xvii–xviii.

8. Serjeant, 2000, 55–57. I have made minor changes in the English version.

9. Khalifa, 2010, 12.

10. Haywood, 1971, 11–14.

11. Pinault, 1992, 25–28.

12. Pinault, 1992, 26–27. I have made minor changes in the quoted translation.

13. Irwin, 2005, 199–200.

14. Irwin, 2005, 49–50.

15. Brugman, 1984, 12; Allen, 1992, 181–184; 2006, 14–15; Moosa, 1997, 97–98, 185–186.

16. Allen, 1992a, 186; Moosa, 138–149.

17. Allen, 1992a, 186.

18. Zaydan, 2010b; 2011, ix–xi; 2012, vii–4.

19. Allen, 2006, 13–15; Enany, 1992, 23.

20. Allen, 2006, 32–33; Kilpatrick, 1922, 223–225.

21. Ghazali, 1995; M. Kramer, 1–35; Malti-Douglas, 1988, 157–159; Allen, 2010, 137–48.

22. Allen, 1995, 38–39; Cachia, 2005, 192–193.

23. Allen, 2006, 39–40; Brugman, 1984, 138–147; Sukkut, 2000, 20–21.

24. Allan, 1995, 40–41; Hakim, 2012.

25. Johnson-Davies, 2008, 1–4, 201–210.

26. Jayyusi, 1988, 34.

27. Mahfouz, 1996, 1984.

28. Mahfouz, 1993; Enany, 1993, 113–115.

29. Mahfouz, 1999, 28–29.

30. Enany, 1993, 110–113; Toowara, 1991, 53–65.

31. Khanafani, 1999, 9–15.

32. Khanafani, 2004, 1–50.

33. Salih, 30–31, 135–136, 141–142.

34. Allen, 2000, 168–9.

35. Salih, 19–53, 83–93, 155–160.

36. Meyer, 2001, 4–8.

37. E. Khoury, 2007, 19–44, 45–80.

38. E. Khoury, 2007b, 313–339.

Bibliography

Abbott, N. 1939. *The Rise of the North Arabic Script and Its Kur'anic Development.* Chicago: University of Chicago Press.
_____. 1957. *Studies in Arabic Literary Papyri.* 1. *Historical Texts.* Chicago: University of Chicago Press.
_____. 1967. *Studies in Arabic Literary Papyri.* 2. *Qur'anic Commentary and Tradition.* Chicago: University of Chicago Press.
_____. 1972. *Studies in Arabic Literary Papyri.* 3. *Language and Literature.* Chicago: University of Chicago Press.
_____. 1983. Hadith Literature-II. In *Arabic Literature to the End of the Umayyad Period*, ed. A.F.L. Beeston et al., 289–298. Cambridge: Cambridge University Press.
'Abbūd, K. 2004. *al-Mūsīqá wa-al-ghinā' 'inda al-'Arab: min al-Jāhilīyah ilá nihāyat al-qarn al-'ishrīn (Music and Song of Arabs from Pre-Islam to the Twentieth Century).* Beirut: Dār al-Ḥarf al-'Arabī.
Abdullah, I. 2006. The Role of the Pre-Modern: The Generic Characteristics of the "Band." In *Arabic Literature in the Post-Classical Period*, ed. R. Allen and D.S. Richards, Chapter Four. Cambridge: Cambridge University Press.
Abed, Shukri B. 1991. *Aristotelian Logic and Arabic Language in Alfârâbî.* Albany: State University of New York Press.
Abi Rabi'a, U.I. 1977. *Poems from the Diwan of 'Umar ibn Abi Rabi'a.* Trans. A. Wormhoudt. Oskaloosa, IA: William Penn College.
Abou-Bakr, O. 1992. The Symbolic Function of Metaphor in Medieval Sufi Poetry: The Case of Shushtari. *Alif: Journal of Comparative Poetics* 12: 40–57.
Abu al-Fadl Ibrahim. M., ed. 1990a. *Dīwān Imra' al-Qays.* Cairo: Dar al-Ma'arif.
_____. 1990b. *Diwan al-Nabighah al-Dhubyani.* Cairo: Dar al-Ma'arif.
Abū al-Khayr, Maḥmūd 'Abd Allāh. 2004.

Dīwān Ḥurūb al-Riddah (Poems of Riddah war). 'Ammān: Juhaynah.
Abū Bakr. 2006. *Dīwān Abī Bakr al-Ṣiddīq (Poems of Abū Bakr al-Ṣiddīq).* Beirut: Dār wa-Maktabat al-Hilāl.
Abu-Deeb, K. 1975. Towards a Structural Analysis of Pre-Islamic Poetry I. *International Journal of Middle East Studies* 6(2): 148–184.
_____. 2007. *The Imagination Unbound: Al-adab al-'Aja'ibi and the Literature of the Fantastic in the Arabic Tradition.* Berkeley: Saqi.
Abu-Haidar, F. 1988. The Poetic Content of the Iraqi Maqām. *Journal of Arabic Literature* 19(2): 128–141.
Abu Haidar, J. 1978. The Kharja of the Muwashshah in a New Light. *Journal of Arabic Literature* 9: 1–14.
_____. 2001. *Hispano-Arabic Literature and the Early Provençal lyrics.* London: Curzon Press.
Abu-Hamdiyyah, M. 2000. *The Qur'an: An Introduction.* London: Routledge.
Abū Nuwās. 1982. *Al-Ḥasan ibn Hānī, Dīwān Abī Nuwās*, ed. A.A.- al-M. al-Ghazālī. Beirut: Dar al-Kitab al-'Arabi.
_____. 2006. *Dīwān Abū Nuwās al-Hasan ibn Hānī*, ed. G. Schoeler. Cairo: al-Hay'ah al-'Ammah li-qusur al-Thaqafah.
Abul Rauf, M. 1983. Hadith Literature-I. In *Arabic Literature to the End of the Umayyad Period*, eds. A.F.L. Beeston et al., 271–288. Cambridge: Cambridge University Press.
Abusch, I.T., 1987. *Babylonian Witchcraft Literature: Case Studies.* Atlanta, GA: Scholars Press.
Abusch, I.T., W.L. Moran, J. Huehnergard, and P. Steinkeller, eds. 1990. *Lingering Over Words: Studies in Ancient Near Eastern Literature in Honor of William L. Moran.* Atlanta, GA: Scholars Press.

Adamson, P. 2005. Al-Kindi and Reception of Greek Philosophy. In *The Cambridge Companion to Arabic Philosophy*, ed. P. Adamson and R. C. Taylor, 32–51. Cambridge: Cambridge University Press.

_____. 2007. *Al-Kindy*. New York: Oxford University Press.

Adang, C. 1996. *Muslim Writers on Judaism and the Hebrew Bible*. Leiden: E.J. Brill.

Addas, C. 1993. *Quest for the Red Sulphur: The Life of Ibn 'Arabi*. Trans. P. Kingsley. Cambridge: Islamic Texts Society.

_____. 2000. *Ibn 'Arabi: The Voyage of No Return*. Cambridge: Islamic Texts Society.

Adūnīs. 1990. *An Introduction to Arab Poetics*. London: Saqi Books.

_____. 2005. *Sufism and Surrealism*. Trans. C. Cobham. London: SAQI.

_____. 2010. *Selected Poems*. Trans. K. Mattawa. New Haven: Yale University Press.

Agha, S.S. 2007. Holistic Poetic Imagery: A Partnership of the Senses in Alliance with Primal Language—Some Considerations from Classical Arabic Desert Poetry. *Middle Eastern Literatures* 10(2): 107–127.

Ahlwardt, A. 2008. *Divans of the Six Ancient Arabic Poet: Ennabiga, Antara, Tharafa, Zuhair, Alquama and Imruulqais*. Piscataway: Gorgias.

Ahmad, I.A. 1995. The Impact of the Qur'anic Conception of Astronomical Phenomena on Islamic Civilization. *Vistas in Astronomy* 39(4): 395–403.

Ahmad, Z. 2003. *The Epistemology of Ibn Khaldun*. New York: RoutledgeCurzon.

Aitken, K. T. 1990. *The Aqhat Narrative: A Study in the Narrative Structure and Composition of an Ugaritic Tale*. Manchester: University of Manchester Press.

Akbar, J. 1990. Khatta and the Territorial Structure of Early Muslim Twon. *Muqamas* 6: 22–32.

Akbarzadeh, P. 1998. *Persian Musicians*. Shiraz: Navid.

_____. 2002. *Persian Musicians*, vol. 2. Tehran: Roshanak.

Akkach, S. 2005. *Cosmology and Architecture in Premodern Islam: An Architectural Reading of Mystical Ideas*. Albany: SUNNY.

Akkermans, P.A., H. Fokker, and H.T. Waterbolk. 1981. Stratigraphy, Architecture and Layout of Bouqras. In *Préhistoire du Levant*, ed. O. Aurenche, M-C. Cauvin and P. Sanlaville, 485–502. Paris: CNRS.

Alatas, S.F. 2006. From Jāmi'ah to University: Multiculturalism and Christian–Muslim Dialogue. *Current Sociology* 54.1: 112–32.

Albright, W.F. 1922. Some Additional Notes on the Song of Deborah. *Journal of the Palestine Oriental Society* (*JPOS*) 2: 284–85.

_____. 1932. New Light on Early Canaanite Language and Literature. *Bulletin of the American Schools of Oriental Research* 46: 15–20.

_____. 1934. *The Vocalization of the Egyptian Syllabic Orthography*. New Haven, CT: Yale University Press.

_____. 1936. The Song of Deborah in the Light of Archaeology. *Bulletin of the American Schools of Oriental Research* (*BASOR*) 62: 26–31.

_____. 1945. The Old Testament and the Canaanite Language and Literature. *The Catholic Biblical Quarterly* 7: 5–31.

_____. 1948. The Early Alphabetic Inscriptions from Sinai and Their Decipherment. *Bulletin of the American Schools of Oriental Research* 110: 6–22.

_____. 1955. New Light on Early Recensions of the Hebrew Bible. *Bulletin of the American Schools of Oriental Research* 140: 27–33.

_____. 1966. *The Proto-Sinaitic Inscriptions and Their Decipherment*. Cambridge, MA: Harvard University Press.

Alchermes, J.D. 2005. Art and Architecture in the Age of Justinian. In *The Cambridge Companion to the Age of Justinian*, ed. M. Maas, 343–375. MA: Cambridge University Press.

Ali, S.M. 2008. The Rise of the Abbasid Public Sphere: The Case of Al-Mutanabbi and Three Middle Ranking Patrons. In *Al-Qantara: Special Issue on Patronage in Islamic History*, vol. 29, no. 2, ed. E.A. Carro, 467–494. Madrid: Consejo Superior de Investigaciones Científicas, Instituto "Miguel Asín."

_____. 2010. *Arabic Literary Salons in the Islamic Middle Ages: Poetry, Public Performance, and the Presentation of the Past (ND Poetics of Orality and Literacy)*. Notre Dame: University of Notre Dame Press.

Allen, R. 1992a. The Beginnings of the Arabic Novel. In *Modern Arabic Literature*, ed. M. M. Badawi, 180–192. Cambridge: Cambridge University Press.

_____. 1992b. The Mature Arabic Novel outside of Egypt. In *Modern Arabic Literature*, ed. M. M. Badawi, 193–222. Cambridge: Cambridge University Press.

_____. 1995. *The Arabic Novel: An Historical and Critical Introduction*. Syracuse, NY: Syracuse University Press.

_____. 1998. *The Arabic Literary Heritage: The Development of Its Genres and Criticism*. Cambridge: Cambridge University Press.

_____. 2000. *An Introduction to Arabic Literature*. Cambridge: Cambridge University Press.

Allen, R., ed. 2010. *Essays in Arabic Literary*

Biography: 1850–1950. Harrassawitz Vergerlag.

Allen, R., and D.S. Richards. 2006. *The Cambridge History of Arabic Literature. Arabic Literature to the Post-Classical Period.* Cambridge: Cambridge University Press.

Alonso-Schökel, L. 1959. Die stilistische Analyse bei den Propheten. *Vetus Testamentum Supplement* 7: 154–64.

_____. 1963. *Estudios de Poitica Hebrea.* Barcelona: Juan Flors.

_____. 1965. *The Inspired Word.* London: Burns and Gates.

Alonso-Schökel, L., and A. Strus. 1980. Salmo 122: Canto al nombre de Jerusalén. *Biblica* 61: 234–50.

_____. 1988. *A Manual of Hebrew Poetics.* Rome: Pontifical Biblical Institute.

Alster, B. 1972. *Dumuzi's Dream. Aspects of Oral Poetry in a Sumerian Myth.* Copenhagen: Akademisk Forlag.

_____. 1974. *The Instructions of Suruppak.* Copenhagen: Akademisk Forlag.

_____. 1976. On the Earliest Sumerian Literary Tradition. *Journal of Cuneiform Studies* 28: 109–126.

_____. 1982. Emesal in Early Dynastic Sumerian? *Acta Sumerologica* 4: 1–6.

_____. 1983. The Mythology of Mourning. *Acta Sumerologica* 5: 1–16.

_____. 1985. Sumerian Love Songs. *Revue d'Assyriologie et d'Archéologie orientale* 79: 127–159.

_____. 1986. A Sumerian Poem About Early Rulers. *Acta Sumerologica* 8: 1–11.

_____. 1988. Sumerian Literary Texts in the National Museum, Copenhagen. *Acta Sumerologica* 10: 1–15.

_____. 1992a. Early Dynastic Proverbs and Other Contributions to the Study of Literary Texts from Abu Salabih. *Archiv für Orientforschung* 38: 1–51.

_____. 1992b. Interaction of Oral and Written Poetry in Early Mesopotamian Literature. In *Mesopotamian Epic Literature,* ed. M. E. Vogelzang and H. L. J. Vanstiphont, 23–69. Lewiston, NY: Edwin Mellen.

_____. 1997a. *Proverbs of Ancient Sumer: The World's Earliest Proverb Collections.* Bethesda: CDL.

_____. 1997b. Sumerian Canonical Compositions. C. Individual Focus. 1. Instructions. In *The Context of Scripture, I: Canonical Compositions from the Biblical World,* ed. W.W. Hallo, 569–570. Leiden: Brill.

_____. 1997c. Sumerian Canonical Compositions. C. Individual Focus. 1. Proverbs. In *The Context of Scripture, I: Canonical Compositions from the Biblical World,* ed. W.W. Hallo, 563–8. Leiden: Brill.

Alster, B., and M.J. Geller. 1990. *Sumerian Literary Texts.* London, British Museum.

Alster, B., and H.L.J. Vanstiphout. 1987. Lahar and Ashnan. Presentation and Analysis of a Sumerian Disputation. *Acta Sumerologica* 9: 1–43.

Alter, R. 1983a. The Dynamics of Parallelism. *Hebrew University Studies in Literature and the Arts* 11(1): 71–101.

_____. 1983b. From Line to Story in Biblical Verse. *Poetics Today* 4: 615–37.

_____. 1985. *The Art of Biblical Poetry.* New York: Basic.

_____. 2007. *The Book of Psalms: A Translation with Commentary.* New York: W.W. Norton.

Alvarez, L.M. 2005. The Mystical Language of Daily Life: The Arabic Vernacular Songs of Abu al-Hsan al-Shushtari. *Exemplaria* 17(1): 1–32.

_____. 2007. *The Vernacular Mystic Poetry of Islam: Spain: Sufi Songs of Andalusia.* Basingstoke: Palgrave.

Alvarez, L.M., ed. and trans. 2009. *Abu al-Hasan al-Shushtari: Songs of Love and Devotion.* New York: Paulist.

Ambros, E. 1979. *Sieben Kapitel des Sarḥ Kitâb Sîbawaihi von ar-Rummânî in Edition und Übersetzung.* Vienna: Verlag des Verbandes der wisschenschaftlichen Gesellschaften Österreichs.

Amir-Moez, A.R. 1962. Khayyam's Solution of Cubic Equations. *Mathematics Magazine* 35(5): 269–271.

Andersen, F.I. 1970a. The Hebrew Verbless Clause in the Pentateuch, *Journal of Biblical Literature* Monograph Series 14. Nashville: Abingdon.

_____. 1970b. Orthography in Repetitive Parallelism. *Journal of Biblical Literature* 89: 343–44.

_____. 1971. Passive and Ergative in Hebrew. In *Near Eastern Studies in Honor of William Foxwell Albright,* ed. H. Goedicke, 1–16. Baltimore: Johns Hopkins.

_____. 1974. *The Sentence in Biblical Hebrew.* The Hague: Mouton.

_____. 1976. *Job. Tyndale O.T. Commentaries.* London: Intervarsity.

Andersen, F.I., and A.D. Forbes. 1983. Prose Particle Counts of the Hebrew Bible. In *The Word of the Lord Shall Go Forth,* ed. C. Meyers and M. O'Connor, 165–83. Winona Lake, IN: Eisenbrauns.

Angoujard, J-P. 1990. *Metrical Structure of Arabic.* Providence, RI: Foris.

Annus, A. 2010. *Divination and Interpretation of Signs in the Ancient World.* Chicago: University of Chicago Press.

Annus, A., and A. Lenzi. 2010. *Ludlul bēl nēmeqi: The Standard Babylonian Poem of the Righteous Sufferer.* Helsinki: Neo-Assyrian Text Corpus Project; Winona Lake, IN: Eisenbrauns.

Ansari, M.A.H. 1983. The Doctrine of One Actor: Junaid's View of Tawhid. *The Muslim World* 1: 33–56.

Anwar, G.C. 1974. *Muslim Spain: Its History and Culture.* Minnesota: University of Minnesota Press.

Arberry, A.J. 1953. *The Legacy of Persia.* Oxford: Clarendon.

_____. 1964. Early Arabic Poetry. In *Anthology of Islamic Literature,* ed. J. Kritzeck, 58–60. New York: Holt, Rinehart and Winston.

_____. 1965. *Arabic Poetry: A Primer for Students.* Cambridge: Cambridge University Press.

_____. 2009. *Poems of Al-Mutanabbi: A Selection with Introduction.* Cambridge: Cambridge University Press.

Armistead, S.G. 2003. Kharjas and Villancicos. *Journal of Arabic Literature,* 34(1–2): 3–19.

Armistead, S.G., and J.T. Monroe. 1985. Beached Whales and Roaring Mice: Additional Remarks on Hispano-Arabic Strophic Poetry. *La Coronica* 13: 206–242.

Arnaldez, R. 1956. *Grammaire et théologie chez Ibn Hazm de Cor doue: Essai sur la structure et les conditions de la pensée musulmane.* Paris: J. Vrin.

Aro, J. 1957. *Studien zur mittelbabylonischen Grammatik.* Studia Orientalia 22. Helsinki: Societas Orientalis Fennica.

Ascalone, E. 2007. *Mesopotamia: Assyrians, Sumerians, Babylonians.* Berkeley: University of California Press.

Atac, M. 2010. *The Mythology of Kingship in Neo-Assyrian Art.* New York: Cambridge University Press.

Atiyeh, G.N. 1995. *The Book in the Islamic World: The Written Word and Communication in the Middle East.* Albany: State University of New York Press.

Aubet, M.E. 2001. *The Phoenicians and the West.* Cambridge: Cambridge University Press.

Auffret, P. 1977. *The Literary Structure of Psalm 2. Journal for the Study of the Old Testament* Supplement Series, 3. Sheffield: JSOT.

Avanzini, A. 2004. *Corpus of South Arabian Inscriptions I–III. Qatabanic, Marginal Qatabanic.* Pisa: Awsanite Inscriptions.

_____. 2005. Some Remarks on the Classification of Ancient South Arabian Languages. *Quaderni di Semitistica* 25: 117–25.

_____. 2006. A Fresh Look at Sabaic. *Journal of the American Oriental Society* 126(2): 153–156.

Avishur, Y. 1972. Addenda to the Expanded Colon in Ugaritic and Biblical Verse. *Ugarit-Forschungen* 4: 1–10.

_____. 1974. Stylistic Common Elements Between Ugaritic Literature and Song of Songs. *Beth Mikra* 59: 508–25.

_____. 1975. Word Pairs Common to Phoenician and Biblical Hebrew. *Ugarit-Forschungen* 7:13–47.

_____. 1976. Studies of Stylistic Features Common to the Phoenician Inscriptions and the Bible. *Ugarit-Forschungen* 8: 1–12.

_____. 1977. *The Construct State of Synonyms in Biblical Rhetoric.* Jerusalem: Kiryat Sepher.

_____. 1994. *Studies in Hebrew and Ugaritic Psalms.* Jerusalem: Magnes.

Ayoub, M. 1992. *The Qur'an and Its interpreters.* Albany: State University of New York Press.

Baalbaki, R. 1979. Some Aspects of Harmony and Hierarchy in Sîbawayhi's Grammatical Analysis. *Journal of Arabic Linguistics (ZAL)* 2: 7–22.

_____. 1981. Arab Grammatical Controversies and the Extant Sources of the Second and Third Centuries A.H. In *Studia Arabica et Islamica,* ed. W. al-Qâdî, 1–26. Beirut: American University.

_____. 1983. The Relation Between *naḥw* and *balāġa*: A Comparative Study of the Methods of Sîbawayhi and Gurğânî." *Journal of Arabic Linguistics (ZAL)* 11: 7–23.

Baasten, M.F.J. 2003. A Note on the History of "Semitic." In *Hamlet on a Hill: Semitic and Greek Studies,* ed. M.F.J. Baasten and W. Th. van Peursen, 57–71. Leuven: Peeters.

Bachra, B.N. 2001. *The Phonological Structure of the Verbal Roots in Arabic and Hebrew.* Leiden: Brill.

Badawi, M.M. 1978. The Function of Rhetoric in Medieval Arabic Poetry: Abū Tammām's Ode on Amorium. *Journal of Arabic Literature* 9: 41–56.

_____. 1980. From Primary to Secondary Qasida: Thoughts on the Development of Classical Arabic Poetry. *Journal of Arabic Literature* 2: 1–31.

_____. 1993. *A Short History of Modern Arabic Literature.* Oxford: Oxford University Press.

_____. 2010. *Early Arabic Drama.* Cambridge: Cambridge University Press.

Badawi, M.M., ed. 1992. *Modern Arabic Literature.* Cambridge: Cambridge University Press.

Baer, E. 1989. *Ayyubid Metalwork with Christian Images.* Leiden: Brill.

_____. 1999. The Human Figure in Early Islamic Art: Some Preliminary Remarks. *Muqarnas: An Annual on the Visual Culture of the Islamic World,* 16: 32–41.

Bahnassi, A. 1989. *The Great Omayyad Mosque of Damascus: The First Masterpieces of Islamic Art*. Damascus: Tlass.

Bakalla, M.H. 1984. *Arabic Culture Through Its Language and Literature*. London: Kegan Paul International.

Baker, H.D. 2001. *The Prosopography of the Neo-Assyrian Empire*. Helsinki: Neo-Assyrian Text Corpus Project, University of Helsinki.

Baker, P. 1980. The Frescoes of Amra. *Saudi Aramco World* 31(4): 22–25.

Baldick, J. 1989. *Mystical Islam*. New York: New York University Press.

Barakāt, H. 1969. *'Awdat at-ṭa'ir ilā at-baḥr* [*The Flying Dutchman's Return to the Sea*]. Beirut: Dār al-Nahār.

_____. 1974. *Days of Dust*. Trans. T. Le Gassick. Wilmette, IL: Medina.

Barakāt, H.I. 2000. *Awdat at-ta'ir ila al-bahr*. Bayrut: al-Markiz al-Thaqaafi al-'Arabi.

_____. 2008. *The Crane*. Trans. B.K. Frangieh and R.M.A. Allen. Cairo: American University of Cairo Press.

Bargnaysi, K. Reflections on a Qur'anic Metaphor: The Meaning of "*khatf al-tayr*" in Verse 31 of Suirat al-Hajj. http://al-quran.info/#22:1. Accessed on May 30, 2012.

Barnett, R.D. 1974. *Assyrian Palace Reliefs in the British Museum*. London: British Museum.

_____. 1976. *Sculptures from the North Palace of Ashurbanipal at Nineveh (668–627 B.C.)* London: British Museum Press.

Barrucand, M. 1992. *Moorish Architecture in Andalusia*. Cologne: Taschen.

Bateson, M.C. 1970. *Structural Continuity in Poetry: A Linguistic Study of Five Pre-Islamic Arabic Odes*. The Hague: Mouton.

_____. 2003. *Arabic Language Handbook*. Washington, DC: Georgetown University Press.

Bauer, G. 1972. *Athanasius von Qus, Qilâdat at-taḥrîr fî 'ilm at-tafsîr: Eine koptische Grammatik in arabischer Sprache aus dem 13./14. Jahrhundert*. Freiburg: K. Schwarz.

Beekes, R.S.P. 1988. *A Grammar of Gatha-Avestan*. Leiden: Brill.

Beeston, A.F.L. 1962. Arabian Sibilants. *Journal of Semitic Studies* 7(2): 222–233.

_____. 1968. *Written Arabic: An Approach to the Basic Structures*. Cambridge: Cambridge University Press.

_____. 1971. The Genesis of the *Maqāmāt* Genre. *Journal of Arabic Literature* 3: 1–12.

_____. 1973. The Inscription Jaussen-Savignac 71. *Proceedings of the Seminar for Arabic Studies* 3: 69–72.

_____. 1976. *Warfare in Ancient South Arabia*. London: Luzac.

_____. 1977. *Selections from the Poetry of Baššār*. Cambridge: Cambridge University Press.

_____. 1980. *The Epistle on Singing Girls by Jāḥiz Warminster*. Warminster, UK: Aris & Phillips.

_____. 1981. Languages of Pre-Islamic Arabia. *Arabica* 28: 178–86.

_____. 1983. The Role of Parallelism in Arabic Prose. In *Arabic Literature to the End of the Umayyad Period*, ed. A.F.L. Beeston et al., 180–185. Cambridge: Cambridge University Press.

_____. 1984. *Sabaic Grammar*. Manchester: University of Manchester.

_____. 1992. Languages: Pre-Islamic South Arabian. In *The Anchor Bible Dictionary*. 4: 223–26. New York: Doubleday.

Beeston, A.F.L., and A. Jones, eds. 1991. *Arabicus Felix: Luminosus Britannicus*. Ithaca: Reading.

Beeston, A.F.L., and M.R. Menocal, eds. 2000. *The Cambridge History of Arabic Literature: The Literature of Al-Andalus*. Cambridge: Cambridge University Press.

Beeston, A.F.L., et al., eds. 1983. *Cambridge History of Arabic Literature to the End of the Umayyad Period*. Cambridge: Cambridge University Press.

Behrens-Abouseif, D. 1992. *Islamic Architecture of Cairo: An Introduction*. Leiden: Brill.

_____. 1997. The Lion-Gazelle Mosaic at Khirbat al-Mafjar. In *Muqarnas XIV: An Annual on the Visual Culture of the Islamic World*, ed. G. Necipoglu, 11–18. Leiden: E.J. Brill.

_____. 2008. *Cairo of the Mamluks: A History of the Architecture and Its Culture*. New York: Macmillan.

Behzadi, L., and W. Bihmardi. 2009. *The Weaving of Words: Approaches to Classical Arabic Prose*. Beirut: Orient-Institut; Würzburg: Ergon in Kommission.

Bekkum, W.J. van. 1983. The Risâla of Yehuda ibn Quraysh and Its Place in Hebrew Linguistics. *History of Linguistics in the Near East*, ed. C.H.M. Versteegh, E.F.K. Koerner, 71–91. Philadelphia: J. Benjamins.

Bekkum, W.J. van, J. Houben, I. Sluiter, and K. Versteegh. 1997. *The Emergence of Semantics in Four Linguistic Traditions: Hebrew, Sanskrit, Greek, Arabic*. Philadelphia: J. Benjamins.

Bellamy, J. 1988. Two Pre-Islamic Arabic Inscriptions Revised: Jabal Ramm and Umm al-Jimal. *Journal of the American Oriental Society* 108(3): 369–78.

Bello, L.A. 1989. *The Medieval Islamic Controversy Between Philosophy and Orthodoxy: Ijma' and Ta'wīl in the Conflict Between Al-Ghazālī and Ibn Rushd*. Leiden: Brill.

Belnap, R.K., and Niloofar, H. 1997. *Structuralist Studies in Arabic Linguistics: Charles A. Fergusonís Papers, 1954–1994.* Leiden: Brill.

Benbabaali, S. 1987. *Poétique du muwashshah dans l'Occident musulman médiéval, thèse de 3e cycle.* Sous la direction de R. Arié, Paris 3.

_____. 2008. *La plume, la voix et le plectra.* Avec Beihdja Rahal, Barzakh, Alger. December.

_____. 2010. *Bahdjat al-Nufûs fī Bahâ'i Djannât al-Andalus (l'Amour, la femme et les jardins dans la poésie andalouse).* Alger: La Société ANEP.

Bennett, P.R. 1998. *Comparative Semitic Linguistics: A Manual.* Winona Lake, IN: Eisenbrauns.

Benveniste, E. 1930. Le texte du Draxt asūrīk et la vérification pehlevie. *Journal Asiatique* 216: 193–225.

_____. 1932a. Le Mémorial de Zarēr, poème pehlevi mazdéen. *Journal Asiatique* 220: 245–93.

Berg, H. 2000. *The Development of Exegesis in Early Islam: The Authenticity of Muslim Literature from the Formative Period.* New York: Routledge.

Berlin, A. 1978. Shared Rhetorical Features in Biblical and Sumerian Literature. *Journal of the Ancient Near Eastern Society* 10: 35–42.

_____. 1979a. Grammatical Aspects of Biblical Parallelism. *Hebrew Union College Annual* 50: 17–43.

_____. 1979b. Isaiah 40:4: Etymological and Poetic Considerations. *Hebrew Union College Annual* 3: 1–6.

_____. 1982a. On the Bible as Literature. *Prooftexts* 2: 323–27.

_____. 1982b. Review of M. O'Connor, Hebrew Verse Structure. *Journal of the American Oriental Society* 102: 392–93.

_____. 1983a. Motif and Creativity in Biblical Poetry. *Prooftexts* 3: 231–41.

_____. 1983b. Parallel Word Pairs: A Linguistic Explanation. *Ugarit-Forschungen* 15: 7–16.

_____. 1985. *The Dynamics of Biblical Parallelism* Bloomington: Indiana University Press.

Bernards, M. 1993. "Establishing a Reputation: The Reception of the Kitâb Sîbawayh." Dissertation, University of Nijmegen.

Bertolacci, A. 2006. *The Reception of Aristotle's Metaphysics in Avicenna's Kitab al-Sifa: A Milestone of Western Metaphysical Thought.* Leiden: Brill.

_____. 2011. On the Latin Reception of Avicenna's Metaphysics Before Albertus Magnus: An Attempt at Periodization. In *The Arabic, Hebrew and Latin Reception of Avicenna's Metaphysics,* ed. D.N. Hasse and A. Bertolacci, 197–224. Berlin: De Guyter.

Beyer, K. 1986. *The Aramaic Language.* Trans. J.F. Healey. Göttingen: Vandenhoeck and Ruprecht.

Bier, L. 1986. *Sarvistan: A Study in Early Iranian Architecture.* University Park: Pennsylvania State University Press.

Bierman, I.A. 1998. *Writing Signs: The Fatimid Public Text.* Berkeley: University of California Press.

Biggs, R.D. 1971. An Archaic Sumerian version of the Kesh Temple Hymn from Tell Abū [S]alābīkh. *Zeitschrift für Assyriologie* 61: 193–207.

_____. 1974. *Inscriptions from Tell Abū Salābīkh.* Chicago: University of Chicago Press.

_____. 1984. Ancient Mesopotamia and the Scholarly Traditions of the Third Millennium. *Sumer* 42: 32–3.

Bīrūnī, M. A. 2001. *Alberuni's India.* Trans. E.C. Cashau. Vol. 2. New York: Routledge.

_____. 2004. *The Book of Instruction in the Elements of the Art of Astrology.* Trans. R.R. Wright. New: Kessinger.

Bisheh, G.I. 1979. "The Mosque of the Prophet at Madinah Throughout the First Century A.H. with Special Emphasis on the Umayyad Mosque." PhD Dissertation, University of Michigan.

el-Bizri, N. el-. 2000. *The Phenomenological Quest Between Avicenna and Heidegger.* Binghamton: State University of New York.

_____. 2001. Avicenna and Essentialism. *Review of Metaphysics* 54: 753–778.

_____. 2003. Avicenna's De Anima Between Aristotle and Husserl. In *The Passions of the Soul in the Metamorphosis of Becoming,* ed. A. Tymieniecka, 67–89. Dordrecht: Kluwer Academic.

Blachere, R. 1960. Metrique et prosodie arabes a la lumiere de publications recentes. *Arabica* 7(3): 225–236.

Black, D. 1990. *Logic and Aristotle's Rhetoric and Poetics in Medieval Arabic Philosophy.* Leiden: Brill.

Black, J.A. 1991. *Sumerian Grammar in Babylonian Theory.* Rome: Biblical Institute.

_____. 1992. Some Structural Features of Sumerian Narrative Poetry. In *Mesopotamian Epic Literature: Oral or Aural?* ed. M.E. Vogelzang and H.L.J. Vanstiphout, 71–101. Lewiston, NY: Edwin Mellen.

_____. 1995. Real and Unreal Conditional Sentences in Sumerian. *Acta Sumerologica* 17: 15–39.

_____. 1996. The Imagery of Birds in Sumerian Poetry. In *Mesopotamian Poetic Language: Sumerian And Akkadian,* ed. M.E. Vogelzang, H.L. Herman, and L.J. Vanstiphout, 23–46. Groningen: Styx.

_____. 1998. *Reading Sumerian Poetry*. Ithaca, NY: Cornell University Press.

_____. 2006. *The Literature of Ancient Sumer.* Oxford: Oxford University Press.

Blair, S.S. 1986. *The Ilkhanid Shrine Complex at Natanz, Iran*. Cambridge, MA: Harvard University Press.

_____. 1990. Sufi Saints and Shrine Architecture in the Early Fourteenth Century. *Muqarnas* 7: 35–49.

_____. 2006. *Islamic Calligraphy*. Edinburgh: Edinburgh University Press.

Blair, S.S., and J.M. Bloom. 1995. *The Art and Architecture of Islam*. Yale University Press.

_____. 2011. *And Diverse Are Their Hues: Color in Islamic Art and Culture*. New Haven: Yale University Press.

Blanc, H. 1975. Linguistics Among the Arabs. In *Current Trends in Linguistics*, vol. 13: *Historiography of Linguistics*, ed. T. Sebeok, 1265–83. The Hague: Mouton.

_____. 1979. Diachronic and Synchronic Ordering in Medieval Arab Grammatical Theory. In *Studia Orientalia Memoriae D.H. Baneth Dedicata*, ed. D. S. Baneth, 155–80. Jerusalem: Magnes.

Blau, J. 1988. *Studies in Middle Arabic and Its Judaeo-Arabic Variety*. Jerusalem: Hebrew University.

_____. 1998. Hebrew and North West Semitic: Reflections on the Classification of the Semitic Languages. In *Topics in Hebrew and Semitic Linguistics*, 308–332. Jerusalem: Magnes.

Bloom, J. 1985. The Origins of Fatimid Art. *Muqarnas* 3: 30–8.

_____. 1988a. The Introduction of the Muqarnas into Egypt. *Muqarnas* 5: 21–28.

_____. 1988b. The Revival of Early Islamic Architecture by the Umayyads of Spain. In *The Medieval Mediterranean: Cross-Cultural Contexts*, ed. M.J. Chiat and K.L. Reyerson, 35–41. Minnesota: St. Cloud.

_____. 1989. *Minaret, Symbol of Islam*. Oxford: Oxford University Press.

_____. 2002. *Early Islamic Art and Architecture*. Burlington, VT: Ashgate.

_____. 2007. *Arts of the City Victorious: Islamic Art and Architecture in Fatimid North Africa and Egypt*. New Haven: Yale University Press.

Bloom, J., and S. Blair. *Islamic Arts*. London: Phaidon.

Bohas, G. 1981. Quelques aspects de l'argumentation et de l'explication chez les grammairiens arabes. *Arabica* 28: 204–21.

_____. 1985. L'explication en phonologie arabe. *Studies in the History of Arabic Grammar* 1: 45–52.

Bohas, G., and J. Guillaume. 1984. *Etude des théories des grammairiens arabes*. I. Morphologie et phonologie. Damascus: Institut Français de Damas.

Bohas, G., J. Guillaume, and D.E. Kouloughli. 1989. L'analyse linguistique dans la tradition arabe. *Histoire des idées linguistiques* 1: 260–82.

_____. 1990. *The Arabic Linguistic Tradition*. New York: Routledge.

Bordreuil, P., and D. Pardee. 2009. *A Manual of Ugaritic: Linguistic Studies in Ancient West Semitic* 3. Winona Lake, IN: Eisenbraun's.

Bosworth, C.E. 1976. *The Mediaeval Islamic Underworld: The Banu Sasan in Arabic Society and Literature*. Leiden: Brill.

_____. 1983. Persian Impact on Arabic Literature. In *Arabic Literature to the End of the Umayyad Period*, ed. A.F.L. Beeston et al., 483–497. Cambridge: Cambridge University Press.

Bottéro, J. 1992. *Mesopotamia: Writing, Reasoning and the Gods*. Trans. Z. Bahrani and M. Van de Mieroop. Chicago: University of Chicago Press.

Bowersock, G., W. Brown, and P. Lamont. 2001. *Interpreting Late Antiquity: Essays on the Postclassical World*. Cambridge, MA: Harvard University Press.

Boyce, M. 1954. *The Manichaean Hymn Cycles in Parthian*. London: Oxford University Press.

_____. 1957. The Parthian *gōsān* and Iranian Minstrel Tradition. *Journal of the Royal Asiatic Society*, 45–52.

_____. 1975a. *A History of Zoroastrianism*. Vol. 1: *The Early Period. Handbuch der Orientalistik* I, viii. Leiden: E.J. Brill.

_____. 1975b. *A Reader in Manichaean Middle Persian and Parthian*. Leiden: Brill.

_____. 1984. *Textual Sources for the Study of Zoroastrianism*. Chicago: University of Chicago Press.

Boyer, C.B. 1989. *A History of Mathematics*. New York: Wiley.

Braun, J. 2002. *Music in Ancient Israel/Palestine: Archaeological, Written, and Comparative Sources Bible in Its World*. Grand Rapids, MI: Wm. B. Eerdmans.

Bravmann, M. 1934. *Materialien und Untersuchungen zu den phonetischen Lehren der Araber*. Göttingen: W.F. Kaestner.

Bravmann, M.M. 1977. *Studies in Semitic Philology*. Leiden: Brill.

Brend, B. 2002. *Perspectives on Persian Painting: Illustrations to Amir Khusrau's Khamsah*. New York: Routledge.

Bright, W., and P. Daniels, eds. 1996. *The World's Writing Systems*. Oxford: Oxford University Press.

Brisch, N.M. 2007. *Tradition and the Poetics of Innovation: Sumerian Court Literature of the Larsa Dynasty (c. 2003–1763 BCE)*. Munster: Ugarit-Verlag.

Brockelmann, C. 1982. *Grundriß der vergleichenden Grammatik der semitischen Sprachen*. Hildesheim: Olms.

Brockett, A. 1988. The Value of Hafs and Warsh Transmissions for the Textual History of the Qur'an. In *Approaches of the History of Interpretation of the Qur'an*, ed. A. Rippins, 33–49. Oxford: Clarendon.

Broemeling, L.D. 2011. An Account of Early Statistical Inference in Arab Cryptology. *The American Statistician* 65(4): 255–257.

Bronznick, N. 1979. Metathetic Parallelism'— An Unrecognized Subtype of Synonymous Parallelism. *Hebrew Annual Review* 3: 25–39.

Broug, E. 2008. *Islamic Geometric Patterns*. London: Thames and Hudson.

Brown, J.A.C. 2004. Criticism of the Proto-Hadith Canon: Al-daraqutni's Adjustment of the Sahihayn. *Journal of Islamic Studies* 15(1): 1–37.

_____. 2007. *The Canonization of Al-Bukhārī and Muslim. The Formation and Function of the Sunnī Ḥadīth.* Leiden: Brill.

Browne, E.G. *Literary History of Persia*. 4 vols. Cambridge: Cambridge University Press.

Bruderlin, M., et al. 2002. *Ornament and Abstraction: The Dialogue Between Non-Western, Modern and Contemporary Art*. New Haven: Yale University Press.

Brugman, J. 1984. *An Introduction to the History of Modern Arabic Literature in Egypt*. Leiden: Brill.

Buccellati, G. 1996. *A Structural Grammar of Babylonian*. Wiesbaden: Harrassowitz.

_____. 1997. Akkadian. In *The Semitic Languages*, ed. R. Hetzron, 69–99. New York: Routledge.

Bukhari, M. ibn. 2008. *Isma'l Hadith of Bukhari*. Vol. I, II, III, IV. Charleston, SC: Forgotten Books.

Burckhardt, T. 1972. *Moorish Culture in Spain*. Trans. A. Jaffa. London: Allen and Unwin.

_____. 1992. *Fez: City of Islam*. Cambridge: Islamic Texts Society.

_____. 2006. *The Foundations of Christian Art: Illustrated*. Bloomington, IN: World Wisdom.

_____. 2009. *Art of Islam: Language and Meaning*. Bloomington, IN: World Wisdom.

Burgh, T.W. 2006. *Listening to the Artifacts: Music Culture in Ancient Palestine*. New York: T. and T. Clark.

Burns, R. 2005. *Damascus: A History*. London: Routledge.

Burrell, D.B. 1986. *Knowing the Unknowable God: Ibn-Sina, Maimonides, Aquinas*. Notre Dame, IN: University of Notre Dame Press.

Bussmann, H. 1996. *Routledge Dictionary of Language and Linguistics*. New York: Routledge.

Butler, H.C. 1907–20. *Ancient Architecture of Syria*. Section A.B., *Syria*. Publications of the Princeton University Archaeological Expedition to Syria. Div. 2, II, A.

Buttner, F. 2006. Verse Structure and Musical Rhythm in Latin Hymn Melodies. *Anuario Musical* 61: 3–22.

Cachia, P. 1968. Bayāwī on the Fawāti. *Journal of Semitic Studies* 13(2): 218–231.

_____. 1989. *Popular Narrative Ballads of Modern Egypt*. Oxford: Clarendon.

_____. 1990. *An Overview of Modern Arabic Literature*. Edinburgh: University of Edinburgh Press.

_____. 2002. *Arabic Literature: An Overview*. London: RoutledgeCurzon.

_____. 2005. *Taha Husayn: His Place in the Egyptian Literary Renaissance*. London: Gorgias.

el-Calamawy, S. 1983. Narrative Elements in the Hadith Literature. In *Arabic Literature to the End of Ummayad Period*, ed. A.F.L. Beeston et al., 308–316. Cambridge: Cambridge University Press.

Cameron, A. 1993. *The Mediterranean World in Late Antiquity, A.D. 395–600*. London: Routledge.

Canby, S. 2005. *Islamic Art in Detail*. Cambridge, MA: Harvard University Press.

Cantarino, V. 1975. *Arabic Poetrics in the Golden Age*. Leiden: Brill.

Campanini, M., and C. Higgitt. 2008. *An Introduction to Islamic Philosophy*. Edinburgh: Edinburgh University Press.

Campbell, L. 1999. *Historical Linguistics: An Introduction*. Cambridge, MA: MIT Press.

Canby, S.R. 2005. *Islamic Art in Detail*. Cambridge, MA: Harvard University Press.

Caplin, W.E. 1998. *Classical Form: A Theory of Formal Functions for the Instrumental Music of Haydn, Mozart, and Beethoven*. New York: Oxford University Press.

Casey, M. 1998. *Aramaic Sources of Mark's Gospel*. Cambridge University Press.

Catford, J.C. 1988. *A Practical Introduction to Phonetics*. Oxford: Oxford University.

Carter, M.G. 1968. A Study of Sîbawaihi's Principles of Grammatical Analysis. Dissertation, University of Oxford.

_____. 1972. Les origines de la grammaire arabe. *Revue des Études Islamiques* 40: 79–97.

_____. 1973. An Arab Grammarian of the Eighth Century A.D. *Journal of the American Oriental Society* 93: 146–57.

_____. 1981. *Arab Linguistics: An Introductory Classical Text with Translation and Notes*. Amsterdam: J. Benjamins.

_____. 1983. Language Control as People

Control in Medieval Islam: The Aims of the Grammarians in Their Cultural Context. In *Arab Language and Culture*, ed. R. Baalbaki, 65–84. Beirut: American University of Beirut.

_____. 1984. Linguistic Science and Orthodoxy in Conflict: The Case of al-Rummânî. *Zeitschrift für Geschichte der Arabisch-Islamischen Wissenschaften* 1:212–32.

_____. 1990. Arabic Grammar. In *Cambridge History of Arabic Literature: Religion, Learning and Science in the 'Abbâsid Period*, ed. M.J.L. Young, J.D. Latham, and R.B. Serjeant, 118–138. Cambridge: Cambridge University Press.

_____. 1994. *Sibawayhi*. New York: I.B. Tauris.

Ceresko, A. 1975. The A:B::B:A Word Pattern in Hebrew and Northwest Semitic with Special Reference to the Book of Job. *Ugarit-Forschungen* 7: 73–88.

_____. 1976. The Chiastic Word Pattern in Hebrew. *Catholic Biblical Quarterly* 38: 303–11.

_____. 1978. The Function of Chiasmus in Hebrew Poetry. *Catholic Biblical Quarterly* 4: 1–10.

_____. 1982. The Function of Antanaclasis (mṣ' 'to find' // mṣ' 'to reach, overtake, grasp') in Hebrew Poetry, Especially in the Book of Qoheleth. *Catholic Biblical Quarterly* 44: 551–69.

Chambers, J.K., and P. Trudgill. 1980. *Dialectology*. Cambridge: Cambridge University Press.

_____. 1994. Writing the History of Arabic Grammar. *Historiographia Linguistica* 21:385–414.

_____. 2008. *A History of Arabic Language*. Cambridge: Cambridge University Press.

Chatman, S. 1960. Comparing Metrical Styles. In *Style in Language*, ed. T. Sebeok, 149–172. Cambridge, MA: MIT Press.

Chatman, S., ed. 1971. *Literary Style: A Symposium*. London: Oxford University Press.

_____. 1973. *Approaches to Poetics*. New York: Columbia University Press.

Chejne, A.G. 1969. *The Arabic Language: Its Role in History*. Minneapolis: University of Minnesota Press.

_____. 1974. *Muslim Spain*. Minneapolis: University of Minnesota Press.

Cheng, J. 2001. "Assyrian Music as Represented and Representations of Assyrian Music." PhD Dissertation, Harvard University.

_____. 2009. A Review of Early Dynastic III Music: Man's Animal Call. *Journal of Near Eastern Studies* 68(3): 163–178.

Chiat, M.J., and K.L. Reyerson, eds. *The Medieval Mediterranean: Cross-Cultural Contexts*. Minnesota: St. Cloud.

Chittick, W.C. 1978. Eschatology. In *Islamic Spirituality: Foundations,* ed. S.H. Nasr, 378–409. New York: Crossroad.

_____. 1982. The Five Divine Presences: From al-Qûnawî to al-Qaysarî. *Muslim World* 72: 107–28.

_____. 1989. *The Sufi Path of Knowledge: Ibn al-'Arabî's Metaphysics of Imagination*. Albany: State University of New York Press.

_____. 1994a. *Imaginal Worlds: Ibn al-'Arabî and the Problem of Religious Diversity*. Albany: State University of New York Press.

_____. 1994b. Rûmî and Wahdat al-wujûd. In *Poetry and Mysticism in Islam: The Heritage of Rûmî*, ed. A. Banani, R. Hovanisian, and G. Sabagh, pp. 70–111. Cambridge, England: Cambridge University Press.

_____. 1996. Ibn 'Arabî and The School of Ibn 'Arabî. In *History of Islamic Philosophy*, ed. S.H. Nasr and O. Leaman, pp. 497–523. London: Routledge.

_____. 1998. *The Self-Disclosure of God: Principles of Ibn al-'Arabî's Cosmology*. Albany: State University of New York Press.

_____. 2004. The Central Point: Qûnawî's Role in the School of Ibn 'Arabî. *Journal of the Muhyiddin Ibn 'Arabi Society* 35: 25–45.

_____. 2005. *Ibn 'Arabi: Heir to the Prophets*. Oxford: Oneworld.

Civil, M. 1973. The Sumerian Writing System: Sumerian Problems. *Orientalia* n.s. 42: 21–34.

Civil, M., and G. Rubio. 1999. An Ebla Incantation Against Insomnia and the Semiticization of Sumerian: Notes ARET 5 8b and 9. *Orientalia* n.s. 68: 254–266.

Clark, E. 2003. Underneath Which Rivers Flow: The Symbolism of the Islamic Garden. *Halı: Carpet, Textile and Islamic Art* 128: 84–89.

Claydon, T. 1992. Kish in the Kassite Period (c. 1650–1150 B.C.). *Iraq* 54: 141–155.

Clevenot, D., and G. Degeorge. 2000. *Ornament and Decoration in Islamic Architecture*. London: Thames and Hudson.

Cohen, A., and S.E. Kangas. 2010. *Assyrian Reliefs from the Palace of Ashurnasirpal I: A Cultural Biography*. Hanover, NH: Hood Museum of Art; Dartmouth College: University Press of New England.

Cohen, D. 1978. *La phrase nominale et l'evolution du systeme verbal en semitique*. Paris: Société de linguistique de Paris.

Cohen, M.E. 1981. *Sumerian Hymnology: The Eršemma*. Cincinnati: Hebrew Union College.

_____. 1988. *The Canonical Lamentations of Ancient Mesopotamia*. Potomac MD: Capital Decisions.

Cole, S.W. 1996. *Nippur IV: The Early Neo-*

Babylonian Governor's Archive from Nippur. Chicago: University of Chicago Press.

Colless, B. 1990. The Proto-Alphabetic Inscriptions of Sinai. *Abr-Nahrain* 28. Louvain: Peeters.

_____. 1991. The Proto-Alphabetic Inscriptions of Canaan. *Abr-Nahrain* 29. Louvain: Peeters.

_____. 1998. The Canaanite Syllabary. *Ancient Near Eastern Studies* 35: 26–46.

Collon, D. 2008. *Playing in Concert in the Ancient Near East: Proceedings of the International Conference of Near Eastern Archaeomusicology.* London: ICONEA.

Comrie, B. 1976. *Aspect.* Cambridge: Cambridge University.

_____. 1985. *Tense.* Cambridge: Cambridge University.

Comrie, B., ed. 1989. *Language Universals and Linguistic Typology.* Chicago: University of Chicago.

Contadini, A. 2012. *A World of Beasts: A Thirteenth-Century Illustrated Arabic Book on Animals (the Kitāb Naʾt al-Ḥayawān) in the Ibn Bakhtishuʾ Tradition.* Boston: Brill.

Coogan, M.D. 2009. *A Brief Introduction to the Old Testament.* Oxford: Oxford University Press.

Cooper, J.S. 1986. *Sumerian and Akkadian Royal Inscriptions.* New Haven: CO: American Oriental Society.

Cooper, J.S., and G.M. Schwartz. 1996. *The Study of the Ancient Near East in the Twenty-First Century: The William Foxwell Albright Centennial Conference.* Winona Lake, IN: Eisenbrauns.

Cooperson, M. 2000. *Classical Arabic Biography: The Heirs of the Prophets in the Age of Al-Mamun.* Cambridge: Cambridge University Press.

Cooperson, M., and S.M. Toorawa. 2005. *Arabic Literary Culture, 500–925.* Detroit: Thomson Gale.

Copeland, R., and I. Sluiter. 2009. *Medieval Grammar and Rhetoric: Language Arts and Literary Theory, A.D. 300–1475.* Oxford: Oxford University Press.

Corbin, H. 1969. *Creative Imagination in the Sufism of Ibn Arabi.* Princeton: Princeton University Press.

_____. 1993. *History of Islamic Philosophy.* Trans. L. Sherrard. London: Kegan Paul International.

_____. 1998. *Alone with the Alone: Creative Imagination in the Sufism of Ibn ʿArabi.* Princeton: Princeton University Press.

Corriente, F. 1997. *Poesía dialectal árabe y romance en Alandalús: cejeles y xarajat de muwassahat.* Madrid: Gredos.

Coulmas, F. 2004. *Writing Systems of the World.* Oxford: Blackwell.

Craig, J.A. 1974. *Assyrian and Babylonian Religious Texts.* Leipzig: Zentralantiquariat d. DDR.

Craig, W.L. 1979. *The Kalam Cosmological Argument.* London: Macmillan.

_____. 1994. *Reasonable Faith: Christian Truth and Apologetics.* Wheaton, IL: Crossway.

Craigie, P.C. 1969. The Song of Deborah and the Epic of Tukulti-Ninurta. *Journal of Biblical Literature* 88: 253–65.

_____. 1971. A Note on "Fixed Pairs" in Ugaritic and Early Hebrew Poetry. *Journal of Theological Studies* 22:140–43.

_____. 1979a. Parallel Word Pairs in Ugaritic Poetry: A Critical Evaluation of Their Relevance for Ps 29. *Ugarit-Forschungen* 11: 135–40.

_____. 1979b. The Problem of Parallel Word Pairs in Ugaritic and Hebrew Poetry. *Semitics* 5: 48–58.

_____. 1983. *Ugarit and the Old Testament.* Grand Rapids: Eerdmans.

Creswell, K.A.C. 1951. The Kaʻba in A.D. 608. *Archaeologia* 94: 97–102.

_____. 1952. *The Muslim Architecture of Egypt.* Oxford: Clarendon.

Creswell, K.A.C., and J.W. Allan. 1989. *A Short Account of Early Muslim Architecture.* Aldershot: Scholar.

Creswell, K.A.C., and M.G. Berchen. 1969. *Early Muslim Architecture umayyadas: A.D. 622–750.* Oxford: Clarendon.

_____. 1978. *Ayyubids and Early Baḥrite Mamlks: A.D. 1171–1326.* New York: Hacker Art Books.

Cross, F.M. 1967. The Origin and Early Evolution of the Alphabet. *Eretz-Israel* 8: 8–24.

_____. 1973. *Canaanite Myth and Hebrew Epic.* Cambridge: Cambridge University Press.

_____. 1979. Early Alphabetic Scripts. In *Symposia*, 97–111. Cambridge, MA: American Schools of Oriental Research.

_____. 2000. *From Epic to Canon: History and Literature in Ancient Israel.* Baltimore: Johns Hopkins University Press.

Cross, F.M., and D.N. Freedman. 1997. *Ancient Yahwistic Poetry.* Livonia, MI: Dove.

Crowley, T. 1992. *An Introduction to Historical Linguistics.* Oxford: Oxford University.

Cruttenden, A.I. 1997. *Intonation.* 2nd ed. Cambridge Textbooks in Linguistics. Cambridge: Cambridge University Press.

Cumming, C.G. 2007. *Assyrian and Hebrew Hymns of Praise.* Piscataway: Gorgias.

Curtius, E.R. 1979. *European Literature and the Latin Middle Ages.* London: Routledge to Kegan Paul.

Czapkiewicz, A. 1988. *The Views of the Medieval Arab Philologists on Language and*

Its Origin in the Light of as-Suyûti's al-Muzhir. Cracow: Uniwersytet Jagiellonski.

Dabousy, S. el-. 1983. "Medieval Linguistics: Ibn Janâh's Comparative Structure of Arabic and Hebrew." Ph.D. dissertation, University of London.

Dalgleish, K. 1973. Some Aspects of the Treatment of Emotion in the *Dīwān* of al-A'shā. *Journal of Arabic Literature* 4: 97–111.

Dallal, A. 1999. Science, Medicine, and Technology: The Making of a Scientific Culture. In *The Oxford History of Islam*, ed. J.L. Esposito, 155–214. New York: Oxford University Press.

_____. 2010. *Islam, Science, and the Challenge of History.* New Haven: Yale University Press.

Dalley, S. 1989. *Myths from Mesopotamia: Creation, the Flood, Gilgamesh, and Others.* Oxford: Oxford University Press.

_____. 1991. *Texts from Kish and Elsewhere.* Oxford: Clarendon.

_____. 2005. *Old Babylonian Texts in the Ashmolean Museum: Mainly from Larsa, Sippir, Kish, and Lagaba.* Oxford: Oxford University Press.

_____. 2007. *Esther's Revenge at Susa: From Sennacherib to Ahasuerus.* Oxford: Oxford University Press.

Dalley, S., ed. 1998. *The Legacy of Mesopotamia.* Oxford: Oxford University Press.

Daniel, N. 2000. *Islam and the West.* Edinburgh: Edinburgh University Press.

Daniels, P.T., and W. Bright. 1996. *The World's Writing Systems.* Oxford: Oxford University Press.

Danner, V. 1987. The Early Development of Sufism. In *Islamic Spirituality: Foundations*, ed. S.H. Nasr, 129–64. New York: Crossroad.

Darnell, J., and C. Dobbs-Allsopp, et al. 2005. Two Early Alphabetic Inscriptions from the Wadi el-Hol: New Evidence for the Origin of the Alphabet from the Western Desert of Egypt. *Annual of the American Schools of Oriental Research* 59: 63–124.

Dean, M.E. 1996. The Grammar of Sound in Greek Texts: Toward a Method for Mapping the Echoes of Speech in Writing. *Australian Biblical Review* 44: 53–70.

De Blois, F. 1990. *Burzōy's Voyage to India and the Origin of the Book of Kalilah wa Dimnah.* London: Royal Asiatic Society.

_____. 2000. A Persian Poem Lamenting the Arab Conquest. In *Studies in Honour of C.E. Bosworth* 2: 82–95, ed. C. Hillebrand. Leiden: Brill.

De Bruijin, J.T.P. 2009. *General Introduction to Persian Literature.* New York: I.B. Tauris.

De Jong, F. 1993. *Verse and the Fair Sex: Studies in Arabic Poetry and in the Representation.* Utrecht: M.Th. Houtsma Stichting.

De Jong, F., and B. Radtke, eds. 1999. *Islamic Mysticism Contested: Thirteen Centuries of Controversies and Polemics.* Leiden: Brill.

De Moor, J.C. 1987. *An Anthology of Religious Texts from Ugarit.* Leiden: Brill.

Der Meer, W. van., and J.C. De Moor. 1988. The Structural Analysis of Biblical and Canaanite Poetry. Sheffield: JSOT.

Deutscher, G. 2005. *The Unfolding of Language: An Evolutionary Tour of Mankind's Greatest Invention.* New York: Metropolitan.

_____. 2006. *The Akkadian Language in Its Semitic Context: Studies in the Akkadian of the Third and Second Millennium BC.* Leiden: Nederlands Instituut voor het Nabije.

_____. 2007. *Syntactic Change in Akkadian: The Evolution of Sentential Complementation.* Oxford: Oxford University Press.

_____. 2010. *Through the Language Glass: Why the World Looks Different in Other Languages.* New York: Metropolitan/Henry Holt.

De Zorzi, N. 2009. Bird Divination in Mesopotamia—New Evidence from BM 108874. *KASKAL: Rivista di storia, ambienti e culture del Vicino Oriente Antico* 6: 91–94.

Diakonoff, I.M. 1976. Ancient Writing and Ancient Written Language: Pitfalls and Peculiarities in the Study of Sumerian. *Assyriological Studies* 20: 99–121.

_____. 1988. *Afrasian languages.* Moscow: Nauka, Central Department of Oriental Literature.

Diem, W. 1974. *Hochsprache und Dialekt im Arabischen: Untersuchungen zur heutigen arabischen Zweisprachigkeit.* Wiesbaden: F. Steiner.

_____. 1975. Gedanken zur Frage der Mimation und Nunation in den semitischen Sprachen. *Zeitschrift der Deutschen Morgenländischen Gesellschaft* (*ZDMG*) 125: 239–58.

Dietrich, M., O. Loretz, and J. Sanmartin, eds. 1995. *The Cuneiform Alphabetic Texts* Münster: Ugarit-Verlag.

Diringer, D. 1968. *The Alphabet.* London: Hutchinson.

Dobbs-Allsopp, F. 2001a. The Enjambing Line in Lamentations: A Taxonomy (Part 1). *Zeitschrift für Geschichte der Arabisch-Islamischen Wissenschaften* 113: 219–39.

_____. 2001b. The Effects of Enjambment in Lamentations (Part 2). *Zeitschrift für Geschichte der Arabisch-Islamischen Wissenschaften* 113: 370–95; 371.

Dobie, R.J. 2010. *Logos and Revelation: Ibn 'Arabi, Meister Eckhart, and Mystical Hermeneutics.* Washington, DC: Catholic University of America Press.

Dodds, J. 1992a. The Mudejar Tradition in Architecture. In *The Legacy of Muslim Spain,* ed. S.K. Jayyusi and M. Marin, 592–98. Leiden: Brill.

_____. 1992b. The Arts of Al-Andalus. In *The Legacy of Muslim Spain,* ed. S.K. Jayyusi and M. Marin, 599–621. Leiden: Brill.

Dodge, B. 1970. *The Fihrist of Al-Nadim: A Tenth-Century Survey of Muslim Culture.* New York: Columbia University Press.

Dold-Samplonius, Y., and S. Harmsen. 2004. Muqarnas: Construction and Reconstruction. In *Nexus V: Architecture and Mathematics,* ed. K. Williams and F.D. Cepeda, 69–77. Florence: Kim Williams.

Donner, F.M. 1998. *Narratives of Islamic Origins: The Beginnings of Islamic Historical Writing.* Princeton: Darwin.

Driver, G.R. 1936. *Problems of the Hebrew Verbal System.* Edinburgh: T &T Clark.

Drory, R. 2000a. *Models and Contacts: Arabic Literature and Its Impact on Medieval Jewish Culture.* Boston: Brill.

_____. 2000b. The *Maqāmā.* In *The Literature of Al-Andalus,* ed. M.R. Menocal, M.A. Sells and R.P. Scheindlin, 190–210. Cambridge: Cambridge University Press.

Duchesne-Guillemin, M. 1980. Sur la restitution de la musique hourrite. *Revue de Musicologie* 66(1): 5–26.

_____. 1981. Music in Ancient Mesopotamia and Egypt. *World Archaeology* 12(3): 287–297.

_____. 1984. *A Hurrian Musical Score from Ugarit: The Discovery of Mesopotamian Music.* Malibu, CA: Undena.

Dumbrill, R.J. 1998. *The Musicology and Organology of the Ancient Near East.* London: Tadema.

_____. 1999. *The Music of the Ancient Near East.* London: Athlone.

_____. 2000. *The Archaeomusicology of the Ancient Near East.* Victoria, BC: Trafford.

_____. 2008a. The Earliest Evidence of Heptatonism in a Late Old Babylonian Text: CBS 1766. *Archaeological Review of the Ancient Near East* 1: 1–18.

_____. 2008b. Evidence and Inference in Texts of Theory in the Ancient Near East. In *Proceedings of the International Conference of Near Eastern Archaeomusicology,* ed. R.J. Dumbrill and I.L. Finkel, 5–116. British Museum, December 4–6.

_____. 2008c. Four Tables from the Temple Library of Nippur: A Source for "Plato's Number" in Relation to the Quantification of Babylonian Tone Numbers. *Archaeomusicological Review of the Ancient Near East* 1: 27–38.

_____. 2008d. Is the Heptagram in CBS 1766 a Dial? *Archaeomusicological Review of the Ancient Near East* 1: 47–50.

_____. 2009. Babylonian Quantification of Pitches and Its Influence on Music Theory of the Abbasids and the Renaissance. In *Musical Traditions in the Middle East: Reminiscences of a Distant Past.* Conference on Ancient Near East Musicology, Leiden University, December 10–12.

_____. 2010a. The Concept of Music Theoricism in the Ancient Middle/Near East and in Egypt in Relation to the Development of Sexagesimal Mathematics. *ICONEA 2010: Proceedings of the International Conference of Near Eastern Archaeomusicology.* University of London, December 15–17.

_____. 2010b. Mesopotamian Origins of Heptatonism. *Music and Numbers,* May 14–15.

_____. 2011. *Idiophones of the Ancient Near East in the Collections of the British Museum* Piscataway. NJ: Gorgias.

Duri, A.A. 1998. *The Rise of Historical Writing Among the Arabs.* Princeton: Princeton University Press.

Ebbling, J., and G. Cunningham. 2007. *Analysing Literary Sumerian: Corpus-Based Approaches.* Oakville, CT: Equinox.

Edzard, D.O. 1987. Deep-Rooted Skyscrapers and Bricks: Ancient Mesopotamian Architecture and Its Imaging. In *Figurative Language in the Ancient Near East,* ed. Midlin et al., 13–24. London: School of Oriental and African Studies, University of London.

_____. 2003. *Sumerian Grammar.* Boston: Brill.

Eickelman, D.F., and A. Salvatore. 2002. The Public Sphere and Muslim Identities. *European Journal of Sociology* 43: 92–115.

Elad, A. 1992. Why Did 'Abd al-Malik Build the Dome of the Rock? A Re-Examination of the Muslim Sources. In *Bayt al-Maqdis: 'Abd al-Malik's Jerusalem,* vol. 1, ed. J. Raby and J. Johns, 33–58. Oxford: Oxford University Press.

Elamrani-Jamal, Abdelali. 1983. *Logique aristotélicienne et grammaire arabe: Étude et documents.* Paris: J. Vrin.

Elgibali, A., ed. 1996. *Understanding Arabic: Essays in Contemporary Arabic Linguistics in Honor of El-Said Badawi.* Cairo: American University of Cairo Press.

Elkaisy-Friemuth, M. 2006. *God and Humans in Islamic Thought: 'Abd al-Jabbar, Ibn Sina and al-Ghazali.* London: Routledge.

Elwell-Sutton, L.P. 1975a. *Colloquial Persian.* London: Routledge and K. Paul.

_____. 1975b. The Foundations of Persian Prosody and Metrics. *Iran* 13: 75–97.

Emery, E. 2006. *Muwashshah: Proceedings of the Conference on Arabic and Hebrew Strophic Poetry and Its Romance Parallels.* School of Oriental and African Studies (SOAS), London, October 8–10, 2004. London: RN Books.

Enan, M.A. 1979. *Ibn Khaldun: His Life and Works*. New Delhi: Kitab Bhavan.

Enany, R. el-. 1993. *Naguib Mahfouz: The Pursuit of Meaning*. London: Routledge.

Endress, G. 1977a. The Debate Between Arabic Grammar and Greek Logic in Classical Islamic Thought. *Journal for the History of Arabic Science* 1: 339–51.

_____. 1977b. *The Works of Yahyâ ibn ʿAdî: An Analytical Inventory*. Wiesbaden: L. Reichert.

_____. 1978. Yahyâ ibn ʿAdî's "Treatise on the Difference Between the Arts of Philosophical Logic and of Arabic Grammar": A Critical Edition. *Journal for the History of Arabic Science* 2: 181–E93.

_____. 1986. Grammatik und Logik: Arabische Philologie und griechische Philosophie im Widerstreit. In *Sprachphilosophie in Antike und Mittelalter*, ed. B. Mojsisch, 163–299. Amsterdam: B.R. Grüner.

Ermers, R. 1995. "Turkic Forms in Arabic Structures: The Description of Turkic by Arabic Grammarians." PhD dissertation, University of Nijmegen.

Ernst, C.W. 1985. *Words of Ecstasy in Sufism*. Albany: State University of New York Press.

Ettinghausen, R., and O. Grabar. 1987. *The Art and Architecture of Islam 650–1250*. New Haven: Yale University Press.

_____. 2001. *Islamic Art and Architecture, 650–1250*. New Haven: Yale University Press.

Everson, M., and R. Pournader. 2007. Revised Proposal to Encode the Avestan Script in the SMP of the UCS. http://std.dkuug.dk/jtc1/sc2/wg2/docs/n3197.pdf, 2007-06-10.

Fakhry, M. 2002. *Al-Farabi: Founder of Islamic Neoplatonism*. Oxford: Oneworld.

_____. 2004. *A History of Islamic Philosophy*. New York: Columbia University Press.

Fancy, N.A.G. 2006. "Pulmonary Transit and Bodily Resurrection: The Interaction of Medicine. Philosophy and Religion in the Works of Ibn al-Nafīs (d. 1288)." Dissertation, University of Notre Dame.

Farhat, H. 2004. *The Dastgah Concept in Persian Music*. Cambridge: Cambridge University Press.

Farmer, H.G. 1926. The Old Persian Musical Modes. *Journal of the Royal Asiatic Society* 58.1: 93–95.

_____. 1929. *A History of Arabian Music to the XIIIth Century*. London, Luzac.

_____. 1931. *The Organ of the Ancients: From Eastern Sources (Hebrew, Syriac and Arabic)*. London: W. Reeves.

_____. 1934. Reciprocal Influences in Music Twixt the Far and Middle East. *Journal of the Royal Asiatic Society* 66.2: 327–42.

_____. 1944. An Anonymous English-Arabic Fragment on Music. In *Islamic Culture* 18: 201–205.

_____. 1955. The Song Captions in the Kitāb al-aghānī. *Transactions: Glasgow University Oriental Society* 15: xv, 1–10.

_____. 1957a. The Music of Ancient Mesopotamia. In *Ancient and Oriental Music*, ed. E. Wellesz, 288–254. Oxford: Oxford University Press.

_____. 1957b. The Music of Islam. In *Ancient and Oriental Music*, ed. E. Wellesz, 421–478. Oxford: Oxford University Press.

_____. 1964. *The Oriental Musical Influence, and Jewish Genizah Fragments on Music*. New York: Hinrichsen.

_____. 1965. *The Sources of Arabian Music: An Annotated Bibliography of Arabic Manuscripts Which Deal with the Theory, Practice, and History of Arabian Music from the Eighth to the Seventeenth Century*. Leiden: Brill.

_____. 1970. *Historical Facts for the Arabian Musical Influence*. New York: Hildesheim.

_____. 1978. *Historical Facts for the Arabian Musical Influence*. New York: Arno.

_____. 1997. *Studies in Oriental Music*, ed. E. Neubauer. 2 vols. Frankfurt: Institute for the History of Arabic-Islamic Science at the Johann Wolfgang Goethe University.

Farrin, R. 2010. *Abundance from the Desert: Classical Arabic Poetry*. Syracuse: Syracuse University Press.

Faruqi, L.I. al-. 1975. Muwashshah: A Vocal Form in Islamic Culture. *Ethnomusicology* 29(1):1–29.

Fassberg, S.E. 2006. *Biblical Hebrew in Its Northwest Semitic Setting: Typological and Historical Perspectives*. Jerusalem: Hebrew University Magnes Press; Winona Lake, IN: Eisenbrauns.

Ferguson, C.A. 1959a. The Arabic Koine. In *Structuralist Studies in Arabic Linguistics: Charles A. Fergusons Papers, 1954–1994*, ed. R.K. Belnap and N. Haeri, 50–68. Leiden: Brill.

_____. 1959b. Diglossia. *Word* 15: 325–40.

_____. 1959c. Myths About Arabic. In *Structuralist Studies in Arabic Linguistics: Charles A. Fergusons Papers, 1954–1994*, ed. R. Kirk Belnap and N. Haeri, 250–256. Leiden: Brill.

Fernandez, M.P. 1997. *An Introductory Grammar of Rabbinic Hebrew*. Leiden: Brill.

Ferrara, A.J. 1995. Topoi and Stock-Strophes in Sumerian Literary Tradition: Some Observations, Part 1. *Journal of Near Eastern Studies* 54(2): 81–117.

Finch, R. 1984. Notes on Arabic Prosody. *Alif: Journal of Comparative Poetics* 1(4): 42–62.

Fiore, S. *Voices from the Clay: The Develop-*

ment of Assyro-Babylonian Literature. Norman: University of Oklahoma Press.

Firestone, R. 1999. *Jihad: The Origin of Holy War in Islam*. New York: Oxford University Press.

Fischer, M.M.J., and M. Abedi. 1990. Qur'an in Dialogics: Islam Poetics and Politics for Muslims and for Us. In *The Interpretation of Dialogue*, ed. T. Maronhao, 120–156. Chicago: University of Chicago Press.

Fischer, S.R. 2001. *A History of Writing*. London: Reaktion.

Fischer, W. 1997. Classical Arabic. In *The Semitic Languages*, ed. R. Hetzron, 182–219. New York: Routledge.

Fish Compton, L. 1976. *Andalusian Lyrical Poetry and Old Spanish Love Songs: The Muwashshaḥ and Its Kharjaḥ*. New York: University Press.

Fitzmyer, J. 1979. *A Wandering Aramean: Collected Aramaic Essays*. Missoula: Scholars.

Fleisch, H. 1961. *Traité de philologie arabe*. 1. *Préliminaires, phonétique, morphologie nominale*. Beirut: Imprimerie Catholique.

_____. 1994. Arabic linguistics. In *History of Linguistics*, vol. 1: *The Eastern Traditions*, ed. G. Lepschy, 164–185. London: Longman.

Fleming, D.E., and S.J. Milstein, eds. 2010. *The Buried Foundation of the Gilgamesh Epic: The Akkadian Huwawa Narrative*. Leiden: Brill.

Fletcher, B., and D. Cruickshank. 1996. *Sir Banister Fletcher's a History of Architecture*. Boston: Architectural.

Flood, F.B. 1997. Umayyad Survivals and Mamluk Revivals: Qalawunid Architecture and the Great Mosque of Damascus. In *Muqarnas XIV: An Annual on the Visual Culture of the Islamic World*, ed. G. Necipoglu, 57–79. Leiden: Brill.

_____. 2001. *The Great Mosque of Damascus: Studies on the Makings of an Ummayad Visual Culture*. Leiden: Brill.

Fokkelman, J.P. 2001. *Reading Biblical Poetry: An Introductory Guide*. Louisville, KY: Westminster John Knox.

Foster, B., ed. and trans. 2001. *The Epic of Gilgamesh*. New York: W.W. Norton.

Foster, J.L. 1975. Thought Couplets in Khety's Hymn to the Inundation. *Journal of Near Eastern Studies* 34: 14–16.

Frangieh, B.K. 1999. *Arabian Love Poems: Full Arabic and English Texts*. Boulder: Lynne Rienner.

_____, trans. 2004. *Love, Death, and Exile* by Abdul Wahab al-Bayati. Washington, DC: Georgetown University Press.

_____. 2005. *Anthology of Arabic Literature, Culture, and Thought from Pre-Islamic Times to the Present*. New Haven: Yale University Press.

Frank, R. 1981. Meanings Are Spoken of in Many Ways: The Earlier Arab Grammarians. *Le Muséon* 94: 259–319.

Friberg, J. 2007. *Amazing Traces of a Babylonian Origin in Greek Mathematics*. London: World Scientific.

Frolov, D. 2000. *Classical Arabic Verse: History and Theory of 'Arud*. Leiden: Brill.

Gadd, C.J. 1972. *History and Monuments of Ur*. New York: Arno.

Gadd, C.J., L. Legrain, and E. Sollberger, eds. 1928. *Royal Inscriptions*. London: Trustees of the Two Museums.

Gadd, C.J., S.N. Kramer, and A. Shaffer, eds. 1963–2006. *Literary and Religious Texts*. London: Trustees of the Two Museums.

Galpin, F.W. 1929. The Sumerian Harp of Ur. *Music and Letters* 10.2: x.

_____. 1937. *The Music of the Sumerians and Their Immediate Successors, the Babylonians and Assyrians*. Cambridge: Cambridge University Press.

_____. 1980. Babylonian Music. In *Grove's Dictionary of Music*, vol. 1, ed. G. Grove and S. Sadie, 282–3. London: Macmillan.

Gamal, A.S. 1993. The Beginnings of Classical Arabic Poetry. In *Literary Heritage of Classical Islam*, ed. J.A. Bellamy, M. Mir and J.E. Fossum, 41–67. Princeton: Darwin Press.

Gandz, S. 1938. The Algebra of Inheritance: A Rehabilitation of Al-Khuwārizmī. *Osiris* 5: 319–391.

Gätje, H. 1971. Die Gliederung der sprachlichen Zeichen nach al-Fârâbî. *Der Islam* 47: 1–24.

_____. 1985. Arabische Lexikographie: Ein historischer Übersicht. *Historia Linguistica* 12: 105–47.

Gelb, I.J. 1960. Sumerians and Akkadians in Their Ethno-Linguistic Relationship. *Compte rendu Recontre Assyriologique Internationale* 8: 258–271.

_____. 1961. *Old Akkadian Writing and Grammar*. Chicago: University of Chicago Press.

Geller, S. 1979. *Parallelism in Early Biblical Poetry*. Missoula, MT: Scholars.

_____. 1982. The Dynamics of Parallel Verse: A Poetic Analysis of Deut 32:6–12. *Harvard Theological Review* 75: 35–56.

_____. 1983. Review of J. Kugel, The Idea of Biblical Poetry. Parallelism and Its History. *Journal of Biblical Literature* 102: 625–26.

George, Alain. 2003. The Geometry of the Qur'an of Amajur: A Preliminary Study of Proportion in Early Arabic Calligraphy. *Muqarnas* 20: 1–15.

_____. 2010. *The Rise of Islamic Calligraphy*. Berkeley: Saqi.

George, Andrew. 2007. Babylonian and Assyrian: A History of Akkadian. In *Languages of Iraq, Ancient and Modern*, ed. J.N. Postgate, 31–71. London: British School of Archaeology in Iraq.

George, A.R. 1999. What's New in the Gilgamesh Epic? *Bulletin of the Canadian Society for Mesopotamian Studies* 34: 51–58.

_____. 2000. *The Babylonian Gilgamesh Epic—Introduction, Critical Edition and Cuneiform Texts*. 2 vols. New York: Penguin.

George, A.R., and F.N.H. Al-Rawi. 1990. Tablets from the Sippar Library. VII. Three Wisdom Texts. *Iraq* 60: 187–206.

Gershevitch, I. 2008. *The Avestan Hymn to Mithra*. Cambridge: Cambridge University Press.

Ghazzālī, al-. 1995. *Deliverance from Error and Mystical Union with the Almighty = al-Munqiḏ min al-ḍalāl*. Trans. G.F. McLean. Washington, DC: Council for Research in Values and Philosophy.

Ghitani, G. al-, and H. Davies. 2007. *The Mahfouz Dialogs*. Cairo: American University in Cairo Press.

Gibb, H. 1963. *Arabic Literature: An Introduction*. Oxford: Clarendon.

Gibson, J.C.L. 1975. *Syrian Semitic Inscriptions. 2. Aramaic Inscriptions*. Oxford: Oxford University Press.

Giegler, N. 2011. Music: The Work of Professionals. In *The Oxford Handbook of Cuneiform Culture*, ed. K. Radner and E. Robson, 288–312. Oxford: Oxford University Press.

Gilliot, C. 1990. *Exégèse, langue, et théologie en Islam: L'exégèse coranique de Ṭabarî (m. 311/923)*. Paris: J. Vrin.

_____. 2006. Creation of a Fixed Text. In *The Cambridge Companion to the Qur'an*, ed. J.D. McAuliffe, 41–58. Cambridge: Cambridge University Press.

Gimaret, D. 1990. *La doctrine d'al-Ash'ari*. Paris: Cerf.

Ginsberg, H.L. 1970. The Northwest Semitic Languages. In *Patriarchs: World History of the Jewish People*, ed. B. Mazar, 2: 102–24. New Brunswick: Rutgers University Press.

Glassner, J.-J. 2003. *The Invention of Cuneiform: Writing in Sumer*. Trans Z. Bahrani and M. van de Mieroop. Baltimore: Johns Hopkins University Press.

Glassner, R. 2009. *Averroes' Physics: A Turning Point in Medieval Natural Philosophy*. Oxford: Oxford University Press.

Goldziher, I. 1967. Muruwwa and Din'. *Muslim Studies* 1: 11–44.

_____. 1970. *Die Richtungen der islamischen Koranauslegung*. Leiden: Brill.

Golombek, L., and D. Wilber. 1988. *The Timurid Architecture of Iran and Turan*. Princeton: Princeton University Press.

Gordon, R.P., and J.C. de Moor, eds. 2005. *The Old Testament in Its World: Papers Read at the Winter Meeting January 2003, the Society for Old Testament Study and at the Joint Meeting, July 2003, the Society for Old Testament Study and the Oudtestamentisch Werkgezelschap in Nederland en België*. Leiden: Brill.

Gorton, T.J. 1975. The Metre of Ibn Quzman: A "Classical Approach." *Journal of Arabic Literature* 6: 1–29.

Goss, C. 2012. Flutes of Gilgamesh and Ancient Mesopotamia. *Flutopedia*. Accessed January 8, 2012.

Grabar, O. 1973. *The Formation of Islamic Art*. New Haven: Yale University Press.

_____. 1987. The Date and Meaning of Mshatta Dumbarton Oaks Papers. *Studies on Art and Archeology in Honor of Ernst Kitzinger on His Seventy-Fifth Birthday* 41: 243–247.

_____. 1992. *The Mediation of Ornament*. New Haven: Yale University Press.

_____. 1996. *The Shape of the Holy: Early Islamic Jerusalem*. Princeton: Princeton University Press.

_____. 2005. *Constructing the Study of Islamic Art*. 4 vols. Burlington, VT: Ashgate.

_____. 2006a. *The Dome of Rock*. Cambridge, MA: Harvard University Press.

_____. 2006b. *Islamic Art and Beyond*. Burlington, VT: Ashgate.

_____. 2006c. *Islamic Visual Culture, 1100–1800*. Burlington, VT: Ashgate.

Gradenwitz, P. 1996. *The Music of Israel: From the Biblical Era to Modern Times*. Portland, OR: Amadeus.

Grafman, R., and M. Rosen-Ayalon. 1999. The Two Great Syrian Umayyad Mosques: Jerusalem and Damascus. *Muqarnas: An Annual on the Visual Culture of the Islamic World* 16: 1–15.

Graham, W.A. 2006. Recitation and Aesthetic Reception. In *The Cambridge Companion to the Qur'an*, ed. J.D. McAuliffe, 115–144. Cambridge: Cambridge University Press.

Grayson, A.K. 2000. *Assyrian and Babylonian Chronicles*. Winona Lake, IN: Eisenbrauns.

Greundler, B. 2003. *Medieval Arabic Praise Poetry: Ibn al-Rūmī and the Patron's Redemption*. Richmond: Curzon.

_____. 2010. *Medieval Arabic Praise Poetry*. London: Routledge.

Griffel, F. 2009. *Al-Ghazālī's Philosophical Theology*. Oxford: Oxford University Press.

Griffith, S.H. 1997. From Aramaic to Arabic: The Languages of the Monasteries of Palestine in the Byzantine and Early Islamic Periods. *Dumbarton Oaks Papers* 51: 11–31.

Grube, E. 1978. *Persian Painting in the Fourteenth Century: A Research Report*. Napoli: Istituto Orientale di Napoli.

Grundler, B. 1993. *The Development of the Arabic Scripts: From the Nabatean Era to the First Islamic Century According to Dated Texts.* Atlanta, GA: Scholars.

_____. 2003. *Medieval Arabic Praise Poetry: Ibn Al-Rūmī and the Patron's Redemption.* London: Routledge.

Grunebaum, G.E. von. 1942. Pre-Islamic Poetry. *The Moslem World* 32: 147–153.

_____. 1944. Growth and Structure of Arabic Poetry, A.D. 500–1000. In *The Arab Heritage*, ed. N.A. Faris, P.K. Hitti, 121–141. Princeton: Princeton University Press.

_____. 1948. Three Arabic Poets of the Early Abbasid Age (The Collected Fragments of Muṭī' b. Iyās, Salm al-Khāsir and Abū 'š-Šamaqmaq). *Orientalia* 17: 160–204.

_____. 1952. Avicenna's Risâla fī '1-'išq and Courtly Love. *Journal of Near Eastern Studies* 11(4): 233–8.

_____. 1961. *Islam: Essays in the Nature and Growth of a Cultural Tradition.* London: Routledge and Kegan Paul.

_____. 1969. Aspects of Arabic Urban Literature Mostly in the Ninth and Tenth Centuries. *Islamic Studies* 8: 281–300.

Grunebaum, G.E. von, and M.C. Bateson. 1973. Review of Structural Continuity in Poetry: A Linguistic Study in Five Pre-Islamic Arabic Odes. *Language* 49(1): 212–215.

Gruntfest, Y. 1999. The Consecutive Imperfect in Semitic Epigraphy. In *Historical, Epigraphical and Biblical Studies in Honor of Prof. Michael Heltzer*, ed. Y. Avishur and R. Deutsch, 171–189. Tel Aviv: Archaeological Center Publications.

Guillaume, A. 1968. *Studies in the Book of Job.* Leiden: Brill.

Gully, A. 1995. *Grammar and Semantics in Medieval Arabic: A Study of Ibn-Hisham's "Mughni 1-Labib."* Richmond: Curzon.

_____. 2008. *The Culture of Letter-Writing in Pre-Modern Islamic Society.* Edinburgh: Edinburgh University Press.

Gunther, S. 2005. *Ideas, Images, and Methods of Portrayal: Insights into Classical Arabic Literature and Islam.* Leiden: Brill.

Gurney, O.R. 1968. An Old Babylonian Treatise on the Tuning of the Harp. *Iraq* 30: 229–233.

_____. 1994. Babylonian Music Again. *Iraq* 56: 101–106.

Gutas, D. 1988. *Avicenna and the Aristotelian Tradition: Introduction to Reading Avicenna's Philosophical Works.* Leiden: Brill.

_____. 1998. *Greek Thought, Arabic Culture: The Graeco-Arabic Translation Movement in Baghdad and Early Abb Asid Society (2nd–4th/8th–10th Centuries).* New York: Routledge.

Gütterbock, H. 1970. Musical Notation in Ugarit. *Revue d'assyriologie et d'archéologie orientale* 64(1): 45–52.

Haeri, N. 2003. *Sacred Language, Ordinary People: Dilemmas of Culture and Politics in Egypt.* New York: Palgrave Macmillan.

Hakim, T. al-. 1966. *Bird of the East.* Trans. B. Winder. Beirut: Khayats.

_____. 1985. *The Return of Consciousness.* Trans. B. Winder. Basingstoke: Macmillan.

_____. 1989. *The Maze of Justice: Diary of a Country Prosecutor.* Trans. A. Eban. Austin: University of Texas Press.

_____. 2008. *The Essential Tawfiq al-Hakim: Plays, Fiction, Autobiography.* Cairo: American University in Cairo Press.

_____. 2012. *Return of the Spirit.* Trans. W. Mhutchins. Boulder, CO: Lynne Rienner.

Hall, M.D. 1985. "A Study of Sumerian Moon God Nanna/Suen." PhD dissertation, University of Pennsylvania.

Hallaq, W.B. 1985–1986. The Logic of Legal Reasoning in Religious and Non-Religious Cultures: The Case of Islamic Law and the Common Law. *Cleveland State Law Review* 34: 79–96.

_____. 1993. *Ibn Taymiyya Against the Greek Logicians.* Oxford: Oxford University Press.

_____. 1999a. The Authenticity of Prophetic Hadîth: A Pseudo-Problem. *Studia Islamica* (89): 75–90.

_____. 1999b. *A History of Islamic Legal Theories: An Introduction to Sunnī Uṣūl Al-fiqh.* Cambridge: Cambridge University Press.

_____. 2004. *The Formation of Islamic Law.* Burlington, VT: Ashgate/Variorum.

_____. 2005. *The Origins and Evolution of Islamic Law.* Cambridge: Cambridge University Press.

Hallo, W.W. 1968. Individual Prayer in Sumerian: The Continuity of a Tradition. *Journal of the American Oriental Society* 88: 71–89.

_____. 1970. The Cultic Setting of Sumerian Poetry. In *Publications de Comité belge de recherches historiques, épigraphiques et archéologiques en Mésopotamie*, vol. 1, ed. A. Finet. Ham-sur-Heure: Comité belge de recherches en Mésopotamie.

_____. 1975. Another Sumerian Literary Catalogue. *Studia Orientalia* 46: 77–80.

_____. 1982. Notes from the Babylonian Collection, II. *Journal of Cuneiform Studies* 34: 81–89.

_____. 1983. Lugalbanda Excavated. *Journal of the American Oriental Society* 103: 165–180.

_____. 1987. The Birth of Kings. In *Love and Death in the Ancient Near East: Essays in Honor of Marvin H. Pope*, ed. J.H. Marks and R.M. Good, 45–52. Guilford: Four Quarters.

_____. 1997. Sumerian Canonical Compositions. A. Divine Focus. 1. Myths: The Exaltation of Inanna; 2. Hymns: The Blessing of Nisaba by Enki (1.1.63) (NIN-MUL-AN-GIM). In *The Context of Scripture*, 1: *Canonical Compositions from the Biblical World*, ed. W.W. Hallo, 518–522, 531–532. Leiden: Brill.

———. 1997–2003. *The Context of Scripture.* 3 vols. Leiden: Brill.

Hamadhani, B.Z. al-. 2002. *Maqāmaāt Badī' al-Zamān al-Hamadhānī.* Bayrut: Dar al-Kutub al-'Ilmiyah.

Hamblin, W., and D. Seely. 2007. *Solomon's Temple: Myth and History.* London: Thames and Hudson.

Hamdani, H. ibn Hamad, and N.A. Faris. 1938. *The Antiquities of South Arabia.* Princeton: Princeton University Library.

Hameen-Anttila, J. 2002. *Maqama: A History of a Genre.* Wiesbaden: Harrassowitz.

Hamilton, G.J. 2006. *The Origins of the West Semitic Alphabet in Egyptian Scripts.* Washington, DC: Catholic Biblical Association.

Hamilton, R.W., and O. Grabar. 1959. *Khirbat al Mafjar: An Arabian Mansion in the Jordan Valley.* Oxford: Clarendon.

———. 1969. Who Built Khirbet Al-Mafjar? *Levant* 1: 61–67.

———. 1978. Khirbet al-Mafjar: The Bath Hall Reconsidered. *Levant* 10: 126–38.

Hammarlund, A., and T. Olsson, eds. 1999. *Sufism, Music and Society in Turkey and the Middle East.* Richmond: Curzon.

Hammond, M. 2008. *Transforming Loss into Beauty: Essays on Arabic Literature and Culture in Honor of Magda Al-Nowaihi.* Cairo: American University in Cairo Press.

———. 2010. *Beyond Elegy: Classical Arabic Women's Poetry in Context.* Oxford: Oxford University Press.

Hamori, A. 1969. Convention in the Poetry of Abū Nuwās. *Studia Islamica* 30: 5–26.

———. 1971. An Allegory from the Arabian Nights: The City of Brass. *Bulletin of the School of Oriental and African Studies* 34(1): 9–19.

———. 1974. *On the Art of Medieval Arabic Literature.* Princeton: Princeton University Press.

———. 1977. Form and Logic in Some Medieval Poems. *Edebiyât* 2(1): 63–72.

———. 1992. *The Composition of Mutanabbī's Panegyrics to Sayf al-Dawla.* Leiden: Brill.

Hanna, S.A., and N. Greis. 1972. *Writing Arabic: A Linguistic Approach, from Sounds to Script.* Leiden: Brill.

Harīrī, A.S. 1980. *The Assemblies of Al-Harīrī: Fifty Encounters*, ed. A. Shah. London: Octagon.

Hasan, M.R. 1974. *Athar al-maqāmā fī nash'at al 'qissah al-Misriyyah al-Hadīthah.* Cairo: Al-Hay'ah al-Misriyyah al-'āmmah li-al-kitab.

Hashmi, A. 1986. *The Worlds of Muslim Imagination.* Islamabad: Gulmohar.

Hasse, D.N., and A. Bertolacci. 2011. *The Arabic, Hebrew and Latin Reception of Avicenna's Metaphysics.* Berlin: De Gruyter.

Haydar, A. 1989. The Development of Lebanese Zajal: Genre, Meter, and Verbal Duel. *Oral Tradition* Fall: 159–212.

Hayes, J.L. 2000. *A Manual of Sumerian Grammar and Texts.* Malibu: Undena.

Haywood, J. 1971. *Modern Arabic Literature 1800–1970.* London: Lund Humphries.

Haywood, J.A. 1965. *Arabic Lexicography: Its History and Its Place in the General History of Lexicography.* Leiden: Brill.

Haywood, N. 1965. *A New Arabic Grammar.* London: Lund Humphries.

Hazen, Ibn al-Haytham al-. 1990. *Ibn al-Haytham's on the Configuration of the World.* Trans. Y.T. Langermann. New York: Garland.

Healey, J.F. 1990. *The Early Alphabet.* Berkeley: University of California Press.

———. 1993. *The Nabataean Tomb Inscriptions of Mada'in Salih: With an Arabic Section.* Oxford: Oxford University Press.

———. 2009. *Aramaic Inscriptions and Documents of the Roman Period.* Oxford: Oxford University Press.

Heath, P. 1992. *Allegory and Philosophy in Avicenna (Ibn Sina).* Philadelphia: University of Pennsylvania Press.

Heidel, A. 1963. *The Gilgamesh Epic and Old Testament Parallels.* Chicago: University of Chicago Press.

Heimpel, W. 1970. *Observations on Rhythmical Structure in Sumerian Literary Texts.* Roma: Pontificium Institutum Biblicum.

Heinle, E., and J. Schlaich. 1996. *Kuppeln aller Zeiten, aller Kulturen.* Stuttgart: Verlagsanstalt.

Heinrichs, W. 1997. The Etymology of Muqarnas: Some Observations. In *Humanism, Culture and Language in the Near East*, ed. G. Krotkoff, A. Afsaruddin, and A.H. M. Zahniser, 175–184. Winona Lake, IN: Eisenbrauns.

Hellyer, P. 1998. *Hidden Riches: An Archaeological Introduction to the United Arab Emirates.* Abu Dhabi: Union National Bank.

Helms, S., A.V.G.W. Betts, F. Lancaster, and C.J. Lenzen. 1990. *Early Islamic Architecture of the Desert: A Bedouin Station in Eastern Jordan.* Edinburgh: Edinburgh University Press.

Henning, W.B. 1933. Geburt und Entsendung des manichäischen Urmenschen. *Nachrichten der Gesellschaft der Wissenschaften zu Göttingen*: 306–318.

_____. 1942. The Disintegration of the Avestic Studies. *Transactions of the Philological Society*: 40–56.

_____. 1950. A Pahlavi Poem. *Bulletin of the School of Oriental and African Studies (BSOAS)* 13: 641–48.

_____. 1971. Pahlavi, pârsi, dari: les langues de l'Iran d'après Ibn al-Muqaffa. In *Iran and Islam in Memory of the Late V. Minorsky*, ed. C.E. Bosworth, 361–391. Edinburgh: Cop.

_____. 1975. The Rise of the New Persian language. In *The Cambridge History of Iran IV*, ed. R.N. Frye, 595–632. Cambridge: Cambridge University Press.

_____. 2001. La versification d'un poème pehlevi. In *Tafazzoli Memorial Volume*, ed. A.A. Sadeghi, 39–47. Tehran: Sokhan.

_____. 2002. Encore la versification pehlevie. *Jerusalem Studies in Arabic and Islam* 26: 130–139.

_____. 2002–2003. Le mètre du Draxt asûrîg. *Orientalia suecana* 51–52: 327–36.

_____. 2003. La versification d'un hymne manichéen en parthe. In *Religious Themes and Texts of Pre-Islamic Iran and Central Asia*, ed. C.G. Cereti, M. Maggi, E. Provasi and G. Gnoli, 223–30. Wiesbaden: Reichert.

Hepokoski, J.A., and W. Darcy. 2006. *Elements of Sonata Theory: Norms, Types, and Deformations in the Late Eighteenth-Century Sonata*. Oxford: Oxford University Press.

Hesk, I. 1994. *Passport to Jewish Music: Its History, Traditions, and Culture*. Westport, CT: Greenwood.

Hetzron, R. 1987. Semitic Languages. In *The World's Major Languages*, ed. B. Comrie, 654–663. New York: Oxford University Press.

Hetzron, R., ed. 1997. *The Semitic Languages*. London: Routledge.

Hickerman, E. 1988. *The Archaeology of Early Music Cultures*. Bonn: Verlag für systematische Musikwissenschaft.

_____. 2000. *Studien zur Musikarchäologie*, vol. 2. Rahden: Verlag Marie Leidorf.

Hill, D.R. 1993. *Islamic Science and Engineering*. Edinburgh: Edinburgh University Press.

Hillenbrand, R. 1992. "The Ornament of the World": Medieval Córdoba as a Cultural Centre. In *The Legacy of Muslim Spain*, ed. S.K. Jayyusi, 112–128. Leiden: Brill.

_____. 1994. *Islamic Architecture: Form, Function, and Meaning*. New York: Columbia University Press.

_____. 1999. *Islamic Art and Architecture*. London: Thames and Hudson.

_____. 2000. *Persian Painting: From the Mongols to the Qajars: Studies in Honour of Basil W. Robinson*. New York: I.B. Tauris

in Association with the Centre of Middle Eastern Studies, University of Cambridge.

_____. 2003. Studying Islamic Architecture: Challenges and Perspectives. *Architectural History* 46: 1–18.

Hillman, M.C. 1971. Sound and Sense in Ghazal of Hafiz. *Muslim World* 61: 11–21.

_____. 1972. Hafiz and Poetic Unity Through Verse Rhythms. *Journal of Near Eastern Studies* 31: 1–10.

_____. 1976. *Unity in the Ghazals of Hafez*. Minneapolis: Bibliotheca Islamica.

_____. 2007. *Persian Vocabulary Acquisition: An Intermediate Reader and Guide to Word Forms and the Arabic Element in Persian*. Hyattsville, MD: Dunwoody.

Hoag, J.D. 1975. *Islamic Architecture*. New York: H.N. Abrams.

Hochberg, G.Z. 2007. *In Spite of Partition: Jews, Arabs, and the Limits of Separatist Imagination*. Princeton: Princeton University Press.

Hock, H.H., and B.D. Joseph. 1996. *Language History, Language Change, and Language Relationship: An Introduction to Historical and Comparative Linguistics*. New York: Mouton de Gruyter.

Hoexter, M., S.N. Eisenstadt, and N. Levtzion, eds. 2000. *The Public Sphere in Muslim Societies*. Albany: State University of New York Press.

Hoffman, J.M. 2004. *In the Beginning: A Short History of the Hebrew Language*. New York: New York University Press.

Holes, C. 1995. *Modern Arabic: Structures, Functions and Varieties*. London: Longman.

_____. 2004. *Modern Arabic: Structures, Functions, and Varieties*. Washington, DC: Georgetown University Press.

Homayoonfarrokh, R. 1992. *History of Persian Poetry*. In Persian. Tehran: Elm.

Homerin, Th.E. 2001a. *From Arab Poet to Muslim Saint: Ibn Al-Fāriḍ, His Verse, and His Shrine*. Cairo: American University in Cairo Press.

_____. 2001b. *'Umar ibn al-Farid: Sufi Verse, Saintly Life*. New York: Paulist.

_____. 2011. *Passion Before Me, My Fate Behind: Ibn al-Farid and the Poetry of Recollection*. Alberny: State University of New York Press.

Horowitz, W., and W.G. Lambert. 2002. A New Exemplar of Ludlul Bēl Nēmeqi Tablet I from Birmingham. *Iraq* 64: 237–245.

Hourani, G. 2007. *Reason and Tradition in Islamic Ethics*. Cambridge: Cambridge University Press.

Hoyland, R.G. 2001. *Arabia and the Arabs: From the Bronze Age to the Coming of Islam*. New York: Routledge.

Huda, Q. 2003. *Striving for Divine Union:*

Spiritual Exercises for Suhrawardi Sufis. London: RoutledgeCurzon.

Huehnergard, J. 1996. New Directions in the Study of Semitic Languages. In *The Study of the Ancient Near East in the Twenty-First Century*, ed. J.S. Cooper and G.M. Schwartz, 251–272. Winona Lake, IN: Eisenbrauns.

_____. 1998. *Grammar of Akkadian.* Atlanta, GA: Scholars.

_____. 2005. *A Key to a Grammar of Akkadian.* Harvard Semitic Studies. Eisenbrauns.

Huehnergard, J., and J.A. Hackett. 2002. The Hebrew and Aramaic Languages. In *The Biblical World* vol. 2, ed. J. Barton, 3–24. London: Routledge.

Huff, T.E. 2003. *The Rise of Early Modern Science: Islam, China, and the West.* Cambridge: Cambridge University Press.

Humbach, H. 1991. *The Gathas of Zarathustra and Other Old Avestan Texts.* 2 vols. Heidelberg: Carl Winter.

Humbert, G. 1995. *Les voies de la transmission du Kitāb de Sîbawayhi.* Leiden: Brill.

Hurvitz, A. 1972. *Biblical Hebrew in Transition: A Study in Post-Exilic and Its Implications for the Dating of the Psalms.* Jerusalem: Bialik.

_____. 2003. [*ro'sh-davar*] and [*sôp dabar*]: Reflexes of Two Scribal Terms Imported into Biblical Hebrew from the Imperial Aramaic Formulary. In *Hamlet on a Hill: Semitic and Greek Studies*, ed. M.F.J. Baasten and W. Th. van Peursen, 281–286. Leuven: Peeters.

Hussin, A. 2006. Towards a Literary and Historical Study of the Old Qasida in Al-Yamama. *Mélanges de l'Université Saint-Joseph* 59: 97–143.

_____. 2008. The *Naqā'iḍ* Poetry in the Age of Its Florescence and Towards Its Eclipse. *Jerusalem Studies in Arabic and Islam* 34: 499–528.

_____. 2009. *The Lightening Scene in Ancient Arabic Poetry.* Wiesbaden: Otto Harrasowitz Verlag.

Ibn al-'Arabī. 2002–2004. *The Meccan Revelations.* Trans. M. Chodkiewicz, W.C. Chittick, et al. New York: Pir.

Ibn al-Farid, U. 2001. '*Umar ibn al-Farid: Sufi Verse, Saintly Life.* Trans. Th.E. Homerin. New York: Paulist.

Ibn al-Jazari. 2007. *Asānīd ibn al-Jazarī al-Imām ilā Khayr al-Anām Bi Riwāyah Hafs ibn Sulaymān.* Western Cape, South Africa: Madbūt Writers and Translators.

Ibn Khaldūn. 2005. *The Muqaddimah: An Introduction to History.* Trans. F. Rosenthal. 3 vols. Princeton: Princeton University Press.

Imamuddin, S.M. 1981. *Muslim Spain.* Leiden: Brill.

Imr' al-Qays. 1984. *Diwan lmr' al-Qays*, ed. Abu al-Fadl Ibrahim. Cairo: Dar al-Ma'arif.

Irwin, R. 2005. *The Arabian Nights: A Companion.* London: Tauris Parke.

Isaksson, B. 1989–1990. The Position of Ugaritic Among the Semitic Languages. *Orientalia Suecana* 38–39: 54–70.

Iskenderoglu, M. 2002. *Fakhr al-Din al-Rāzī and Thomas Aquinas on the Question of the Eternity of the World.* Boston: Brill.

Jacobi, R. 1982. The Camel-Section of the Panegyrical Ode. *Journal of Arabic Literature* 13: 122.

_____. 1984. Die Anfänge der arabischen Ġazalpoesie: Abū Du'aib alHudalī. *Der Islam* 61: 218–50.

_____. 1985. Time and Reality in Nasīb and Ghazal. *Journal of Arabic Literature* 16: 1–17.

_____. 1992. Theme and Variations in Umayyad Ghazal Poetry. *Journal of Arabic Literature* 23(2): 109–19.

_____. 1994. Zur Ġazalpoesie des Walids Ibn Yazīd. In *Festschrift Ewald Wagner zum 65, Geburtstag*, vol. 2: *Studien zur Arabischen Dichtung*, ed. W. Heinrichs and G. Schoeler, 145–161. Stuttgart: Steiner.

_____. 1996. The Origins of the Qasida Form. In *Qasida Poetry in Islamic Asia and Africa*, vol. 1: *Classical Traditions and Modern Meanings*, ed. S. Stefan and S. Christopher, 21–34. Leiden: Brill.

Jacobsen, J. 2002. *Chanting the Hebrew Bible: The Art of Cantillation.* Philadelphia: Jewish Publication Society.

Jacobsen, T. 1987a. *The Harps That Once—: Sumerian Poetry in Translation.* New Haven: Yale University Press.

_____. 1987b. Pictures and Pictorial Language. In *Figurative Language in the Ancient Near East*, ed. M. Mindlin, M.J. Geller, and J.E. Wansbrough, 1–13. London: School of Oriental and African Studies, University of London.

_____. 1997. *The Harps That Once: Sumerian Poetry in Translation.* New Haven: Yale University Press.

Jairazbhoy, R.A. 1962. The History of the Shrines at Mecca and Medina. *Islamic Culture* 1: 1–23.

Jamal, M. 2009. *Islamic Mystical Poetry: Sufi Verse from the Mystics to Rumi.* New York: Penguin.

James, D. 1974. Space-Forms in the Work of the Baghdād "Maqāmāt" Illustrators, 1225–58. *Bulletin of the School of Oriental and African Studies* (London) 37(2): 305–320.

Jamil, N. 1999. Caliph and Qutb. In *Bayt al-Maqdis*, vol. 2: *Jerusalem and Early Islam*, ed. J. Raby and J. Johns, 11–58. Oxford: Oxford University Press.

Jastrow, M., and A.T. Clay. 1920. *An Old Babylonian Version of the Gilgamesh Epic on the Basis of Recently Discovered Texts.* New Haven: Yale University Press.

Jayyusi, S.K. 1977. *Trends and Movements in Modern Arabic Poetry.* Leiden: Brill.

———. 1987. *Modern Arabic Poetry.* New York: Columbia University Press.

———. 1996. Persistence of the Qaṣīda Form. In *Qasida Poetry in Islamic Asia and Africa,* vol. 1: *Classical Traditions and Modern Meanings,* ed. S. Sperl and C. Shakle, 1–20. Leiden: Brill.

———. 2006. Arabic Poetry in the Post-Classical Age. In *The Cambridge History of Arabic Literature,* ed. R. Allen and D.S. Richards, 25–59. MA: Cambridge University Press.

Jayyusi, S.K., ed. 1987. *Modern Arabic Poetry: An Anthology.* New York: Columbia University Press.

———. 1988. *The Literature of Modern Arabia: An Anthology.* New York: Kegan Paul.

———. 1992–94. *The Legacy of Muslim Spain.* 2 vols. Leiden: Brill.

———. 2010. *Classical Arabic Stories.* New York: Columbia University Press.

Jayyusi, S.K., and A. Roger, eds. 1995. *Modern Arabic Drama: An Anthology.* Bloomington: Indiana University Press.

Jeffers, A. 1996. *Magic and Divination in Ancient Palestine and Syria.* Leiden: Brill.

Jensen, H. 1969. *Sign, Symbol, and Script.* London: George Allen and Unwin.

Johns, J. 1999. The "House of the Prophet" and the Concept of the Mosque. In *Bayt al-Maqdis. Jerusalem and Early Islam,* ed. J. Johns, 59–112. Oxford: Oxford University Press.

Johnson-Davies, D. 2008. *The Essential Tawfiq al-Hakim: Plays, Fiction, Autobiography.* Cairo: American University in Cairo Press.

Johnstone, T.M. 1972. Nasīb and Mansöngur. *Journal of Arabic Literature* 3: 90–95.

Jones, A. 1987. *Romance Kharjas in Andalusian Arabic Muwassah Poetry: A Palaeographic Analysis.* London: Ithaca.

———. 1991a. Final Taḍmīn in the Poems of Abū Nuwās. In *Arabicus Felix,* ed. A.F.L. Beeston and A. Jones, 61–73. Reading: Ithaca.

———. 1991b. Studies on the Muwashshah and the Kharja. In *Proceedings of the Exeter International Colloquium,* ed. A. Jones et al. Reading: Ithaca.

———. 1992. *Marathi and ṣu'luk Poems.* Reading: Ithaca.

———. 1992–1996. *Early Arabic Poetry.* 2 vols. Reading: Ithaca.

———. 1996. The Prose Literature of Pre-Islamic Arabia. In *Tradition and Modernity in Arabic Language and Literature,* ed. J.R. Smart, 229–241. Richmond (Surrey): Curzon.

———. 1997. The Qur'an in the Light of Earlier Arabic Prose. In *University Lectures in Islamic Studies,* ed. A Jones, 67–83. London: Altajir World of Islam Trust.

Jones, A., and R. Hitchcock. 1991. *Studies on the Muwassah and the Kharja: Proceedings of the Exeter International Colloquium.* Reading: Published by Ithaca for the Board of the Faculty of Oriental Studies, Oxford University.

Kafescioglu, C. 2009. *Constantinopolis/Istanbul: Cultural Encounter, Imperial Vision, and the Construction of the Ottoman Capital.* University Park: Pennsylvania State University Press.

Kanazi G. 1989. *Studies in the Kitāb a'-'inā'atayn of Abū Hilāl al-'Askarī.* Leiden: Brill.

Kaplan, R.B., and R.B. Baldauf. 2007. *Language Planning and Policy in Africa.* Clevedon, UK: Multilingual Matters.

Karamustafa, A.K. 2007. *Sufism: The Formative Period.* Berkeley: University of California Press.

Katib, A.H. al-. 1983. The Beginnings of Arabic Prose: Epistolary Genre. In *Arabic Literature to the End of the Umayyad Period,* ed. A.F.L. Beeston et al., 154–179. Cambridge: Cambridge University Press.

Katsumata, N. 2002. The Style of the *Maqāmā*: Arabic, Persian, Hebrew, Syriac. *Arabic and Middle Eastern Literatures* 5(2): 117–37.

Katz, V.J. 1995. Ideas of Calculus in Islam and India. *Mathematics Magazine* 68(3): 163–74.

———. 1998. *A History of Mathematics: An Introduction.* Reading, MA: Addison-Wesley.

Kaye, A.S. 1987. Arabic. In *The World's Major Languages,* ed. B. Comrie, 664–685. New York: Oxford University Press.

———. 1991. The Hamzat al-Waṣl in Contemporary Modern Standard Arabic. *Journal of the American Oriental Society* 111(3): 572–574.

Kemal, S. 2003. *The Philosophical Poetics of Alfarabi, Avicenna and Averroes: The Aristotelian Reception.* London: RoutledgeCurzon.

Kennedy, P.F. 1989. Khamr and Ḥikma in Jāilī Poetry. *Journal of Arabic Literature* 20/2: 97–114.

———. 1991a. Labīd, al-Nābigha, al-Akhṭal and the Oryx. In *Arabicus Felix,* ed. A.F.L. Beeston and A. Jones, 74–89. Reading: Ithaca.

———. 1991b. Thematic Patterning in the

Muwaššaḥāt: The Case of the Gazelle Motif. In *Poesía Estrófica*, ed. F. Corriente and A. Saenz-Badillos, 201–16. Madrid: Instituto de Cooperación con edl Mundo Arabe.

———. 1994. Perspectives of a *hamriyya*. In *Festschrift Ewald Wagner zum 65, Geburtstag*, vol. 2: *Studien zur Arabiscben Dicbtung*, ed. W. Heinrichs and G. Schoeler, 258–76. Beirut: Orient-Institut der Deutschen Morgenländischen Gesellschaft.

———. 1997. *The Wine Song in Classical Arabic Poetry: Abu Nuwas and the Literary Tradition*. Oxford: Clarendon.

———. 2005. *Abu Nuwas: A Genius of Poetry*. Oxford: Oneorld.

Khalifah, A.M. al-S. 2010. *Al-Fukāhah fī Maqāmāt Badī' al-Zamān al-Hamadhānī: dirāsah taḥlīlīyah*. Alexandria: Dar al-Wafa' li-Dunya al-Ṭiba'ah wa-al-Nashr.

Khanafānī, G. 1999. *Men in the Sun and Other Palestinian Stories*. Trans. H. Kilpatrick. Boulder, CO: Lynne Rienner.

———. 2004. *All That's Left to You*. Trans. R. Allen, M. Jayyusi, and J. Reed. Northampton, MA: Interlink World Fiction.

Khansā', R.A. 1973. *Diwan al Khansa*. Trans. A. Wormhoudt. Oskaloosa, IW: William Penn College.

Kho'I, Abu al-Qasem al-. 1998. *The Prolegomena to the Qur'an*. Trans. A.A. Sachedina. New York: Oxford University Press.

Khouri, R. 1990. Qasr'Amra. *Saudi Aramco World* 41(5): 33.

Khoury, E. 2007a. *Little Mountain*. New York: Picador.

———. 2007b. *Gate of the Sun*. New York: Picador.

Khoury, N.N. 1992. The Mihrab Image: Commemorative Themes in Medieval Islamic Architecture. *Muqarnas* 9: 11–28.

———. 1993. The Dome of the Rock, the Ka'ba, and Ghumdan: Arab Myths and Umayyad Monuments. *Muqarnas* 10: 57–65.

Kienast, B., and I.J. Gelb. 1990. *Die Altakkadischen Königsinschriften des dritten Jahrtausends v. Chr.* Stuttgart: F. Steiner.

Kilmer, A.D. 1959. The String of Musical Instruments: Their Names, Numbers, and Significance. *Studies in Honor of Benno Landsberger, Assyriological Studies* (16): 261–268.

———. 1971. The Discovery of an Ancient Mesopotamian Theory of Music. *Proceedings of the American Philosophical Society* 115: 131–49.

———. 1974. The Cult Song with Music from Ancient Ugarit: Another Interpretation. *Revue d'Assyriologie* 68: 69–82.

———. 1996. Old Babylonian Music Instruction Texts. *Journal of Cuneiform Studies* 48: 49–56.

———. 1997. Musik, A: Philologisch. In *Reallexikon der Assyriologie und vorderasiatischen Archäologie* 8, ed. D.O. Edzard, 463–82. Berlin: De Gruyter.

———. 1998a. Correction to Kilmer/Tinney "Old Babylonian Music Instruction Texts," *Journal of Cuneiform Studies*, 50: 118.

———. 1998b. The Musical Instruments from Ur and Ancient Mesopotamian Music. *Expedition* 40(2): 12–19.

———. 2000. Continuity and Change in Ancient Mesopotamian Terminology for Music and Musical Instruments. In *Studien zur Musikarcheologie, Orient-Archäologie*, 7. Rahden/Westf.: M. Leidorf.

———. 2001. Mesopotamia §8(ii). In *The New Grove Dictionary of Music and Musicians*, ed. S. Sadie and J. Tyrrell. London: Macmillan.

———. 2002. Die musikalische Ausformung von Tonalität und Genre in Mesopotamian [Modal music, tonality and genre in Mesopotamian musical performance]. In *Studien zur Musikarchaologie* III, ed. E. Hickmann; R. Eichmann, and A.D. Kilmer, 481–486. Rahden/Westf.: M. Leidorf.

———. 2007. Music in Ancient Mesopotamia. In *Sounds of Ancient Music*, ed. J.C. Linsider and F. Skolnik, 24–37. Jerusalem: Bible Lands Museum.

———. 2009. More Old Babylonian Music-Instruction Fragments from Nippur. *Journal of Cuneiform Studies* 61: 93–96.

Kilmer, A.D., and M. Civil. 1986. Old Babylonian Musical Instructions Relating to Hymnody. *Journal of Cuneiform Studies* 38(1): 94–98.

Kilmer, A.D., R.L. Crocker, and R.R. Brown. 1976. *Sounds from Silence: Recent Discoveries in Ancient Near Eastern Music*. Berkeley: Bit Enki.

Kilpatrick, H. 1976. Tradition and Innovation in the Fiction of Ghassān Kanafānī. *Journal of Arabic Literature* (7): 53–64.

———. 1992. The Egyptian Novel from Zaynab to 1980. In *Modern Arabic Literature*, ed. M.M. Badawi, 223–269. Cambridge: Cambridge University Press.

King, D.A. 2005. *In Synchrony with the Heavens, Studies in Astronomical Timekeeping and Instrumentation in Medieval Islamic Civilization: Instruments of Mass Calculation*. Leiden: Brill.

Klein, J. 1981a. *Three Shulgi Hymns. Sumerian Royal Hymns Glorifying King Shulgi of Ur*. Ramat-Gan: Bar Ilan University Press.

———. 1981b. *The Royal Hymns of Shulgi King of Ur: Man's Quest for Immortal Fame*. Philadelphia: American Philosophical Society.

_____. 1982. "Personal God" and Individual Prayer in Sumerian Religion. *Archiv für Orientforschung Beiheft* 19: 295–306.

_____. 1983. The Capture of Akka by Gilgamesh (GA 81 and 99*). Journal of the American Oriental Society* 103: 201–203.

_____. 1986. On Writing Monumental Inscriptions in Ur III Scribal Curriculum. *Revue d'assyriologie et d'archéologie orientale* 80: 1–7.

_____. 1997a. The God Martu in Sumerian Literature. In *Sumerian Gods and Their Representation*, ed. I.J. Finkel and M.J. Geller, 99–116. Groningen: Styx.

_____. 1997b. Sumerian Canonical Compositions. A. Divine Focus. 4. Lamentations: Lamentation Over the Destruction of Sumer and Ur (1.166). In *The Context of Scripture*, vol. 1: *Canonical Compositions from the Biblical World*, ed. W.W. Hallo, 535–539. Leiden: Brill.

_____. 1997c. Sumerian Canonical Compositions. A. Divine Focus. 1. Myths: Enki and Ninmah (1.159*).* In *The Context of Scripture*, vol. 1: *Canonical Compositions from the Biblical World*, ed. W.W. Hallo, 516–522. Leiden: Brill.

Klein-Frank, F. 2001. *Al-Kindi: History of Islamic Philosophy, ed.* O. Leaman and H. Nasr. London: Routledge.

Kogan, L., and A. Korotayev. 1997. *Sayhadic Languages (Epigraphic South Arabian). Semitic Languages.* London: Routledge.

Kojaman, Y. 2001. *The Maqam Music Tradition of Iraq.* London: Y. Kojaman.

Kovacs, M.G. 1989. *The Epic of Gilgamesh.* Stanford: Stanford University Press.

Kramer, S.N. 1940. *Lamentation Over the Destruction of Ur.* Chicago: Chicago University Press.

_____. 1942. The Oldest Literary Catalogue. A Sumerian List of Literary Compositions Compiled About 2000 B.C. *Bulletin of the American Schools of Oriental Research* 88: 10–19.

_____. 1944a. The Death of Gilgamesh. *Bulletin of the American Schools of Oriental Research* 94: 2–12.

_____. 1944b. *Sumerian Mythology.* Philadelphia: American Philosophical Society.

_____. 1944c. *Sumerian Literary Texts from Nippur in the Museum of the Ancient Orient at Istanbul.* New Haven: American Schools of Oriental Research.

_____. 1949. Gilgamesh and Akka. *American Journal of Archaeology* 53: 1–18.

_____. 1952. Five New Sumerian Literary Texts. *Belleten* 16: 345–365.

_____. 1955. Man and His God: A Sumerian Variation on the "Job" Motif. In *Wisdom in Israel and in the Ancient Near East*, ed. M.

Noth and D.W. Thomas, 170–182. Leiden: Brill.

_____. 1963a. Cuneiform Studies and the History of Literature: The Sumerian Sacred Marriage Texts. *Proceedings of the American Philosophical Society* 107: 485–527.

_____. 1963.b *The Sumerians*. Chicago: University of Chicago Press.

_____. 1969a. Sumerian Hymns. In *Ancient Near Eastern Texts Relating to the Old Testament*, ed. J.B. Pritchard, 573–586. Princeton: Princeton University Press.

_____. 1969b. Sumerian Lamentation. In *Ancient Near Eastern Texts Relating to the Old Testament*, ed. J.B. Pritchard, 611–619. Princeton: Princeton University Press.

_____. 1969c. Inanna and Shulgi: A Sumerian Fertility Song. *Iraq* 31: 18–23.

_____. 1989. BM 100042: A Hymn to Shu-Sin and an Adab of Nergal. In *DUMU-E2-DUB-BA-A*, ed. H. Behrens, D. Loding, and M.T. Roth, 303–316. Philadelphia: University Museum, Philadelphia.

Korotayev, A. 1995. *Ancient Yemen*. Oxford: Oxford University Press.

_____. 1996. *Pre-Islamic Yemen: Socio-Political Organization of the Sabaean Cultural Area in the 2nd and 3rd Centuries* A.D. Wiesbaden: Harrassowitz.

Kovacs, M.G. 1989. *The Epic of Gilgamesh.* Stanford: Stanford University Press.

Kramer, M. 1991. *Middle Eastern Lives: The Practice of Biography and Self-Narrative.* Syracuse: Syracuse University Press.

Kramer, S.N. 1944. *Sumerian Literary Texts from Nippur in the Museum of Istanbul.* New Haven, CT: Yale University Press.

_____. 1963. *The Sumerians: Their History, Culture and Character*. Chicago: University of Chicago Press.

Kramer, S.N., and J.R. Maier. 1989. *Myths of Enki, the Crafty God.* Oxford: Oxford University Press.

Krautheimer, R. 1986. *Early Christian and Byzantine Architecture.* New Haven: Yale University Press.

Krispijn, T.J.H. 1990. Beitrage zur altorientalischen Musikforschung. 1. Sulgi und die Musik [Contributions to Ancient Oriental Music Research. First Shulgi and the music]. *Akkadica* 70: 1–27.

_____. 2008a. Music in School and Temple in the Ancient Near East. In *What Was Old Is New Again—A Meeting of Art and Scholarship*, 14–17. ZKM Center for Art and Technology, November 21–23. Karlsruhe, Germany.

_____. 2008b. Music and Healing for Someone Far Away from Home HS 1556, A Remarkable Ur III Incantation Revisited. In *Studies in Ancient Near Eastern World View and Society*, ed. R.J. van der Spek, 173–194. Bethesda: CDL.

_____. 2008c. Musical Ensembles in Ancient Mesopotamia. In *Proceedings of the International Conference of Near Eastern Archaeomusicology (ICONEA)*, ed. R.J. Dumbrill, 125–150. British Museum, December 4–6.

_____. 2009. The Old Babylonian Tuning Text UET VI/3 899. *Iraq* 71: 43.

Kselman, J.S. 1975. Psalm 72: Some Observations on Structure. *Bulletin of the American Schools of Oriental Research* 220: 77–81.

_____. 1977. Semantic-Sonant Chiasmus in Biblical Poetry. *Biblica* 58: 219–23.

_____. 1978a. RB // KBD: A New Hebrew-Akkadian Formulaic Pair. *Bulletin of the American Schools of Oriental Research* 29: 110–13.

_____. 1978b. The Recovery of Poetic Fragments from the Pentateuchal Priestly Source. *Journal of Biblical Literature* 97: 161–73.

_____. 1982. The ABCB Pattern: Further Examples. *Vetus Testamentum* 32: 224–29.

Kuban, D. 1974. *The Mosque and Its Early Development*. Leiden: Brill.

Kubiak, W. 1987. *Al-Fustāt, Its Foundation and Early Urban Development*. Cairo: American University in Cairo Press.

Kugel, J. 1981a. *The Idea of Biblical Poetry. Parallelism and Its History*. New Haven: Yale University Press.

_____. 1981b. On the Bible and Literary Criticism. *Prooftexts* 1: 217–36.

_____. 1984. Some Thoughts on Future Research into Biblical Style: Addenda to the Idea of Biblical Poetry. *Journal for the Study of the Old Testament* 28: 107–17.

Kühnel, E. 1976. *The Arabesque Meaning and Transformation of an Ornament*. Verlag für Sammler.

Kuhrt, A. 1995. *The Ancient Near East c. 3000–330 B.C.* London: Routledge.

Kurylowicz, J. 1972. *Studies in Semitic Grammar and Metrics*. Poland: Zaklad Narodowy imienia Ossplinskich.

Lacoste, Y. 1984. *Ibn Khaldun: The Birth of History and the Past of the Third World*. London: Verso.

Lambert, W.G. 1960. *Babylonian Wisdom Literature*. Oxford: Clarendon.

_____. 1966. *Enuma Elis: The Babylonian Epic of Creation*. Oxford: Clarendon.

_____. 1992. *Catalogue of the Cuneiform Tablets in the Kouyunjik Collection of the British Museum: Third Supplement*. London: British Museum.

_____. 2007. *Babylonian Oracle Questions*. Winona Lake, IN: Eisenbrauns.

Lancioni, G., and L. Bettini. 2011. *The Word in Arabic*. Leiden: Brill.

Langdon, S. 1909. *Sumerian and Babylonian Psalms*. New York: G.E. Stechert.

_____. 1913. *Babylonian Liturgies*. Paris: Paul Geuthne.

_____. 1914. *Tammuz and Ishtar*. Oxford: Oxford University Press.

_____. 1921a. Babylonian and Hebrew Musical Terms. *Journal of the Royal Asiatic Society of Great Britain and Ireland* 53(2): 169–191.

_____. 1921b. Sumerian and Babylonian Songs. *Journal of the Royal Asiatic Society of Great Britain and Ireland* 53(1): 1–22.

_____. 1923a. *The Babylonian Epic of Creation Restored from the Recently Recovered Tablets of Assur*. Oxford: Clarendon.

_____. 1923b. *Sumerian and Semitic Religious and Historical Texts*. Vol. 1 of *The H. Weld-Blundell Collection in the Ashmolean Museum*. Oxford: Oxford University Press.

_____. 1923c. Two Sumerian Hymns from Eridu and Nippur. *The American Journal of Semitic Languages and Literatures* 39(3): 161–186.

_____. 1927. *Babylonian Penitential Psalms*. Paris: Paul Geuthne.

_____. 1973. *Sumerian Liturgies and Psalms*. Philadelphia: The University Museum.

Larkin, M. 1995. *The Theology of Meaning: 'Abd al-Qâhir al-Jurjâni's Theory of Discourse*. New Haven, CT: American Oriental Society.

_____. 2008. *Al-Mutanabbi: Voice of the 'Abbasid Poetic Ideal*. Oxford: Oneworld.

Lasater, A.E. 1974. *Spain to England: A Comparative Study of Arabic, European, and English Literature of the Middle Ages*. Jackson: University Press of Mississippi.

Latham, J.D. 1983. The Beginning of Arabic Prose Literature. In *Arabic Literature to the End of the Umayyad Period*, ed. A.F.L. Beeston et al., 154–179. Cambridge: Cambridge University Press.

_____. 1990. Ibn al-Muqaffa' and Early Abbasid Prose. In *The Cambridge History of Arabic Literature. 'Abbasid belles-lettres*, ed. Ashtiany et al., 48–78. Cambridge: Cambridge University Press.

_____. 2000. The Prosody of an Andalusian Muwashshah Re-Examined. In *Arabian and Islamic Studies*, ed. R.L. Bidwell and G.R. Smith, 86–99. London: Longman.

Law, V. 1990. Indian Influence on Early Arab Phonetics: Or Coincidence? *Studies in the History of Arabic Grammar* 2: 215–227.

Lawergren, B. 1983. *Harmonicis of S Motion on Bowed Strings*. New York: Acoustical Society of America.

_____. 1988. The Origin of Musical Instruments and Sounds. *Anthropos* Bd. 83: 31–45.

_____. 1993. Lyres in the West (Italy, Greece)

and East (Egypt, the Near East), ca 2000 to 400 B.C. *Opuscula Romana* 19(6): 55–76.

———. 2000a A "Cycladic" Harpist in the Metropolitan Museum of Art. *History of Art* 20(1): 2–9.

———. 2000b. Extant Silver Pipes from Ur, 2450 B.C. In *Studien zur Musikarchäologie*, 2: ed. E. Hickman, 121–132. Rahden: Verlag Marie Leidorf.

———. 2008. Bull Lyres, Silver Lyres, Silver Pipes and Animals in Sumer, Circa 2500 B.C. In *Proceedings of the International Conference of Near Eastern Archaeomusicology (ICONEA)*, ed. R.J. Dumbrill: 83–88. British Museum, December 4–6.

Lazard, G. 1975. The Rise of the New Persian Language. In *The Cambridge History of Iran* IV, ed. R.N. Frye, 595–632. Cambridge: Cambridge University Press.

———. 1993. *The Origins of Literary Persian.* Bethesda, MD: Foundation for Iranian Studies.

Leaman, O. 1985. *An Introduction to Medieval Islamic Philosophy.* Cambridge: Cambridge University Press.

———. 1988. *Averroes and His Philosophy.* New York: Oxford University Press.

Lehrman, J.B. 1980. *Earthly Paradise: Garden and Courtyard in Islam.* Berkeley: University of California Press.

Leick, G. 1994. *Sex and Eroticism in Mesopotamian Literature.* London: Routledge.

———. 2003. *The Babylonians: An Introduction.* London: Routledge.

LeMon, J. 2005. The Power of Parallelism in KTU2 1.119: Another "Trial Cut." *Ugarit-Forschungen* 37: 375–394.

Levin, A. 1985. The Distinction Between Nominal and Verbal Sentences According to the Arab Grammarians. *Studies in the History of Arabic Grammar* 1: 118–27.

———. 1986. The Mediaeval Arabic Term Kalima and the Modern Linguistic Term Morpheme: Similarities and Differences. In *Studies in Islamic History and Civilization*, ed. D. Ayalon and M. Sharon, 423–46. Leiden: Brill.

———. 1994. Sîbawayhi's Attitude to the Spoken Language. *Jerusalem Studies in Arabic and Islam* 17: 204–43.

Levin, Y. 2002. Nimrod the Mighty, King of Kish, King of Sumer and Akkad. *Vetus Testamentum* 52: 350–366.

Levine, J.A. 2010. Judaism and Music. In *The Historiography of Music in Global Perspective*, ed. S. Mirelman, 29–56. Piscataway, NJ: Gorgias.

Lewis, B. 1966. *The Arabs in History.* Oxford: Oxford University Press.

———. 1984. *The Sargon Legend: A Study of the Akkadian Text and the Tale of the Hero*

Who Was Exposed at Birth. Ann Arbor: University Microfilms International.

———. 2006. Ibn Khaldun in Turkey. *Ibn Khaldun: The Mediterranean in the 14th Century: Rise and Fall of Empires*, 376–380. Seville, Spain: Foundation El Legado Andalusí.

Liebhaber, S. 2010. Rhythm and Beat: Re-Evaluating Arabic Prosody in the Light of Mahri Oral Poetry. *Journal of Semitic Studies* 55(1): 163–182.

Limet, H. 1976. *Textes sumériens de la IIIe dynastye d'Ur.* Bruxelles: Musées royaux d'art et d'histoire.

Lindberg, D.C. 1967. Alhazen's Theory of Vision and Its Reception in the West. *Isis* 58(3): 321–341.

———. 1976. *Theories of Vision from al-Kindi to Kepler.* Chicago: University of Chicago Press.

Liverani, M. 1993. *Akkad: The First World Empire.* Padova: Sargon.

Lockyer, H. 2004. *All the Music of the Bible: The Minstrelsy and Music of God's People.* Peabody, MA: Hendrickson.

Loprieno, A. 1995. *Ancient Egyptian: A Linguistic Introduction.* New York: Cambridge University Press.

———. 1996. *Ancient Egyptian Literature: History and Forms.* Leiden: Brill.

Loucel, H. 1963–4. L'origine ad du langage d'après les grammairiens arabes. *Arabica.* 10: 188–208, 253–81; 11: 57–72, 151–87.

Lucas, S.C. 2002. *The Arts of Hadith Compilation and Criticism.* Chicago: University of Chicago Press.

Luckenbill, D.D. 1924. *The Annals of Sennacherib.* Chicago: University of Chicago Press.

———. 1927. *Ancient Records of Assyria and Babylonia.* Vol. 2: *Historical Records of Assyria from Sargon to the End.* Chicago: University of Chicago Press.

Lunde, P. 1992. Al-Farghani and the "Short Degree." *Saudi Aramco World* 43.2: 6–17.

Luz, N. 1997. The Construction of an Islamic City in Palestine: The Case of Umayyad al-Ramla. *Journal of the Royal Asiatic Society* 7(1): 27–54.

Lyall, C. 1930. *Translations of Ancient Arabic Poetry: Chiefly Pre-Islamic.* London: William and Norgate.

Lyons, M.C. 1995. *The Arabian Epic.* 3 vols. Cambridge: Cambridge University Press.

Maalouf, S. 2002. *History of Arabic Music Theory: Change and Continuity in the Tone Systems, Genres, and Scales.* Kaslik, Lebanon: Université Saint-Esprit de Kaslik.

———. 2011. *History of Arabic Music Theory: Change and Continuity in the Tone Systems, Genres, and Scales.* Shelbyville, KY: Wasteland.

Mack, R., ed. 2009. Introduction. *Arabian Nights' Entertainments*, ix–xxiii. Oxford: Oxford University Press.

Madhloom, T. 1967. Excavations at Nineveh: A Preliminary Report. *Sumer* 23: 76–79.

_____. 1968. Excavations at Nineveh: The 1967–68 Campaign. *Sumer* 24: 45–51.

_____. 1969. Excavations at Nineveh: The 1968–69 Campaign. *Sumer* 25: 43–49.

Magee, P. 1999. Writing in the Iron Age: the earliest south Arabian inscription from southeastern Arabia. *Arabian Archaeology and Epigraphy* 10: 43–50.

Mahdi, M. 1970. Language and Logic in Classical Islam. In *Logic in Classical Islamic Culture*, ed. G.E. von Grunebaum, 51–83. Wiesbaden: O. Harrassowitz.

_____. 2001. *Alfarabi and the Foundation of Islamic Political Philosophy*. Chicago: University of Chicago Press.

_____. 2002. *Music in Muslim Civilization*. London: Al-Furqam Islamic Heritage Foundation.

Mahfouz, N. 1984. *The Thief and the Dogs*. Cairo: American University in Cairo Press.

_____. 1993. *Mirmar*. Trans. F.M. Mahmoud, ed. M. El Kommos and J. Rodenbeck. New York: Ancor.

_____. 1996. *Children of the Alley*. Cairo: American University in Cairo Press.

_____. 1999. *Adrift on the Nile*. Cairo: American University in Cairo Press.

_____. 2003a. *Rhadopis of Nubia*. Cairo: American University in Cairo Press.

_____. 2003b. *Khufu's Wisdom*. Cairo: American University in Cairo Press.

_____. 2006. *Thebes at War*. Cairo: American University in Cairo Press.

Maigret, A. de. 1988. *The Sabaean Archaeological Complex in the Wadi Yala*. Rome: IsMEO.

Mainstone, R.J. 1997. *Hagia Sophia: Architecture, Structure, and Liturgy of Justinian's Great Church*. New York: W.W. Norton.

Makdisi, G. 1984. The Juridical Theology of Shâfi'î: Origins and Significance of the *usûl al-fiqh*. *Studia Islamica* 59: 5–47.

_____. 1986. The Diary in Islamic Historiography: Some Notes. *History and Theory* 25(2): 173–85.

Makdisi, S., and F. Nussbaum. 2008. *The Arabian Nights in Historical Context: Between East and West*. New York: Oxford University Press.

Malti-Douglas, F. 1985. *Structures of Avarice: The Bukhalā in Medieval Arabic Literature*. Leiden: Brill.

Mansour, N., and M. Allen. 2011. *Sacred Script: Muhaqqaq in Islamic Calligraphy*. London: I.B. Tauris.

Mansur, S.H. 1977. *The World-View of Al-Jāhiz in Kitāb al-Hayawān*. Bloomington: Indiana University Press.

Marcus, S.L. 2007. *Music in Egypt: Experiencing Music, Expressing Culture*. New York: Oxford University Press.

Markoe, G.E. 2000. *Phoenicians*. Berkeley: University of California Press.

Marrassini, P. 2003. Sur le sud-semitique: problemes de definition. In *Melanges David Cohen*, ed. J. Lentin and A. Lonnet, 461–70. Paris: Maisonneuve & Larose.

Martin, R.C., and M.R. Woodward. 1997. *Defenders of Reason in Islam: Mu'tazilism from Medieval School to Modern Symbol*. Oxford: Oneworld.

Marzolph, U., ed. 2006. *The Arabian Nights Reader*. Detroit: Wayne State University Press.

Mas, R. 1998. Qiyas: A Study in Islamic Logic. *Folia Orientalia* 34: 113–128.

Masood, E. 2009. *Science and Islam: A History*. New York: Icon.

Mathiesen, T.J. 1999. *Apollo's Lyre: Greek Music and Music Theory in Antiquity and the Middle Ages*. Lincoln: University of Nebraska.

Mathiesen, T.J., and I. Greece. 2001. *The New Grove Dictionary of Music and Musicians*, vol. 10, 327–48.

McAuliffe, J.D. 2006a. *The Cambridge Companion to the Qur'an*. Cambridge: Cambridge University Press.

_____. 2006b. The Tasks and Traditions of Interpretation. In *The Cambridge Companion to the Qur'an*, ed. J.D. McAuliffe, 181–210. Cambridge: Cambridge University Press.

McCarthy, J., and A. Prince. 1986. *Prosodic Morphology*. Waltham: Brandeis University.

_____. 1990. Foot and Word in Prosodic Morphology: The Arabic Broken Plural. *Natural Language and Linguistic Theory* 8: 209–84.

_____. 1993a. *Generalized Alignment*. Amherst: University of Massachusetts.

_____. 1993b. *Prosodic Morphology*. New Jersey: Rutgers University Press.

_____. 1994a. *Optimality in Prosodic Morphology: The Emergence of the Unmarked*. Handout from a talk presented at NELS (North-Eastern Linguistic Society) 24. University of Massachusetts, Amherst and Rutgers University.

_____. 1994b. *Prosodic Morphology*, parts 1 and 2. Utrecht: Prosodic Morphology Workshop.

McCreesh, T.P. 1991. *Biblical Sound and Sense: Poetic Sound Patterns*. Sheffield: JSOT.

McDonald, M.V.M. 1978. Orally Transmitted Poetry in Pre-Islamic Arabia and Other Pre-Literate Societies. *Journal of Arabic Literature* 9: 14–31.

McKinnon, J. 1988. *Music in Early Christian Literature*. Cambridge: Cambridge University Press.

_____. 1998. *The Temple, the Church Fathers, and Early Western Chant*. Aldershot: Ashgate.

Méhiri, A. 1973. *Les théories grammaticales d'Ibn Jinnî*. Tunis: Université de Tunis.

Meisami, J.S. 1985. The Uses of the Qaṣīda: Thematic and Structural Patterns in a Poem of Baššār. *Journal of Arabic Literature* 16: 40–60.

_____. 1987. *Medieval Persian Court Poetry*, Princeton: Princeton University Press.

_____. 1993. Arabic Mujūn Poetry: The Literary Dimension. In *Studies in Arabic Poetry and in the Representation of Women in Arabic Literature Verse and the Fair Sex*, ed. F. de Jong, 8–30. Utrecht: Stitching.

Melchert, C. 1997. *The Formation of the Sunni Schools of Law, 9th–10th Centuries C.E.* Leiden: Brill.

Mendelsohn, I. 1955. *Religions of the Ancient Near East: Sumero-Akkadian Religious Texts and Ugaritic Epics*. New York: Liberal Arts.

Mendenhall, G.E. 2000. Arabic in Semitic Linguistic History. *American Oriental Society* 126(1): 17–26.

Menocal, M.R., R.P. Scheindlin, and M.A. Sells, eds. 2000. *The Literature of Al-Andalus*. New York: Cambridge University Press.

Merx, A. 1966. *Historia artis grammaticae apud Syros*. Nendeln: Kraus.

Meyer, S.G. 2001. *The Experimental Arabic Novel: Postcolonial Literary Modernism in the Levant*. Albany: State University of New York Press.

Mez, A. 1975. *The Renaissance of Islam*. New York: AMS.

Michalowski, P. 1981. Carminative Magic: Towards an Understanding of Sumerian Poetics. *Zeitschrift für Assyriologie und vorderasiatische Archäologie* 71(1): 1–18.

_____. 1989. *The Lamentation Over the Destruction of Sumer and Ur*. Winona Lake: Eisenbrauns.

_____. 1996. Sailing to Babylon: Reading the Dark Side of the Moon. In *The Study of the Ancient Near East in the Twenty-First Century*, ed. C. Schwartz, 179–198. Winona Lake, IN: Eisenbrauns.

_____. 2004. Sumerian. In *The Cambridge Encyclopedia of the World's Ancient Languages*, ed. R.D. Woodard, 19–59. Cambridge: Cambridge University Press.

_____. 2008. The Mortal Kings of Ur: A Short Century of Divine Rule in Ancient Mesopotamia. *Oriental Institute Seminars* 4: 33–45.

Michalowski, P., and E. Reiner. 1993. *Letters from Early Mesopotamia*. Atlanta, GA: Scholars.

Michalowski, P., and N. Veldhuis, eds. 2006. *Approaches to Sumerian Literature: Studies in Honor of Stip (H.L.J. Vanstiphout)*. Leiden: Brill.

Michaud, R., S. Michaud, and M. Barry. 1996. *Design and Color in Islamic Architecture: Eight Centuries of the Tile-Makers's Art*. New York: Vendome.

Michell, G., ed. 1978. *Architecture of the Islamic World: Its History and Social Meaning*. London: Thames and Hudson.

Miller, L.C. 2004. *Music and Song in Persia: The Art of Avaz*. London: New York: RoutledgeCurzon.

Miller, P.J. 1980a. Studies in Hebrew Word Patterns. *Harvard Theological Review* 73: 79–89.

_____. 1980b. Synonymous-Sequential Parallelism in the Psalms. *Biblica* 61: 256–60.

_____. 1983. Review of Hebrew Verse Structure by M. O'Connor. *Journal of Biblical Literature* 102: 628–29.

Mindlin, M., M.J. Geller, and J.E. Wansbrough, eds. 1987. *Figurative Language in the Ancient Near East*. London: University of London, School of Oriental and African Studies.

Molan, P.D. 1978. "Medieval Western Arabic: Reconstructing Elements of the Dialects of Al-Andalus, Sicily, and North Africa from the laḥn al-'âmma Literature." PhD dissertation, University of California, Berkeley.

Momen, M. 1985. *An Introduction to Shi'i Islam: The History and Doctrines of Twelve*. New Haven, CT: Yale University Press.

Monroe, J.T. 1972. Oral Composition in Pre-Islamic Poetry. *Journal of Arabic Literature* 3: 1–53.

_____. 1974. *Hispano-Arabic Poetry*. Berkeley: University of California Press.

_____. 1975. Formulaic Diction and the Common Origins of Romance Lyric Traditions. *Hispanic Review* 43: 341–350.

_____. 1983. *The Art of Badī' az-Zaman al-Hamadhānī as Picaresque Narrative*. Beirut: Center for Arab and Middle East Studies, American University of Beirut.

_____. 1997. Al-Saraqusī, ibn al-Aštarkūwī: Andalusī Lexicographer, Poet, and Author of "al-Maqāmāt al-Luzumiyya." *Journal of Arabic Literature* 28.1: 1–37.

Monroe, J.T., and Abu l-Tahir Muḥammad Ibn Yusuf al-Tamimi al-Saraqusti Ibn al-Astarkuwi. 2001. *Al-Maqāmā al-luzumiyah*. Leiden: Brill.

Monteil, V. 1967–68. *Ibn Khaldûn, Discours sur l'Histoire Universelle (al-Muqaddima): Traduction nouvelle, préface, notes et index*.

3 vols. Beirut: Commission Libanaise pour la Traduction des Chefs-d'Oeuvre.

Montgomery, J.E. 1997. *The Vagaries of the Qasidah: The Tradition and Practice of Early Arabic Poetry.* Cambridge: E.J.W. Gibb Memorial Trust.

Moorey, R.R.S. 1991. *A Century of Biblical Archaeology.* Cambridge: Cambridge University Press.

Moosa, M. 1997. *The Origins of Modern Arabic Fiction.* Boulder, CO: Lynn Rienner.

Morag, S. 1962. *The Vocalization Systems of Arabic, Hebrew, and Aramaic: Their Phonetic and Phonemic Principles.* 's-Gravenhage: Mouton.

_____. 1974. On the Historical Validity of the Vocalization of the Hebrew Bible. *Journal of the American Oriental Society* 94: 307–15.

Moran, W.L. 1983. Notes on the Hymn to Marduk in Ludlul Bel Nemeqi. *Journal of the American Oriental Society* 103(1): 255–260.

Moreh, S. 1986. Live Theater in Medieval Islam. In *Studies in Islamic History and Civilization*, ed. D. Ayalon and S. Moshe, 565–601. Leiden: Brill.

_____. 1992. *Live Theatre and Dramatic Literature in the Arab World.* Edinburgh: Edinburgh University Press.

Mukhopadhyaya, S. 1986. Preface. *A Grammar of the Classical Arabic Language.* Trans. M.S. Howell. 4 vols. Delhi, India: Gian.

Murray, P., and P. Wilson. 2004. *Music and the Muses; The Culture of Mousike in the Classical Athenian City.* Oxford: Oxford University Press.

Musa, A. 2008. *Hadith as Scripture: Discussions on the Authority of Prophetic Traditions in Islam.* New York: Palgrave Macmillan.

Musawi, M.J. al-. 2005. *The Postcolonial Arabic Novel: Debating Ambivalence.* Leiden: Brill.

_____. 2006. Elite Prose. In *The Cambridge History of Arabic Literature. Arabic Literature to the Post-Classical Period*, ed. R. Allen and D.S. Richards, 101–133. Cambridge: Cambridge University Press.

Mustansir, M. 1992. Dialogue in the Qur'an. *Religion and Literature* 24(1): 1–22.

Nasr, S.H. 2006. *Islamic Philosophy from Its Origin to the Present: Philosophy in the Land of Prophecy.* Albany: State University of New York Press.

Nasr, S.H., and O. Learnan. 2001. *History of Islamic Philosophy.* New York: Routledge.

Nassir, M.J. al-. 1993. *Sibawayh the Phonologist: A Critical Study of the Phonetic and Phonological Theory of Sibawayh as Presented in His Treatise Al-Kitāb.* New York: Kegan Paul International.

Naudé, J.A. 2000. The Language of the Book of Ezekiel: Biblical Hebrew in Transition? *Old Testament Essays* 13: 46–71.

Naveh, J. 1970. *The Development of the Aramaic Script.* Jerusalem: Israel Academy of Sciences and Humanities.

_____. 1978. *On Stone and Mosaic: The Aramaic and Hebrew Inscriptions from Ancient Synagogues.* Jerusalem: Israel Exploration Society.

_____. 1982. *Early History of the Alphabet: An Introduction to West Semitic Epigraphy and Palaeography.* Jerusalem: Hebrew University.

_____. 1993. *Magic Spells and Formulae: Aramaic Incantations of Late Antiquity.* Jerusalem: Hebrew University.

Naveh, J., and S. Shaked. 2006. *Ancient Aramaic Documents from Bactria.* Oxford: Khalili Collections.

Nebes, N. 1988. The Infinitive in Sabaean and Qatabanian Inscriptions. *Proceedings of the Seminar for Arabian Studies* 18: 63–78.

_____. 1994. Verwendung und Funktion der Prafixkonjugation im Sabaischen. In *Arabia Felix: Beiträge zur Sprache und Kultur des vorislamischen Arabien*, ed. N. Nebes, 191–211. Wiesbaden: O. Harrassowitz.

_____. 1997. Stand und Aufgaben einer Grammatik des Altsudarabischen. In *Aktualisierte Beitrage zum I. Internationalen Symposion Sudarabien interdisziplindr an der Universitat Graz mit kurzen Einfuhrung zu Sprach- und Kulturgeschichte*, ed. R.G. Stiegner, 111–131. University of Graz.

_____. 2001. Zur Genese der altsudarabischen Kultur: Eine Arbeitshypothese. In *Migration und Kulturtransfer: Der Wandel vorder- und zentralasiatischen Kulturen im Umbruch vom 2. zum 1. vorchristlichen Jahrtausend. Akten des Internationalen Kolloquiums. Berlin, 23. bis 26 November 1999*, ed. R. Eichmann and H. Parzinger, 427–435. Bonn.

Nebes, N., and P. Stein. 2003. Ancient South Arabian. In *The Cambridge Encyclopedia of the World's Ancient Languages*, ed. R.D. Woodard, 454–487. Cambridge: Cambridge University Press.

Necipoglu, G. 1991. *Architecture, Ceremonial, and Power: The Topkapi Palace in the Fifteenth and Sixteenth Centuries.* Cambridge, MA: MIT Press.

_____. 1995. *The Topkapi Scroll: Geometry and Ornament in Islamic Architecture.* Santa Monica, CA: Getty Center for the History of Art and the Humanities.

_____. 2003. *Muqarnas.* Vol. 20: *An Annual on the Visual Culture of the Islamic World.* Leiden: Brill.

_____. 2005. *The Age of Sinan: Architectural*

Culture in the Ottoman Empire. Princeton: Princeton University Press.

_____. 2008. *Frontiers of Islamic Art and Architecture: Essays in Celebration of Oleg Grabar's Eightieth Birthday*. Leiden: Brill.

_____. 2010. *Muqarnas: An Annual on the Visual Cultures of the Islamic World*. Leiden: Brill.

Nelson, K. 2001. *Art of Reciting the Qur'an*. Cairo: University of Cairo Press.

Netton, L.R. 1982. *Muslim Neoplatonists: An Introduction to the Thought of the Brethren of Purity (Ikhwân al-safâ')*. London: G. Allen & Unwin.

Neuwirth, A. 2006. Structural, Linguistic and Literary Features. In *The Cambridge Companion to the Qur'an*, ed. J.D. McAuliffe, 97–114. Cambridge: Cambridge University Press.

Neuwirth, A., A. Pflitsch, and B. Winckler. 2010. *Arabic Literature: Postmodern Perspectives*. Saint Paul, MI: Saqi.

Nicholson, R.A. 1969. *A Literary History of the Arabs*. London: Cambridge University Press.

_____. 1987. *Translations of Eastern Poetry and Prose*. London: Curzon.

Nissen, H.J. 1988. *The Early History of the Ancient Near East 9000–2000 B.C.* Chicago: University of Chicago Press.

Nissen, H.J., P. Damerow, and R.K. Englund. 1993. *Archaic Bookkeeping*. Chicago: University of Chicago Press.

Nizami, G. 1995. *The Haft Paykar: A Medieval Persian Romance*. Oxford: Oxford University Press.

Norborg, A. 1995. *Ancient Middle Eastern Lyres*. Stockholm: Musikmuseets.

Norris, H.T. 1983. Qisas Elements in the Qur'an. In *Arabic Literature to the End of Umayyad Period*, ed. Beeston et al., 246–259. Cambridge: Cambridge University Press.

Northedge, A. 2001. The Palaces of Abbasids in Samarra. In *A Medieval Islamic City Reconsidered: An Interdisciplinary Approach to Samarra*, ed. C.F. Robinson, 29–68. Oxford: Oxford University Press.

_____. 2005. *The Historical Topography of Samarra*. London: British School of Archaeology in Iraq.

Nykl, A.R. 1946. *Hispano-Arabic Poetry and Its Relations with the Old Provençal Troubadours*. Baltimore: J.H. Furst.

O'Connor, M. 1977. The Rhetoric of the Kilamuwa Inscription. *Bulletin of the American Schools of Oriental Research* 226: 15–29.

_____. 1980a. *Hebrew Verse Structure*. Winona Lake, IN: Eisenbrauns.

_____. 1980b. Review of T. Collins, Line-Forms in Hebrew Poetry. *Catholic Biblical Quarterly* 42: 91–92.

_____. 1981. *The Role of Syntax in Hebrew Verse*. Paper read at the Annual Meeting of the American Oriental Society, Boston.

_____. 1982. "Unanswerable the Knack of Tongues": The Linguistic Study of Verse. In *Exceptional Language and Linguistics*, ed. L. Obler and L. Menn, 143–168. New York.

Ohlander, E.S. 2008. *Sufism in an Age of Transition: Umar al-Suhrawardi and the Rise of the Islamic*. Leiden: Brill.

O'Kane, B. 1995. *Studies in Persian Art and Architecture*. Cairo: American University in Cairo Press.

_____. 2003. *Early Persian Painting: Kalila and Dimna Manuscripts of the Late Fourteenth Century*. New York: I.B. Tauris.

_____. 2005. *The Iconography of Islamic Art: Studies in Honour of Robert Hillenbrand*. Edinburgh: Edinburgh University Press.

_____. 2006. *The Treasures of Islamic Art in the Museums of Cairo*. Cairo: American University in Cairo Press.

Oppenheim, A.L. 1969. *Ancient Near Eastern Texts Relating to the Old Testament*, ed. J.B. Pritchard. Princeton: Princeton University Press.

Orfali, B. 2009. The Works of Abū Mansūr al-Thālibī (350–429/961–1039). *Journal of Arabic Literature* 40(3): 273–318.

_____, ed. 2011. *In the Shadow of Arabic*. Leiden: Brill.

Orton, D.E., ed. 1999a. *The Composition of John's Gospel: Selected Studies from "Novum Testamentum."* Leiden, Boston: Brill.

_____. 1999b. *The Composition of Mark's Gospel: Selected Studies from "Novum Testamentum."* Leiden: Brill.

_____. 1999c. *The Composition of Luke's Gospel: Selected Studies from "Novum Testamentum."* Leiden: Brill.

_____. 2000. *Poetry in the Hebrew Bible: Selected Studies from "Vetus Testamentum."* Leiden: Brill.

Osborne, H. 1975. *The Oxford Companion to the Decorative Arts*. Oxford: Oxford University Press.

Owens, J. 1988. *The Foundations of Grammar: An Introduction to Medieval Arabic Grammatical Theory*. Amsterdam amd Philadelphia: J. Benjamins.

_____. 1989. The Syntactic Basis of Arabic Word Classification. *Arabica* 36: 211–34.

_____. 1990. *Early Arabic Grammatical Theory: Heterogeneity and Standardization*. Amsterdam and Philadelphia: J. Benjamins.

_____. 1995. The Comparative Study of Medieval Arabic Grammatical Theory: A Mollusc Replies to A.E. Houseman, Jr. *HL* 22: 425–40.

_____. 2006. *A Linguistic History of Arabic.* Oxford: Oxford University Press.

Pardee, D. 1984. The Semantic Parallelism of Psalm 89. In *The Shelter of Elyon: Essays on Ancient Palestinian Life and Literature,* ed. W.B. Barrick and J.R. Spenser, 121–137. Sheffield: JSOT.

_____. 1988. *Ugaritic and Hebrew Poetic Parallelism: A Trial Cut ('nt 1 and Proverbs 2).* Leiden: Brill.

_____. 2007. The Ugaritic Alphabetic Cuneiform Writing System in the Context of Other Alphabetic Systems. *Studies in Ancient Oriental Civilization* 60: 181–200.

Pardee, D., and P. Bordreuil, eds. 2009. *A Manual of Ugaritic.* Winona Lake, IN: Eisenbrauns.

Pardee, D., and T.J. Lewis, eds. 2002. *Ritual and Cult at Ugarit.* Atlanta: Society of Biblical Literature.

Paret, R. 1983. Qur'an I and II. In *Cambridge History of Arabic Literature to the End of the Umayyad Period,* ed. A.F.L. Beeston, et al., 186–245. Cambridge: Cambridge University Press.

Parker, S. 1974. Parallelism and Prosody in Ugaritic Narrative Verse. *Ugarit-Forschungen* 6: 283–94.

_____. 1989. *The Pre-Biblical Narrative Tradition: Essays on the Ugaritic Poems Keret and Aqhat.* Atlanta: Scholars.

_____. 2000. Ugaritic Literature and the Bible. *Near Eastern Archaeology* 63(4): 228–231.

Parpola, S. 1988. Proto-Assyrian. *Wirtschaft und Gesellschaft von Ebla. Heidelberger Studien zum alten Orient (HSAO)* 2: 293–98. Heidelberg: Heidelberger Orientverlag.

Parrot, A. 1961. *The Arts of Assyria.* New York: Golden.

Pasnau, R. 2010. Introduction. In *The Cambridge History of Medieval Philosophy,* ed. N. Kretzmann; A. Kenny and J. Pinborg. Cambridge: Cambridge University Press.

Payne, S.G. 2011. *Spain: A Unique History.* Madison: University of Wisconsin Press.

Peters, F.E. 1968. *Aristotle and the Arabs: The Aristotelian Tradition in Islam.* New York: New York University Press.

Peters, J.R.T.M. 1976. *God's Created Speech: A Study in the Speculative Theology of the Mu'tazilî Qâdî l-Qudât Abû l-Hasan 'Abd al-Jabbâr bn. Ahmad al-Hamadânî.* Leiden: Brill.

Petruccioli, A., and K.K. Pirani. 2002. *Understanding Islamic Architecture.* London: RoutledgeCurzon.

Pinault, D. 1992. *Story-Telling Techniques in the Arabian Nights.* Leiden: Brill.

Polak, F. 2002. Poetic Style and Parallelism in the Creation Account (Gen. 1:1–2:3). In *Creation in Jewish and Christian Tradition,* ed.

H. Reventlow and Y. Hoffman, 2–31. Sheffield: Sheffield Academic.

Popper, W. *Studies in Biblical Parallelism.* Part II: *Parallelism in Isaiah.* Berkeley: University of California Press.

Postgate, J.N. 1969. *Neo-Assyrian Royal Grants and Degrees.* Rome: Biblical Institute.

Potts, D.T. 1990. *The Arabian Gulf in Antiquity.* 2 vols. Oxford: Clarendon.

Qabbani, N. 1995. *On Entering the Sea: The Erotic and Other Poetry of Nizar Qabbani.* New York: Interlink.

_____. 1999. *Arabian Love Poems: Full Arabic and English Texts.* Boulder: Lynne Rienner.

Qadir, C.A. 1990. *Philosophy and Science in the Islumic World.* New York: Routledge.

Qassim, H. 1980. *Les instruments de musique en Irak et leur rôle dans la societé traditionnelle.* Paris: Éditions de l'École des hautes etudes en sciences sociales.

Quaknin, M. 1999. *Mysteries of the Alphabet: The Origins of Writing.* New York: Abbeville.

Rabbat, N. 1995. *The Citadel of Cairo: A New Interpretation of Royal Mamluk Architecture.* Leiden: Brill.

_____. 1996. Al-Azhar Mosque: An Architectural Chronicle of Cairo's History. In *Muqarnas: An Annual on the Visual Culture of the Islamic World,* vol. 13, ed. G. Necipogulu, 45–67. Leiden: Brill.

Rabin, C. 1951. *Ancient West-Arabian.* London: Taylor's Foreign Press.

_____. 1981. The Language of Amos and Hosea. In *Iyyunim be-Sefer Tre-'Asar,* ed. B.Z. Luria, 117–136. Jerusalem: Kiryath Sepher.

Raby, J., and J. Johns. 1993–99. *Bayt-al-Maqdis: Abd-al-Malik's Jerusalem.* Oxford: Oxford University Press.

Racy, A.J. 2003. *Making Music in the Arab World: The Culture and Artistry of Arab.* New York: Cambridge University Press.

Radner, K., and E. Robson, eds. 2011. *The Oxford Handbook of Cuneiform Culture.* New York: Oxford University Press.

Rainey, A.F. 1971. Observations on Ugaritic Grammar. *Ugarit-Forschungen* 3: 151–72.

Rammuny, R.M. 1985. Al-Jurjânî: A Pioneer of Grammatical and Linguistic Studies. *Historiographia Linguistica* 12:351–71.

Rashed, R., and A. Armstrong. 1994. *The Development of Arabic Mathematics.* London: Springer.

Rasmussen, A.K. 2010. *Women, the Recited Qur'an, and Islamic Music in Indonesia.* Berkeley: University of California Press.

Reade, J. 2009. *Assyrian Palace Sculptures.* Austin: University of Texas Press.

Rees, R. 2002. *Layers of Loyalty in Latin Pan-egyric: A.D. 289–307.* New York: Oxford University Press.

Reiner, E. 1970. *Surpu: A Collection of Sumer-ian and Akkadien Incantations.* Osnabruck: Neudr. der Ausg.

_____. 1985. *Your Thwarts in Pieces, Your Mooring Rope Cut: Poetry from Babylonia and Assyria.* Ann Arbor: Horace H. Rack-ham School of Graduate Studies at the Uni-versity of Michigan.

Reisman, D.C. 2002. *The Making of the Avi-cennan Tradition.* Leiden: Brill.

Reuschel, W. 1959. *Al-Halīl ibn-Ahmad, der Lehrer Sîbawaihs, als Grammatiker.* Berlin: Akademie-Verlag.

Reynold, E.D. 2000. Music. In *The Literature of Al-Andalus,* ed. M.R. Menocal, R.P. Scheindlin and M.A. Sells, 60–82. New York: Cambridge University Press.

_____. 2004. *Innovations in Hebrew Poetry: Parallelism and the Poems of Sirach.* Lei-den: Brill.

Rice, D.S. 1958. Deacon or Drink: Some Paint-ings from Samarra Re-Examined. *Arabic* 5: 15–33.

Richmond, D. 1978. *Antar and Abla: A Be-douin Romance.* London: Quartet.

Riegl, A. 1992a. *The Arabesque: Problems of Style.* Princeton: Princeton University Press.

_____. 1992b. *Problems of Style: Foundations for a History of Ornament.* Princeton: Princeton University Press.

_____. 2004. *Historical Grammar of the Vi-sual Arts.* New York: Zone.

Rimmer, J. 1969. *Ancient Musical Instruments of Western Asia in the Department of West-ern Asiatic Antiquities.* London: British Mu-seum.

Rippin, A. 1982. The Present Status of Tafsîr Studies. *Muslim World* 72: 224–38.

_____. 1988. Origins and Development of Early Tafsil Tradition. In *Approaches to the History of Interpretation of Qur'an,* 13–30. Oxford: Oxford University Press.

_____. 1999. *The Qur'an: Formative Interpre-tation.* Brookfield, VT: Ashgate.

Ritter, H. 1959. *Die Geheimnisse der Wort-kunst (Asrar al-balaga) des Abdalqahir al-Curcani.* Wiesbaden: F. Steiner.

Roberts, R. 1977. Old Testament Poetry: The Translatable Structure. *Publications of the Modern Language Association* 92: 987–1004.

Robinson, A. 1995. *The Story of Writing.* Lon-don: Thames and Hudson.

Robinson, C. 2002. *In Praise of Song: The Making of Courtly Culture in Al-Andalus and Provence, 1005–1134 A.D.* Leiden: Brill.

_____. 2003. *Islamic Historiography.* Cam-bridge: Cambridge University Press.

_____. 2007. *Medieval Andalusian Courtly Culture in the Mediterranean: Ḥadith Bayad wa-Riyaḍ.* London: Routledge.

_____. 2008. Marginal Ornament: Poetics, Memesis, and Devotion in the Palace of Lion. In *Frontiers of Islamic Art and Archi-tecture,* ed. G, Necipoğlu et al., 185–214. Leiden: Brill.

Rogers, J.H. 1998. Origins of the ancient con-stellations: I. The Mesopotamian traditions. *Journal of the British Astronomical Associ-ation* 108(1): 9–28.

Rosen, C. 1988. *Sonata Form.* New York: Nor-ton.

Rosen, T. 2000. Muwashshah. In *The Litera-ture of Al-Andalus,* ed. M.R. Menocal, R.P. Scheindlin, and M.A. Sells, 165–189. New York: Cambridge University Press.

Rosen-Ayalon, M. 1989. *The Early Islamic Monuments of al-Ḥaram al-Sharīf.* Jerusa-lem: Institute of Archaeology, Hebrew Uni-versity of Jerusalem.

Rosenbaum, M. 1999. *Word-Order Variation in Isaiah 40–55: A Functional Perspective* (SSN 36; Assen: Van Gorcum, 1997). Re-view: J.A. Naudé. *Old Testament Essays* 12: 216–18.

Rosenbaum, S.N. 1977. Northern Amos Revis-ited: Two Philological Suggestions, *Hebrew Studies* 18: 132–48.

Rosenberg, J. 1987. Jeremiah and Ezekiel. In *The Literary Guide to the Bible,* ed. R. Alter and F. Kermode, 105–106. Cambridge, MA: Harvard University Press.

Rosenthal, F. 1958. *The Muqaddima of Ibn Khaldûn: An Introduction to History.* 3 vols. New York: Pantheon.

Rozenfeld, B.A. 1988. *A History of Non-Eu-clidean Geometry: Evolution of the Concept of a Geometric Space.* New York: Springer Verlag.

Rubin, U. 1990. *Ḥanīfiyya* and *Ka'ba:* An In-quiry into the Arabian Pre-Islamic Back-ground of *Dīn Ibrāhīm.* Jerusalem Studies in Arabic and Islam 13: 85–112.

Rubio, G. 1999. On the Alleged "Pre-Sumer-ian" Substratun. *Journal of Cuneiform Stud-ies* 51: 1–16.

_____. 2005. *Writing in Another Tongue: Al-logiottography in the Ancient Near East,* 33–66. http://oi.uchicago.edu/pdf/Rubio_abstract.pdf. Oxford: British Institute for the Study of Iraq.

_____. 2007a. The Language of the Ancient Near East. In *Companion to the Ancient Near East,* ed. D.C. Snell, 79–94. New York: Wiley-Blackwell.

_____. 2007b. From Sumer to Babylonia. In *Current Issues in the History of the Ancient Near East,* ed. M.W. Chavalas, 5–51. Clare-mont, CA: Regina.

_____. 2009. Sumerian Literature. In *From an Antique Land: An Introduction to Ancient Near Eastern Literature*, ed. C.S. Ehrlich, 11–75. Lanham, MD: Rowman and Littlefield.

_____. 2010. Scribal Secrets and Antiquarian Anxiety: Writing and Scholarship in Cuneiform Tradition. In *Your Praise Is Sweet*, ed. H.D. Baker, E. Robson, and G. Zolyomi. London: British Institute for the Study of Iraq.

Ruggles, D.F. 2008. *Islamic Gardens and Landscapes*. Philadelphia: University of Pennsylvania Press.

Rumi, J. al-D. 1968. *Mystical Poems of Rumi: First Selection: Poems 1–200*. Trans. A.J. Arberry. Chicago: University of Chicago Press.

_____. 1983. Rumi's Path to Love. In *The Sufi Path of Love: The Spiritual Teachings of Rumi*. Albany: State University of New York Press.

_____. 1993. *Discourses of Rumi*. Trans. A.J. Arberry. Richard, Surrey: Curzon.

_____. 1996. *The Essential Rumi*. Trans. C. Barks with J. Moyne, A.J. Arberry and R. Nicholson. San Francisco: HarperCollins.

_____. 2008. *Say Nothing: Poems of Jalal al-Din Rumi in Persian and English*. Sandpoint, ID: Morning Light.

Rundgren, F. 1976. Über den griechischen Einfluss auf die arabische Nationalgrammatik." *Acta Universitatis Upsaliensis (AUU)* n.s. 2, 5: 119–44.

Russell, J.M. 1991. *Sennacherib's Palace Without Rival at Nineveh*. Chicago: University of Chicago Press.

Ryckmans, J. 1951. *L'Institution monarchique en Arabie méridionale avantl'Islam (Ma'in et Saba)*, Louvain: Publications universitaires.

_____. 1983. Biblical and Old South Arabian Institutions: Some Parallels. In *Arabian and Islamic Studies,* ed. R. Bidwell and G.R. Smith, 14–25. London: Longman.

Ryding, K.C. 1998. *Early Medieval Arabic: Studies on Al-Khalil Ibn Ahmad*. Washington, DC: Georgetown University Press.

Sabatino, M. 1980. *An Introduction to Comparative Grammar of Semitic Languages Phonology and Morphology*. Wiesbaden: Harrassowitz Verlag.

Sabra, A.I. 1971. Al-Farghānī. In *Dictionary of Scientific Biography*, vol. 4, ed. C.C. Gillispie, 541–545. New York: Scribner's.

_____. 1978. An Eleventh-Century Refutation of Ptolemy's Planetary Theory. *Science and History: Studies in Honor of Edward Rosen*, ed. E. Hilfstein and P. Czartoryski, 117–131. Wrocław: Ossolineum.

_____. 1981. *Theories of Light from Descartes to Newton*. Cambridge: Cambridge University Press.

_____. 1996. Greek Science in Medieval Islam. In *Tradition, Transmission, Transformation: Proceedings of Two Conferences on Pre-Modern Science*, ed. R.J. Ragep, S.P. Ragep, and S.J. Livesey, 3–30. University of Oklahoma. Leiden: Brill.

_____. 1998. Configuring the Universe: Aporetic, Problem Solving, and Kinematic Modeling as Themes of Arabic Astronomy. *Perspectives on Science* 6(3): 288–330.

_____. 2000. Situating Arab Science: Locality Versus Essence. In *The Scientific Enterprise in Antiquity and the Middle Ages*, ed. M.H. Shank, 215–231. Chicago: University of Chicago Press.

_____. 2003. Ibn al-Haytham: Brief Life of an Arab Mathematician. *Harvard Magazine* (Sept.–Oct.). Accessed January 23, 2008.

Sabra, A.I., and J.P. Hogendijk. 2003. *The Enterprise of Science in Islam: New Perspectives*. Cambridge, MA: MIT Press.

Sachedina, A.A. 1988. *The Just Ruler (al-sultan al-adil) in Shiite Islam: The Comprehensive Authority of the Jurist in Imamite Jurisprudence*. New York: Oxford University Press.

Sadan, J. 1977. Vin-fait de civilisation. In *Studies in Memory of Gaston Wiet,* ed. M. Rosen-Ayalon, 129–60. Jerusalem: Institute of Asian and African Studies, Hebrew University of Jerusalem.

_____. 1991. Maiden's Hair and Starry Skies. In *Israel Oriental Studies*, vol. 11, ed. S. Somekh, 57–88. Leiden: Brill.

_____. 2009. In the Eyes of the Christian Writer al-Hārit ibn Sinān Poetics and Eloquence as a Platform of Inter-Cultural Contacts and Contrasts. *Arabica* 56(1): 1–26.

Sáenz-Badillos, A. 1993 *A History of the Hebrew Language*. Trans. J. Elwolde. Cambridge: Cambridge University Press.

Said, I. el-. 2008. *Islamic Art and Architecture: The System of Geometric Design*. Reading: Garnet.

Sakkut, H. 2000. *The Arabic Novel: Bibliography and Critical Introduction, 1865–1995*, vol. 1. Trans. R. Monroe. Cairo: American University in Cairo Press.

Saliba, G. 1994. *A History of Arabic Astronomy: Planetary Theories During the Golden Age of Islam*. New York: University of New York Press.

Salih, al-T. 1978. *Season of Migration to the North*. Trans. D. Johnson-Davies. London: Heinemann.

Sallam, M.Z. 1971–1999. *Al- Adab fi 'l-'asr al-mamluki [The Literature of the Mamluk Period]*. 4 vols. Cairo: Dar al-Ma'arif.

_____. 1977. *Al-Adab fi al-'aṣr al-Ayyubi* [*The Literature of the Ayyubi Period*]. Alexandria: Munsa'at al- Ma'arif.

_____. 1988–1994. *Al- Adab fi 'l- 'aṣr al-fāṭimi* [*The Literature of Fatimi Period*]. 4 vols. Alexandria: Munsa'at al-Ma'arif.

Salvesen, A. 1998. The Legacy of Babylon and Niveveh in Aramaic Sources. In *The Legacy of Mesopotamia*, ed. S. Dalley, 139–162. Oxford: Oxford University Press.

Sanders, S.L. 2006. *Margins of Writing, Origins of Cultures.* Chicago: Oriental Institute of the University of Chicago.

_____. 2009. *The Invention of Hebrew.* Urbana: University of Illinois Press.

Sanders, S.L., W. Horowitz, and T. Oshima. 2006. *Cuneiform in Canaan: Cuneiform Sources from the Land of Israel in Ancient Times.* Jerusalem: Israel Exploration Society: Hebrew University of Jerusalem.

Sanni, A. 1998. *The Arabic Theory of Prosification and Versification: On Ḥall and naẓm in Arabic Theoretical Discourse.* Stuttgart: Steiner Verlag.

Sass, B. 1991. Studia alphabetica: *On the Origin and Early History of the Northwest Semitic, South Semitic and Greek Alphabets.* Göttingen: Vandenhoeck and Ruprecht.

Sasson, J.M., ed. 1995. *Civilizations of the Ancient Near East.* 5 vols. New York: Scribner's.

Sasson, J.M., and S.N. Kramer. 1983. *Studies in Literature from the Ancient Near East.* New Haven: American Oriental Society.

Savage-Smith, E. 1985. *Islamicate Celestial Globes: Their History, Construction, and Use.* Washington, DC: Smithsonian Institution.

_____. 1995. Attitudes Toward Dissection in Medieval Islam. *Journal of the History of Medicine and Allied Sciences* 50(1): 67–110.

Savory, R. 1980. *Iran Under the Safavids.* New York: Cambridge University Press.

Sawaie, M. 1987. Jurjî Zaydân (1861–1914): A Modernist in Arabic Linguistics. *Historiographia Linguistica* 14: 283–304.

_____. 1990. An Aspect of 19th-Century Arabic Lexicography: The Modernizing Role and Contribution of Faris al-Shidyak (1804?–1887). In *History and Historiography of Linguistics*, vol. l, ed. H. Niederehe and K. Koerner, 157–171. Amsterdam and Philadelphia: J. Benjamins.

Sayyad, N. al-. 1991. *Cities and Caliphs: On the Genesis of Arab Muslim Urbanism.* New York: Greenwood.

Scheindlin, R.P. 1974. *Form and Structure in the Poetry of Al-Mu'tamid Ibn 'Abba'd.* Leiden: Brill.

Schimmel, A. 1984. *Calligraphy and Islamic Culture.* New York: New York University Press.

_____. 1992. *Islamic Calligraphy.* New York: Metropolitan Museum of Art.

Schmandt-Besserat, D. 1992. *Before Writing: From Counting to Cuneiform.* Austin: University of Texas Press.

Schniedewind, W.M., and J.H. Hunt. 2007. *A Primer on Ugaritic: Language, Culture, and Literature.* Cambridge: Cambridge University Press.

Schoeler, G. 1969. *Arabische Dichtung und griechische Poetik: Hâzim al-Qartâğannîs Grundlegung der Poetik mit Hilfe aristotelischer Begriffe.* Beirut and Wiesbaden: F. Steiner.

_____. 2006. *The Oral and the Written in Early Islam.* New York: Routledge.

_____. 2008. *The Genesis of Literature in Islam: From the Aural to the Written.* Trans. S. Toorawa. Edinburgh: Edinburgh University Press.

Schwadron, A.A. 1983. Jewish Music. In *Music of Many Cultures: An Introduction*, ed. E. May, 284–306. Berkeley: University of California Press.

Schwemer, D. 2011. Magic Rituals: Conceptualization and Performance. In *The Oxford Handbook of Cuneiform Culture*, ed. K. Radner and E. Robson, 418–446. Oxford: Oxford University Press.

Segert, S. 1983a. Parallelism in Ugaritic Poetry. *Journal of American Oriental Society* 103: 295–306.

_____. 1983b. Prague Structuralism in American Biblical Scholarship: Performance and Potential. In *The Word of the Lord Shall Go Forth*, ed. C. Meyers and M. O'Connor, 697–708. Winona Lake, IN: Eisenbrauns.

_____. 1985. *A Basic Grammar of the Ugaritic Language.* Berkeley: University of California Press.

_____. 1960. Problems of Hebrew Prosody. *Vetus Testamentum Supplement* 7: 283–91.

_____. 1979. Ugaritic Poetry and Poetics: Some Preliminary Observations. *Ugarit-Forschungen* 11: 729–38.

Sells, M.A. 1989. *Desert Tracings: Six Classic Arabian Odes.* Middletown, CO: Wesleyan University Press.

_____. 1994a. Guises of the Ghul. In *Reorientctions: Arabic and Persian Poetry*, ed. S.P. Stetkevych, 130–164. Bloomington: Indiana University Press.

_____. 1994b. *Mystical Languages of Unsaying.* Chicago: University of Chicago Press.

_____. 1996a. *Early Islamic Mysticism: Sufi, Qur'an, Miraj, Poetic and Theological Writings.* New York: Paulist.

_____. 1996b. Toward a Multidimensional Understanding of Islam: The Poetic Key. *Journal of the American Academy of Religion* 64(1): 145–166.

_____. 1999. *Approaching the Qur'an: The Early Revelations.* Ashland, OR: White Cloud.

_____. 2000. *Stations of Desire.* Jerusalem: Ibis Editions.

_____. 2009. Foreword. In *Abu al-Hasan al-Shushtari: Songs of Love and Devotion,* ed. L.M. Alvarez, xi–xix. Mahwah, NJ: Paulist.

Sells, M.A., and C. Ernst. 1996. *Early Islamic Mysticism: Sufi, Qur'an, Miraj, Poetic and Theological Writings.* New York: Paulist.

Semaan, K. 1968. *Linguistics in the Middle Ages: Phonetic Studies in Early Islam.* Leiden: Brill.

Sendrey, A. 1964. *David's Harp: The Story of Music in Biblical Times.* New York: New American Library.

_____. 1969. *Music in Ancient Israel.* New York: Philosophical Library.

_____. 1974. *Music in the Social and Religious Life of Antiquity.* Fairleigh Dickinson University Press.

Serjeant, R.B. 1959. Mihrab. *Bulletin of the School of Oriental and African Studies* 22(1/3): 439–453.

_____. 1983. Early Arabic Prose. In *Arabic Literature to the End of the Umayyad Period,* ed. A.F.L. Beeston et al., 114–153. Cambridge: Cambridge University Press.

_____. 2000. Introduction. In *The Book of Misers,* ed. al-Gāhiz, E. Ibrahim, and R.B. Serjeant, xvii–xix. Reading: Garnet.

Setia, A. 2004. Fakhr Al-Din Al-Razi on Physics and the Nature of the Physical World: A Preliminary Survey. *Islam and Science* 2. http://www.questia.com/library/1G1-128606463/fakhr-al-din-al-razi-on-physics-and-the-nature-of. Accessed March 2, 2010.

Sezgin, F. 1967–2010. *Geschichte des arabischen Schrifttums.* Vol. 9. *Grammatik bis ca. 430 H.* Leiden: Brill.

Sezgin, F., C. Ehrig-Eggert, and E. Neubauer. 2007. *The Great Mosque of the Prophet in Medina.* Frankfurt am Main: Institute for the History of Arabic-Islamic Science.

Shaffer, A. 1963. "Sumerian Sources of Tablet XII of the Epic of Gilgameš. Dissertation, University of Pennsylvania." Ann Arbor, MI: University Microfilms International.

Shahid, I. 1984. *Byzantium and the Arabs in the Fourth Century.* Washington, DC: Dumbarton Oaks Research Library and Collection.

_____. 1989. *Byzantium and the Arabs in the Fifth Century.* Washington, DC: Dumbarton Oaks Research Library and Collection.

_____. 1995. *Byzantium and the Arabs in the Sixth Century.* Washington, DC: Dumbarton Oaks Research Library and Collection.

Shamy, H. el-. 1980. *Folktales of Egypt.* Chicago: University of Chicago Press.

_____. 1995. *Folk Traditions of the Arab World: A Guide to Motif Classification.* Bloomington: Indiana University Press.

Sharif, M., and B.K. Thapar. 1999. Food-Producing Communities in Pakistan and Northern India. In *History of Civilizations of Central Asia,* vol. 1, ed. V.M. Masson and A.H. Dani, 128–137. Delhi: Motilal Banarsidass.

Sharkawi, M. al-. 2010. *The Ecology of Arabic: A Study of Arabicization.* Leiden: Brill.

Sheehan, P. 2010. *Babylon of Egypt: The Archaeology of Old Cairo and the Origins of the City.* Cairo: American University in Cairo Press.

Shihah, M.A. 2001. *Islamic Architecture in Egypt.* Cairo: Prism.

Shiloah, A. 1992. *Jewish Musical Traditions.* Detroit: Wayne State University Press.

_____. 1995. *Music in the World of Islam: A Socio-Cultural Study.* Detroit: Wayne State University Press.

_____. 2003. *The Theory of Music in Arabic Writings (c. 900–1900).* Munich: G. Henle Verlag.

_____. 2007. *Music and Its Virtues in Islamic and Judaic Writings.* Burlington, VT: Ashgate.

Shireen, M. 2002. *History of Arabic Music Theory: Change and Continuity in the Tone Systems, Genres, and Scales.* Kaslik, Lebanon: Université Saint-Esprit.

Shlonsky, U. 1997. *Clause Structure and Word Order in Hebrew and Arabic: An Essay in Comparative Semitic Syntax.* New York: Oxford University Press.

Shvidkovskii, D.O., and E. Shorban. 2007. *Russian Architecture and the West.* New Haven: Yale University Press.

Sībawayh, Amr ibn Uthmān, ed. 1988. *Al-Kitāb Kitāb Sībawayh Abī Bishr 'Abd al-Salām Muhammad Hārūn.* Cairo: Maktabat al-Khānjī.

Sidarus, A. 1993. Medieval Coptic Grammars in Arabic: The Coptic *muqaddimât. Journal of Coptic Studies* 3: 1–10.

Signell, K.L. 1986. *Makam: Modal Practice in Turkish Art Music.* New York: Da Capo.

Simon, U.G. 1993. *Mittelalterliche arabische Sprachbetrachtung zwischen Grammatik und Rhetorik: 'ilm al-ma'ânî bei as-Sakkâkî.* Heidelberg: Heidelberger Orientverlag.

Simpson, St. J. 2002. *Queen of Sheba: Treasures from Ancient Yemen.* London: British Museum.

Sivan, D.A. 1984. *Grammatical Analysis and Glossary of the Northwest Semitic Vocables in Akkadian Texts of the 15th–13th* C.B.C. *from Canaan and Syria* Kevelaer: Bercker and Butzon; Neukirchen-Vluyn: Neukirchener Verlag.

_____. 1997. *Grammar of the Ugaritic Language*. Leiden: Brill.

Sivan, D.A., and S. Yona. 1998. Pivot Words or Expressions in Biblical Hebrew and in Ugaritic Poetry. *Vetus Testamentum* 48(3): 399–407.

Skjærvo, P.O. 2002. An Introduction to Old Persian. http://www.fas.harvard.edu/~iranian/OldPersian/index.html.

_____. 2006a. Old Avestan. http://www.fas.harvard.edu/~iranian/OldAvestan/index.html.

_____. 2006b. Introduction to Young Avestan. http://www.fas.harvard.edu/~iranian/Avesta/index.html.

Smith, J.A. 1984. The Ancient Synagogue, the Early Church and Singing. *Music & Letters* 65: 1–16.

_____. 1998. Musical Aspects of Old Testament Canticles in the Biblical Setting. *Early Music* 17: 221–284.

_____. 2010. *Music in Ancient Judaism and Early Christianity*. Burlington, VT: Ashgate.

Smith, M. 1984. *Rabi'a The Mystic and Her Fellow-Saints in Islam*. Cambridge: Cambridge University Press.

Smith, M.S., et al. 1997. *Ugaritic Narrative Poetry*. Atlanta: Scholars.

Smith, S. 1932. Notes on the Gutian Period. *Journal of the Royal Asiatic Society of Great Britain and Ireland* 64(2): 295–308.

Smith, W.S. 1962. *Musical Aspects of the New Testament*. Amsterdam: Uitgeverij W. ten Have, N.V.

Somekh, S. 1991. *Studies in Medieval Arabic and Hebrew Poetics*. Leiden: Brill.

Sonn, T. 2006. Art and the Qur'an. In *The Qur'an: An Encyclopedia*, ed. O. Leaman, 71–81. London: Routledge.

Speight, T.M. 2000. Narrative Structures in the Hadīth. *Journal of Near Eastern Studies* 59(4): 265–271.

Sperl, S. 1977. Islamic Kingship and Arabic Panegyric Poetry in the Early Ninth Century. *Journal of Arabic Literature* 8: 20–35.

_____. 1989. *Mannerism in Arabic Poetry: A Structural Analysis of Selected Texts*. Cambridge: Cambridge University Press.

Sperl, S., and C. Shackle. 1996. *Qasida Poetry in Islamic Asia and Africa*. Leiden: Brill.

Stainer, J. 1970. *The Music of the Bible, with Some Account of the Development of Modern Musical Instruments from Ancient Types*. New York: Da Capo.

Stein, P. 2002a. Gibt es Kasus im Sabäischen? In *Neue Beiträge zur Semitistik,* ed. N. Nebes, 201–222. Wiesbaden: Harrassowitz.

_____. 2002b. Zur Morphologie des sabäischen Infinitivs. *Orientalia* 71: 393–414.

_____. 2004a. Zur Dialektographie des Sabäischen. *Journal of Semitic Studies* 49: 225–45.

_____. 2004b. Zur Dialektgeographie des Sabäischen. Oxford: Oxford University Press.

_____. 2005a. Linguistic Contribution to Sabaean Chronology. *Archdologische Berichte aus dem Yemen* 10: 179–89.

_____. 2005b. The Ancient South Arabian Minuscule Inscriptions on Wood: A New Genre of Pre-Islamic Epigraphy. *Jaarbericht van het Vooraziatisch-Egyptisch Genootschap "Ex Oriente Lux"* 39: 181–199.

Stephenson, F.R. 2009. *Historical Eclipses and Earth's Rotation*. Cambridge: Cambridge University Press.

Stern, S.M. 1974. *Hispano-Arabic Strophic Poetry*. Oxford: Clarendon.

Stetkevych, J. 1989. Space of Delight: A Symbolic Topoanalysis of the Classical Arabic Nasib. *Studies in the Arabic Literary Tradition* 25: 5–27.

_____. 1993. *The Zephyrs of Najd: The Poetics of Nostalgia in the Classical Arabic Nasib*. Chicago: University of Chicago Press.

_____. 1996. *Muhammad and the Golden Bough: Reconstructing Arabian Myth*. Bloomington: Indiana University Press.

Stetkevych, S.P. 1983. Structuralist Interpretations of Pre-Islamic Poetry: Critique and New Directions. *Journal of Near Eastern Studies* 42(2): 85–107.

_____. 1993a. *The Mute Immortals Speak: Pre-Islamic Poetry and the Poetics of Ritual* Ithaca, NY: Cornell University Press.

_____. 1993b. *The Zephyrs of Najd: The Poetics of Nostalgia in the Classical Arabic Nasib*. Chicago: University of Chicago Press.

_____. 1994a. *Reorientations: Arabic and Persian Poetry*. Bloomington: Indiana University Press.

_____. 1994b. Pre-Islamic Panegyric and the Poetics of Redemption. In *Reorientations: Arabic and Persian Poetry*, ed. S.P. Stetkevych, 1–49. Bloomington: Indiana University Press.

_____. 2002. *The Poetics of Islamic Legitimacy: Myth, Gender, and Ceremony in the Classical Arabic Ode*. Bloomington: Indiana University Press.

_____. 2006. From Text to Talisman: Al-Busiri's Qasidat al-Burdah (Mantle Ode) and the Supplicatory Ode. *Journal of Arabic Literature* 37(2): 145–189.

_____. 2007. From Sirah to Qasidah: Poetics and Polemics in Al-Busiri's Qasidat Al-Burdah (Mantle Ode). *Journal of Arabic Literature* 38(1): 1–52.

_____. 2009. *Early Islamic Poetry and Poetics*. Burlington, VT: Ashgate.

_____. 2010. *The Mantle Odes: Arabic Praise Poems to the Prophet Muhammad*. Bloomington: Indiana University Press.

Steward, D.J. 1990. Saj' in the Qur'an: Prosody and Structure. *Journal of Arabic Literature* 21(2): 101–139.

Stierlin, H. 2005. *Masterworks of Islamic Architecture: From Damascus to Granada and from Cairo to Istanbul.* Cairo, Egypt: American University in Cairo Press.

_____. 2007. *Islamic Architecture: Design and Decoration in the Service of Faith.* London: Thames and Hudson.

Stoetzer, W.F.G.J. 1986. "Theory and Practice in Arabic Metrics." Dissertation, Leiden University.

Stol, M. 1993. *Epilepsy in Babylonia.* Groningen: Styx.

Strange, G. 1900. *Baghdad During the Abbasid Caliphate from Contemporary Arabic and Persian Sources.* Oxford: Clarendon.

Struik, D.J. 1987. *A Concise History of Mathematics.* New York: Dover.

Stuart, D.K. 1976. *Studies in Early Hebrew Meter.* Missoula: Scholars.

Sulaiman Ali Mourad, S.A. 2005. *Early Islam Between Myth and History: Al-Hasan Al-Basrī (d. 110H/728 CE) and the Formation of His Legacy in the Formation of Classical IslamicScholarship.* Leiden: Brill.

Suleiman, M.Y. 1990. Sîbawaihi's "Parts of Speech" According to Zajjâjî: A New Interpretation. *Journal of Semitic Studies* 35: 245–63.

Sumi, A.M. 2004. *Description in Classical Arabic Poetry: Waṣf, Ekphrasis, and Interarts Theory.* Leiden: Brill.

Swainson, H. 2005. *The Church of Sancta Sophia Constantinople: A Study of Byzantine Building.* Boston, MA: Adamant Media.

Swelim, M.T. 1994. "The Mosque of Ibn Tulun: A New Perspective." PhD dissertation, Harvard University.

Tabbaa, Y. 1985. The Muqarnas Dome: Its Origin and Meaning. *Muqarnas* 3: 61–74.

_____. 2001. *The Transformation of Islamic Art During the Sunni Revival.* Seattle: University of Washington Press.

Taha, Z.A. 1995. "Issues of Syntax and Semantics: A Comparative Study of Sibawayhi, Al-Mubarrad, and Ibn as-Sarraaj." PhD dissertation, Georgetown University.

Talmon, R. 1985. "Who Was the First Arab Grammarian? A New Approach to an Old Problem." *Studies in the History of Arabic Grammar (SHAG)* 1: 128–45.

_____. 1988. *"Al-kalâm mâ kâna muktafiyan bi-nafsihi wa-huwa ǧumla"*: A Study in the History of Sentence Concept and the Sîbawaihian Legacy in Arabic Grammar. *Zeitschrift der Deutshcen Morgenländischen Gesellschaft (ZDMG)* 138: 74–98.

_____. 1990. The Philosophizing Farrâ': An Interpretation of an Obscure Saying Attributed to the Grammarian Ta'lab. *Studies in the History of Arabic Grammar (SHAG)* 2: 265–79.

Termanini, K. 2004. Singing in the Jahili Period. http://www.khaledtrm.net/. Accessed March 23, 2012.

Thacker, T.W. 1954. *The Relationship of the Semitic and Egyptian Verbal Systems.* Oxford: Oxford University Press.

Thackston, W.M. 1990. *An Introduction to Koranic Arabic.* Cambridge, MA: Harvard University Press.

Thomas, E. 2007. *Monumentality and the Roman Empire: Architecture in the Antonine Age.* Oxford: Oxford University Press.

Thomason, S.G. 2001. *Language Contact: An Introduction.* Washington, DC: Georgetown University Press.

Thompson, R.C. 1929. *The Excavations on the Temple of Nabu at Nineveh.* Oxford: John Johnson for the Society of Antiquaries of London.

Thompson, R.C., and R.W. Hutchinson. 1931. The Site of the Palace of Ashurnasirpal II at Nineveh Excavated in 1929–30. *Liverpool Annals of Archaeology and Anthropology* 18: 79–112.

_____. 1932. The British Museum Excavations on the Temple of Ishtar at Nineveh 1930–31. *Liverpool Annals of Archaeology and Anthropology* 19: 55–116.

Thompson, R.C., and M.E.L. Mallowan. 1933. The British Museum Excavations at Nineveh 1931–32. *Liverpool Annals of Archaeology and Anthropology* 20: 71–186.

Tigay, J.H. 1982. *The Evolution of the Gilgamesh Epic.* Philadelphia: University of Pennsylvania Press.

Tinney, S. 1996. *The Nippur Lament: Royal Rhetoric and Divine Legitimation in the Reign of Isme-Dagan of Isin (1953–1935 B.C.).* Philadelphia: University of Pennsylvania Museum.

Tobi, J. 2004. *Proximity and Distance: Medieval Hebrew and Arabic Poetry.* Leiden: Brill.

_____. 2010. *Between Hebrew and Arabic Poetry: Studies in Spanish Medieval Hebrew Poetry.* Leiden: Brill.

Toorawa, S.M. 1991. Movement in Mahfūz's "Tharthara Fawq an-Nīl." *Journal of Arabic Literature* 22(1): 53–65.

_____. 1997. Review of Suzanne P. Stetkevych (ed.), Reorientations: Arabic and Persian Poetry. *Journal of the American Oriental Society* 117: 759–762.

Touati, H., and L. Cochrane. 2010. *Islam and Travel in the Middle Ages.* Chicago: University of Chicago Press.

Touma, H.H. 1975. *Maqam Bayati in the Arabian Taqsim: A Study in the Phenomenology*

of the Maqam. [S.l.]: International Monograph.
_____. 1996. *The Music of the Arabs.* Trans. Laurie Schwartz. Portland, OR: Amadeus.
Tropper, J. 1994. Present *yaqtulum in Central Semitic. *Journal of Semitic Studies* 39: 1–6.
Troupeau, G. 1962. La grammaire à Bagdad du IXe au XIIIe siècle. *Arabica.* 9: 397–405.
_____. 1976. *Lexique-index du Kitâb de Sibawayhi.* Paris: Klincksieck.
Tunkel, V. 2004. *The Music of the Hebrew Bible—The Western Ashkenazi Tradition.* London: Tymsder.
Turner, H.R. 1997. *Science in Medieval Islam: An Illustrated Introduction.* Austin: University of Texas Press.
Ullendorff, E. 1955. *The Semitic Languages of Ethiopia: A Comparative Phonology.* London: Taylor's.
Utas, B. 1975. On the Composition of the Ayyātkār i Zarērān. In *Monumentum H.S. Nyberg,* vol. 2, ed. H.S. Nyberg, 399–418. Leiden: Brill.
_____. 1994. Arabic and Iranian Elements in New Persian Prosody. In *Arabic Prosody and Its Applications in Muslim Poetry,* ed. L. Johanson and B. Utas, 129–141. Stockholm: Almqvist & Wiksell Internat.
Van Der Linden, N. 2001. The Classical Iraqi Maqam and Its Survival. In *Colors of Enchantment: Theater, Dance, Music and the Visual Arts of the Middle East,* ed. S. Zuhur, 321–335. Cairo: American University Press.
Van der Lugt, P. 2006. *Cantos and Strophes in Biblical Hebrew Poetry: With Special Reference to the First Book of the Psalter.* Leiden: Brill.
Van de Mieroop, M. 1999. *Cuneiform Texts and the Writing of History.* New York: Routledge.
_____. 2006. *History of the Ancient Near East, ca. 3000–323 B.C.* Malden, MA: Blackwell.
Van Dijk, H.J. 1968. *Ezekiel's Prophecy on Tyre (Ez 26, 1–28, 19): A New Approach.* Rome: Pontifical Biblical Institute.
Van Gelder, G.J.H. 1982. *Beyond the Line: Classical Arabic Literary Critics on the Coherence and Unity of the Poem.* Leiden: Brill.
Van Gelder, G.J.H., and M. Hammond. 2008. *Takhyil: The Imaginary in Classical Arabic Poetics.* Cambridge: Gibb Memorial Trust.
Vanstiphout, H.L.J. 1988. *Mihiltum, or the Image of Cuneiform Writing.* Leiden: Brill.
_____. 1996. *Mesopotamian Poetic Language: Sumerian and Akkadian: Proceedings of the Groningen Group for the Study of Mesopotamian Literature.* Vol. 2. Groningen: Styx Publications.
_____. 2001. *Genre in Mesopotamian Literature.* Leiden: Brill.

_____. 2003. *Epics of Sumerian Kings: The Matter of Aratta.* Atlanta, GA: Society of Biblical Literature.
Veldhuis, N. 1990. The Haret Grassand Related Matters. *Orientalia Lovaniensia Periodica* 21: 27–44.
_____. 2004. *Religion, Literature and Scholarship: The Sumerian Composition "Nanse and the Birds": With a Catalogue of Sumerian Bird Names.* Leiden: Brill.
Versteegh, K. 1977. *Greek Elements in Arabic Linguistic Thinking.* Leiden: Brill.
_____. 1980. Logique et grammaire au dixième siècle. *Histoire Epistémologie Langage* 2: 39–52, 67–75.
_____. 1983. A Dissenting Grammarian: Quṭrub on Declension. *Historiographia Linguistica* 8.2: 403–429.
_____. 1984. *Pidginization and Creolization: The Case of Arabic.* Amsterdam: J. Benjamins.
_____. 1985. The Development of Argumentation in Arabic Grammar: The Declension of the Dual and the Plural. *Studies in the History of Arabic Grammar (SHAG)* 2: 152–73.
_____. 1987. Arabische Sprachwissenschaft (Grammatik). *Grundriß der Arabischen Philologie (GAP)* 2: 148–76.
_____. 1989c. Early and Late Grammarians in the Arab Grammatical Tradition: The Morphonology of the Hollow Verb. *Zeitschrift für arabische Linguistik (ZAL)* 20: 9–22.
_____. 1990. Freedom of the Speaker: The Term *ittisâ'* and Related Notions in Arabic Grammar. *Studies in the History of Arabic Grammar (SHAG)* 2: 281–93.
_____. 1992. Grammar and Rhetoric: Gurğânî on the Verbs of Admiration. *Jerusalem Studies in Arabic and Islam (JSAI)* 15: 113–33.
_____. 1993. *Arabic Grammar and Qur'ânic Exegesis in Early Islam.* Leiden: Brill.
_____. 1994. The Notion of "Underlying Levels" in the Arabic Grammatical Tradition. *Historiographia Linguistica (HL)* 21: 271–96.
_____. 1995. *The Explanation of Linguistic Causes: Az-Zaǧǧâǧî's Theory of Grammar, Introduction, Translation and Commentary.* Amsterdam and Philadelphia: J. Benjamins.
_____. 1996. Linguistic Attitudes and the Origin of Speech in the Arab World. In *Festschrift Badawi,* ed. A. El-Gibali, 15–31. Cairo: American University Press.
_____. 1997a. *The Arabic Language.* Edinburgh: Edinburgh University Press.
_____. 1997b. *The Arabic Linguistic Tradition.* London: Routledge.
_____. 2001. *The Arabic Language.* Edinburgh: Edinburgh University Press.
Versteegh, K., E. Ditters, and H. Motzki. 2007.

Approaches to Arabic Linguistics. Leiden: Brill.

Vitale, R. 1982. La Musique suméro-accadienne: gamme et notation musicale. *Ugarit-Forschungen* 14: 241–63.

Vogelzang, M.E., and H.L.J. Vanstiphout. 1992. *Mesopotamian Epic Literature: Oral or Aural?* Lewiston: Edwin Mellen.

———. 1996. *Mesopotamian Poetic Language: Sumerian and Akkadian.* Groningen: Styx.

Voigt, R.M. 1987. The Classification of Central Semitic. *Journal of Semitic Studies* 32: 1–27.

Von Soden, 1974–1981. *Akkadisches Handworterbuch.* 3 vols. Wiesbaden: O. Harrassowitz.

———. 1984. *Reflektierte und konstruierte Mythen in Babylonien und Assyrien.* Helsinki: Finnish Oriental Society.

———. 1994. *The Ancient Orient: An Introduction to the Study of the Ancient Near East.* Grand Rapids, MI: W.B. Eerdmans.

Wacks, D.A. 2003. The Performativity of Ibn al-Muqaffas Kalila wa-Dimna and Al-Maqāmāt al-Luzumiyya of al-Saraqusti. *Journal of Arabic Literature* 34 (1–2): 178–89.

———. 2006. Reading Jaume Roig's Spill and the Libro de buen amor in the Iberian *maqāma* Tradition. *Bulletin of Spanish Studies* 83(5): 597–616.

———. 2007. *Framing Iberia: Maqamat and Frametale Narratives in Medieval Spain.* Leiden: Brill.

Walker, C.B.F. 1987. *Cuneiform.* London: British Museum.

Wansbrough, J. 1977. *Quranic Studies: Sources and Methods of Scriptural Interpretation.* London: Oxford University Press.

———. 1978. *The Sectarian Milieu: Content and Composition of Islamic Salvation History.* New York: Oxford University Press.

Wansbrough, J., and A. Rippin. 2004. *Quranic Studies: Sources and Methods of Scriptural Interpretation.* Amherst, NY: Prometheus.

Watson, J. 2002. *The Phonology and Morphology of Arabic.* New York: Oxford University Press.

Watson, W.G.E. 1972. Fixed Pairs in Ugaritic and Isaiah. *Vetus Testamentum* 22: 460–68.

———. 1975. Verse Patterns in Ugaritic, Akkadian, and Hebrew Poetry. *Ugarit-Forschungen* 7: 483–92.

———. 1976. Pivot Pattern in Hebrew, Ugaritic, Akkadian. *Zeitschrift für die Alttestamentliche Wissenschaft* 88: 239–53.

———. 1980. Gender-Matched Synonymous Parallelism in the OT. *Journal of Biblical Literature* 99: 321–41.

———. 1980. Review of T. Collins, Line-Forms in Hebrew Poetry. *Biblica* 61: 581–83.

———. 1981a. Gender-Matched Synonymous Parallelism in Ugaritic Poetry. *Ugarit-Forschungen* 13: 181–87.

———. 1981b. Reversed Word-Pairs in Ugaritic Poetry. *Ugarit-Forschungen* 13: 189–92.

———. 1982a. Lineation (Stichometry) in Ugaritic Verse. *Ugarit-Forschungen* 14: 311–312.

———. 1982b. Trends in the Development of Classical Hebrew Poetry: A Comparative Study. *Ugarit-Forschungen* 14: 265–79.

———. 1983a. Classical Hebrew Poetry: A Guide to Its Techniques. *Journal for the Study of the Old Testament*, Supplement Series 26.

———. 1983b. Review of James L. Kugel, The Idea of Biblical Poetry: Parallelism and Its History. *Biblica* 64: 134–36.

———. 1983c. Review of M. O'Connor, Hebrew Verse Structure. *Biblica* 64: 131–34.

———. 1984. A Review of Kugel's The Idea of Biblical Poetry. *Journal for the Study of the Old Testament* 28: 89–98.

———. 1994. *Traditional Techniques in Classical Hebrew Verse.* Sheffield: Sheffield Academic Press.

———. 1999. Ugaritic Poetry. In *Handbook of Ugaritic Studies*, ed. W.G.E. Watson and N. Wyatt, 165–194. Leiden: Brill.

Watt, W.M. 1970. *Bell's Introduction to the Qur'ân.* Revised and enlarged ed. Edinburgh: Edinburgh University Press.

Weil, G. 1913. *Die grammatischen Fragen der Basrer und Kufer.* Leiden: Brill.

———. 1915. Zum Verständnis der Methode der moslemischen Grammatiker. In *Festschrift E. Sachau gewidmet*, 380–92. Berlin.

Weiss, B.G. 1966. "Language in Orthodox Muslim Thought: A Study of wad' al-lughah and Its Development." PhD dissertation, Princeton University.

———. 1974. The Medieval Muslim Discussions of the Origin of Language. *Zeitschrift der Deutshcen Morgenländischen Gesellschaft (ZDMG)* 125: 33–41.

———. 1976. A Theory of the Parts of Speech in Arabic (Noun, Verb and Particle): A Study in 'ilm al-wad'. *Arabica* 23: 23–36.

———. 1984. Language and Tradition in Medieval Islam: The Question of al-tarîq ilâ ma'rifat al-lugha. *Der Islam* 61: 91–99.

———. 2002. *Studies in Islamic Legal Theory.* Boston: Brill.

Weiss, D. 1995. Ibn Khaldun on Economic Transformation. *International Journal of Middle East Studies* 27(1): 29–37.

Weiss, J. 1910. Die arabische Nationalgrammatik und die Lateiner. *Zeitschrift der Deutshcen Morgenländischen Gesellschaft (ZDMG)* 64: 349–90.

Wellesz, E, ed. 1957. *New Oxford History of*

Music. Vol. 1: *Ancient and Oriental Music.* Oxford: Oxford University Press.

Wells, P.S. 1980. *Culture Contact and Culture Change: Early Iron Age Europe and the Mediterranean World.* Cambridge: Cambridge University Press.

Werner, E. 1976. *Contributions to a Historical Study of Jewish Music.* New York: Ktav.

_____. 1984. *The Sacred Bridge: The Interdependence of Liturgy and Music in Synagogue and Church During the First Millennium.* New York: Columbia University Press.

Werner, L. 2001. A Gift of Ghazals. *Saudi Aramco World,* July/August, 38–45.

West, M.L. 1994. The Babylonian Musical Notation and the Hurrian Melodic Texts. *Music and Letters* 75(2): 161–79.

_____. 1997. Akkadian Poetry: Metre and Performance. *Iraq* 59: 175–187.

Westenholz, J.G. 2007. *Three Faces of Monotheism* = [Sheloshah panim le-eḥad]. Jerusalem: Bible Lands Museum.

Westenholz, J.G., J.A. Linsider, and F. Skolnik. 2007. *Sounds of Ancient Music.* Jerusalem: Bible Lands Museum.

Westenholz, J.G., and A. Westenholz. 2006. *Cuneiform Inscriptions in the Collection of the Bible Lands Museum Jerusalem: The Old Babylonian Inscriptions.* Leiden: Brill.

Wheatley, P. 2001. *The Places Where Men Pray Together: Cities in Islamic Lands.* Chicago: University of Chicago Press.

Wheeler, J. 1989a. Music of the Temple. *Archaeology and Biblical Research* 2/1: 12–20.

_____. 1989b. The Music of the Temple. *Archaeology and Biblical Research* 4/2: 13–122.

_____. 1991. Recovery of Biblical Chant: The Music of the Bible Revealed by Suzanne Haik-Vantoura. *Journal of Jewish Music and Liturgy* 14: 25–35.

_____. 1993. The Hebrew Old Testament as a Vocal Score. *The Hymn* 44/3: 10–15.

Wild, S. 1965. *Das Kitâb al-'ain und die arabische Lexikographie.* Wiesbaden: O. Harrassowitz.

_____. 1987. Arabische Lexikographie. *Grundriß der Arabischen Philologie (GAP)* 2: 136–47.

Wilkinson, T.J. 2005. The Other Side of Sheba: Early Towns in the Highlands of Yemen. *Bibliotheca Orientalis* 62: 1–14.

Williams, C. 2002. *Islamic Monuments in Cairo: The Practical Guide.* Cairo: American University of Cairo Press.

Williams, J.A. 1994. *The Word of Islam.* Austin: University of Texas Press.

Williams, W. 2002. Aspects of the Creed of Imam Ahmad Ibn Hanbal: A Study of Anthropomorphism in Early Islamic Discourse. *International Journal of Middle East Studies* 34: 441–463.

Wiseman, D.J. 1980. A New Text of the Babylonian Poem of the Righteous Sufferer. *Anatolian Studies* 30: 101–107.

Wolfe, R.G. 1984. "Ibn Madâ' al-Qurtubî and the Book in Refutation of the Grammarians." PhD dissertation, Indiana University.

_____. 1990. Ibn Madâ' al-Qurtubî's Kitâb arradd 'alâ n-nuhât: An Historical Misnomer. *Studies in the History of Arabic Grammar (SHAG)* 2: 295–304.

Wolfson, H.A. 1976. *The Philosophy of the Kalam.* Cambridge, MA: Harvard University Press.

Woodard, R.D. 2008. *The Ancient Languages of Mesopotamia, Egypt and Aksum.* Cambridge: Cambridge University Press.

Woods, C. 2006. Bilingualism, Scribal Learning, and the Death of Sumerian. In *Margins of Writing, Origins of Cultures,* ed. S.L. Sanders, 91–120. Chicago: Oriental Institute of the University of Chicago.

Woolley, C.L. 1934. *The Excavations at Ur.* Vol. 2. London: The British Museum Press.

Wu, Y., and S. Dalley. 1990. The Origins of the Manana Dynasty at Kish and the Assyrian King List. *Iraq* 52: 159–165.

Wulstan, D. 1968. The Tuning of the Babylonian Harp. *Iraq* 30: 215–28.

_____. 1971. The Earliest Musical Notation. *Music and Letters* 52: 365–82.

Wyatt, N. *Religious Texts from Ugarit.* London: Sheffield Academic Press.

Yâqubi, A. al-. 1969. *Tarikh Ahmad ibn Abi Yaqubi.* Trans. M. Th. Houtsma. Lugduni Batavorum: Brill.

Yaron E. 2005. *God's Mountain: The Temple Mount in Time, Place and Memory.* Baltimore: Johns Hopkins University Press.

Yarshater, E., ed. 1983. *The Cambridge History of Iran.* 3.1: *The Seleucid, Parthian and Sasanian Periods.* Cambridge: Cambridge University Press.

Yeomans, R. 2000. *The Story of Islamic Architecture.* New York: New York University Press.

Young, D.C. 2004a. *Rogues and Genres: Generic Transformation in the Spanish Picaresque and Arabic Maqama.* Newark, DE: Juan de la Cuesta.

_____. 2004b. Wine and Genre: Khamriyya in the Andalusi *Maqāmā.* In *Wine, Women and Song: Hebrew and Arabic Poetry of Medieval Iberia,* ed. M.M. Hamilton, S.J. Portnoy and D.A. Wacks, 87–100. Newark, DE: Juan de la Cuesta Hispanic Monographs.

Young, I. 1998. The "Archaic" Poetry of the Pentateuch in the MT, Samaritan Pentateuch and 4Qexodc. *Abr-Nahrain* 35: 74–83.

Yushmanov, N.V. 1961. *The Structure of the Arabic Language.* Washington: Center for

Applied Linguistics of the Modern Language Association of America.

Zaydan, J. 2010. *The Conquest of Andalusia.* Trans. R. Allen. Bethesda, MD: Zaidan Foundation.

_____. 2011a. *The Battle of Poitiers: Charles Martel and Abd al-Rahman.* Trans. W. Granara. Bethesda, MD: Zaidan Foundation.

_____. 2011b. *Caliph's Sister: Harun al-Rashid and the Fall of the Persians.* Trans. A.J. Boullata. Bethesa, MD: Zaidan Foundation.

Zaynahum, M. 2004. *Islamic Architecture in Egypt.* Cairo: Ministry of Culture, Egypt, Prism.

Ziadeh, F.J. 1986. Prosody and the Initial Formation of Classical Arabic. *Journal of the American Oriental Society* 106(2): 333–338.

Zimmermann, F.W. 1972. Some Observations on Al-Fârâbî and Logical Tradition. In *Islamic Philosophy and the Classical Tradition,* ed. S.M. Stern, A. Hourani and V. Brown, 517–546. Oxford: Cassirer.

_____. 1981. *Al-Fârâbî's Commentary and Short Treatise on Aristotle's De Interpretatione.* Oxford: Oxford University Press.

Zubaidi, A.M. 1983. The Impact of the Qur'an and Hadith on Medieval Arabic. In *The Cambridge History of Arabic Literature,* ed. A.F.L. Beeston, 322–342. Cambridge: Cambridge University Press.

Zuhur, S. 1998. *Images of Enchantment: Visual and Performing Arts of the Middle East.* Cairo: American University of Cairo.

Zwartjez, O. 1997. *Love Songs from al-Andalus: History, Structure, and Meaning of the Kharja.* Leiden: Brill.

Zwartjez, O., and Heijkoop, H. 2004. *Muwassah, Zajal, Kharja: Bibliography of Eleven Centuries of Strophic Poetry and Music from Al-Andalus and Their Influence on East and West.* Leiden: Brill.

Zwettler, M. 1978. *The Oral Tradition of Classical Arabic Poetry: Its Character and Implications.* Columbus: Ohio State University Press.

Zwiep, I.E. 1995. "Aristotle, Galen, God: A Short History of Medieval Jewish Linguistic Thought." PhD dissertation, University of Amsterdam.

Index

277